Treaties
establishing the
European Communities

Treaties amending these Treaties

Single European Act

Resolutions — Declarations

I

This publication is also available in

ES — Vol. I + II: ISBN 92-77-19290-9
       Vol. I: ISBN 92-77-19221-6
DA — Vol. I + II: ISBN 92-77-19291-7
       Vol. I: ISBN 92-77-19222-4
DE — Vol. I + II: ISBN 92-77-19292-5
       Vol. I: ISBN 92-77-19223-2
GR — Vol. I + II: ISBN 92-77-19293-3
       Vol. I: ISBN 92-77-19224-0
FR — Vol. I + II: ISBN 92-77-19295-X
       Vol. I: ISBN 92-77-19226-7
GA — Vol. I + II: ISBN 92-77-19299-2
       Vol. I: ISBN 92-77-19230-5
IT — Vol. I + II: ISBN 92-77-19296-8
       Vol. I: ISBN 92-77-19227-5
NL — Vol. I + II: ISBN 92-77-19297-6
       Vol. I: ISBN 92-77-19228-3
PT — Vol. I + II: ISBN 92-77-19298-4
       Vol. I: ISBN 92-77-19229-1

Cataloguing data can be found at the end of this publication

Luxembourg: Office for Official Publications of the European
Communities, 1987

Vol. I + II: ISBN 92-77-19294-1 — Vol. I: ISBN 92-77-19225-9

Catalogue number (Vol. I): FX-80-86-001-EN-C

Introductory Note

This edition of the Treaties establishing the European Communities and documents concerning Accessions to those Communities is published in two volumes. It has been brought up to date as at 1 July 1987 by the services of the Community Institutions on the basis of the official texts in force on that date and is published in the Spanish, Danish, German, Greek, English, French, Irish, Italian, Dutch and Portuguese languages. (¹)

This first volume contains the Treaties establishing the European Communities, the Treaties amending those Treaties and the Single European Act. It also contains a certain number of Resolutions and Declarations.

The second volume contains the documents concerning the Accessions to the Communities of Denmark, Ireland, the United Kingdom of Great Britain and Northern Ireland, Greece, Spain and Portugal.

Throughout the texts reproduced in the two volumes, the term 'Assembly' has, where necessary, been replaced, in accordance with Article 3 of the Single European Act, by the terms 'European Parliament'.

The two collections of texts have been prepared for documentation purposes and do not involve the responsibility of the Institutions.

(¹) Castellano, Dansk, Deutsch, Ellinika, English, Français, Gaeilge, Italiano, Nederlands, Português.

Convention on Common Institutions	Convention on certain institutions common to the European Communities
Merger Treaty	Treaty establishing a Single Council and a Single Commission of the European Communities (*Official Journal of the European Communities,* No 152, 13 July 1967)
Treaty amending Certain Budgetary Provisions	Treaty amending Certain Budgetary Provisions of the Treaties establishing the European Communities and of the Treaty establishing a Single Council and a Single Commission of the European Communities (*Official Journal of the European Communities,* No L 2, 2 January 1971)
Treaty amending the Protocol on the Statute of the Bank	Treaty amending Certain Provisions of the Protocol on the Statute of the European Investment Bank (*Official Journal of the European Communities,* No L 91, 6 April 1978)
Treaty amending Certain Financial Provisions	Treaty amending Certain Financial Provisions of the Treaty establishing the European Communities and of the Treaty establishing a Single Council and a Single Commission of the European Communities (*Official Journal of the European Communities,* No L 359, 31 December 1977)
Act concerning the election of the representatives of the Assembly	Act concerning the election of the representatives of the Assembly by direct universal suffrage (*Official Journal of the European Communities,* No L 278, 8 October 1976)
Greenland Treaty	Treaty amending, with regard to Greenland, the Treaties establishing the European Communities (*Official Journal of the European Communities,* No L 29, 1 February 1985)
SEA	Single European Act (*Official Journal of the European Communities,* No L 169, 29 June 1987)

AA DK/IRL/UK	Act concerning the Conditions of Accession and the Adjustments to the Treaties — Accession to the European Communities of the Kingdom of Denmark, Ireland and the United Kingdom of Great Britain and Northern Ireland (*Official Journal of the European Communities*, No L 73, 27 March 1972)
Protocol No 1 annexed to the Act of Accession DK/IRL/UK	Protocol No 1 on the Statute of the European Investment Bank annexed to the Act concerning the Conditions of Accession and the Adjustments to the Treaties (*Official Journal of the European Communities*, No L 73, 27 March 1972)
AD AA DK/IRL/UK	Decision of the Council of the European Communities of 1 January 1973 adjusting the documents concerning the accession of new Member States to the European Communities (*Official Journal of the European Communities*, No L 2, 1 January 1973)
AA GR	Act concerning the Conditions of Accession and the Adjustments to the Treaties — Accession to the European Communities of the Hellenic Republic (*Official Journal of the European Communities*, No L 291, 19 November 1979)
AA ESP/PORT	Act concerning the Conditions of Accession and the Adjustments to the Treaties — Accession to the European Communities of the Kingdom of Spain and the Portuguese Republic (*Official Journal of the European Communities*, No L 302, 15 November 1985)

General table of contents

---

* The Protocol on the Privileges and Immunities of the European Coal and Steel Community has been repealed by the second paragraph of Article 28 of the Merger Treaty; see Protocol on the Privileges and Immunities of the European Communities (p. 853).

---

* The Protocol on the Privileges and Immunities of the European Economic Community has been repealed by the second paragraph of Article 28 of the Merger Treaty; see Protocol on the Privileges and Immunities of the European Communities (p. 853).

---

* The Protocol on the Privileges and Immunities of the European Atomic Energy Community has been repealed by the second paragraph of Article 28 of the Merger Treaty; see Protocol on the Privileges and Immunities of the European Communities (p. 853).

13

E. **Resolutions and Declarations** 1085

Treaty
establishing the
European Coal and Steel
Community

Contents

---

* The Protocol on the Privileges and Immunities of the European Coal and Steel Community has
  been replaced by the second paragraph of Article 28 of the Merger Treaty; see Protocol on the
  Privileges and Immunities of the European Communities (p. 853).

I — TEXT OF THE TREATY

THE PRESIDENT OF THE FEDERAL REPUBLIC OF GERMANY, HIS ROYAL HIGHNESS THE PRINCE ROYAL OF BELGIUM, THE PRESIDENT OF THE FRENCH REPUBLIC, THE PRESIDENT OF THE ITALIAN REPUBLIC, HER ROYAL HIGHNESS THE GRAND DUCHESS OF LUXEMBOURG, HER MAJESTY THE QUEEN OF THE NETHERLANDS,

CONSIDERING that world peace can be safeguarded only by creative efforts commensurate with the dangers that threaten it,

CONVINCED that the contribution which an organized and vital Europe can make to civilization is indispensable to the maintenance of peaceful relations,

RECOGNIZING that Europe can be built only through practical achievements which will first of all create real solidarity, and through the establishment of common bases for economic development,

ANXIOUS to help, by expanding their basic production, to raise the standard of living and further the works of peace,

RESOLVED to substitute for age-old rivalries the merging of their essential interests; to create, by establishing an economic community, the basis for a broader and deeper community among peoples long divided by bloody conflicts; and to lay the foundations for institutions which will give direction to a destiny henceforward shared,

HAVE DECIDED to create a European Coal and Steel Community and to this end have designated as their plenipotentiaries:

25

THE PRESIDENT OF THE FEDERAL REPUBLIC OF GERMANY:

Dr Konrad ADENAUER, Chancellor and Minister for Foreign Affairs;

HIS ROYAL HIGHNESS THE PRINCE ROYAL OF BELGIUM:

Mr Paul VAN ZEELAND, Minister for Foreign Affairs,
Mr Joseph MEURICE, Minister for Foreign Trade;

THE PRESIDENT OF THE FRENCH REPUBLIC:

Mr Robert SCHUMAN, Minister for Foreign Affairs;

THE PRESIDENT OF THE ITALIAN REPUBLIC:

Mr Carlo SFORZA, Minister for Foreign Affairs;

HER ROYAL HIGHNESS THE GRAND DUCHESS OF LUXEMBOURG:

Mr Joseph BECH, Minister for Foreign Affairs;

HER MAJESTY THE QUEEN OF THE NETHERLANDS:

Mr D. U. STIKKER, Minister for Foreign Affairs,
Mr J. R. M. VAN DEN BRINK; Minister for Economic Affairs;

WHO, having exchanged their Full Powers, found in good and due form, have agreed as follows.

The European Coal and Steel Community

Article 1

By this Treaty, the HIGH CONTRACTING PARTIES establish among themselves a EUROPEAN COAL AND STEEL COMMUNITY, founded upon a common market, common objectives and common institutions.

Article 2

The European Coal and Steel Community shall have as its task to contribute, in harmony with the general economy of the Member States and through the establishment of a common market as provided in Article 4, to economic expansion, growth of employment and a rising standard of living in the Member States.

The Community shall progressively bring about conditions which will of themselves ensure the most rational distribution of production at the highest possible level of productivity, while safeguarding continuity of employment and taking care not to provoke fundamental and persistent disturbances in the economies of Member States.

Article 3

The institutions of the Community shall, within the limits of their respective powers, in the common interest:

(a) ensure an orderly supply to the common market, taking into account the needs of third countries;

(b) ensure that all comparably placed consumers in the common market have equal access to the sources of production;

(c) ensure the establishment of the lowest prices under such conditions that these prices do not result in higher prices charged by the same undertakings in other transactions or in a higher general price level at another time, while allowing necessary amortization and normal return on invested capital;

(d) ensure the maintenance of conditions which will encourage undertakings to expand and improve their production potential and to promote a policy of using natural resources rationally and avoiding their unconsidered exhaustion;

(e) promote improved working conditions and an improved standard of living for the workers in each of the industries for which it is responsible, so as to make possible their harmonization while the improvement is being maintained;

(f) promote the growth of international trade and ensure that equitable limits are observed in export pricing;

(g) promote the orderly expansion and modernization of production, and the improvement of quality, with no protection against competing industries that is not justified by improper action on their part or in their favour.

Article 4

The following are recognized as incompatible with the common market for coal and steel and shall accordingly be abolished and prohibited within the Community, as provided in this Treaty:

(a) import and export duties, or charges having equivalent effect, and quantitative restrictions on the movement of products;

(b) measures or practices which discriminate between producers, between purchasers or between consumers, especially in prices and delivery terms or transport rates and conditions, and measures or practices which interfere with the purchaser's free choice of supplier;

(c) subsidies or aids granted by States, or special charges imposed by States, in any form whatsoever;

(d) restrictive practices which tend towards the sharing or exploiting of markets.

Article 5

The Community shall carry out its task in accordance with this Treaty, with a limited measure of intervention.

To this end the Community shall:

— provide guidance and assistance for the parties concerned, by obtaining information, organizing consultations and laying down general objectives;

— place financial resources at the disposal of undertakings for their investment and bear part of the cost of readaptation;

— ensure the establishment, maintenance and observance of normal competitive conditions and exert direct influence upon production or upon the market only when circumstances so require;

— publish the reasons for its actions and take the necessary measures to ensure the observance of the rules laid down in this Treaty.

The institutions of the Community shall carry out these activities with a minimum of administrative machinery and in close cooperation with the parties concerned.

Article 6

The Community shall have legal personality.

In international relations, the Community shall enjoy the legal capacity it requires to perform its functions and attain its objectives.

In each of the Member States, the Community shall enjoy the most extensive legal capacity accorded to legal persons constituted in that State; it may, in particular, acquire or dispose of movable and immovable property and may be a party to legal proceedings.

The Community shall be represented by its institutions, each within the limits of its powers.

The institutions of the Community

Article 7

The institutions of the Community shall be:

— a HIGH AUTHORITY, assisted by a *Consultative Committee;*

— a COMMON ASSEMBLY (hereinafter called the 'European Parliament');

— a SPECIAL COUNCIL OF MINISTERS (hereinafter called the 'Council');

— a COURT OF JUSTICE (hereinafter called the 'Court').

The audit shall be carried out by a Court of Auditors acting within the limits of the powers conferred upon it by this Treaty.*

CHAPTER I

THE HIGH AUTHORITY

Article 8

It shall be the duty of the High Authority to ensure that the objectives set out in this Treaty are attained in accordance with the provisions thereof.

---

* Second paragraph added by Article 1 of the Treaty amending Certain Financial Provisions.

Article 9

(Article repealed by Article 19 of the Merger Treaty)

[*See Article 10 of the Merger Treaty, which reads as follows:*

1. The Commission shall consist of seventeen members, who shall be chosen on the grounds of their general competence and whose independence is beyond doubt.*

The number of members of the Commission may be altered by the Council, acting unanimously.

Only nationals of Member States may be members of the Commission.

The Commission must include at least one national of each of the Member States, but may not include more than two members having the nationality of the same State.

2. The members of the Commission shall, in the general interest of the Communities, be completely independent in the performance of their duties.

In the performance of these duties, they shall neither seek nor take instructions from any Government or from any other body. They shall refrain from any action incompatible with their duties. Each Member State undertakes to respect this principle and not to seek to influence the members of the Commission in the performance of their tasks.

The members of the Commission may not, during their term of office, engage in any other occupation, whether gainful or not. When entering upon their duties they shall give a solemn undertaking that, both during and after their term of office, they will respect

_____

* First subparagraph of paragraph 1 as amended by Article 15 of the Act of Accession ESP/PORT.

the obligations arising therefrom and in particular their duty to behave with integrity and discretion as regards the acceptance, after they have ceased to hold office, of certain appointments or benefits. In the event of any breach of these obligations, the Court of Justice may, on application by the Council or the Commission, rule that the member concerned be, according to the circumstances, either compulsorily retired in accordance with the provisions of Article 13* or deprived of his right to a pension or other benefits in its stead.]

Article 10

(Article repealed by Article 19 of the Merger Treaty)

[*See Article 11 of the Merger Treaty, which reads as follows:*

The members of the Commission shall be appointed by common accord of the Governments of the Member States.

Their term of office shall be four years. It shall be renewable.]

Article 11

(Article repealed by Article 19 of the Merger Treaty)

[*See Article 14 of the Merger Treaty, which reads as follows:*

The President and the six Vice-Presidents of the Commission shall be appointed from among its members for a term of two years in accordance with the same procedure as that laid down for the appointment of members of the Commission. Their appointments may be renewed.**

The Council, acting unanimously, may amend the provisions concerning Vice-Presidents.***

---

   * Article 13 of the Merger Treaty. See also footnote to Article 12.
  ** First paragraph as amended by Article 16 of the Act of Accession ESP/PORT.
*** Second paragraph as amended by Article 16 of the said Act.

Save where the entire Commission is replaced, such appointments shall be made after the Commission has been consulted.

In the event of retirement or death, the President and the Vice-President shall be replaced for the remainder of their term of office in accordance with the preceding provisions.]

Article 12

(Article repealed by Article 19 of the Merger Treaty)

[*See Article 12 of the Merger Treaty, which reads as follows:*

Apart from normal replacement, or death, the duties of a member of the Commission shall end when he resigns or is compulsorily retired.

The vacancy thus caused shall be filled for the remainder of the member's term of office. The Council may, acting unanimously, decide that such a vacancy need not be filled.

Save in the case of compulsory retirement under the provisions of Article 13,* members of the Commission shall remain in office until they have been replaced.]

Article 13

(Article repealed by Article 19 of the Merger Treaty)

[*See Article 17 of the Merger Treaty, which reads as follows:*

The Commission shall act by a majority of the number of members provided for in Article 10.**

---

* Article 13 of the Merger Treaty stipulates:
  'If any member of the Commission no longer fulfils the conditions required for the performance of his duties or if he has been guilty of serious misconduct, the Court of Justice may, on application by the Council or the Commission, compulsorily retire him.'

** Article 10 of the Merger Treaty. See also Article 9 above.

A meeting of the Commission shall be valid only if the number of members laid down in its rules of procedure is present.]

Article 14

In order to carry out the tasks assigned to it the High Authority shall, in accordance with the provisions of this Treaty, take decisions, make recommendations or deliver opinions.

Decisions shall be binding in their entirety.

Recommendations shall be binding as to the aims to be pursued but shall leave the choice of the appropriate methods for achieving these aims to those to whom the recommendations are addressed.

Opinions shall have no binding force.

In cases where the High Authority is empowered to take a decision, it may confine itself to making a recommendation.

Article 15

Decisions, recommendations and opinions of the High Authority shall state the reasons on which they are based and shall refer to any opinions which were required to be obtained.

Where decisions and recommendations are individual in character, they shall become binding upon being notified to the party concerned.

In all other cases, they shall take effect by the mere fact of publication.

The High Authority shall determine the manner in which this Article is to be implemented.

Article 16

The High Authority shall make all appropriate administrative arrangements for the operation of its departments.

It may set up study committees, including an economic study committee.

(Third paragraph repealed by Article 19 of the Merger Treaty)

[*See Article 16 of the Merger Treaty, which reads as follows:*

The Commission shall adopt its rules of procedure so as to ensure that both it and its departments operate in accordance with the provisions of the Treaties establishing the European Coal and Steel Community, the European Economic Community and the European Atomic Energy Community, and of this Treaty. It shall ensure that these rules are published.]

Article 17

(Article repealed by Article 19 of the Merger Treaty)

[*See Article 18 of the Merger Treaty, which reads as follows:*

The Commission shall publish annually, not later than one month before the opening of the session of the European Parliament, a general report on the activities of the Communities.]

Article 18

A Consultative Committee shall be attached to the High Authority. It shall consist of not less than seventy-two and not more than ninety-six members and shall comprise equal numbers of producers, of workers and of consumers and dealers.*

The members of the Consultative Committee shall be appointed by the Council.

---

* First paragraph as amended by Article 22 of the Act of Accession ESP/PORT.

In the case of the producers and workers, the Council shall designate representative organizations among which it shall allocate the seats to be filled. Each organization shall be required to draw up a list containing twice as many names as there are seats allotted to it. Appointment shall be made from this list.

The members of the Consultative Committee shall be appointed in their personal capacity for two years. They shall not be bound by any mandate or instructions from the organizations which nominated them.

The Consultative Committee shall elect its chairman and officers from among its members for a term of one year. The Committee shall adopt its rules of procedure.

(Sixth paragraph repealed by Article 19 of the Merger Treaty)

[*See Article 6 of the Merger Treaty, which reads as follows:*

The Council shall, acting by a qualified majority, determine the salaries, allowances and pensions of the President and members of the Commission, and of the President, Judges, Advocate-General and Registrar of the Court of Justice. It shall also, again by a qualified majority, determine any payment to be made instead of remuneration.]

Article 19

The High Authority may consult the Consultative Committee in all cases in which it considers this appropriate. It must do so whenever such consultation is prescribed by this Treaty.

The High Authority shall submit to the Consultative Committee the general objectives and the programmes drawn up under Article 46 and shall keep the Committee informed of the broad lines of its action under Articles 54, 65 and 66.

Should the High Authority consider it necessary, it may set the Consultative Committee a time limit for the submission of its opinion. The period allowed may not be less than ten days from the date on which the chairman receives notification to this effect.

The Consultative Committee shall be convened by its chairman, either at the request of the High Authority or at the request of a majority of its members, for the purpose of discussing a specific question.

The minutes of the proceedings shall be forwarded to the High Authority and to the Council at the same time as the opinions of the Committee.

CHAPTER II

THE EUROPEAN PARLIAMENT

Article 20

The European Parliament, which shall consist of representatives of the peoples of the States brought together in the Community, shall exercise the supervisory powers which are conferred upon it by this Treaty.

Article 21

(Paragraphs 1 and 2 lapsed on 17 July 1979 in accordance with Article 14 of the Act concerning the election of the representatives of the European Parliament)

[See Article 1 of that Act which reads as follows:

1. The representatives in the European Parliament of the peoples of the States brought together in the Community shall be elected by direct universal suffrage.]

[See Article 2 of that Act which reads as follows:

2. The number of representatives elected in each Member State shall be as follows:

Belgium	24
Denmark	16
Germany	81
Greece	24
Spain	60
France	81
Ireland	15
Italy	81
Luxembourg	6
Netherlands	25
Portugal	24
United Kingdom	81 .]*

3. The European Parliament shall draw up proposals for elections by direct universal suffrage in accordance with a uniform procedure in all Member States.**

The Council shall, acting unanimously, lay down the appropriate provisions, which it shall recommend to Member States for adoption in accordance with their respective constitutional requirements.***

---

* Number of representatives as fixed by Article 10 of the Act of Accession ESP/PORT.

** See also Article 7 (1) and (2) of the Act concerning the election of the representatives of the European Parliament.

*** Paragraph (3) as amended by Article 2 (2) of the Convention on Common Institutions.

Article 22

The European Parliament shall hold an annual session. It shall meet, without requiring to be convened, on the second Tuesday in March.* **

The European Parliament may be convened in extraordinary session at the request of the Council in order to deliver an opinion on such questions as may be put to it by the Council.

It may also meet in extraordinary session at the request of a majority of its members or of the High Authority.

Article 23

The European Parliament shall elect its President and its officers from among its members.

Members of the High Authority may attend all meetings. The President of the High Authority or such of its members as it may designate shall be heard at their request.

The High Authority shall reply orally or in writing to questions put to it by the European Parliament or its members.

The members of the Council may attend all meetings and shall be heard at their request.

---

* First paragraph as amended by Article 27 (1) of the Merger Treaty.
** With regard to the second sentence of this paragraph, see also Article 10 (3) of the Act concerning the election of the representatives of the European Parliament.

Article 24

The European Parliament shall discuss in open session the general report submitted to it by the High Authority.

If a motion of censure on the activities of the High Authority is tabled before it, the European Parliament shall not vote thereon until at least three days after the motion has been tabled and only by open vote.*

If the motion of censure is carried by a two-thirds majority of the votes cast, representing a majority of the Members of the European Parliament, the members of the High Authority shall resign as a body. They shall continue to deal with current business until they are replaced in accordance with Article 10.

Article 25

The European Parliament shall adopt its rules of procedure, acting by a majority of its members.

The proceedings of the European Parliament shall be published in the manner laid down in its rules of procedure.

---

* Second paragraph as amended by Article 27 (2) of the Merger Treaty.

CHAPTER III

THE COUNCIL

Article 26

The Council shall exercise its powers in the cases provided for and in the manner set out in this Treaty, in particular in order to harmonize the action of the High Authority and that of the Governments, which are responsible for the general economic policies of their countries.

To this end, the Council and the High Authority shall exchange information and consult each other.

The Council may request the High Authority to examine any proposals or measures which the Council may consider appropriate or necessary for the attainment of the common objectives.

Article 27

(Article repealed by Article 7 of the Merger Treaty)

[*See Article 2 of the Merger Treaty, which reads as follows:*

The Council shall consist of representatives of the Member States. Each Government shall delegate to it one of its members.

The office of President shall be held in turn by each Member State in the Council for a term of six months in the following order of Member States:

— for a first cycle of six years: Belgium, Denmark, Germany, Greece, Spain, France, Ireland, Italy, Luxembourg, Netherlands, Portugal, United Kingdom;

— for the following cycle of six years: Denmark, Belgium, Greece, Germany, France, Spain, Italy, Ireland, Netherlands, Luxembourg, United Kingdom, Portugal.]*

---

* Second paragraph as amended by Article 11 of the Act of Accession ESP/PORT.

Article 28*

When the Council is consulted by the High Authority, it shall consider the matter without necessarily taking a vote. The minutes of its proceedings shall be forwarded to the High Authority.

Wherever this Treaty requires that the assent of the Council be given, that assent shall be considered to have been given if the proposal submitted by the High Authority receives the approval:

— of an absolute majority of the representatives of the Member States, including the votes of the representatives of two Member States which each produce at least one ninth of the total value of the coal and steel output of the Community; or

— in the event of an equal division of votes and if the High Authority maintains its proposal after a second discussion, of the representatives of three Member States which each produce at least one ninth of the total value of the coal and steel output of the Community.

Wherever this Treaty requires a unanimous decision or unanimous assent, such decision or assent shall have been duly given if all the members of the Council vote in favour. However, for the purposes of applying Articles 21, 32, 32a, 78e and 78h of this Treaty, and Article 16, the third paragraph of Article 20, the fifth paragraph of Article 28 and Article 44 of the Protocol on the Statute of the Court of Justice, abstention by members present in person or represented shall not prevent the adoption by the Council of acts which require unanimity.

---

* Text as replaced by Article 12 of the Act of Accession ESP/PORT.

Decisions of the Council, other than those for which a qualified majority or unanimity is required, shall be taken by a vote of the majority of its members; this majority shall be considered to be attained if it represents an absolute majority of the representatives of two Member States, including the votes of the representatives of two Member States which each produce at least one ninth of the total value of the coal and steel output of the Community. However, for the purpose of applying Articles 78, 78b and 78e of this Treaty which require a qualified majority, the votes of the members of the Council shall be weighted as follows:

Belgium	5
Denmark	3
Germany	10
Greece	5
Spain	8
France	10
Ireland	3
Italy	10
Luxembourg	2
Netherlands	5
Portugal	5
United Kingdom	10

For their adoption, acts shall require at least 54 votes in favour, cast by not less than eight members.

Where a vote is taken, any member of the Council may act on behalf of not more than one other member.

The Council shall deal with the Member States through its President.

The acts of the Council shall be published in such a manner as it may decide.

Article 29

(Article repealed by Article 7 of the Merger Treaty)

[*See Article 6 of the Merger Treaty, which reads as follows:*

The Council shall, acting by a qualified majority, determine the salaries, allowances and pensions of the President and members of the Commission, and of the President, Judges, Advocates-General and Registrar of the Court of Justice. It shall also, again by a qualified majority, determine any payment to be made instead of remuneration.]

Article 30

(Article repealed by Article 7 of the Merger Treaty)

[*See Article 5 of the Merger Treaty, which reads as follows:*

The Council shall adopt its rules of procedure.]

CHAPTER IV

THE COURT

Article 31

The Court shall ensure that in the interpretation and application of this Treaty, and of rules laid down for the implementation thereof, the law is observed.

Article 32

The Court of Justice shall consist of thirteen judges.*

---

* First paragraph as amended by Article 17 of the Act of Accession ESP/PORT.

The Court shall sit in plenary session. It may, however, form Chambers, each consisting of three or five Judges, either to undertake certain preparatory inquiries or to adjudicate on particular categories of cases in accordance with rules laid down for these purposes.*

Whenever the Court of Justice hears cases brought before it by a Member State or by one of the institutions of the Community or, to the extent that the Chambers of the Court do not have the requisite jurisdiction under the Rules of Procedure, has to give preliminary rulings on questions submitted to it pursuant to Article 41, it shall sit in plenary session.**

Should the Court so request, the Council may, acting unanimously, increase the number of Judges and make the necessary adjustments to the second and third paragraphs of this Article and to the second paragraph of Article 32b.*

Article 32 a***

The Court of Justice shall be assisted by six Advocates-General.****

It shall be the duty of the Advocate-General acting with complete impartiality and independence, to make, in open court, reasoned submissions on cases brought before the Court, in order to assist the Court in the performance of the task assigned to it in Article 31.

---

* Second and fourth paragraphs as amended by Article 4 (2) *(a)* of the Convention on Common Institutions.

** Third paragraph as amended by Article 1 of the Council Decision of 26 November 1974 (*Official Journal of the European Communities,* No L 318, 28 November 1974).

*** Article added by Article 4 (2) *(a)* of the Convention on Common Institutions.

**** First paragraph as amended by Article 18 of the Act of Accession ESP/PORT.

Should the Court so request, the Council may, acting unanimously, increase the number of Advocates-General and make the necessary adjustments to the third paragraph of Article 32b.

Article 32 b*

The Judges and Advocates-General shall be chosen from persons whose independence is beyond doubt and who possess the qualifications required for appointment to the highest judicial offices in their respective countries or who are jurisconsults of recognized competence; they shall be appointed by common accord of the Governments of the Member States for a term of six years.

Every three years there shall be a partial replacement of the Judges. Seven and six Judges shall be replaced alternately.**

Every three years there shall be a partial replacement of the Advocates-General. Three Advocates-General shall be replaced on each occasion.**

Retiring Judges and Advocates-General shall be eligible for reappointment.

The Judges shall elect the President of the Court from among their number for a term of three years. He may be re-elected.

Article 32 c*

The Court shall appoint its Registrar and lay down the rules governing his service.

---

* Article added by Article 4 (2) *(a)* of the Convention on Common Institutions.
**Second and third paragraphs as amended by Article 19 of the Act of Accession ESP/PORT.

Article 32 d*

1. At the request of the Court of Justice and after consulting the Commission and the European Parliament, the Council may, acting unanimously, attach to the Court of Justice a court with jurisdiction to hear and determine at first instance, subject to a right of appeal to the Court of Justice on points of law only and in accordance with the conditions laid down by the Statute, certain classes of action or proceeding brought by natural or legal persons. That court shall not be competent to hear and determine actions brought by Member States or by Community Institutions or questions referred for a preliminary ruling under Article 41.

2. The Council, following the procedure laid down in paragraph 1, shall determine the composition of that court and adopt the necessary adjustments and additional provisions to the Statute of the Court of Justice. Unless the Council decides otherwise, the provisions of this Treaty relating to the Court of Justice, in particular the provisions of the Protocol on the Statute of the Court of Justice, shall apply to that court.

3. The members of that court shall be chosen from persons whose independence is beyond doubt and who possess the ability required for appointment to judicial office; they shall be appointed by common accord of the Governments of the Member States for a term of six years. The membership shall be partially renewed every three years. Retiring members shall be eligible for reappointment.

4. That court shall establish its rules of procedure in agreement with the Court of Justice. Those rules shall require the unanimous approval of the Council.

---

* Article added by Article 4 of the SEA.

Article 33

The Court shall have jurisdiction in actions brought by a Member State or by the Council to have decisions or recommendations of the High Authority declared void on grounds of lack of competence, infringement of an essential procedural requirement, infringement of this Treaty or of any rule of law relating to its application, or misuse of powers. The Court may not, however, examine the evaluation of the situation, resulting from economic facts or circumstances, in the light of which the High Authority took its decisions or made its recommendations, save where the High Authority is alleged to have misused its powers or to have manifestly failed to observe the provisions of this Treaty or any rule of law relating to its application.

Undertakings or the associations referred to in Article 48 may, under the same conditions, institute proceedings against decisions or recommendations concerning them which are individual in character or against general decisions or recommendations which they consider to involve a misuse of powers affecting them.

The proceedings provided for in the first two paragraphs of this Article shall be instituted within one month of the notification or publication, as the case may be, of the decision or recommendation.

Article 34

If the Court declares a decision or recommendation void, it shall refer the matter back to the High Authority. The High Authority shall take the necessary steps to comply with the judgment. If direct and special harm is suffered by an undertaking or group of undertakings by reason of a decision or recommendation held by the Court to involve a fault of such a nature as to render the Community liable, the High Authority shall, using the powers conferred upon it by this Treaty, take steps to ensure equitable redress for the harm resulting directly from the decision or recommendation declared void and, where necessary, pay appropriate damages.

If the High Authority fails to take within a reasonable time the necessary steps to comply with the judgment, proceedings for damages may be instituted before the Court.

Article 35

Wherever the High Authority is required by this Treaty, or by rules laid down for the implementation thereof, to take a decision or make a recommendation and fails to fulfil this obligation, it shall be for States, the Council, undertakings or associations, as the case may be, to raise the matter with the High Authority.

The same shall apply if the High Authority, where empowered by this Treaty, or by rules laid down for the implementation thereof, to take a decision or make a recommendation, abstains from doing so and such abstention constitutes a misuse of powers.

If at the end of two months the High Authority has not taken any decision or made any recommendation, proceedings may be instituted before the Court within one month against the implied decision of refusal which is to be inferred from the silence of the High Authority on the matter.

Article 36

Before imposing a pecuniary sanction or ordering a periodic penalty payment as provided for in this Treaty, the High Authority must give the party concerned the opportunity to submit its comments.

The Court shall have unlimited jurisdiction in appeals against pecuniary sanctions and periodic penalty payments imposed under this Treaty.

In support of its appeal, a party may, under the same conditions as in the first paragraph of Article 33 of this Treaty, contest the legality of the decision or recommendation which that party is alleged not to have observed.

Article 37

If a Member State considers that in a given case action or failure to act on the part of the High Authority is of such a nature as to provoke fundamental and persistent disturbances in its economy, it may raise the matter with the High Authority.

The High Authority, after consulting the Council, shall, if there are grounds for so doing, recognize the existence of such a situation and decide on the measures to be taken to end it, in accordance with the provisions of this Treaty, while at the same time safeguarding the essential interests of the Community.

When proceedings are instituted in the Court under this Article against such a decision or against an express or implied decision refusing to recognize the existence of the situation referred to above, it shall be for the Court to determine whether it is well founded.

If the Court declares the decision void, the High Authority shall, within the terms of the judgment of the Court, decide on the measures to be taken for the purposes indicated in the second paragraph of this Article.

Article 38

The Court may, on application by a Member State or the High Authority, declare an act of the European Parliament or of the Council to be void.

Application shall be made within one month of the publication of the act of the European Parliament or the notification of the act of the Council to the Member States or to the High Authority.

The only grounds for such application shall be lack of competence or infringement of an essential procedural requirement.

Article 39

Actions brought before the Court shall not have suspensory effect.

The Court may, however, if it considers that circumstances so require, order that application of the contested decision or recommendation be suspended.

The Court may prescribe any other necessary interim measures.

Article 40

Without prejudice to the first paragraph of Article 34, the Court shall have jurisdiction to order pecuniary reparation from the Community, on application by the injured party, to make good any injury caused in carrying out this Treaty by a wrongful act or omission on the part of the Community in the performance of its functions.

The Court shall also have jurisdiction to order the Community to make good any injury caused by a personal wrong by a servant of the Community in the performance of his duties. The personal liability of its servants towards the Community shall be governed by the provisions laid down in their Staff Regulations or the Conditions of Employment applicable to them.*

All other disputes between the Community and persons other than its servants to which the provisions of this Treaty or the rules laid down for the implementation thereof do not apply shall be brought before national courts or tribunals.

---

* Second paragraph as amended by Article 26 of the Merger Treaty.

Article 41

The Court shall have sole jurisdiction to give preliminary rulings on the validity of acts of the High Authority and of the Council where such validity is in issue in proceedings brought before a national court or tribunal.

Article 42

The Court shall have jurisdiction to give judgment pursuant to any arbitration clause contained in a contract concluded by or on behalf of the Community, whether that contract be governed by public or private law.

Article 43

The Court shall have jurisdiction in any other case provided for by a provision supplementing this Treaty.

It may also rule in all cases which relate to the subject matter of this Treaty where jurisdiction is conferred upon it by the law of a Member State.

Article 44

The judgments of the Court shall be enforceable in the territory of Member States under the conditions laid down in Article 92.

Article 45

The Statute of the Court is laid down in a Protocol annexed to this Treaty.

The Council may, acting unanimously at the request of the Court of Justice and after consulting the Commission and the European Parliament, amend the provisions of Title III of the Statute.*

---

* Second paragraph added by Article 5 of the SEA.

TITLE THREE

Economic and social provisions

CHAPTER I

GENERAL PROVISIONS

Article 46

The High Authority may at any time consult Governments, the various parties concerned (undertakings, workers, consumers and dealers) and their associations, and any experts.

Undertakings, workers, consumers and dealers, and their associations, shall be entitled to present any suggestions or comments to the High Authority on questions affecting them.

To provide guidance, in line with the tasks assigned to the Community, on the course of action to be followed by all concerned, and to determine its own course of action, in accordance with the provisions of this Treaty, the High Authority shall, in consultation as provided above:

1. conduct a continuous study of market and price trends;

2. periodically draw up programmes indicating foreseeable developments in production, consumption, exports and imports;

3. periodically lay down general objectives for modernization, long-term planning of manufacture and expansion of productive capacity;

4. take part, at the request of the Governments concerned, in studying the possibilities for re-employing, in existing industries or through the

creation of new activities, workers made redundant by market developments or technical changes;

5. obtain the information it requires to assess the possibilities for improving working conditions and living standards for workers in the industries within its province, and the threats to those standards.

The High Authority shall publish the general objectives and the programmes after submitting them to the Consultative Committee.

It may publish the studies and information mentioned above.

Article 47

The High Authority may obtain the information it requires to carry out its tasks. It may have any necessary checks made.

The High Authority must not disclose information of the kind covered by the obligation of professional secrecy, in particular information about undertakings, their business relations or their cost components. Subject to this reservation, it shall publish such data as could be useful to Governments or to any other parties concerned.

The High Authority may impose fines or periodic penalty payments on undertakings which evade their obligations under decisions taken in pursuance of this Article or which knowingly furnish false information. The maximum amount of such fines shall be 1 per cent of the annual turnover, and the maximum amount of such penalty payments shall be 5 per cent of the average daily turnover for each day's delay.

Any breach of professional secrecy by the High Authority which has caused damage to an undertaking may be the subject of an action for compensation before the Court, as provided in Article 40.

Article 48

The right of undertakings to form associations shall not be affected by this Treaty. Membership of such associations must be voluntary. Associations may engage in any activity which is not contrary to the provisions of this Treaty or to the decisions or recommendations of the High Authority.

Where this Treaty requires the Consultative Committee to be consulted, any association shall have the right to submit to the High Authority, within such time as the latter may set, the comments of its members on the proposed course of action.

To obtain information which it requires, or to facilitate the performance of the tasks entrusted to it, the High Authority shall normally call upon producers' associations on condition either that they provide for accredited representatives of workers and consumers to sit on their governing bodies or on advisory committees attached to them, or that they make satisfactory provision in some other way in their organization for the interests of workers and consumers to be voiced.

The associations referred to in the preceding paragraphs shall furnish the High Authority with such information on their activities as it may consider necessary. The comments referred to in the second paragraph of this Article and the information furnished in pursuance of this paragraph shall also be forwarded by those associations to the Government concerned.

CHAPTER II

FINANCIAL PROVISIONS

Article 49

The High Authority is empowered to procure the funds it requires to carry out its tasks:

— by imposing levies on the production of coal and steel;

— by contracting loans.

It may receive gifts.

Article 50

1. The levies are intended to cover:

— the administrative expenditure provided for in Article 78;

— the non-repayable aid towards readaptation provided for in Article 56;

— in the case of the financing arrangements provided for in Articles 54 and 56, and after recourse to the reserve fund, any portion of the amounts required for servicing loans raised by the High Authority which may not be covered by receipts from the servicing of loans granted by it, and any payments to be made under guarantees granted by the High Authority on loans contracted directly by undertakings;

— expenditure on the promotion of technical and economic research as provided for in Article 55 (2).

2. The levies shall be assessed annually on the various products according to their average value; the rate thereof shall not, however, exceed 1 per cent unless previously authorized by the Council, acting by a two-thirds majority. The mode of assessment and collection shall be determined by a general decision of the High Authority taken after consulting the Council; cumulative imposition shall be avoided as far as possible.

3. The High Authority may impose upon undertakings which do not comply with decisions taken by it under this Article surcharges of not more than 5 per cent for each quarter's delay.

Article 51

1. The High Authority may not use the funds obtained by borrowing except to grant loans.

The issue of loans by the High Authority on the markets of Member States shall be subject to the rules and regulations in force on these markets.

If the High Authority considers the guarantee of Member States necessary in order to contract certain loans, it shall approach the Government or Governments concerned after consulting the Council; no State shall be obliged to give its guarantee.

2. The High Authority may, as provided in Article 54, guarantee loans granted direct to undertakings by third parties.

3. The High Authority may so determine its conditions for loans or guarantees as to enable a reserve fund to be built up for the sole purpose of reducing whatever amounts may have to be paid out of the levies in accordance with the third subparagraph of Article 50 (1): the sums thus accumulated must not however, be used for any form of lending to undertakings.

4. The High Authority shall not itself engage in the banking operations which its financial tasks entail.

Article 52

Member States shall make all appropriate arrangements to enable transfers of funds derived from the levies, from pecuniary sanctions and periodic penalty payments and from the reserve fund to be effected within the territories referred to in the first paragraph of Article 79 in accordance with the procedure for commercial payments, to the extent necessary to make it possible for them to be used for the purposes intended by this Treaty.

The procedure for effecting transfers, both between Member States and to third countries, arising out of other financial operations carried out or guaranteed by the High Authority, shall be determined by agreement between the High Authority and the Member States concerned or the appropriate agencies; there shall, however, be no obligation upon any Member State which applies exchange controls to permit transfers where it has not expressly undertaken to do so.

Article 53

Without prejudice to the provisions of Article 58 or Chapter V of Title III, the High Authority may:

(a) after consulting the Consultative Committee and the Council, authorize the making, on conditions which it shall determine and under its supervision, of any financial arrangements common to several undertakings which it recognizes to be necessary for the performance of the tasks set out in Article 3 and compatible with this Treaty, and in particular with Article 65;

(b) with the unanimous assent of the Council, itself make any financial arrangements serving the same purposes.

Similar arrangements made or maintained by Member States shall be notified to the High Authority, which, after consulting the Consultative Committee and the Council, shall make the necessary recommendations to the States concerned where such arrangements are inconsistent, in whole or in part, with the application of this Treaty.

CHAPTER III

INVESTMENT AND FINANCIAL AID

Article 54

The High Authority may facilitate the carrying out of investment programmes by granting loans to undertakings or by guaranteeing other loans which they may contract.

With the unanimous assent of the Council, the High Authority may by the same means assist the financing of works and installations which contribute directly and primarily to increasing the production, reducing the production costs or facilitating the marketing of products within its jurisdiction.

In order to encourage coordinated development of investment, the High Authority may, in accordance with Article 47, require undertakings to inform it of individual programmes in advance, either by a special request addressed to the undertaking concerned or by a decision stating what kind and scale of programme must be communicated.

The High Authority may, after giving the parties concerned full opportunity to submit their comments, deliver a reasoned opinion on such programmes within the framework of the general objectives provided for in Article 46. If application is made by the undertaking concerned, the High Authority must deliver a reasoned opinion. The High Authority shall notify the opinion to the undertaking concerned and shall bring the opinion to the attention of its Government. Lists of such opinions shall be published.

If the High Authority finds that the financing of a programme or the operation of the installations therein planned would involve subsidies, aids, protection or discrimination contrary to this Treaty, the adverse opinion delivered by it on these grounds shall have the force of a decision within the meaning of Article 14 and the effect of prohibiting the undertaking concerned from drawing on resources other than its own funds to carry out the programme.

The High Authority may impose on undertakings which disregard the prohibition referred to in the preceding paragraph fines not exceeding the amounts improperly devoted to carrying out the programme in question.

Article 55

1. The High Authority shall promote technical and economic research relating to the production and increased use of coal and steel and to occupational safety in the coal and steel industries. To this end it shall organize all appropriate contacts among existing research bodies.

2. After consulting the Consultative Committee, the High Authority may initiate and facilitate such research:

(a) by inducing joint financing by the undertakings concerned; or *(b)* by allotting for that purpose any funds received as gifts; or

(c) with the assent of the Council, by allotting for that purpose funds derived from the levies provided for in Article 50; the limit laid down in paragraph 2 of that Article must not, however, be exceeded.

The results of research financed as provided in subparagraphs *(b)* and *(c)* shall be made available to all concerned in the Community.

3. The High Authority shall deliver any opinions which serve to make technical improvements more widely known, particularly with regard to the exchange of patents and the granting of licences for using them.

Article 56

1. If the introduction, within the framework of the general objectives of the High Authority, of new technical processes or equipment should lead to an exceptionally large reduction in labour requirements in the coal or the steel industry, making it particularly difficult in one or more areas to re-employ redundant workers, the High Authority, on application by the Governments concerned:

(a) shall obtain the opinion of the Consultative Committee;

(b) may facilitate, in the manner laid down in Article 54, either in the industries within its jurisdiction or, with the assent of the Council, in any other industry, the financing of such programmes as it may approve for the creation of new and economically sound activities capable of reabsorbing the redundant workers into productive employment;

(c) shall provide non-repayable aid towards:

— the payment of tideover allowances to workers;

— the payment of resettlement allowances to workers;

— the financing of vocational retraining for workers having to change their employment.

The High Authority shall make the provision of non-repayable aid conditional upon payment by the State concerned of a special contribution of not less than the amount of that aid, unless an exception is authorized by the Council, acting by a two-thirds majority.

2.   * If fundamental changes, not directly connected with the establishment of the common market, in market conditions for the coal or the steel industry should compel some undertakings permanently to discontinue, curtail or change their activities, the High Authority, on application by the Governments concerned:

(a) may facilitate, in the manner laid down in Article 54, either in the industries within its jurisdiction or, with the assent of the Council, in any other industry, the financing of such programmes as it may approve for the creation of new and economically sound activities or for the conversion of existing undertakings capable of reabsorbing the redundant workers into productive employment;

(b) may provide non-repayable aid towards:

— the payment of tideover allowances to workers;

---

* Paragraph (2) added in accordance with the procedure under the third and fourth paragraphs of Article 95 of this Treaty (*Official Journal of the European Communities* No 33, 16 May 1960).

— the payment of allowances to undertakings to enable them to continue paying such of their workers as may have to be temporarily laid off as a result of the undertakings' change of activity;

— the payment of resettlement allowances to workers;

— the financing of vocational retraining for workers having to change their employment.

The High Authority shall make the provision of non-repayable aid conditional upon payment by the State concerned of a special contribution of not less than the amount of that aid, unless an exception is authorized by the Council, acting by a two-thirds majority.

CHAPTER IV

PRODUCTION

Article 57

In the sphere of production, the High Authority shall give preference to the indirect means of action at its disposal, such as:

— cooperation with Governments to regularize or influence general consumption, particularly that of the public services;

— intervention in regard to prices and commercial policy as provided for in this Treaty.

Article 58

1. In the event of a decline in demand, if the High Authority considers that the Community is confronted with a period of manifest crisis

and that the means of action provided for in Article 57 are not sufficient to deal with this, it shall, after consulting the Consultative Committee and with the assent of the Council, establish a system of production quotas, accompanied to the necessary extent by the measures provided for in Article 74.

If the High Authority fails to act, a Member State may bring the matter before the Council, which may, acting unanimously, require the High Authority to establish a system of quotas.

2. The High Authority shall, on the basis of studies made jointly with undertakings and associations of undertakings, determine the quotas on an equitable basis, taking account of the principles set out in Articles 2, 3 and 4. It may in particular regulate the level of activity of undertakings by appropriate levies on tonnages exceeding a reference level set by a general decision.

The funds thus obtained shall be used to support undertakings whose rate of production has fallen below that envisaged, in order, in particular, to maintain employment in these undertakings as far as possible.

3. The system of quotas shall be ended on a proposal made to the Council by the High Authority after consulting the Consultative Committee, or by the Government of a Member State, unless the Council decides otherwise, acting unanimously if the proposal emanates from the High Authority or by a simple majority if the proposal emanates from a Government. An announcement on the ending of the quota system shall be made by the High Authority.

4. The High Authority may impose upon undertakings which do not comply with decisions taken by it under this Article fines not exceeding the value of the tonnages produced in disregard thereof.

Article 59

1. If, after consulting the Consultative Committee, the High Authority finds that the Community is confronted with a serious shortage of any or all of the products within its jurisdiction, and that the means of action provided for in Article 57 are not sufficient to deal with this, it shall bring the situation to the attention of the Council and shall, unless the Council, acting unanimously, decides otherwise, propose to it the necessary measures.

If the High Authority fails to act, a Member State may bring the matter before the Council, which may, acting unanimously, recognize that the situation in question does in fact exist.

2. The Council shall, acting unanimously on a proposal from and in consultation with the High Authority, establish consumption priorities and determine the allocation of the coal and steel resources of the Community to the industries within its jurisdiction, to export and to other sectors of consumption.

On the basis of the consumption priorities thus established, the High Authority shall, after consulting the undertakings concerned, draw up the production programmes with which the undertakings shall be required to comply.

3. If the Council does not reach a unanimous decision on the measures referred to in paragraph 2, the High Authority shall itself allocate the resources of the Community among the Member States on the basis of consumption and exports, irrespective of the place of production.

Within each of the Member States allocation of the resources assigned by the High Authority shall be carried out on the responsibility of the Government, provided that the deliveries scheduled to be supplied to other Member States are not affected and that the High Authority is consulted concerning the portions to be allotted to export and to the operation of the coal and steel industries.

If the portion allotted by a Government to export is less than the amount taken as the basis for calculating the total tonnage to be assigned to the Member State concerned, the High Authority shall, to the necessary extent, at the next allocation, redivide among the Member States the resources thus made available for consumption.

If the portion allotted by a Government to the operation of the coal and steel industries is similarly less and the result is a decrease in Community production of one of these, the tonnage assigned to the Member State concerned shall, at the next allocation, be reduced by the amount of the decrease in production so caused.

4. In all cases, the High Authority shall be responsible for allocating equitably among undertakings the quantities assigned to the industries within its jurisdiction, on the basis of studies made jointly with undertakings and associations of undertakings.

5. Should the situation provided for in paragraph 1 of this Article arise, the High Authority may, in accordance with Article 57, after consulting the Consultative Committee and with the assent of the Council, decide that restrictions on exports to third countries shall be imposed in all the Member States, or, if the High Authority fails to act, the Council may, acting unanimously, so decide on a proposal from a Government.

6. The High Authority may end the arrangements made under this Article after consulting the Consultative Committee and the Council. It shall not do so if the Council unanimously dissents.

If the High Authority fails to act, the Council may, acting unanimously, itself end the arrangements.

7. The High Authority may impose upon undertakings which do not comply with decisions taken under this Article fines not exceeding twice the value of prescribed production or deliveries either not effected or diverted from their proper use.

CHAPTER V

PRICES

Article 60

1. Pricing practices contrary to Articles 2, 3 and 4 shall be prohibited, in particular:

— unfair competitive practices, especially purely temporary or purely local price reductions tending towards the acquisition of a monopoly position within the common market;

— discriminatory practices involving, within the common market, the application by a seller of dissimilar conditions to comparable transactions, especially on grounds of the nationality of the buyer.

The High Authority may define the practices covered by this prohibition by decisions taken after consulting the Consultative Committee and the Council.

2. For these purposes:

(a) the price lists and conditions of sale applied by undertakings within the common market must be made public to the extent and in the manner prescribed by the High Authority after consulting the Consultative Com-

mittee. If the High Authority finds that an undertaking's choice of point on which it bases its price lists is abnormal and in particular makes it possible to evade the provisions of subparagraph *(b)*, it shall make appropriate recommendations to that undertaking;

(b) the methods of quotation used must not have the effect that prices charged by an undertaking in the common market, when reduced to their equivalent at the point chosen for its price lists, result in:

— increases over the price shown in the price list in question for a comparable transaction; or

— reductions below that price the amount of which exceeds either:

— the extent enabling the quotation to be aligned on the price list, based on another point which secures the buyer the most advantageous delivered terms; or

— the limits fixed, by decision of the High Authority after the Consultative Committee has delivered its opinion, for each category of product, with due regard, where appropriate, for the origin and destination of products.

Such decisions shall be taken when found necessary, to avoid disturbances in the whole or any part of the common market or disequilibria resulting from a difference between the methods of quotation used for a product and for materials involved in making it. Such decisions shall not preclude undertakings from aligning their quotations on those of undertakings outside the Community, on condition that the transactions are notified to the High Authority, which may, in the event of abuse, restrict or abrogate the right of the undertakings concerned to take advantage of this exception.

Article 61

On the basis of studies made jointly with undertakings and associations of undertakings, in accordance with the first paragraph of Article 46 and the third paragraph of Article 48, and after consulting the Consultative Committee and the Council as to the advisability of so doing and the price level to be so determined, the High Authority may, for one or more of the products within its jurisdiction:

(a) fix maximum prices within the common market, if it finds that such a decision is necessary to attain the objectives set out in Article 3, and particularly in paragraph *(c)* thereof;

(b) fix minimum prices within the common market, if it finds that a manifest crisis exists or is imminent and that such a decision is necessary to attain the objectives set out in Article 3;

(c) after consulting the associations to which the undertakings concerned belong, or the undertakings themselves, fix, by methods appropriate to the nature of the export markets, minimum or maximum export prices, if such an arrangement can be effectively supervised and is necessary both in view of the dangers to the undertakings resulting from the state of the market and in order to secure the acceptance in international economic relations of the objective set out in Article 3 *(f)*; any fixing of minimum prices shall be without prejudice to the measures provided for in the last subparagraph of Article 60 (2).

In fixing prices, the High Authority shall take into account the need to ensure that the coal and steel industries and the consumer industries remain competitive, in accordance with the principles laid down in Article 3 *(c)*.

If in these circumstances the High Authority fails to act, the Government of a Member State may bring the matter before the Council, which may, acting unanimously, call upon the High Authority to fix such maximum or minimum prices.

Article 62

If the High Authority considers this the most appropriate way of preventing coal from being priced at the level of the production costs of the mines which have the highest costs but which it is recognized should be temporarily maintained in service in order that the tasks laid down in Article 3 may be performed, it may, after consulting the Consultative Committee, authorize equalization payments:

— between undertakings in the same coalfield to which the same price lists apply;

— after consulting the Council, between undertakings in different coalfields.

These equalization payments may, moreover, be instituted as provided in Article 53.

Article 63

1. If the High Authority finds that discrimination is being systematically practised by purchasers, in particular under provisions governing contracts entered into by bodies dependent on a public authority, it shall make appropriate recommendations to the Governments concerned.

2. Where the High Authority considers it necessary, it may decide that:

(a) undertakings must frame their conditions of sale in such a way that their customers and commission agents acting on their behalf shall be under an obligation to comply with the rules made by the High Authority in application of this Chapter;

(b) undertakings shall be held responsible for infringements of this obligation by their direct agents or by commission agents acting on their behalf.

In the event of an infringement of this obligation by a purchaser, the High Authority may restrict or, should the infringement be repeated, temporarily prohibit dealings with that purchaser by Community undertakings. If this is done, the purchaser shall have the right, without prejudice to Article 33, to bring an action before the Court.

3. In addition, the High Authority is empowered to make to the Member States concerned any appropriate recommendations to ensure that the rules laid down for the application of Article 60 (1) are duly observed by all distributive undertakings and agencies in the coal and steel sectors.

Article 64

The High Authority may impose upon undertakings which infringe the provisions of this Chapter or decisions taken thereunder fines not exceeding twice the value of the sales effected in disregard thereof. If the infringement is repeated, this maximum shall be doubled.

CHAPTER VI

AGREEMENTS AND CONCENTRATIONS

Article 65

1. All agreements between undertakings, decisions by associations of undertakings and concerted practices tending directly or indirectly to prevent, restrict or distort normal competition within the common market shall be prohibited, and in particular those tending:

(a) to fix or determine prices;

(b) to restrict or control production, technical development or investment;

(c) to share markets, products, customers or sources of supply.

2.   However, the High Authority shall authorize specialization agreements or joint-buying or joint-selling agreements in respect of particular products, if it finds that:

(a) such specialization or such joint-buying or -selling will make for a substantial improvement in the production or distribution of those products;

(b) the agreement in question is essential in order to achieve these results and is not more restrictive than is necessary for that purpose; and

(c) the agreement is not liable to give the undertakings concerned the power to determine the prices, or to control or restrict the production or marketing, of a substantial part of the products in question within the common market, or to shield them against effective competition from other undertakings within the common market.

If the High Authority finds that certain agreements are strictly analogous in nature and effect to those referred to above, having particular regard to the fact that this paragraph applies to distributive undertakings, it shall authorize them also when satisfied that they meet the same requirements.

Authorizations may be granted subject to specified conditions and for limited periods. In such cases the High Authority shall renew an authorization once or several times if it finds that the requirements of subparagraphs *(a)* to *(c)* are still met at the time of renewal.

The High Authority shall revoke or amend an authorization if it finds that as a result of a change in circumstances the agreement no longer meets these requirements, or that the actual results of the agreement or of the application thereof are contrary to the requirements for its authorization.

Decisions granting, renewing, amending, refusing or revoking an authorization shall be published together with the reasons therefor; the restrictions imposed by the second paragraph of Article 47 shall not apply thereto.

3. The High Authority may, as provided in Article 47, obtain any information needed for the application of this Article, either by making a special request to the parties concerned or by means of regulations stating the kinds of agreement, decision or practice which must be communicated to it.

4. Any agreement or decision prohibited by paragraph 1 of this Article shall be automatically void and may not be relied upon before any court or tribunal in the Member States.

The High Authority shall have sole jurisdiction, subject to the right to bring actions before the Court, to rule whether any such agreement or decision is compatible with this Article.

5. On any undertaking which has entered into an agreement which is automatically void, or has enforced or attempted to enforce, by arbitration, penalty, boycott or any other means, an agreement or decision which is automatically void or an agreement for which authorization has been refused or revoked, or has obtained an authorization by means of information which it knew to be false or misleading, or has engaged in practices prohibited by paragraph 1 of this Article, the High Authority may impose fines or periodic penalty payments not exceeding twice the turnover on the products which were the subject of the agreement, decision or practice prohibited by this Article; if, however, the purpose of the agreement, decision or practice is to restrict production, technical development or investment, this maximum may be raised to 10 per cent of the annual turnover of the undertakings in question in the case of fines, and 20 per cent of the daily turnover in the case of periodic penalty payments.

Article 66

1. Any transaction shall require the prior authorization of the High Authority, subject to the provisions of paragraph 3 of this Article, if it has in itself the direct or indirect effect of bringing about within the territories referred to in the first paragraph of Article 79, as a result of action by any person or undertaking or group of persons or undertakings, a concentration between undertakings at least one of which is covered by Article 80, whether the transaction concerns a single product or a number of different products, and whether it is effected by merger, acquisition of shares or parts of the undertaking or assets, loan, contract or any other means of control. For the purpose of applying these provisions, the High Authority shall, by regulations made after consulting the Council, define what constitutes control of an undertaking.

2. The High Authority shall grant the authorization referred to in the preceding paragraph if it finds that the proposed transaction will not give to the persons or undertakings concerned the power, in respect of the product or products within its jurisdiction:

— to determine prices, to control or restrict production or distribution or to hinder effective competition in a substantial part of the market for those products; or

— to evade the rules of competition instituted under this Treaty, in particular by establishing an artificially privileged position involving a substantial advantage in access to supplies or markets.

In assessing whether this is so, the High Authority shall, in accordance with the principle of non-discrimination laid down in Article 4 *(b)*, take account of the size of like undertakings in the Community, to the extent it considers justified in order to avoid or correct disadvantages resulting from unequal competitive conditions.

The High Authority may make its authorization subject to any conditions which it considers appropriate for the purposes of this paragraph.

Before ruling on a transaction concerning undertakings at least one of which is not subject to Article 80, the High Authority shall obtain the comments of the Governments concerned.

3. The High Authority shall exempt from the requirement of prior authorization such classes of transactions as it finds should, in view of the size of the assets or undertakings concerned, taken in conjunction with the kind of concentration to be effected, be deemed to meet the requirements of paragraph 2. Regulations made to this effect, with the assent of the Council, shall also lay down the conditions governing such exemption.

4. Without prejudice to the application of Article 47 to undertakings within its jurisdiction, the High Authority may, either by regulations made after consultation with the Council stating the kind of transaction to be communicated to it or by a special request under these regulations to the parties concerned, obtain from the natural or legal persons who have acquired or regrouped or are intending to acquire or regroup the rights or assets in question any information needed for the application of this Article concerning transactions liable to produce the effect referred to in paragraph 1.

5. If a concentration should occur which the High Authority finds has been effected contrary to the provisions of paragraph 1 but which nevertheless meets the requirements of paragraph 2, the High Authority shall make its approval of that concentration subject to payment by the persons who have acquired or regrouped the rights or assets in question of the fine provided for in the second subparagraph of paragraph 6; the amount of the fine shall not be less than half of the maximum determined in that subparagraph should it be clear that authorization ought to have been applied for. If the fine is not paid, the High Authority shall take the steps hereinafter provided for in respect of concentrations found to be unlawful.

If a concentration should occur which the High Authority finds cannot fulfil the general or specific conditions to which an authorization under paragraph 2 would be subject, the High Authority shall, by means of a reasoned decision, declare the concentration unlawful and, after giving the parties concerned the opportunity to submit their comments, shall order separation of the undertakings or assets improperly concentrated or cessation of joint control, and any other measures which it considers appropriate to return the undertakings or assets in question to independent operation and restore normal conditions of competition. Any person directly concerned may institute proceedings against such decisions, as provided in Article 33. By way of derogation from Article 33, the Court shall have unlimited jurisdiction to assess whether the transaction effected is a concentration within the meaning of paragraph 1 and of regulations made in application thereof. The institution of proceedings shall have suspensory effect. Proceedings may not be instituted until the measures provided for above have been ordered, unless the High Authority agrees to the institution of separate proceedings against the decision declaring the transaction unlawful.

The High Authority may at any time, unless the third paragraph of Article 39 is applied, take or cause to be taken such interim measures of protection as it may consider necessary to safeguard the interests of competing undertakings and of third parties, and to forestall any step which might hinder the implementation of its decisions. Unless the Court decides otherwise, proceedings shall not have suspensory effect in respect of such interim measures.

The High Authority shall allow the parties concerned a reasonable period in which to comply with its decisions, on expiration of which it may impose daily penalty payments not exceeding one tenth of one per cent of the value of the rights or assets in question.

Furthermore, if the parties concerned do not fulfil their obligations, the High Authority shall itself take steps to implement its decision; it may in particular suspend the exercise, in undertakings within its jurisdiction, of the rights attached to the assets acquired irregularly, obtain the appointment by the judicial authorities of a receiver of such assets, organize the forced sale of such assets subject to the protection of the legitimate interests of their owners, and annul with respect to natural or legal persons who have acquired the rights or assets in question through the unlawful transac-

85

tion, the acts, decisions, resolutions or proceedings of the supervisory and managing bodies or undertakings over which control has been obtained irregularly.

The High Authority is also empowered to make such recommendations to the Member States concerned as may be necessary to ensure that the measures provided for in the preceding subparagraphs are implemented under their own law.

In the exercise of its powers, the High Authority shall take account of the rights of third parties which have been acquired in good faith.

6. The High Authority may impose fines not exceeding:

— 3 per cent of the value of the assets acquired or regrouped or to be acquired or regrouped, on natural or legal persons who have evaded the obligations laid down in paragraph 4;

— 10 per cent of the value of the assets acquired or regrouped, on natural or legal persons who have evaded the obligations laid down in paragraph 1; this maximum shall be increased by one twenty-fourth for each month which elapses after the end of the twelfth month following completion of the transaction until the High Authority establishes that there has been an infringement;

— 10 per cent of the value of the assets acquired or regrouped or to be acquired or regrouped, on natural or legal persons who have obtained or attempted to obtain authorization under paragraph 2 by means of false or misleading information;

— 15 per cent of the value of the assets acquired or regrouped, on undertakings within its jurisdiction which have engaged in or been party to transactions contrary to the provisions of this Article.

Persons fined under this paragraph may appeal to the Court as provided in Article 36.

7. If the High Authority finds that public or private undertakings which, in law or in fact, hold or acquire in the market for one of the products within its jurisdiction a dominant position shielding them against effective competition in a substantial part of the common market are using that position for purposes contrary to the objectives of this Treaty, it shall make to them such recommendations as may be appropriate to prevent the position from being so used. If these recommendations are not implemented satisfactorily within a reasonable time, the High Authority shall, by decisions taken in consultation with the Government concerned, determine the prices and conditions of sale to be applied by the undertaking in question or draw up production or delivery programmes with which it must comply, subject to liability to the penalties provided for in Articles 58, 59 and 64.

CHAPTER VII

INTERFERENCE WITH CONDITIONS OF COMPETITION

Article 67

1. Any action by a Member State which is liable to have appreciable repercussions on conditions of competition in the coal or the steel industry shall be brought to the knowledge of the High Authority by the Government concerned.

2.   If the action is liable, by substantially increasing differences in production costs otherwise than through changes in productivity, to provoke a serious disequilibrium, the High Authority, after consulting the Consultative Committee and the Council, may take the following steps:

— if the action taken by that State is having harmful effects on the coal or steel undertakings within the jurisdiction of that State, the High Authority may authorize it to grant aid to these undertakings, the amount, conditions and duration of which shall be determined in agreement with the High Authority. The same shall apply in the case of any change in wages and working conditions which would have the same effects, even if not resulting from any action by that State;

— if the action taken by that State is having harmful effects on the coal or steel undertakings within the jurisdiction of other Member States, the High Authority shall make a recommendation to that State with a view to remedying these effects by such measures as that State may consider most compatible with its own economic equilibrium.

3.   If the action taken by that State reduces differences in production costs by allowing special benefits to or imposing special charges on the coal or steel undertakings within its jurisdiction in comparison with the other industries in the same country, the High Authority is empowered to make the necessary recommendations to that State after consulting the Consultative Committee and the Council.

CHAPTER VIII

WAGES AND MOVEMENT OF WORKERS

Article 68

1.   The methods used for fixing wages and welfare benefits in the sev-

eral Member States shall not, in the case of the coal and steel industries, be affected by this Treaty, subject to the following provisions.

2.   If the High Authority finds that one or more undertakings are charging abnormally low prices because they are paying abnormally low wages compared with the wage level in the same area, it shall, after consulting the Consultative Committee, make appropriate recommendations to them. If the abnormally low wages are the result of governmental decisions, the High Authority shall confer with the Government concerned, and failing agreement it may, after consulting the Consultative Committee, make a recommendation to that Government.

3.   If the High Authority finds that wage reduction entails a lowering of the standard of living of workers and at the same time is being used as a means for the permanent economic adjustment of undertakings or as a means of competition between them, it shall, after consulting the Consultative Committee, make a recommendation to the undertaking or Government concerned with a view to securing, at the expense of the undertakings, benefits for the workers in order to compensate for the reductions.

This provision shall not apply to:

(a) overall measures taken by a Member State to restore its external equilibrium, without prejudice in such case to any action under Article 67;

(b) wage reductions resulting from the application of a sliding scale established by law or by contract;

(c) wage reductions resulting from a fall in the cost of living;

(d) wage reductions to correct abnormal increases that occurred previously in exceptional circumstances which no longer obtain.

4. Save in the cases referred to in paragraph 3 *(a)* and *(b)*, any wage reduction affecting all or a substantial number of the workers in an undertaking shall be notified to the High Authority.

5. The recommendations provided for in the preceding paragraphs may be made by the High Authority only after consulting the Council, unless they are addressed to undertakings smaller than a minimum size to be defined by the High Authority in agreement with the Council.

If in one of the Member States a change in the arrangements for the financing of social security or for dealing with unemployment and its effects, or a change in wages, produces the effects referred to in Article 67 (2) or (3), the High Authority is empowered to take the steps provided for in that Article.

6. The High Authority may impose upon undertakings which do not comply with recommendations made to them under this Article fines and periodic penalty payments not exceeding twice the amount of the saving in labour costs improperly effected.

Article 69

1. Member States undertake to remove any restriction based on nationality upon the employment in the coal and steel industries of workers who are nationals of Member States and have recognized qualifications in a coalmining or steelmaking occupation, subject to the limitations imposed by the basic requirements of health and public policy.

2. For the purpose of applying this provision, Member States shall draw up common definitions of skilled trades and qualifications therefor, shall determine by common accord the limitations provided for in paragraph 1, and shall endeavour to work out arrangements on a Community-wide basis for bringing offers of employment into touch with applications for employment.

3.   In addition, with regard to workers not covered by paragraph 2, they shall, should growth of coal or steel production be hampered by a shortage of suitable labour, adjust their immigration rules to the extent needed to remedy this state of affairs; in particular, they shall facilitate the re-employment of workers from the coal and steel industries of other Member States.

4.   They shall prohibit any discrimination in remuneration and working conditions between nationals and migrant workers, without prejudice to special measures concerning frontier workers; in particular, they shall endeavour to settle among themselves any matters remaining to be dealt with in order to ensure that social security arrangements do not inhibit labour mobility.

5.   The High Authority shall guide and facilitate action by Member States in applying this Article.

6.   This Article shall not affect the international obligations of Member States.

CHAPTER IX

TRANSPORT

Article 70

It is recognized that the establishment of the common market necessitates the application of such rates and conditions for the carriage of coal and steel as will afford comparable price conditions to comparably placed consumers.

Any discrimination in rates and conditions of carriage of every kind which is based on the country of origin or destination of products shall be prohibited in traffic between Member States. For the purpose of eliminating such discrimination it shall in particular be obligatory to apply to the carriage of coal and steel to or from another country of the Community the scales, rates and all other tariff rules of every kind which are applicable to the internal carriage of the same goods on the same route.

The scales, rates and all other tariff rules of every kind applied to the carriage of coal and steel within each Member State and between Member States shall be published or brought to the knowledge of the High Authority.

The application of special internal rates and conditions in the interest of one or more coal- or steel-producing undertakings shall require the prior agreement of the High Authority, which shall verify that they are in accordance with the principles of this Treaty; it may make its agreement temporary or conditional.

Subject to the provisions of this Article, and to the other provisions of this Treaty, transport policy, including the fixing and altering of rates and conditions of carriage of every kind and the making of rates on a basis calculated to secure for the transport undertakings concerned a properly balanced financial position, shall continue to be governed by the laws or regulations of the individual Member States, as shall measures relating to coordination or competition between different modes of transport or different routes.

CHAPTER X

COMMERCIAL POLICY

Article 71

The powers of the Governments of Member States in matters of commercial policy shall not be affected by this Treaty, save as otherwise provided therein.

The powers conferred on the Community by this Treaty in matters of commercial policy towards third countries may not exceed those accorded to Member States under international agreements to which they are parties, subject to the provisions of Article 75.

The Governments of Member States shall afford each other such mutual assistance as is necessary to implement measures recognized by the High Authority as being in accordance with this Treaty and with existing international agreements. The High Authority is empowered to propose to the Member States concerned the methods by which this mutual assistance may be provided.

Article 72

Minimum rates below which Member States undertake not to lower their customs duties on coal and steel as against third countries, and maximum rates above which they undertake not to raise them, may be fixed by decision of the Council, acting unanimously on a proposal from the High Authority made on the latter's own initiative or at the request of a Member State.

Within the limits so fixed, each Government shall determine its tariffs according to its own national procedure. The High Authority may, on its own initiative or at the request of a Member State, deliver an opinion suggesting amendment of the tariffs of the State.

Article 73

The administration of import and export licences for trade with third countries shall be a matter for the Government in whose territory the place of destination for imports or the place of origin for exports is situated.

The High Authority is empowered to supervise the administration and verification of these licences with respect to coal and steel. Where necessary it shall, after consulting the Council, make recommendations to Member States to ensure that the arrangements in this connection are not more restrictive than the circumstances governing their adoption or retention require, and to secure the coordination of measures taken under the third paragraph of Article 71 or under Article 74.

Article 74

In the cases set out below, the High Authority is empowered to take any measures which is in accordance with this Treaty, and in particular with the objectives set out in Article 3, and to make to Governments any recommendation which is in accordance with the second paragraph of Article 71:

(1) if it is found that countries not members of the Community or undertakings situated in such countries are engaging in dumping or other practices condemned by the Havana Charter;

(2) if a difference between quotations by undertakings outside and by undertakings within the jurisdiction of the Community is due solely to the fact that those of the former are based on conditions of competition contrary to this Treaty;

(3) if one of the products referred to in Article 81 of this Treaty is imported into the territory of one or more Member States in relatively increased quantities and under such conditions that these imports cause or threaten to cause serious injury to production within the common market of like or directly competing products.

However, recommendations for the introduction of quantitative restrictions under subparagraph 2 may be made only with the assent of the Council, and under subparagraph 3 only under the conditions laid down in Article 58.

Article 75

The Member States undertake to keep the High Authority informed of proposed commercial agreements or arrangements having similar effect where these relate to coal and steel or to the importation of other raw materials and specialized equipment needed for the production of coal and steel in Member States.

If a proposed agreement or arrangement contains clauses which would hinder the implementation of this Treaty, the High Authority shall make the necessary recommendations to the State concerned within ten days of receiving notification of the communication addressed to it; in any other case it may deliver opinions.

TITLE FOUR

General provisions

Article 76

(Article repealed by the second paragraph of Article 28 of the Merger Treaty)

[*See Merger Treaty, first paragraph of Article 28, which reads as follows:*

The European Communities shall enjoy in the territories of the Member States such privileges and immunities as are necessary for the performance of their tasks, under the conditions laid down in the Protocol annexed to this Treaty. The same shall apply to the European Investment Bank.]

Article 77

The seat of the institutions of the Community will be determined by common accord of the Governments of the Member States.

Article 78* **

1. The financial year shall run from 1 January to 31 December.

The administrative expenditure of the Community shall comprise the expenditure of the High Authority, including that relating to the functioning of the Consultative Committee, and that of the European Parliament, the Council, and of the Court of Justice.

---

* Text as amended by Article 2 of Treaty amending Certain Financial Provisions.

** EDITORIAL NOTE:
The Joint Declaration by the European Parliament, the Council and the Commission, adopted on 30 June 1982, on various measures to improve the budgetary procedure is reproduced on page 1103 of this volume.

2. Each institution of the Community shall, before 1 July, draw up estimates of its administrative expenditure. The High Authority shall consolidate these estimates in a preliminary draft administrative budget. It shall attach thereto an opinion which may contain different estimates.

The preliminary draft budget shall contain an estimate of revenue and an estimate of expenditure.

3. The High Authority shall place the preliminary draft administrative budget before the Council not later than 1 September of the year preceding that in which the budget is to be implemented.

The Council shall consult the High Authority and, where appropriate, the other institutions concerned whenever it intends to depart from the preliminary draft budget.

The Council shall, acting by a qualified majority, establish the draft administrative budget and forward it to the European Parliament.

4. The draft administrative budget shall be placed before the European Parliament not later than 5 October of the year preceding that in which the budget is to be implemented.

The European Parliament shall have the right to amend the draft administrative budget, acting by a majority of its members and to propose to the Council, acting by an absolute majority of the votes cast, modifications to the draft budget relating to expenditure necessarily resulting from this Treaty or from acts adopted in accordance therewith.

If, within 45 days of the draft administrative budget being placed before it, the European Parliament has given its approval, the administrative budget shall stand as finally adopted. If within this period the European Parliament has not amended the draft administrative budget nor proposed any modifications thereto, the administrative budget shall be deemed to be finally adopted.

If within this period the European Parliament has adopted amendments or proposed modifications, the draft administrative budget together with the amendments or proposed modifications shall be forwarded to the Council.

5.   After discussing the draft administrative budget with the High Authority and, where appropriate, with the other institutions concerned, the Council shall act under the following conditions:

(a) the Council may, acting by a qualified majority, modify any of the amendments adopted by the European Parliament;

(b) with regard to the proposed modifications:

— where a modification proposed by the European Parliament does not have the effect of increasing the total amount of the expenditure of an institution, owing in particular to the fact that the increase in expenditure which it would involve would be expressly compensated by one or more proposed modifications correspondingly reducing expenditure, the Council may, acting by a qualified majority, reject the proposed modification. In the absence of a decision to reject it, the proposed modification shall stand as accepted,

— where a modification proposed by the European Parliament has the effect of increasing the total amount of the expenditure of an institution, the Council may, acting by a qualified majority, accept this proposed modification. In the absence of a decision to accept it, the proposed modification shall stand as rejected,

— where, in pursuance of one of the two preceding subparagraphs, the Council has rejected a proposed modification, it may, acting by a qualified majority, either retain the amount shown in the draft administrative budget or fix another amount.

The draft administrative budget shall be modified on the basis of the proposed modifications accepted by the Council.

If, within 15 days of the draft administrative budget being placed before it, the Council has not modified any of the amendments adopted by the European Parliament and if the modifications proposed by the latter have been accepted, the administrative budget shall be deemed to be finally adopted. The Council shall inform the European Parliament that it has not modified any of the amendments and that the proposed modifications have been accepted.

If within this period the Council has modified one or more of the amendments adopted by the European Parliament or if the modifications proposed by the latter have been rejected or modified, the modified draft administrative budget shall again be forwarded to the European Parliament. The Council shall inform the European Parliament of the results of its deliberations.

6. Within 15 days of the draft administrative budget being placed before it, the European Parliament, which shall have been notified of the action taken on its proposed modification, may, acting by a majority of its members and three-fifths of the votes cast, amend or reject the modifications to its amendments made by the Council and shall adopt the administrative budget accordingly. If within this period the European Parliament has not acted, the administrative budget shall be deemed to be finally adopted.

7. When the procedure provided for in this Article has been completed, the President of the European Parliament shall declare that the administrative budget has been finally adopted.

8. However, the European Parliament, acting by a majority of its members and two-thirds of the votes cast, may, if there are important reasons, reject the draft administrative budget and ask for a new draft to be submitted to it.

9.   A maximum rate of increase in relation to the expenditure of the same type to be incurred during the current year shall be fixed annually for the total expenditure other than that necessarily resulting from this Treaty or from acts adopted in accordance therewith.

The High Authority shall, after consulting the Economic Policy Committee, declare what this maximum is as it results from:

— the trend, in terms of volume, of the gross national product within the Community,

— the average variation in the budgets of the Member States,

and

— the trend of the cost of living during the preceding financial year.

The maximum rate shall be communicated, before 1 May, to all the institutions of the Community. The latter shall be required to conform to this during the budgetary procedure, subject to the provisions of the fourth and fifth subparagraphs of this paragraph.

If, in respect of expenditure other than that necessarily resulting from this Treaty or from acts adopted in accordance therewith, the actual rate of increase on the draft administrative budget established by the Council is over half the maximum rate, the European Parliament may, exercising its right of amendment, further increase the total amount of that expenditure to a limit not exceeding half the maximum rate.

Where the European Parliament, the Council or the High Authority considers that the activities of the Communities require that the rate determined according to the procedure laid down in this paragraph should be exceeded, another rate may be fixed by agreement between the Council, acting by a qualified majority, and the European Parliament, acting by a majority of its members and three-fifths of the votes cast.

10. Each institution shall exercise the powers conferred upon it by this Article, with due regard for the provisions of this Treaty and for acts adopted in accordance therewith, in particular those relating to the Communities' own resources and to the balance between revenue and expenditure.

11. Final adoption of the administrative budget shall have the effect of authorizing and requiring the High Authority to collect the corresponding revenue in accordance with the provisions of Article 49.

Article 78a*

The administrative budget shall be drawn up in the unit of account determined in accordance with the provisions of the regulations made pursuant to Article 78h.

The expenditure shown on the budget shall be authorized for one financial year, unless the regulations made pursuant to Article 78h provide otherwise.

In accordance with conditions to be laid down pursuant to Article 78h any appropriations, other than those relating to staff expenditure, that are unexpended at the end of the financial year may be carried forward to the next financial year only.

Appropriations shall be classified under different chapters grouping items of expenditure according to their nature or purpose and subdivided, as far as may be necessary, in accordance with the regulations made pursuant to Article 78h.

The expenditure of the European Parliament, the Council, the High Authority and the Court shall be set out in separate parts of the administrative budget, without prejudice to special arrangements for certain common items of expenditure.

---

* Text as amended by Article 3 of the Treaty amending Certain Financial Provisions.

Article 78b*

1. If, at the beginning of a financial year, the administrative budget has not yet been voted, a sum equivalent to not more than one-twelfth of the budget appropriations for the preceding financial year may be spent each month in respect of any chapter or other subdivision of the administrative budget in accordance with the provisions of the regulations made pursuant to Article 78h; this arrangement shall not, however, have the effect of placing at the disposal of the High Authority appropriations in excess of one-twelfth of those provided for in the draft administrative budget in course of preparation.

The High Authority is authorized and required to impose the levies up to the amount of the appropriations for the preceding financial year, but shall not thereby exceed the amount which would have resulted from the adoption of the draft administrative budget.

2. The Council may, acting by a qualified majority, provided that the other conditions laid down in paragraph 1 are observed, authorize expenditure in excess of one-twelfth. The authorization and requirement to impose the levies may be adjusted accordingly.

If the decision relates to expenditure which does not necessarily result from this Treaty or from acts adopted in accordance therewith, the Council shall forward it immediately to the European Parliament; within 30 days the European Parliament, acting by a majority of its members and three-fifths of the votes cast, may adopt a different decision on the expenditure in excess of the one-twelfth referred to in paragraph 1. This part of the decision of the Council shall be suspended until the European Parliament

---

* Text as amended by Article 4 of the Treaty amending Certain Financial Provisions.

has taken its decision. If within the said period the European Parliament has not taken a decision which differs from the decision of the Council, the latter shall be deemed to be finally adopted.

Article 78c*

The High Authority shall implement the administrative budget, in accordance with the provisions of the regulations made pursuant to Article 78h on its own responsibility and within the limits of the appropriations.

The regulations shall lay down detailed rules for each institution concerning its part in effecting its own expenditure.

Within the administrative budget, the High Authority may, subject to the limits and conditions laid down in the regulations made pursuant to Article 78h, transfer appropriations from one chapter to another or from one subdivision to another.

Article 78d**

The High Authority shall submit annually to the Council and to the European Parliament the accounts of the preceding financial year relating to the implementation of the administrative budget. The High Authority shall also forward to them a financial statement of the assets and liabilities of the Community in the field covered by that budget.

---

* Text as amended by Article 5 of the Treaty amending Certain Financial Provisions.

** Text as amended by Article 6 of the Treaty amending Certain Financial Provisions.

1. A Court of Auditors is hereby established.

2. The Court of Auditors shall consist of twelve members.**

3. The members of the Court of Auditors shall be chosen from among persons who belong or have belonged in their respective countries to external audit bodies or who are especially qualified for this office. Their independence must be beyond doubt.

4. The members of the Court of Auditors shall be appointed for a term of six years by the Council, acting unanimously after consulting the European Parliament.

However, when the first appointments are made, four members of the Court of Auditors, chosen by lot, shall be appointed for a term of office of four years only.

The members of the Court of Auditors shall be eligible for reappointment.

They shall elect the President of the Court of Auditors from among their number for a term of three years. The President may be re-elected.

5. The members of the Court of Auditors shall, in the general interest of the Community, be completely independent in the performance of their duties.

In the performance of these duties, they shall neither seek nor take instructions from any government or from any other body. They shall refrain from any action incompatible with their duties.

6. The members of the Court of Auditors may not, during their term of office, engage in any other occupation, whether gainful or not. When en-

---

* Text, excepting paragraph 2, as amended by Article 7 of the Treaty amending Certain Financial Provisions.

** Paragraph 2 as amended by Article 20 of the Act of Accession ESP/PORT.

tering upon their duties they shall give a solemn undertaking that, both during and after their term of office, they will respect the obligations arising therefrom and in particular their duty to behave with integrity and discretion as regards the acceptance, after they have ceased to hold office, of certain appointments or benefits.

7. Apart from normal replacement, or death, the duties of a member of the Court of Auditors shall end when he resigns, or is compulsorily retired by a ruling of the Court of Justice pursuant to paragraph 8.

The vacancy thus caused shall be filled for the remainder of the member's term of office.

Save in the case of compulsory retirement, members of the Court of Auditors shall remain in office until they have been replaced.

8. A member of the Court of Auditors may be deprived of his office or of his right to a pension or other benefits in its stead only if the Court of Justice, at the request of the Court of Auditors, finds that he no longer fulfils the requisite conditions or meets the obligations arising from his office.

9. The Council, acting by a qualified majority, shall determine the conditions of employment of the President and the members of the Court of Auditors and in particular their salaries, allowances and pensions. It shall also, by the same majority, determine any payment to be made instead of remuneration.

10. The provisions of the Protocol on the Privileges and Immunities of the European Communities applicable to the Judges of the Court of Justice shall also apply to the members of the Court of Auditors.

Article 78f*

1. The Court of Auditors shall examine the accounts of all administrative expenditure and administrative revenue of the Community, including the revenue from the tax for the benefit of the Community levied on the salaries, wages and emoluments of officials and other servants of the latter. It shall also examine the accounts of all revenue and expenditure of all bodies set up by the Community in so far as the relevant constituent instrument does not preclude such examination.

2. The Court of Auditors shall examine whether all revenue referred to in paragraph 1 has been received and all expenditure referred to in that paragraph has been incurred in a lawful and regular manner and whether the financial management has been sound.

The audit of revenue shall be carried out on the basis both of the amounts established as due and the amounts actually paid to the Community.

The audit of expenditure shall be carried out on the basis both of commitments undertaken and payments made.

These audits may be carried out before the closure of accounts for the financial year in question.

3. The audit shall be based on records and, if necessary, performed on the spot in the institutions of the Community and in the Member States. In the Member States the audit shall be carried out in liaison with the national audit bodies or, if these do not have the necessary powers, with the competent national departments. These bodies or departments shall inform the Court of Auditors whether they intend to take part in the audit.

The institutions of the Community and the national audit bodies or, if these do not have the necessary powers, the competent national depart-

---

* Text as amended by Article 8 of the Treaty amending Certain Financial Provisions.

ments, shall forward to the Court of Auditors, at its request, any document or information necessary to carry out its task.

4. The Court of Auditors shall draw up an annual report after the close of each financial year. It shall be forwarded to the institutions of the Community and shall be published, together with the replies of these institutions to the observations of the Court of Auditors, in the *Official Journal of the European Communities.*

The Court of Auditors may also, at any time, submit observations on specific questions and deliver opinions at the request of one of the institutions of the Community.

It shall adopt its annual reports or opinions by a majority of its members.

It shall assist the European Parliament and the Council in exercising their powers of control over the implementation of the budget.

5. The Court of Auditors shall also draw up a separate annual report stating whether the accounting other than that for the expenditure and revenue referred to in paragraph 1 and the financial management by the High Authority relating thereto have been effected in a regular manner. It shall draw up this report within six months of the end of the financial year to which the accounts refer and shall submit it to the High Authority and the Council. The High Authority shall forward it to the European Parliament.

Article 78g*

The European Parliament, acting on a recommendation from the Council which shall act by a qualified majority, shall give a discharge to the High Authority in respect of the implementation of the administrative budget. To this end, the Council and the European Parliament in turn shall

---

* Text added by Article 9 of the Treaty amending Certain Financial Provisions.

examine the accounts and the financial statement referred to in Article 78d, and the annual report by the Court of Auditors together with the replies of the institutions under audit to the observations of the Court of Auditors.

Article 78h*

The Council, acting unanimously on a proposal from the High Authority and after consulting the European Parliament and obtaining the opinion of the Court of Auditors, shall:

(a) make Financial Regulations specifying in particular the procedure to be adopted for establishing and implementing the administrative budget and for presenting and auditing accounts;

(b) lay down rules concerning the responsibility of authorizing officers and accounting officers and concerning appropriate arrangements for inspection.

Article 79

This Treaty shall apply to the European territories of the High Contracting Parties. It shall also apply to European territories for whose external relations a signatory State is responsible; as regards the Saar, an exchange of letters between the Government of the Federal Republic of Germany and the Government of the French Republic is annexed to this Treaty.

** Notwithstanding the preceding paragraph:

(a) This Treaty shall not apply to the Faroe Islands. The Government of the Kingdom of Denmark may, however, give notice, by a declaration deposited by 31 December 1975 at the latest with the Government

---

* Text added by Article 10 of the Treaty amending Certain Financial Provisions.

** Second paragraph, with the exception of the second subparagraph of point (a), added by Article 25 of the Act of Accession DK/IRL/UK, modified by Article 14 of the AD AA DK/IRL/UK.

of the French Republic, which shall transmit a certified copy thereof to each of the Governments of the other Member States, that this Treaty shall apply to those Islands. In that event, this Treaty shall apply to those Islands from the first day of the second month following the deposit of the declaration.

This Treaty shall not apply to Greenland.*

(b) This Treaty shall not apply to the Sovereign Base Areas of the United Kingdom of Great Britain and Northern Ireland in Cyprus.

(c) This Treaty shall apply to the Channel Islands and the Isle of Man only to the extent necessary to ensure the implementation of the arrangements for those islands set out in the Decision of the Council of the European Communities of 22 January 1972 concerning the accession of new Member States to the European Coal and Steel Community.

Each High Contracting Party undertakes to extend to the other Member States the preferential treatment which it enjoys with respect to coal and steel in the non-European territories under its jurisdiction.

Article 80

For the purposes of this Treaty, 'undertaking' means any undertaking engaged in production in the coal or the steel industry within the territories referred to in the first paragraph of Article 79, and also, for the purposes of Articles 65 and 66 and of information required for their application and proceedings in connection with them, any undertaking or agency regularly engaged in distribution other than sale to domestic consumers or small craft industries.

Article 81

The expressions 'coal' and 'steel' are defined in Annex I to this Treaty.

---

* Subparagraph added by Article 1 of the Greenland Treaty.

Additions to the lists in that Annex may be made by the Council, acting unanimously.

Article 82

The turnover taken as the basis for calculating any fines and periodic penalty payments imposed on undertakings under this Treaty shall be the turnover on products within the jurisdiction of the High Authority.

Article 83

The establishment of the Community shall in no way prejudice the system of ownership of the undertakings to which this Treaty applies.

Article 84

For the purposes of this Treaty, the words 'this Treaty' mean the provisions of the Treaty and its Annexes, of the Protocols annexed thereto and of the Convention on the Transitional Provisions.

Article 85

The initial and transitional measures agreed by the High Contracting Parties to enable the provisions of this Treaty to be applied are laid down in a Convention annexed to this Treaty.

Article 86

Member States undertake to take all appropriate measures, whether general or particular, to ensure fulfilment of the obligations resulting from decisions and recommendations of the institutions of the Community and to facilitate the performance of the Community's tasks.

Member States undertake to refrain from any measures incompatible with the common market referred to in Articles 1 and 4.

They shall make all appropriate arrangements, as far as lies within their powers, for the settlement of international accounts arising out of trade in coal and steel within the common market and shall afford each other mutual assistance to facilitate such settlements.

Officials of the High Authority entrusted by it with tasks of inspection shall enjoy in the territories of Member States, to the full extent required for the performance of their duties, such rights and powers as are granted by the laws of these States to their own revenue officials. Forthcoming visits of inspection and the status of the officials shall be duly notified to the State concerned. Officials of that State may, at its request or at that of the High Authority, assist the High Authority's officials in the performance of their task.

Article 87

The High Contracting Parties undertake not to avail themselves of any treaties, conventions or declarations made between them for the purpose of submitting a dispute concerning the interpretation or application of this Treaty to any method of settlement other than those provided for therein.

Article 88

If the High Authority considers that a State has failed to fulfil an obligation under this Treaty, it shall record this failure in a reasoned decision after giving the State concerned the opportunity to submit its comments. It shall set the State a time limit for the fulfilment of its obligation.

The State may institute proceedings before the Court within two months of notification of the decision; the Court shall have unlimited jurisdiction in such cases.

If the State has not fulfilled its obligation by the time limit set by the High Authority, or if it brings an action which is dismissed, the High Authority may, with the assent of the Council acting by a two-thirds majority:

(a) suspend the payment of any sums which it may be liable to pay to the State in question under this Treaty;

(b) take measures, or authorize the other Member States to take measures, by way of derogation from the provisions of Article 4, in order to correct the effects of the infringement of the obligation.

Proceedings may be instituted before the Court against decisions taken under subparagraphs (a) and (b) within two months of their notification; the Court shall have unlimited jurisdiction in such cases.

If these measures prove ineffective, the High Authority shall bring the matter before the Council.

Article 89

Any dispute between Member States concerning the application of this Treaty which cannot be settled by another procedure provided for in this Treaty may be submitted to the Court on application by one of the States which are parties to the dispute.

The Court shall also have jurisdiction in any dispute between Member States which relates to the subject matter of this Treaty, if the dispute is submitted to it under a special agreement between the parties.

Article 90

If failure to fulfil an obligation under this Treaty on the part of an undertaking also constitutes an infringement of its obligations under the law of its State and judicial or administrative action is being taken under that law against the undertaking, the State in question shall so inform the High Authority, which may defer its decision.

If the High Authority defers its decision, it shall be kept informed of the progress of the action taken by national authorities and shall be permitted to produce all relevant documents and expert and other evidence. It shall also be informed of the final decision on the case and shall take account of this decision in determining any penalty it may itself impose.

Article 91

If an undertaking does not pay by the time limit set a sum which it is liable to pay to the High Authority either under this Treaty or rules laid down for the implementation thereof or in discharge of a pecuniary sanction or periodic penalty payment imposed by the High Authority, the High Authority may suspend payment of sums which it is liable to pay to that undertaking, up to the amount of the outstanding payment.

Article 92

Decisions of the High Authority which impose a pecuniary obligation shall be enforceable.

Enforcement in the territory of Member States shall be carried out by means of the legal procedure in force in each State, after the order for enforcement in the form in use in the State in whose territory the decision is to be enforced has been appended to the decision, without other formality than verification of the authenticity of the decision. This formality shall be carried out at the instance of a Minister designated for this purpose by each of the Governments.

Enforcement may be suspended only by a decision of the Court.

Article 93

The High Authority shall maintain all appropriate relations with the United Nations and the Organization for European Economic Cooperation and shall keep these organizations regularly informed of the activities of the Community.

Article 94

Relations shall be maintained between the institutions of the Community and the Council of Europe as provided in a Protocol annexed to this Treaty.

Article 95

In all cases not provided for in this Treaty where it becomes apparent that a decision or recommendation of the High Authority is necessary to attain, within the common market in coal and steel and in accordance with Article 5, one of the objectives of the Community set out in Articles 2, 3 and 4, the decision may be taken or the recommendation made with the unanimous assent of the Council and after the Consultative Committee has been consulted.

Any decision so taken or recommendation so made shall determine what penalties, if any, may be imposed.

If, after the end of the transitional period provided in the Convention on the Transitional Provisions, unforeseen difficulties emerging in the light of experience in the application of this Treaty, or fundamental economic or technical changes directly affecting the common market in coal and steel, make it necessary to adapt the rules for the High Authority's exercise of its powers, appropriate amendments may be made; they must not, however, conflict with the provisions of Articles 2, 3 and 4 or interfere with the relationship between the powers of the High Authority and those of the other institutions of the Community.

These amendments shall be proposed jointly by the High Authority and the Council, acting by a ten-twelfths majority of its members, and shall be submitted to the Court for its opinion. In considering them, the Court shall have full power to assess all points of fact and of law. If as a result of such consideration it finds the proposals compatible with the provisions of the preceding paragraph, they shall be forwarded to the European Parliament and shall enter into force if approved by a majority of three quarters of the votes cast and two thirds of the members of the European Parliament.*

Article 96

After the end of the transitional period, the Government of any Member State or the High Authority may propose amendments to this Treaty. Such proposals shall be submitted to the Council. If the Council, acting by a two-thirds majority, delivers an opinion in favour of calling a conference of representatives of the Governments of the Member States, the conference shall be convened forthwith by the President of the Council for the

---

* Fourth paragraph as amended by Article 13 of the Act of Accession ESP/PORT.

purpose of determining by common accord the amendments to be made to the Treaty.

Such amendments shall enter into force after being ratified by all the Member States in accordance with their respective constitutional requirements.

Article 97

This Treaty is concluded for a period of fifty years from its entry into force.

Article 98

Any European State may apply to accede to this Treaty. It shall address its application to the Council, which shall act unanimously after obtaining the opinion of the High Authority; the Council shall also determine the terms of accession, likewise acting unanimously. Accession shall take effect on the day when the instrument of accession is received by the Government acting as depositary of this Treaty.

Article 99

This Treaty shall be ratified by all the Member States in accordance with their respective constitutional requirements; the instruments of ratification shall be deposited with the Government of the French Republic.

This Treaty shall enter into force on the date of deposit of the instrument of ratification by the last signatory State to take this step.

If all the instruments of ratification have not been deposited within six months of the signature of this Treaty, the Governments of the

States which have deposited their instruments shall consult each other on the measures to be taken.

Article 100

This Treaty, drawn up in a single original, shall be deposited in the archives of the Government of the French Republic, which shall transmit a certified copy thereof to each of the Governments of the other signatory States.

IN WITNESS WHEREOF, the undersigned plenipotentiaries have signed this Treaty and affixed thereto their seals.

Done at Paris this eighteenth day of April in the year one thousand nine hundred and fifty-one.

ADENAUER

Paul VAN ZEELAND
J. MEURICE

SCHUMAN

SFORZA

JOS. BECH

STIKKER
VAN DEN BRINK

Annexes

ANNEX I

DEFINITION OF THE EXPRESSIONS
'COAL' AND 'STEEL'

1. The expressions 'coal' and 'steel' cover the products listed below.

2. In the exercise of its functions in relation to special steels, coke and scrap the High Authority shall take account of the special features of production of these materials or of trade in them.

3. The High Authority shall exercise its functions in relation to gas coke, and to brown coal other than for the making of briquettes and semi-coke, only where this is necessary by reason of appreciable disturbances caused by these products on the market in fuels.

4. The High Authority shall take account of the fact that the production of some of the products listed is directly linked with the production of by-products which are not listed but whose selling prices may influence those of the principal products.

OEEC Code No (for reference)	PRODUCT
3000	FUELS
3100	*Hard coal*
3200	*Hard coal briquettes*
3300	*Coke, excluding electrode and petroleum coke*
	Semi-coke derived from hard coal
3400	*Brown coal briquettes*
3500	*Run-of-mine brown coal*
	Semi-coke derived from brown coal
4000	IRON AND STEEL
4100 *	*Raw materials for iron and steel production*[1]
	Iron ore (except pyrites)
	Sponge iron and steel[1a]
	Ferrous scrap
	Manganese ore
4200	*Pig iron and ferro-alloys*
	Pig iron for steelmaking
	Foundry and other pig iron
	Spiegeleisen and high-carbon ferro-manganese[2]

[1]   Not including the raw materials under OEEC Code No 4190 ('Other raw materials not elsewhere classified for iron and steel production') which are not contained in this list. Not including refractories.

[1a]   Including sponge iron proper or in briquetted form, Renn balls and similar products.

[2]   Not including other ferro-alloys.

*   EDITORIAL NOTE:
    Text of heading as amended by Article 1 of the Decision of the Council of the European Coal and Steel Community (*Official Journal of the European Communities*, No 129, 6 December 1962, p. 2810).

OEEC Code No (for reference)	PRODUCT
4300	*Crude and semi-finished products of iron, ordinary steel or special steel, including products for re-use and re-rolling* Liquid steel cast or not cast into ingots, including ingots for forging[3] Semi-finished products: blooms, billets and slabs; sheet bars and tinplate bars; hot-rolled wide coils (other than coils classed as finished products)
4400	*Hot finished products of iron, ordinary steel or special steel*[4] Rails, sleepers, fishplates, soleplates, joists, heavy sections 80 mm and over, sheet piling Bars and sections of less than 80 mm and flats of less than 150 mm Wire rod Tube rounds and squares

[3] The High Authority shall concern itself with production of liquid steel for castings only where this is to be regarded as an activity of the steel industry propoer.
Any other production of liquid steel for castings, such as that at small and medium-sized independent foundries, shall be subject to statistical coverage only, such coverage not to give rise to any discriminatory action in respect thereof.

[4] Not including steel castings, forgings and powder metallurgy products.

OEEC Code No (for reference)	PRODUCT
4400 *(cont'd)*	Hot-rolled hoop and strip (including tube strip)
	Hot-rolled sheet under 3 mm (coated or uncoated)
	Plates and sheets of 3 mm thickness and over, universal plates of 150 mm and over
4500	*End products of iron, ordinary steel or special steel[5]*
	Tinplate, terneplate, blackplate, galvanized sheets, other coated sheets
	Cold-rolled sheets under 3 mm
	Electrical sheets
	Strip for tinplate
	Cold-rolled plate, in coil and in strips, of a thickness of 3 mm or more*

---

[5] Not including steel tubes (seamless or welded), cold-rolled strip less than 500 mm in width (other than for tinplating), wire and wire products, bright bars and iron castings (tubes, pipes and fittings, and other iron castings).

---

* EDITORIAL NOTE:
Text of the heading as supplemented by the Single Article of the Council Decision of 21 February 1983 adding a number of products to the list in Annex I to the ECSC Treaty (*Official Journal of the European Communities*, No L 56, 3 March 1983).

ANNEX II

SCRAP

The provisions of this Treaty shall apply to ferrous scrap, but account shall be taken of the following practical arrangements necessitated by the special features of the recovery of and trade in scrap:

(a) any prices fixed by the High Authority under Chapter V of Title III shall apply to purchases by Community undertakings; Member States shall cooperate with the High Authority in ensuring that sellers comply with the decisions taken;

(b) Article 59 shall not apply to:

— cast iron scrap usable only in foundries outside the jurisdiction of the Community;

— undertakings' own arisings, availabilities of which shall, however, be taken into account in calculating the bases for allocations of bought scrap;

(c) for the application of Article 59 to bought scrap, the High Authority shall, in cooperation with the Governments of Member States, obtain the necessary information on availabilities and requirements, including exports to third countries.

On the basis of the information thus obtained, the High Authority shall allocate availabilities among Member States in accordance with Article 59, in such a way as to enable the most efficient use to be made of them and taking into account all the operating and supply conditions in the different parts of the steel industry within its jurisdiction.

To ensure that shipments of scrap so allocated from one Member State to another, or purchases by undertakings in one Member State of the tonnages to which they are entitled on the market of another Member State, will not involve discrimination harmful to undertakings in either State, the following measures shall be taken:

1. Each Member State shall authorize the shipment from its territory to other Member States of tonnages in accordance with the allocation made by the High Authority; in return, each Member State shall be authorized to effect the necessary checks to establish that outgoing shipments are not in excess of the amounts provided for. The High Authority is empowered to ensure that the arrangements made are not more restrictive than is necessary for this purpose.

2. The allocation among Member States shall be reviewed at as frequent intervals as may be necessary to maintain a relation fair both to local purchasers and to purchasers from other Member States between the recorded availabilities in each Member State and the tonnages it is required to ship to other Member States.

3. The High Authority shall ensure that the regulations made by each Member State concerning sellers within its jurisdiction do not lead to the application of dissimilar conditions to comparable transactions, especially on grounds of the nationality of the buyers.

ANNEX III

SPECIAL STEELS

Special steels and high carbon steels, as defined in the draft European customs nomenclature finalized by the Tariff Committee at its meeting in Brussels on 15 July 1950, shall be treated according to which of the following groups they fall within:

(a) special steels commonly called structural steels, containing less than 0.6 per cent of carbon and not more than 8 per cent of two or more alloying elements taken together or 5 per cent of a single alloying element;[1]

(b) high carbon steels, containing between 0.6 and 1.6 per cent of carbon; special steels other than those defined in *(a)* above, containing less than 40 per cent of two or more alloying elements taken together or 20 per cent of a single alloying element;[1]

(c) special steels not covered by *(a)* or *(b)*.

Products in groups *(a)* and *(b)* shall come within the jurisdiction of the High Authority, but to enable study to be made of appropriate arrangements for the application of this Treaty to them, given the special features

---

[1] Sulphur, phosphorus, silicon and manganese in the amounts normally accepted in ordinary steels are not counted as alloying elements.

of their production and of trade in them, the date for the abolition of import and export duties or equivalent charges and of all quantitative restrictions on their movement within the Community shall be deferred until one year after the date the establishment of the common market in steel.

As to products in group *(c)*, the High Authority shall, upon taking up its duties, enter into a series of studies to determine appropriate arrangements for the application of the Treaty to them, taking into account the special features of their production and of trade in them; as and when the findings are forthcoming, and within three years of the establishment of the common market at the latest, the arrangements suggested for each of the products in question shall be submitted by the High Authority to the Council, which shall pronounce upon them in accordance with the Article 81. During this period products in group *(c)* shall be subject only to statistical checks by the High Authority.

K. A.

P. v. Z.
J. M.

Sch.

Sf.

B.

S.
v. d. B.

II — PROTOCOLS

Protocol
on the Statute
of the Court of Justice
of the European Coal and
Steel Community

EDITORIAL NOTE:
Article 4 (2) *(b)* of the Convention on Certain Institutions Common to the European Communities states:
'The provisions of the Protocol on the Statute of the Court of Justice annexed to the Treaty establishing the European Coal and Steel Community, in so far as they are in conflict with Articles 32 to 32c of that Treaty, shall be repealed.'

THE HIGH CONTRACTING PARTIES,

DESIRING to lay down the Statute of the Court of Justice provided for in Article 45 of this Treaty,

HAVE AGREED as follows:

Article 1

The Court of Justice established by Article 7 of the Treaty shall be constituted and shall function in accordance with the provisions of this Treaty and of this Statute.

TITLE I

JUDGES

OATH OF OFFICE

Article 2

Before taking up his duties each Judge shall, in open court, take an oath to perform his duties impartially and conscientiously and to preserve the secrecy of the deliberations of the Court.

PRIVILEGES AND IMMUNITIES

Article 3

The Judges shall be immune from legal proceedings. After they have ceased to hold office, they shall continue to enjoy immunity in respect of acts performed by them in their official capacity, including words spoken or written.

The Court, sitting in plenary session, may waive the immunity.

Where immunity has been waived and criminal proceedings are instituted against a Judge, he shall be tried, in any of the Member States, only by the court competent to judge the members of the highest national judiciary.

(Fourth paragraph repealed by the second paragraph of Article 28 of the Merger Treaty)

[*See Article 21 of the Protocol on the Privileges and Immunities of the European Communities, which reads as follows:*

Articles 12 to 15 and Article 18 shall apply to the Judges, the Advocates-General, the Registrar and the Assistant Rapporteurs of the Court of Justice, without prejudice to the provisions of Article 3 of the Protocols on the Statute of the Court of Justice concerning immunity from legal proceedings of Judges and Advocates-General.]

DISQUALIFICATIONS

Article 4

The Judges may not hold any political or administrative office.

They may not engage in any occupation, whether gainful or not, unless exemption is exceptionally granted by the Council, acting by a two-thirds majority.

They may not acquire or retain, directly or indirectly, any interest in any business related to coal and steel during their term of office and for three years after ceasing to hold office.

REMUNERATION

Article 5

(Article repealed by Article 8 (3) (a) of the Merger Treaty)

[*See Article 6 of the Merger Treaty, which reads as follows:*

The Council shall, acting by a qualified majority, determine the salaries, allowances and pensions of the President, and members of the Commission, and of the President, Judges, Advocates-General and Registrar of the Court of Justice. It shall also, again by a qualified majority, determine any payment to be made instead of remuneration.]

TERMINATION OF APPOINTMENT

Article 6

Apart from normal replacement, the duties of a Judge shall end on his death or resignation.

Where a Judge resigns, his letter of resignation shall be addressed to the President of the Court for transmission to the President of the Council. Upon this notification a vacancy shall arise on the bench.

Save where Article 7 applies, a Judge shall continue to hold office until his successor takes up his duties.

Article 7

A Judge may be deprived of his office only if, in the unanimous opinion of the other Judges, he no longer fulfils the requisite conditions.

The President of the Council, the President of the High Authority and the President of the European Parliament shall be notified thereof by the Registrar.

A vacancy shall arise on the bench upon this notification.

Article 8

A Judge who is to replace a member of the Court whose term of office has not expired shall be appointed for the remainder of his predecessor's term.

TITLE II

ORGANIZATION

Article 9

The Judges, the Advocates-General and the Registrar shall be required to reside at the place where the Court has its seat.

*Article 10**

The Court shall be assisted by two Advocates-General and a Registrar.

ADVOCATES-GENERAL

Article 11

It shall be the duty of the Advocate-General, acting with complete impartiality and independence, to make, in open court, oral and reasoned submissions on cases brought before the Court, in order to assist the Court in the performance of the task assigned to it in Article 31 of this Treaty.

*Article 12**

The Advocates-General shall be appointed for a term of six years in the same manner as the Judges. Every three years there shall be a partial replacement. The Advocate-General whose term of office is to expire at the end of the first three years shall be chosen by lot. The provisions *of the third and fourth paragraphs of Article 32 of this Treaty*** and the provisions of Article 6 of this Statute shall apply to the Advocates-General.

---

* See note on p. 133.
** EDITORIAL NOTE:
    Since the new version of Article 32 of the Treaty establishing the European Coal and Steel Community this reference is no longer accurate; see Articles 32a and 32b of this Treaty.

Article 13

The provisions of Articles 2 to 5 and of Article 8 shall apply to the Advocates-General.

An Advocate-General may be deprived of his office only if he no longer fulfils the requisite conditions. The decision shall be taken by the Council, acting unanimously, after the Court has delivered its opinion.

REGISTRAR

Article 14

The Court shall appoint its Registrar and lay down the rules governing his service, account being taken of the provisions of Article 15. The Registrar shall take an oath before the Court to perform his duties impartially and conscientiously and preserve the secrecy of the deliberations of the Court.

(Second paragraph repealed by the second paragraph of Article 28 of the Merger Treaty)

[*See Article 21 of the Protocol on the Privileges and Immunities of the European Communities, which reads as follows:*

Articles 12 to 15 and Article 18 shall apply to the Judges, the Advocates-General, the Registrar and the Assistant Rapporteurs of the Court of Justice, without prejudice to the provisions of Article 3 of the Protocols on the Statute of the Court of Justice concerning immunity from legal proceedings of Judges and Advocates-General.]

Article 15

(Article repealed by Article 8 (3) (a) of the Merger Treaty)

[*See Article 6 of the Merger Treaty, which reads as follows:*

The Council shall, acting by a qualifed majority, determine the salaries, allowances and pensions of the President and members of the Commission, and of the President, Judges, Advocates-General and Registrar of the Court of Justice. It shall also, again by a qualified majority, determine any payment to be made instead of remuneration.]

STAFF OF THE COURT

Article 16*

1. Officials and other servants shall be attached to the Court to enable it to function. They shall be responsible to the Registrar under the authority of the President.

2. On a proposal from the Court, the Council may, acting unanimously, provide for the appointment of Assistant Rapporteurs and lay down the rules governing their service. The Assistant Rapporteurs may be required, under conditions laid down in the rules of procedure, to participate in preparatory inquiries in cases pending before the Court and to cooperate with the Judge who acts as Rapporteur.

---

* Text as amended by Article 8 (3) *(b)* of the Merger Treaty.

The Assistant Rapporteurs shall be chosen from persons whose independence is beyond doubt and who possess the necessary legal qualifications; they shall be appointed by the Council. They shall take an oath before the Court to perform their duties impartially and conscientiously and to preserve the secrecy of the deliberations of the Court.

FUNCTIONING OF THE COURT

Article 17

The Court shall remain permanently in session. The duration of the judicial vacations shall be determined by the Court with due regard to the needs of its business.

COMPOSITION OF THE COURT

Article 18*

The Court shall sit in plenary session. It may, however, form two Chambers, each consisting of three Judges, either to undertake certain preparatory inquiries or to adjudicate on particular categories of cases in accordance with rules laid down for these purposes.

Decisions of the Court shall be valid only when an uneven number of its members is sitting in the deliberations. Decisions of the full Court shall

---

* See note on p. 133.

be valid if seven members are sitting. Decisions of the Chambers shall be valid only if three Judges are sitting; in the event of one of the Judges of a Chamber being prevented from attending, a Judge of another Chamber may be called upon to sit in accordance with conditions laid down in the rules of procedure.*

Actions brought by States or by the Council shall in all cases be tried in plenary session.

SPECIAL RULES

Article 19

No Judge or Advocate-General may take part in the disposal of any case in which he has previously taken part as agent or adviser or has acted for one of the parties, or on which he has been called upon to pronounce as a member of a court or tribunal, of a commission of inquiry or in any other capacity.

If, for some special reason, any Judge or Advocate-General considers that he should not take part in the judgment or examination of a particular case, he shall so inform the President. If, for some special reason, the President considers that any Judge or Advocate-General should not sit or make submissions in a particular case, he shall notify him accordingly.

Any difficulty arising as to the application of this Article shall be settled by decision of the Court.

A party may not apply for a change in the composition of the Court or of one of its Chambers on the grounds of either the nationality of a Judge or the absence from the Court or from the Chamber of a Judge of the nationality of that party.

---

* Second paragraph as amended by Article 20 of the Act of Accession DK/IRL/UK.

TITLE III

PROCEDURE

REPRESENTATION OF AND ASSISTANCE TO THE PARTIES

Article 20

The States and the institutions of the Community shall be represented before the Court by an agent appointed for each case; the agent may be assisted by a lawyer entitled to practise before a court of a Member State.

Undertakings and all other natural or legal persons must be assisted by a lawyer entitled to practise before a court of a Member State.

Such agents and lawyers shall, when they appear before the Court, enjoy the rights and immunities necessary to the independent exercise of their duties under conditions laid down in rules drawn up by the Court and submitted for the approval of the Council, acting unanimously.*

As regards such lawyers who appear before it, the Court shall have the powers normally accorded to courts of law, under conditions laid down in those rules.

University teachers being nationals of a Member State whose law accords them a right of audience shall have the same rights before the Court as are accorded by this Article to lawyers entitled to practise before a court of a Member State.

---

* Third paragraph as amended by Article 8 (3) *(c)* of the Merger Treaty.

144

STAGES OF PROCEDURE

Article 21

The procedure before the Court shall consist of two parts: written and oral.

The written procedure shall consist of the communication to the parties and to the institutions of the Community whose decisions are in dispute of applications, statements of case, defences and observations, and of replies, if any, as well as of all papers and documents in support or of certified copies of them.

Communications shall be made by the Registrar in the order and within the time laid down in the rules of procedure.

The oral procedure shall consist of the reading of the report presented by a Judge acting as Rapporteur, the hearing by the Court of witnesses, experts, agents, and lawyers entitled to practise before a court of a Member State and of the submissions of the Advocate-General.

APPLICATIONS

Article 22

A case shall be brought before the Court by a written application addressed to the Registrar. The application shall contain the name and address of the party and the description of the signatory, the subject matter of the dispute, the submissions and a brief statement of the grounds on which the application is based.

The application shall be accompanied, where appropriate, by the decision the annulment of which is sought or, in the case of proceedings against an implied decision, by documentary evidence of the date on which the request was lodged. If the documents are not submitted with the application, the Registrar shall ask the party concerned to produce them within a reasonable period, but in that event the rights of the party shall not lapse even if such documents are produced after the time limit for bringing proceedings.

TRANSMISSION OF DOCUMENTS

Article 23

Where proceedings are instituted against a decision of one of the institutions of the Community, that institution shall transmit to the Court all the documents relating to the case before the Court.

PREPARATORY INQUIRIES

Article 24

The Court may require the parties, their representatives or agents or the Governments of the Member States to produce all documents and to supply all information which the Court considers desirable. Formal note shall be taken of any refusal.

Article 25

The Court may at any time entrust any individual, body, authority, committee or other organization it chooses with the task of holding an inquiry or giving an expert opinion; to this end it may compile a list of individuals or bodies approved as experts.

HEARING TO BE PUBLIC

Article 26

The hearing in court shall be public, unless the Court decides otherwise for serious reasons.

MINUTES

Article 27

Minutes shall be made of each hearing and signed by the President and the Registrar.

HEARINGS

Article 28

The case list shall be established by the President.

Witnesses may be heard under conditions laid down in the rules of procedure. They may be heard on oath.

During the hearings the Court may also examine experts, persons entrusted with holding an inquiry, and the parties themselves. The latter, however, may address the Court only through their representatives or their lawyers.

Where it is established that a witness or expert has concealed facts or falsified evidence on any matter on which he has testified or been examined by the Court, the Court is empowered to report the misconduct to the Minister for Justice of the State of which the witness or expert is a national, in order that he may be subjected to the relevant penal provisions of the national law.

With respect to defaulting witnesses the Court shall have the powers generally granted to courts and tribunals, under conditions laid down in rules drawn up by the Court and submitted for the approval of the Council, acting unanimously.*

SECRECY OF THE DELIBERATIONS OF THE COURT

Article 29

The deliberations of the Court shall be and shall remain secret.

JUDGMENTS

Article 30

Judgments shall state the reasons on which they are based. They shall contain the names of the Judges who took part in the deliberations.

Article 31

Judgments shall be signed by the President, the Judge acting as Rapporteur and the Registrar. They shall be read in open court.

---

* Fifth paragraph as amended by Article 8 (3) *(c)* of the Merger Treaty.

COSTS

Article 32

The Court shall adjudicate upon costs.

SUMMARY PROCEDURE

Article 33

The President of the Court may, by way of summary procedure, which may, in so far as necessary, differ from some of the rules contained in this Statute and which shall be laid down in the rules of procedure, adjudicate upon applications to suspend execution, as provided for in the second paragraph of Article 39 of this Treaty, or to prescribe interim measures in pursuance of the last paragraph of Article 39, or to suspend enforcement in accordance with the third paragraph of Article 92.

Should the President be prevented from attending, his place shall be taken by another Judge under conditions laid down in the rules provided for in Article 18 of this Statute.

The ruling of the President or of the Judge replacing him shall be provisional and shall in no way prejudice the decision of the Court on the substance of the case.

INTERVENTION

Article 34

Natural or legal persons establishing an interest in the result of any case submitted to the Court may intervene in that case.

Submissions made in an application to intervene shall be limited to supporting or requesting the rejection of the submissions of one of the parties.

JUDGMENT BY DEFAULT

Article 35

Where the defending party in proceedings in which the Court has unlimited jurisdiction, after having been duly summoned, fails to file written submissions in defence, judgment shall be given against that party by default. An objection may be lodged against the judgment within one month of it being notified. The objection shall not have the effect of staying enforcement of the judgment by default unless the Court decides otherwise.

THIRD-PARTY PROCEEDINGS

Article 36

Natural or legal persons and the institutions of the Community may, in cases and under conditions to be determined by the rules of procedure, institute third-party proceedings to contest a judgment rendered without their being heard.

INTERPRETATION

Article 37

If the meaning or scope of a judgment is in doubt, the Court shall construe it on application by any party or any institution of the Community establishing an interest therein.

REVISION OF A JUDGMENT

Article 38

An application for revision of a judgment may be made to the Court only on discovery of a fact which is of such a nature as to be a decisive factor, and which, when the judgment was given, was unknown to the Court and to the party claiming the revision.

The revision shall be opened by a judgment of the Court expressly recording the existence of a new fact, recognizing that it is of such a character as to lay the case open to revision and declaring the application admissible on this ground.

No application for revision may be made after the lapse of ten years from the date of the judgment.

TIME LIMITS

Article 39

The proceedings provided for in Articles 36 and 37 of this Treaty must be instituted within the time limit of one month provided for in the last paragraph of Article 33.

Periods of grace based on considerations of distance shall be laid down in the rules of procedure.

No right shall be prejudiced in consequence of the expiry of a time limit if the party concerned proves the existence of unforeseeable circumstances or of *force majeure*.

PERIODS OF LIMITATION

Article 40

Proceedings provided for in the first two paragraphs of Article 40 of this Treaty shall be barred after a period of five years from the occurrence of the event giving rise thereto. The period of limitation shall be interrupted if proceedings are instituted before the Court or if prior to such proceedings an application is made by the aggrieved party to the relevant institution of the Community. In the latter event the proceedings must be instituted within the time limit of one month provided for in the last paragraph of Article 33; the provisions of the last paragraph of Article 35 shall apply where appropriate.

SPECIAL RULES RELATING TO DISPUTES BETWEEN MEMBER STATES

Article 41*

Where a dispute between Member States is brought before the Court under Article 89 of this Treaty, the other Member States shall be notified forthwith by the Registrar of the subject matter of the dispute.

Each Member State shall have the right to intervene in the proceedings.

The disputes referred to in this Article must be dealt with in plenary session.

---

* See note on p. 133.

Article 42

If a State intervenes in a case before the Court as provided for in the preceding Article, the interpretation contained in the judgment shall be binding upon the State.

PROCEEDINGS BY THIRD PARTIES

Article 43

Decisions taken by the High Authority under Article 63 (2) of this Treaty must be notified to the purchaser and to the undertakings concerned; if the decision concerns all or a large number of undertakings, publication may be substituted for individual notification.

Appeals may be brought, under Article 36 of this Treaty, by any person on whom a periodic penalty payment has been imposed under the fourth subparagraph of Article 66 (5).

RULES OF PROCEDURE

Article 44*

The Court of Justice shall adopt its rules of procedure. These shall require the unanimous approval of the Council. The rules of procedure shall contain all the provisions necessary for applying and, where required, supplementing this Statute.

------

* As amended by Article 8 (3) *(d)* of the Merger Treaty.

TRANSITIONAL PROVISION

Article 45

Immediately after the oath has been taken, the President of the Council shall proceed to choose by lot the Judges and the Advocates-General whose terms of office are to expire at the end of the first three years in accordance with Article 32 of this Treaty.

Done at Paris this eighteenth day of April in the year one thousand nine hundred and fifty-one.

ADENAUER

Paul VAN ZEELAND
J. MEURICE

SCHUMAN

SFORZA

JOS. BECH

STIKKER
VAN DEN BRINK

Protocol
on relations with
the Council of Europe

THE HIGH CONTRACTING PARTIES,

FULLY AWARE of the need to establish ties as close as possible between the European Coal and Steel Community and the Council of Europe, particularly between the European Parliament and the Consultative Assembly of the Council of Europe,

TAKING NOTE of the recommendations of the Assembly of the Council of Europe,

HAVE AGREED upon the following provisions:

Article 1

The Governments of the Member States are invited to recommend to their respective Parliaments that the members of the Assembly* whom these Parliaments are called upon to designate should preferably be chosen from among the representatives to the Consultative Assembly of the Council of Europe.

Article 2

The European Parliament of the Community shall forward each year to the Consultative Assembly of the Council of Europe a report on its activities.

Article 3

The High Authority shall communicate each year to the Committee of Ministers and to the Consultative Assembly of the Council of Europe the general report provided for in Article 17 of this Treaty.

---

* EDITORIAL NOTE:
  Notwithstanding the provisions of Article 3 of the SEA, and for historical reasons, the term 'Assembly' has not been replaced by the terms 'European Parliament'.

157

Article 4

The High Authority shall inform the Council of Europe of the action which it has been able to take on any recommendations that may have been sent to it by the Committee of Ministers of the Council of Europe under Article 15 *(b)* of the Statute of the Council of Europe.

Article 5

The present Treaty establishing the European Coal and Steel Community and the Annexes thereto shall be registered with the Secretariat of the Council of Europe.

Article 6

Agreements between the Community and the Council of Europe may, among other things, provide for any other type of mutual assistance and cooperation between the two organizations and indicate the appropriate forms thereof.

Done at Paris this eighteenth day of April in the year one thousand nine hundred and fifty-one.

ADENAUER

Paul VAN ZEELAND
J. MEURICE

SCHUMAN

SFORZA

JOS. BECH

STIKKER
VAN DEN BRINK

III — EXCHANGE OF LETTERS
BETWEEN THE GOVERNMENT OF THE FEDERAL
REPUBLIC OF GERMANY AND THE GOVERNMENT
OF THE FRENCH REPUBLIC CONCERNING THE
SAAR

[TRANSLATION]

THE FEDERAL CHANCELLOR
AND
MINISTER FOR FOREIGN AFFAIRS

Paris, 18 April 1951

His Excellency President Robert Schuman,
Minister for Foreign Affairs,
Paris

Sir,

The representatives of the Federal Government have several times declared in the course of the negotiations on the European Coal and Steel Community that the status of the Saar can be finally settled only by the Peace Treaty or a similar Treaty. Furthermore, they have declared in the course of the negotiations that in signing the Treaty the Federal Government is not expressing recognition of the present status of the Saar.

I would repeat this declaration and would ask you to confirm that the French Government agrees with the Federal Government that the status of the Saar can be finally settled only by the Peace Treaty or a similar Treaty and that the French Government does not view the Federal Government's signature of the European Coal and Steel Community Treaty as recognition by the Federal Government of the present status of the Saar.

I am, Sir,
(Signed) ADENAUER

Paris, 18 April 1951

Sir,

In reply to your letter of 18 April 1951, the French Government notes that the Federal Government in signing the Treaty establishing the European Coal and Steel Community does not intend recognition of the present status of the Saar.

The French Government declares, in accordance with its own point of view, that it is acting on behalf of the Saar by virtue of the present status of the latter but does not view the Federal Government's signature of the Treaty as recognition by the Federal Government of the present status of the Saar. It is not its understanding that the Treaty establishing the European Coal and Steel Community prejudges the final status of the Saar, which is a matter for the Peace Treaty or a Treaty in place thereof.

I am, Sir,
(Signed) SCHUMAN

Dr Konrad ADENAUER,
Chancellor and Minister for Foreign Affairs
of the Federal Republic of Germany

IV — CONVENTION
ON THE TRANSITIONAL PROVISIONS

THE HIGH CONTRACTING PARTIES,

DESIRING to draw up the Convention on the Transitional Provisions provided for in Article 85 of the Treaty,

HAVE AGREED as follows:

Purpose of the Convention

Article 1

1. The purpose of this Convention, drawn up in pursuance of Article 85 of the Treaty, is to provide for the measures required in order to establish the common market and enable production to be progressively adapted to the new conditions, while helping to eliminate disequilibria arising out of the former conditions.

2. To this end, the implementation of the Treaty shall be effected in two stages — a preparatory period and a transitional period.

3. The preparatory period shall extend from the date of entry into force of the Treaty to the date of the establishment of the common market.

During this period:

(a) all the institutions of the Community shall be set up and contacts established between them and undertakings and associations of undertakings, trade unions, and associations of consumers and dealers, in order to place the functioning of the Community on a basis of regular

consultation and to develop a common approach and mutual understanding among all concerned;

(b) the High Authority shall conduct:

1. studies and consultations;

2. negotiations with third countries.

The purpose of the studies and consultations shall be to enable an overall survey to be drawn up, in regular contact with Governments, with undertakings and associations of undertakings, with workers and with consumers and dealers, of the situation of the coal and steel industries in the Community and the problems arising therefrom, and the way to be prepared for the actual measures which will have to be taken to deal with these during the transitional period.

The purpose of the negotiations with third countries shall be:

— first, to lay the foundations for cooperation between the Community and these countries;

— second, to obtain, before the elimination of customs duties and quantitative restrictions within the Community, the necessary derogations from:

— most-favoured-nation treatment under the General Agreement on Tariffs and Trade and under bilateral agreements;

— the principle of non-discrimination in liberalization of trade within the Organization for European Economic Cooperation.

4. The transitional period shall begin on the date of the establishment of the common market and shall end five years after the establishment of the common market in coal.

5. Upon the entry into force of the Treaty in accordance with Article 99, the provisions thereof shall apply subject to the derogations allowed by this Convention and without prejudice to the supplementary provisions contained in this Convention for the ends set out above.

Save where this Convention expressly provides otherwise, these derogations and supplementary provisions shall cease to apply, and measures taken to implement them shall cease to have effect, at the end of the transitional period.

PART ONE

Implementation of the Treaty

CHAPTER I

SETTING UP OF THE INSTITUTIONS OF THE COMMUNITY

THE HIGH AUTHORITY

Article 2

1. The High Authority shall take office upon the appointment of its members.

2. In order to perform the tasks assigned to it by Article 1 of this Convention, the High Authority shall exercise forthwith the information and study functions assigned to it by the Treaty, in the manner and with the powers provided in Articles 46, 47 and 48 and the third paragraph of Article 54. Once the High Authority has taken office, the Governments shall notify it in accordance with Article 67 of any action liable to have repercussions on conditions of competition, and in accordance with Article 75 of any provisions in trade agreements or arrangements having similar effect where these relate to coal and steel.

On the basis of information obtained concerning facilities existing and planned, the High Authority shall determine the date from which the provisions of Article 54 other than those referred to in the preceding subparagraph shall apply to investment programmes and to projects already in process of execution on that date. The penultimate paragraph of Article 54 shall not apply, however, to projects for which orders were placed before 1 March 1951.

Once the High Authority has taken office, it shall exercise where necessary, in consultation with the Governments, the powers provided in Article 59 (3).

It shall not exercise the other functions assigned to it by the Treaty until the opening date of the transitional period for each of the products in question.

3. On each of the opening dates referred to in the preceding paragraph, the High Authority shall notify Member States that it is ready to assume the functions concerned. Until such notification the relevant powers shall continue to be exercised by Member States.

However, from a date which the High Authority shall appoint on taking office, prior consultations shall be held between it and Member States concerning any laws or regulations which Member States may be planning to introduce on matters assigned to the jurisdiction of the High Authority by the Treaty.

4. Without prejudice to the provisions of Article 67 relating to the effect of new measures, the High Authority shall examine with the Governments concerned the effect on the coal and steel industries of existing laws and regulations, including any which fix prices for by-products not coming within its jurisdiction, and of such contractual social security schemes as are equivalent in effect to regulations. If it finds that some of these, by reason either of their own effects or of differences in them between two or more Member States, are liable seriously to distort conditions of competition in the coal or the steel industry, whether in the market of the country in question or in the rest of the common market or in export markets, it

shall, after consulting the Council, propose to the Governments concerned any action which it considers will correct them or offset their effects.

5.   In order to have a working basis which is independent of the practices of the various undertakings, the High Authority shall seek to establish, in consultation with Governments, undertakings and associations of under-takings, workers, and consumers and dealers, by what means it will be pos-sible to make comparable:

— the price ranges for different qualities relative to the average price for the products, or for the successive stages of their production;

— the calculation of provision for depreciation.

6.   During the preparatory period the main task of the High Authority shall be to establish relations with undertakings and associations of under-takings, trade unions, and associations of consumers and dealers, in order to obtain practical knowledge of the general situation and of particular situations in the Community.

In the light of the information it obtains on markets, supplies, the pro-duction conditions of undertakings, the living conditions of workers, and modernization and equipment programmes, the High Authority shall, in contact with all concerned, draw up an overall survey of the situation of the Community to guide their work together.

On the basis of these consultations and the overall picture thus formed, the measures shall be prepared which will be needed to establish the com-mon market and facilitate the adaptation of production.

173

THE COUNCIL

Article 3

The Council shall meet within one month after the High Authority takes office.

THE CONSULTATIVE COMMITTEE

Article 4

To enable the Consultative Committee to be set up as provided in Article 18 of the Treaty, Governments shall forward to the High Authority upon its taking office all information on the producers', workers' and consumers' organizations for coal and steel in each country, particularly on their membership, geographical coverage, statutes, powers and functions.

On the basis of this information, the High Authority shall, within two months of taking office, obtain a decision of the Council designating the producers' and workers' associations which are to put forward candidates.

The Consultative Committee shall be set up within one month of this decision.

THE COURT

Article 5

The Court shall take office upon the appointment of its members. Its first President shall be appointed in the same manner as the President of the High Authority.

The Court shall adopt its rules of procedure within three months.

No matter may be brought before the Court until its rules of procedure have been published. The imposition of periodic penalty payments and the collection of fines shall be suspended until the date of that publication.

The time within which an action must be brought shall run only from the same date.

THE ASSEMBLY*

Article 6

The Assembly* shall meet, having been convened by the President of the High Authority, one month after the High Authority takes office, in order to elect its officers and draw up its rules of procedure. Pending the election of its officers, the oldest member shall take the chair.

The Assembly shall hold a second meeting five months after the High Authority takes office in order to consider a general report on the situation of the Community, together with the first budget estimates.

ADMINISTRATIVE AND FINANCIAL PROVISIONS

Article 7

The first financial year shall run from the date on which the High Authority takes office to 30 June of the following year.

The levy provided for in Article 50 of the Treaty may be collected upon the adoption of the first budget estimates. As a transitional measure to

---

* EDITORIAL NOTE:
  Notwithstanding the provisions of Article 3 of the SEA, and for historical reasons, the term 'Assembly' has not been replaced by the terms 'European Parliament'.

meet initial administrative expenditure, Member States shall make repayable interest-free advances, the amount of which shall be calculated in proportion to their contributions to the Organization for European Economic Cooperation.

(Third paragraph repealed by Article 24(2) of the Merger Treaty)

[*See Article 24(1) of the Merger Treaty, which reads as follows:*

1. The officials and other servants of the European Coal and Steel Community, the European Economic Community and the European Atomic Energy Community shall, at the date of entry into force of this Treaty, become officials and other servants of the European Communities and form part of the single administration of those Communities.

The Council shall, acting by a qualified majority on a proposal from the Commission and after consulting the other institutions concerned, lay down the Staff Regulations of officials of the European Communities and the Conditions of Employment of other servants of those Communities.]

CHAPTER II

ESTABLISHMENT OF THE COMMON MARKET

Article 8

The common market will be established as effect is given to Article 4 of the Treaty, once all the institutions of the Community have been set up and the High Authority has consulted Governments, undertakings and associations of undertakings, workers and consumers, and an overall picture of the situation in the Community has been established on the basis of the information thus obtained.

This shall be done, without prejudice to the special provisions contained in this Convention;

(a) in the case of coal, upon notification by the High Authority that the equalization machinery provided for in Chapter II of Part Three of this Convention has been set up;

(b) in the case of iron ore and scrap, on the same date as for coal;

(c) in the case of steel, two months after that date.

The equalization machinery for coal provided for in Part Three of this Convention shall be set up within six months, after the High Authority takes office.

If more time should be needed, revised dates shall be fixed by the Council acting on a proposal from the High Authority.

ELIMINATION OF CUSTOMS DUTIES AND QUANTITATIVE RESTRICTIONS

Article 9

Subject to the special provisions contained in this Convention, Member States shall abolish all import and export duties or charges having equivalent effect and all quantitative restrictions on the movement of coal and steel within the Community on the dates appointed for the establishment of the common market in coal, iron ore and scrap, and the common market in steel, as provided in Article 8.

TRANSPORT

Article 10

A Committee of Experts designated by the Governments of the Member States shall be convened forthwith by the High Authority to study the arrangements to be proposed to the Governments for the carriage of coal and steel, in order to attain the objectives set out in Article 70 of the Treaty.

The negotiations required to obtain the agreement of the Governments concerning the various measures proposed shall, without prejudice to the last paragraph of Article 70, be initiated by the High Authority, as shall any necessary negotiations with third countries concerned.

The Committee of Experts shall study:

1. measures to eliminate discriminatory practices contrary to the second paragraph of Article 70;

2. measures to establish through international tariffs incorporating a degressive factor taking account of total distance for carriage within the Community, without prejudice to the apportionment of the receipts among the carriers concerned;

3. examination of the rates and conditions of every kind for the carriage of coal and steel by the different modes of transport, with a view to their harmonization on a Community-wide basis to the extent necessary to

the proper functioning of the common market, taking account *inter alia* of transport costs.

The Committee of Experts shall have not more than:

— three months for its studies of the measures referred to under 1;

— two years for its studies of the measures referred to under 2 and 3.

The measures referred to under 1 shall enter into force on the date of the establishment of the common market in coal at the latest.

The measures referred to under 2 and 3 shall enter into force simultaneously as soon as the Governments are agreed. If, however, two and a half years after the High Authority is set up the Governments of Member States are still not agreed concerning the measures referred to under 3, the measures referred to under 2 shall enter into force separately on a date to be determined by the High Authority. In that case the High Authority shall, on a proposal from the Committee of Experts, make such recommendations as it considers necessary to avoid any serious disturbances in the transport sector.

The rates and conditions referred to in the fourth paragraph of Article 70 which are in force when the High Authority is set up shall be notified to the High Authority, which shall allow such time for their modification as may be necessary to avoid any serious economic disturbance.

The Committee of Experts shall work out and propose to the Governments concerned the derogations which they will authorize the Luxembourg Government to make from the measures and principles set out above so as to take account of the special position of Luxembourg Railways.

The Governments concerned shall, after consulting the Committee of Experts, authorize the Luxembourg Government, in so far as the special position of Luxembourg Railways makes it necessary, to continue after the transitional period to operate the arrangements adopted.

Until such time as agreement is reached among the Governments concerned on the measures referred to in the preceding paragraphs, the Luxembourg Government shall be authorized not to give effect to the principles set out in Article 70 of the Treaty and in this Article.

SUBSIDIES, DIRECT OR INDIRECT AIDS, SPECIAL CHARGES

Article 11

The Governments of the Member States shall notify the High Authority upon its taking office of all aids and subsidies to or special charges on the coal and steel industries in their respective countries. Unless the High Authority agrees to the continuance of such aids, subsidies or special charges and to the terms on which they are to be continued, they shall be withdrawn, when and in the manner which the High Authority shall determine after consulting the Council, though it shall not be mandatory to withdraw them until the opening date of the transitional period for the products in question.

RESTRICTIVE AGREEMENTS AND ARRANGEMENTS

Article 12

All information concerning agreements or arrangements coming under Article 65 shall be communicated to the High Authority as provided in Article 65 (3).

Where the High Authority does not grant authorization under Article 65 (2), it shall set reasonable time limits after which the prohibitions contained in this Article shall apply.

To facilitate the winding-up of arrangements prohibited by Article 65, the High Authority may appoint liquidators, who shall be responsible to it and shall act under its instructions.

With the assistance of these liquidators, the High Authority shall study the problems involved and the means to be employed:

— to ensure the most economic distribution and use of the products, and particularly of the different grades and qualities of coal;

— in the event of a fall in demand, to avoid any cutback in production capacity, and particularly in colliery capacity, which is needed to keep the common market supplied in times of normal or high demand;

— to avoid inequitable distribution among workers of any reductions in employment arising out of a fall in demand.

On the basis of these studies the High Authority shall, in accordance with the tasks assigned to it, establish such procedures or bodies to which it is authorized to have recourse under the Treaty as it considers appropriate for the purpose of solving the problems through the exercise of its powers, in particular under Articles 53, 57 and 58, and Chapter V of Title III; recourse to these procedures or bodies need not be confined to the transitional period.

Article 13

The provisions of Article 66 (5) shall apply from the entry into force of the Treaty. They may also be applied to transactions bringing about concentrations effected between the signature and the entry into force of the Treaty if the High Authority can show that they were effected in order to evade the application of Article 66.

Until the regulations provided for in paragraph 1 of Article 66 have been made, transactions of the kind referred to in that paragraph shall not automatically require prior authorization. The High Authority shall not be obliged to rule immediately on applications for authorization submitted to it.

Until the regulations provided for in paragraph 4 of Article 66 have been made, the information referred to in that paragraph may be required only from undertakings within the jurisdiction of the High Authority in accordance with the provisions of Article 47.

The regulations provided for in Article 66 (1) and (4) shall be made within four months after the High Authority takes office.

The High Authority shall obtain from Governments, from associations of producers and from undertakings all information relevant to the application of Article 66 (2) and (7) concerning the situation in the different areas of the Community.

The provisions of Article 66 (6) shall apply from the entry into force of the provisions in the case of which legal sanctions are provided for non-compliance.

The provisions of Article 66 (7) shall apply from the date of the establishment of the common market as provided in Article 8 of this Convention.

PART TWO

Relations between the Community
and third countries

CHAPTER I

NEGOTIATIONS WITH THIRD COUNTRIES

Article 14

Once the High Authority has taken office, Member States shall open negotiations with the Governments of third countries, and in particular with the British Government, on the whole range of economic and commercial relations concerning coal and steel between the Community and these countries. In these negotiations the High Authority shall act, upon instructions unanimously agreed by the Council, for the Member States jointly. Representatives of Member States may be present at the negotiations.

Article 15

In order to leave Member States entirely free to negotiate concessions from third countries, including in particular concessions in return for a lowering of customs duties on steel so as to harmonize with the least protective tariffs in the Community, Member States agree to the following arrangements, to take effect upon the establishment of the common market in steel:

— the Benelux countries shall continue to charge on products which are imported from third countries under tariff quotas and are bound for their own home markets the duties which they are charging at the date of entry into force of the Treaty;

— on imports in excess of the quota which are deemed to be bound for other Community countries, they shall charge duties equal to the lowest duty being applied in the other Member States, by reference to the Brussels Nomenclature of 1950, at the date of entry into force of the Treaty.

The tariff quota for each heading of the Benelux customs tariff shall be fixed by the Governments of the Benelux countries, in agreement with the High Authority, for a year at a time subject to quarterly revision, taking into account movements in demand and in trade flows. The initial quotas shall be fixed on the basis of the average imports of the Benelux countries from third countries over an appropriate reference period, account being taken where necessary of any intended change from importation to home production as newly installed capacity comes into service. Any imports in excess of the quota in response to unforeseen demand shall be notified forthwith to the High Authority, which, should it find that shipments from the Benelux countries to other Member States show a substantial increase accounted for entirely by the importation of tonnages in excess of the quota, may prohibit such importation unless temporary controls are imposed on these shipments. Benelux importers shall be entitled to pay the lowest rate of duty only if they undertake not to re-export the products in question to other Community countries.

The undertaking by the Benelux countries to operate a tariff quota shall cease to apply as provided in the agreement concluding the negotiations with Great Britain, and at latest at the end of the transitional period.

If the High Authority finds, at the end of the transitional period or on the abolition of the tariff quota in advance of that date, that one or more Member States are justified in charging on imports from third countries customs duties above the rates which would be chargeable if harmonized with the least protective tariffs in the Community, it shall, as provided in Article 29, authorize these States to take appropriate steps of their own to afford their indirect imports through Member States with lower tariffs the same degree of protection as that afforded by their own tariffs to their direct imports.

To facilitate the harmonization of the tariffs, the Benelux countries agree, where the High Authority in consultation with their Governments finds it necessary, to raise their present duties on steel by up to two points. They shall not be bound to do so until the tariff quotas provided for in the second, third and fourth paragraphs of this Article have been abolished and until one or more of the Member States bordering on the Benelux countries forgo the corresponding arrangements provided for in the preceding paragraph.

Article 16

Save with the agreement of the High Authority, the undertaking given under Article 72 of the Treaty shall debar Member States from binding by international agreements the customs duties in force at the date of entry into force of the Treaty.

Earlier bindings under bilateral or multilateral agreements shall be notified to the High Authority, which shall examine whether their retention is compatible with the proper functioning of the common arrangements and may if necessary make to Member States the appropriate recommendations for terminating the bindings by the procedure provided in the agreements containing them.

Article 17

Trade agreements which still have more than one year to run at the date of entry into force of the Treaty, or which contain a clause for tacit extension, shall be notified to the High Authority, which may make to the Member State concerned appropriate recommendations for bringing the provisions of these agreements into line where necessary with Article 75 under the procedure provided in these agreements.

CHAPTER II

EXPORTS

Article 18

Until such time as the provisions of the exchange control regulations of the various Member States concerning foreign currency left at the disposal of exporters have been made uniform, special measures must be taken to ensure that the elimination of customs duties and quantitative restrictions between Member States does not have the effect of depriving some of them of the foreign currency which is earned when their undertakings export to a third country.

In application of this principle, the Member States undertake not to give exporters of coal or steel, under the regulations referred to above, greater advantages in the use of foreign currency than those accorded under the regulations of the Member State in which the products originate.

The High Authority is empowered to see to it that this is done by making recommendations to Governments after consulting the Council.

If the High Authority finds that the establishment of the common market, by causing a change from direct exporting to re-exporting, is leading to a shift in the pattern of trade with third countries which causes substantial injury to one of the Member States, it may, at the request of the Government concerned, require producers in that State to insert a destination clause in their sales contracts.

CHAPTER III

EXCEPTIONS FROM MOST-FAVOURED-NATION TREATMENT

Article 20

1. As regards the countries entitled to most-favoured-nation treatment under Article I of the General Agreement on Tariffs and Trade, Member States shall jointly approach the Contracting Parties to the Agreement to arrange that the provisions of that Article shall not be a bar to the application of the provisions of the Treaty. If necessary, a special session of the GATT shall be requested for this purpose.

2. As regards countries not parties to the General Agreement on Tariffs and Trade but entitled nevertheless to most-favoured-nation treatment under bilateral agreements in force, negotiations shall be opened once the Treaty has been signed. Should the countries concerned not consent, the agreements shall be amended or denounced as provided therein.

If any country refuses its consent to Member States or to any one of them, the other Member States undertake to give each other effective assistance, which may extend to the denunciation by all Member States of agreements with the country in question.

CHAPTER IV

LIBERALIZATION OF TRADE

Article 21

The Member States of the Community recognize that they constitute a special customs system such as is referred to in Article 5 of the Code of Liberalization of Trade of the Organization for European Economic Cooperation as in force on the date of the signature of the Treaty. They therefore agree to notify the Organization accordingly in due course.

CHAPTER V

SPECIAL PROVISION

Article 22

Notwithstanding the expiry of the transitional period, trade in coal and steel between the Federal Republic of Germany and the Soviet Zone of Occupation shall be regulated, as far as the Federal Republic is concerned, by the Federal Government in agreement with the High Authority.

PART THREE

General safeguards

CHAPTER I

GENERAL PROVISIONS

READAPTATION

Article 23

1. If in consequence of the establishment of the common market some undertakings or parts of undertakings should be compelled to discontinue or alter their activities during the transitional period defined in Article 1 of this Convention, the High Authority shall, on application by the Governments concerned, assist as provided below in ensuring that the workers do not have to bear the brunt of the readaptation and in affording them productive employment, and may provide non-repayable aid to some undertakings.

2. On application by the Governments concerned, the High Authority shall take part, as provided in Article 46, in studying the possibilities for re-employing redundant workers in existing undertakings or through the creation of new activities.

3. The High Authority shall facilitate, in the manner laid down in Article 54, the financing of programmes submitted by the Governments concerned and approved by itself for the conversion of undertakings or for the creation, either in the industries within its jurisdiction or, with the assent of the Council, in any other industry, of new and economically sound activities capable of reabsorbing the redundant workers into productive employment. Subject to the approval of the Government concerned, the High Authority shall give preference to programmes submitted by undertakings which have to close as a result of the establishment of the common market.

4. The High Authority shall provide non-repayable aid towards:

   (a) the payment of tideover allowances to workers, where undertakings are closing altogether or in part;

   (b) the payment of allowances to undertakings to enable them to continue paying such of their workers as may have to be temporarily laid off as a result of the undertakings' change of activity;

   (c) the payment of resettlement allowances to workers;

   (d) the financing of vocational retraining for workers having to change their employment.

5. The High Authority may also provide non-repayable aid to undertakings which have to close as a result of the establishment of the common market, provided that this state of affairs is directly and solely due to the fact that the common market is confined to the coal and steel sectors, and is leading to a relative increase in the production of other Community undertakings. The aid shall be limited to the amount required to enable the undertakings to meet their immediate liabilities.

The undertakings concerned must make all applications for aid through their Governments. The High Authority may decline to provide any aid to an undertaking which has not informed its Government and the High Authority that a situation was developing which might lead it to close or change its activity.

6. The High Authority shall make the provision of non-repayable aid under paragraphs 4 and 5 conditional upon payment by the State concerned of a special contribution at least equal in amount, unless an exception is authorized by the Council, acting by a two-thirds majority.

7. The financing arrangements laid down for the application of Article 56 shall apply to this Article.

8. Assistance under this Article may be provided during the two years following the end of the transitional period by decision of the High Authority with the assent of the Council.

CHAPTER II

SPECIAL PROVISIONS FOR COAL

Article 24

It is agreed that, during the transitional period, safeguards will be necessary to avoid sudden and harmful shifts in production levels. The safeguards shall take account of the position as it is when the common market is established.

Furthermore, if it should become apparent that in one or more areas some price increases are liable to be so sudden and of such extent as to be harmful, precautions will have to be taken to ensure that they do not occur.

To deal with these problems, the High Authority shall, to the necessary extent, authorize during the transitional period, under its supervision:

(a) practices referred to in Article 60 (2) *(b)* and zone prices in cases not covered by Chapter V of Title III;

(b) the retention or institution of national equalization schemes or arrangements financed by a levy on home production, without prejudice to the exceptional expedients provided for below.

Article 25

The High Authority shall impose an equalization levy per saleable metric ton, fixed at a uniform percentage of producers' receipt, on the coal production of those countries whose average costs are below the weighted average of the Community.

The ceiling of the equalization levy shall be 1.5 per cent of these receipts for the first year that the common market is operating and shall be regularly lowered each year by 20 per cent of the initial ceiling.

Taking into account needs recognized by it, in accordance with Articles 26 and 27 below and excluding any special charges in connection with exports to third countries, the High Authority shall periodically determine the amount of the levy to be actually charged and of the Government subsidies related to it in accordance with the following rules:

1. Within the ceiling defined above, it shall calculate the amount to be actually levied in such a way that the Government subsidies to be actually paid shall be at least equal to that amount;

2. It shall fix the maximum permitted amount of the Government subsidies, on the understanding that:

— the Governments may, but need not, grant subsidies up to that amount;

— aid received from outside may in no circumstances exceed the amount of the subsidy actually paid.

Extra charges in connection with exports to third countries shall be allowed for neither in calculating the equalization payments required nor in assessing the offsetting subsidies.

BELGIUM

Article 26

1. It is agreed that net Belgian coal production:

— need not be reduced each year by more than 3 per cent as compared with the level of the preceding year if total Community production is the same or is above the level of the preceding year; or,

— if total Community production is below the level of the preceding year, need not be lower than the figure obtained by applying to the level of

Belgian production in the preceding year less 3 per cent the same coefficient of decrease as that in total Community production.*

The High Authority, as the body responsible for ensuring that the Community is kept regularly supplied, shall make an assessment of the long-term production and sales prospects and, after consulting the Consultative Committee and the Council, shall make to the Belgian Government, for as long as the Belgian market is insulated under paragraph 3 of this Article, a recommendation as to the shifts in production levels which it finds possible on the basis of this assessment. The Belgian Government shall decide, in agreement with the High Authority, what arrangements are to be made to cause these possible shifts to come about within the limits defined above.

2. The equalization arrangements shall be designed, from the beginning of the transitional period:

(a) to enable all consumers of Belgian coal within the common market to be charged prices more nearly in line with the ruling common market prices, reducing Belgian prices to the approximate figure of the estimated production costs at the end of the transitional period. The price list so fixed shall not be changed without the agreement of the High Authority;

(b) to ensure that the Belgian steel industry is not prevented by the special arrangements for Belgian coal from being integrated into the

---

* Example — 1952, total Community production 250 million metric tons, total Belgian production 30 million metric tons; 1953, total Community production 225 million metric tons, i.e. coefficient of decrease 0.9. Hence, Belgian production in 1953 need not be lower than $30 \times 0.97 \times 0.9 = 26.19$ million metric tons.

Of this reduction, 900 000 metric tons represents a permanent shift and the remaining 2 910 000 a downturn due to the business situation.

common market in steel and reducing its prices accordingly to the level ruling in that market.

The High Authority shall periodically fix the amount of such additional equalization payments in respect of Belgian coal sold to the Belgian steel industry as it considers necessary for this purpose in view of all the operational factors involved for that industry, taking care, however, that these equalization payments do not bear unfairly on the steel industries of the neighbouring countries. Also, having regard to the price of the coke used by the Belgian steel industry to below the delivered price it could obtain if supplied with coke from the Ruhr;

(c) to allow, in respect of exports of Belgian coal within the common market considered by the High Authority to be necessary in view of the production and demand prospects in the Community, additional equalization payments to cover 80 per cent of the difference which the High Authority finds to exist between the pithead price plus carriage to destination of Belgian coal and of coal from other Community countries.

3. The Belgian Government may, by way of derogation from the provisions of Article 9 of this Convention, retain or institute, under the supervision of the High Authority, machinery for insulating the Belgian market from the common market.

Imports of coal from third countries shall require the approval of the High Authority.

These special arrangements shall end as provided below.

4. The Belgian Government undertakes to remove the machinery for insulating the Belgian market under paragraph 3 of this Article by the end of the transitional period at the latest. If the High Authority considers it necessary by reason of exceptional circumstances not now foreseeable, it may, after consulting the Consultative Committee and with the assent of the Council, allow the Belgian Government an additional year which may be extended by a further year.

The integration thus provided for shall take place after consultation between the Belgian Government and the High Authority, which shall both determine the ways and means therefor; these may include allowing the Belgian Government, notwithstanding Article 4 *(c)* of the Treaty, to grant subsidies covering the extra operating costs due to the natural conditions of the coalfields, taking into account any charges due to manifest disequilibria which add to these costs. The procedure for granting of subsidies and their maximum amount shall require the approval of the High Authority, which shall see to it that the maximum amount of subsidies and the tonnage subsidized are lowered as quickly as possible, taking into account the facilities for readaptation and the extension of the common market to products other than coal and steel, and ensuring that the scale of such production cutbacks as may be made does not give rise to fundamental disturbances in the Belgian economy.

The High Authority shall every two years submit to the Council for approval proposals as to the tonnage which may be subsidized.

ITALY

Article 27

1. The Sulcis mines shall be entitled to equalization payments under Article 25 to enable them to meet competition in the common market pending completion of the plant installation operations now in progress; the High Authority shall periodically determine the amount of aid required, but outside aid may not be continued for more than two years.

2.   In view of the special position of the Italian coking plants, the High Authority is empowered to authorize the Italian Government to continue, to the necessary extent during the transitional period defined in Article 1 of this Convention, to charge customs duties on coke from other Member States; however, in the first year of the transitional period these may not exceed the rates of duty under Presidential Decree No 442 of 7 July 1950, this ceiling being reduced by 10 per cent in the second year, 25 per cent in the third, 45 per cent in the fourth and 70 per cent in the fifth, and the duties being abolished altogether at the end of the transitional period.

FRANCE

Article 28

1.   It is agreed that coal production in the French mines:

— need not be reduced each year by more than one million metric tons as compared with the level of the preceding year if total Community production is the same or is above the level of the preceding year; or,

— if total Community production is below the level of the preceding year, need not be lower than the figure obtained by applying to the level of French production in the preceding year less one million metric tons the same coefficient of decrease as that in total Community production.

2. To ensure that shifts in production levels are kept within these limits, the arrangements referred to in Article 24 of this Convention may be supplemented by the exceptional expedient of a special levy imposed by the High Authority on increases in the net deliveries from other collieries as shown in French customs statistics, to the extent that these increases represent shifts in production levels.

Accordingly, the levy shall be chargeable on the amounts by which net deliveries in each period exceed those in 1950, up to the amount of the decrease in the coal production of French mines since 1950 or, if total Community production is also down, to the figure obtained by applying to that amount the same coefficient of decrease as that in total Community production. The special levy shall be fixed at a maximum of 10 per cent of the producers' receipts on the amounts in question and shall be used, in agreement with the High Authority, to reduce, in the appropriate zones, the price for certain coals produced by the French mines.

CHAPTER III

SPECIAL PROVISIONS FOR THE STEEL INDUSTRY

Article 29

1. It is agreed that, during the transitional period, special safeguards may be necessary in the case of the steel industry to ensure that shifts in production levels due to the establishment of the common market neither create difficulties for undertakings which would be in a position to meet competition following the adaptation provided for in Article 1 of this Con-

vention, nor lead to more redundancies than can benefit under Article 23. Where the High Authority finds that the provisions of the Treaty, and in particular Articles 57, 58, 59 and 60 (2) *(b)*, cannot be applied, it is empowered, in the following order of preference:

(a) after consulting the Consultative Committee and the Council, to limit by direct or indirect means the net increase in deliveries from one area to another within the common market;

(b) after consulting the Consultative Committee and with the assent of the Council both as to the advisability and the details of the proposed action, to use the powers of intervention provided in Article 61 *(b)*, but, by way of derogation from that Article, without the requirement that a manifest crisis should exist or be imminent;

(c) after consulting the Consultative Committee and with the assent of the Council, to establish a system of production quotas, which shall not, however, affect production for export;

(d) after consulting the Consultative Committee and with the assent of the Council, to authorize a Member State to take the steps referred to in the sixth paragraph of Article 15 of this Convention, in the manner provided therein.

2. For the purpose of applying these provisions, the High Authority shall during the preparatory period defined in Article 1 of this Convention, in consultation with associations of producers, the Consultative Committee and the Council, fix the technical details for the application of the safeguard arrangements.

3. If during part of the transitional period, either because of a shortage, or because the funds earned by undertakings or placed at their disposal are insufficient, or because of exceptional circumstances not now fore-

seeable, it has not been possible to effect the necessary adaptation of or alterations in production conditions, the provisions of this Article may, after the Consultative Committee has been consulted and the assent of the Council obtained, be applied after the end of the transitional period for as long as, but no longer than, this state of affairs continues, up to a maximum of two years.

ITALY

Article 30

1. In view of the special position of the Italian steel industry, the High Authority is empowered to authorize the Italian Government to continue, to the necessary extent during the transitional period defined in Article 1 of this Convention, to charge customs duties on steel products from other Member States; however, in the first year of the transitional period these may not exceed the rates of duty under the Annecy Convention of 10 October 1949, this ceiling being reduced by 10 per cent in the second year, 25 per cent in the third, 45 per cent in the fourth and 70 per cent in the fifth, and the duties being abolished altogether at the end of the transitional period.

2. The prices charged by undertakings for sales of steel on the Italian market, when reduced to their equivalents at the point chosen for their price lists, may not be lower than the prices shown in the lists in question for comparable transactions, save where authorized by the High Authority in agreement with the Italian Government, without prejudice to the last subparagraph of Article 60 (2) *(b)*.

LUXEMBOURG

Article 31

In the operation of the safeguards provided for in Article 29 of this Convention, the High Authority shall take account of the exceptional importance of the steel industry to the general economy of Luxembourg and the need to avoid serious disturbances in the marketing of Luxembourg steel, given the special conditions under which this is effected by reason of the Belgo-Luxembourg Economic Union.

Failing other action, the High Authority may if necessary draw on the funds at its disposal under Article 49 of the Treaty up to the amount needed to deal with any repercussions on the Luxembourg steel industry of the arrangements provided for in Article 26 of this Convention.

Done at Paris this eighteenth day of April in the year one thousand nine hundred and fifty-one.

ADENAUER

Paul VAN ZEELAND
J. MEURICE

SCHUMAN

SFORZA

Jos. BECH

STIKKER
VAN DEN BRINK

Treaty
establishing the
European Economic Community

Contents

---

* The Protocol on the Privileges and Immunities of the European Economic Community has been repealed by the second paragraph of Article 28 of the Merger Treaty; see Protocol on the Privileges and Immunities of the European Communities (p. 853).

I — TEXT OF THE TREATY

HIS MAJESTY THE KING OF THE BELGIANS, THE PRESIDENT OF THE FEDERAL REPUBLIC OF GERMANY, THE PRESIDENT OF THE FRENCH REPUBLIC, THE PRESIDENT OF THE ITALIAN REPUBLIC, HER ROYAL HIGHNESS THE GRAND DUCHESS OF LUXEMBOURG, HER MAJESTY THE QUEEN OF THE NETHERLANDS,

DETERMINED to lay the foundations of an ever closer union among the peoples of Europe,

RESOLVED to ensure the economic and social progress of their countries by common action to eliminate the barriers which divide Europe,

AFFIRMING as the essential objective of their efforts the constant improvement of the living and working conditions of their peoples,

RECOGNIZING that the removal of existing obstacles calls for concerted action in order to guarantee steady expansion, balanced trade and fair competition,

ANXIOUS to strengthen the unity of their economies and to ensure their harmonious development by reducing the differences existing between the various regions and the backwardness of the less favoured regions,

DESIRING to contribute, by means of a common commercial policy, to the progressive abolition of restrictions on international trade,

INTENDING to confirm the solidarity which binds Europe and the overseas countries and desiring to ensure the development of their prosperity, in accordance with the principles of the Charter of the United Nations,

RESOLVED by thus pooling their resources to preserve and strengthen peace and liberty, and calling upon the other peoples of Europe who share their ideal to join in their efforts,

HAVE DECIDED to create a European Economic Community and to this end have designated as their Plenipotentiaries:

HIS MAJESTY THE KING OF THE BELGIANS:

Mr Paul-Henri SPAAK, Minister for Foreign Affairs,
Baron J. Ch. SNOY ET D'OPPUERS, Secretary-General of the Ministry of Economic Affairs, Head of the Belgian Delegation to the Intergovernmental Conference;

THE PRESIDENT OF THE FEDERAL REPUBLIC OF GERMANY:

Dr Konrad ADENAUER, Federal Chancellor,
Professor Dr Walter HALLSTEIN, State Secretary of the Federal Foreign Office;

THE PRESIDENT OF THE FRENCH REPUBLIC:

Mr Christian PINEAU, Minister for Foreign Affairs,
Mr Maurice FAURE, Under-Secretary of State for Foreign Affairs;

THE PRESIDENT OF THE ITALIAN REPUBLIC:

Mr Antonio SEGNI, President of the Council of Ministers,
Professor Gaetano MARTINO, Minister for Foreign Affairs;

HER ROYAL HIGHNESS THE GRAND DUCHESS OF LUXEMBOURG:

Mr Joseph BECH, President of the Government, Minister for Foreign Affairs,
Mr Lambert SCHAUS, Ambassador, Head of the Luxembourg Delegation to the Intergovernmental Conference;

HER MAJESTY THE QUEEN OF THE NETHERLANDS:

Mr Joseph LUNS, Minister for Foreign Affairs,
Mr J. LINTHORST HOMAN, Head of the Netherlands Delegation to the
Intergovernmental Conference;

WHO, having exchanged their Full Powers, found in good and due form,
have agreed as follows.

PART ONE

PRINCIPLES

Article 1

By this Treaty, the HIGH CONTRACTING PARTIES establish among themselves a EUROPEAN ECONOMIC COMMUNITY.

Article 2

The Community shall have as its task, by establishing a common market and progressively approximating the economic policies of Member States, to promote throughout the Community a harmonious development of economic activities, a continuous and balanced expansion, an increase in stability, an accelerated raising of the standard of living and closer relations between the States belonging to it.

Article 3

For the purposes set out in Article 2, the activities of the Community shall include, as provided in this Treaty and in accordance with the timetable set out therein

(a) the elimination, as between Member States, of customs duties and of quantitative restrictions on the import and export of goods, and of all other measures having equivalent effect;

(b) the establishment of a common customs tariff and of a common commercial policy towards third countries;

(c) the abolition, as between Member States, of obstacles to freedom of movement for persons, services and capital;

(d) the adoption of a common policy in the sphere of agriculture;

(e) the adoption of a common policy in the sphere of transport;

(f) the institution of a system ensuring that competition in the common market is not distorted;

(g) the application of procedures by which the economic policies of Member States can be coordinated and disequilibria in their balances of payments remedied;

(h) the approximation of the laws of Member States to the extent required for the proper functioning of the common market;

(i) the creation of a European Social Fund in order to improve employment opportunities for workers and to contribute to the raising of their standard of living;

(j) the establishment of a European Investment Bank to facilitate the economic expansion of the Community by opening up fresh resources;

(k) the association of the overseas countries and territories in order to increase trade and to promote jointly economic and social development.

Article 4

1. The tasks entrusted to the Community shall be carried out by the following institutions:

a EUROPEAN PARLIAMENT,
a COUNCIL,
a COMMISSION,
a COURT OF JUSTICE.

Each institution shall act within the limits of the powers conferred upon it by this Treaty.

2. The Council and the Commission shall be assisted by an Economic and Social Committee acting in an advisory capacity.

3. The audit shall be carried out by a Court of Auditors acting within the limits of the powers conferred upon it by this Treaty.*

---

* Paragraph 3 added by Article 11 of the Treaty amending Certain Financial Provisions.

Article 5

Member States shall take all appropriate measures, whether general or particular, to ensure fulfilment of the obligations arising out of this Treaty or resulting from action taken by the institutions of the Community. They shall facilitate the achievement of the Community's tasks.

They shall abstain from any measure which could jeopardize the attainment of the objectives of this Treaty.

Article 6

1. Member States shall, in close cooperation with the institutions of the Community, coordinate their respective economic policies to the extent necessary to attain the objectives of this Treaty.

2. The institutions of the Community shall take care not to prejudice the internal and external financial stability of the Member States.

Article 7

Within the scope of application of this Treaty, and without prejudice to any special provisions contained therein, any discrimination on grounds of nationality shall be prohibited.

The Council may, on a proposal from the Commission and in cooperation with the European Parliament, adopt, by a qualified majority, rules designed to prohibit such discrimination.*

Article 8

1. The common market shall be progressively established during a transitional period of twelve years.

---

* Second paragraph as amended by Article 6 (2) of the SEA.

This transitional period shall be divided into three stages of four years each; the length of each stage may be altered in accordance with the provisions set out below.

2.   To each stage there shall be assigned a set of actions to be initiated and carried through concurrently.

3.   Transition from the first to the second stage shall be conditional upon a finding that the objectives specifically laid down in this Treaty for the first stage have in fact been attained in substance and that, subject to the exceptions and procedures provided for in this Treaty, the obligations have been fulfilled.

This finding shall be made at the end of the fourth year by the Council, acting unanimously on a report from the Commission. A Member State may not, however, prevent unanimity by relying upon the non-fulfilment of its own obligations. Failing unanimity, the first stage shall automatically be extended for one year.

At the end of the fifth year, the Council shall make its finding under the same conditions. Failing unanimity, the first stage shall automatically be extended for a further year.

At the end of the sixth year, the Council shall make its finding, acting by a qualified majority on a report from the Commission.

4.   Within one month of the last-mentioned vote any Member State which voted with the minority or, if the required majority was not obtained, any Member State shall be entitled to call upon the Council to appoint an arbitration board whose decision shall be binding upon all Member States and upon the institutions of the Community. The arbitration board shall consist of three members appointed by the Council acting unanimously on a proposal from the Commission.

If the Council has not appointed the members of the arbitration board within one month of being called upon to do so, they shall be appointed by the Court of Justice within a further period of one month.

The arbitration board shall elect its own Chairman.

The board shall make its award within six months of the date of the Council vote referred to in the last subparagraph of paragraph 3.

5. The second and third stages may not be extended or curtailed except by a decision of the Council, acting unanimously on a proposal from the Commission.

6. Nothing in the preceding paragraphs shall cause the transitional period to last more than fifteen years after the entry into force of this Treaty.

7. Save for the exceptions or derogations provided for in this Treaty, the expiry of the transitional period shall constitute the latest date by which all the rules laid down must enter into force and all the measures required for establishing the common market must be implemented.

Article 8a*

The Community shall adopt measures with the aim of progressively establishing the internal market over a period expiring on 31 December 1992, in accordance with the provisions of this Article and of Articles 8b, 8c, 28, 57 (2), 59, 70 (1), 84, 99, 100a and 100b and without prejudice to the other provisions of this Treaty.

The internal market shall comprise an area without internal frontiers in which the free movement of goods, persons, services and capital is ensured in accordance with the provisions of this Treaty.

---

* Article added by Article 13 of the SEA.

Article 8b*

The Commission shall report to the Council before 31 December 1988 and again before 31 December 1990 on the progress made towards achieving the internal market within the time limit fixed in Article 8a.

The Council, acting by a qualified majority on a proposal from the Commission, shall determine the guidelines and conditions necessary to ensure balanced progress in all the sectors concerned.

Article 8c**

When drawing up its proposals with a view to achieving the objectives set out in Article 8a, the Commission shall take into account the extent of the effort that certain economies showing differences in development will have to sustain during the period of establishment of the internal market and it may propose appropriate provisions.

If these provisions take the form of derogations, they must be of a temporary nature and must cause the least possible disturbance to the functioning of the common market.

---

* Article added by Article 14 of the SEA.
** Article added by Article 15 of the SEA.

PART TWO

FOUNDATIONS OF THE COMMUNITY

TITLE I

Free movement of goods

Article 9

1. The Community shall be based upon a customs union which shall cover all trade in goods and which shall involve the prohibition between Member States of customs duties on imports and exports and of all charges having equivalent effect, and the adoption of a common customs tariff in their relations with third countries.

2. The provisions of Chapter 1, Section 1, and of Chapter 2 of this Title shall apply to products originating in Member States and to products coming from third countries which are in free circulation in Member States.

Article 10

1. Products coming from a third country shall be considered to be in free circulation in a Member State if the import formalities have been complied with and any customs duties or charges having equivalent effect which are payable have been levied in that Member State, and if they have not benefited from a total or partial drawback of such duties or charges.

2. The Commission shall, before the end of the first year after the entry into force of this Treaty, determine the methods of administrative cooperation to be adopted for the purpose of applying Article 9 (2), taking into account the need to reduce as much as possible formalities imposed on trade.

Before the end of the first year after the entry into force of this Treaty, the Commission shall lay down the provisions applicable, as regards trade between Member States, to goods originating in another Member State in whose manufacture products have been used on which the exporting Member State has not levied the appropriate customs duties or charges having equivalent effect, or which have benefited from a total or partial drawback of such duties or charges.

In adopting these provisions, the Commission shall take into account the rules for the elimination of customs duties within the Community and for the progressive application of the common customs tariff.

Article 11

Member States shall take all appropriate measures to enable Governments to carry out, within the periods of time laid down, the obligations with regard to customs duties which devolve upon them pursuant to this Treaty.

CHAPTER 1

THE CUSTOMS UNION

Section 1

Elimination of customs duties between Member States

Article 12

Member States shall refrain from introducing between themselves any new customs duties on imports or exports or any charges having equivalent effect, and from increasing those which they already apply in their trade with each other.

Article 13

1. Customs duties on imports in force between Member States shall be progressively abolished by them during the transitional period in accordance with Articles 14 and 15.

2. Charges having an effect equivalent to customs duties on imports, in force between Member States, shall be progressively abolished by them during the transitional period. The Commission shall determine by means of directives the timetable for such abolition. It shall be guided by the rules contained in Article 14 (2) and (3) and by the directives issued by the Council pursuant to Article 14 (2).

Article 14

1. For each product, the basic duty to which the successive reductions shall be applied shall be the duty applied on 1 January 1957.

2. The timetable for the reductions shall be determined as follows:

(a) during the first stage, the first reduction shall be made one year after the date when this Treaty enters into force; the second reduction, eighteen months later; the third reduction, at the end of the fourth year after the date when this Treaty enters into force;

(b) during the second stage, a reduction shall be made eighteen months after that stage begins; a second reduction, eighteen months after the preceding one; a third reduction, one year later;

(c) any remaining reductions shall be made during the third stage; the Council shall, acting by a qualified majority on a proposal from the Commission, determine the timetable therefor by means of directives.

3. At the time of the first reduction, Member States shall introduce between themselves a duty on each product equal to the basic duty minus 10 %.

At the time of each subsequent reduction, each Member State shall reduce its customs duties as a whole in such manner as to lower by 10 % its total customs receipts as defined in paragraph 4 and to reduce the duty on each product by at least 5 % of the basic duty.

In the case, however, of products on which the duty is still in excess of 30 %, each reduction must be at least 10 % of the basic duty.

4. The total customs receipts of each Member State, as referred to in paragraph 3, shall be calculated by multiplying the value of its imports from other Member States during 1956 by the basic duties.

5. Any special problems raised in applying paragraphs 1 to 4 shall be settled by directives issued by the Council acting by a qualified majority on a proposal from the Commission.

6. Member States shall report to the Commission on the manner in which effect has been given to the preceding rules for the reduction of duties. They shall endeavour to ensure that the reduction made in the duties on each product shall amount:

— at the end of the first stage, to at least 25 % of the basic duty;

— at the end of the second stage, to at least 50 % of the basic duty.

If the Commission finds that there is a risk that the objectives laid down in Article 13, and the percentages laid down in this paragraph, cannot be attained, it shall make all appropriate recommendations to Member States.

7. The provisions of this Article may be amended by the Council, acting unanimously on a proposal from the Commission and after consulting the European Parliament.

Article 15

1. Irrespective of the provisions of Article 14, any Member State may, in the course of the transitional period, suspend in whole or in part the collection of duties applied by it to products imported from other Member States. It shall inform the other Member States and the Commission thereof.

2. The Member States declare their readiness to reduce customs duties against the other Member States more rapidly than is provided for in Article 14 if their general economic situation and the situation of the economic sector concerned so permit.

To this end, the Commission shall make recommendations to the Member States concerned.

Article 16

Member States shall abolish between themselves customs duties on exports and charges having equivalent effect by the end of the first stage at the latest.

Article 17

1. The provisions of Articles 9 to 15 (1) shall also apply to customs duties of a fiscal nature. Such duties shall not, however, be taken into consideration for the purpose of calculating either total customs receipts or the reduction of customs duties as a whole as referred to in Article 14 (3) and (4).

Such duties shall, at each reduction, be lowered by not less than 10 % of the basic duty. Member States may reduce such duties more rapidly than is provided for in Article 14.

2. Member States shall, before the end of the first year after the entry into force of this Treaty, inform the Commission of their customs duties of a fiscal nature.

3. Member States shall retain the right to substitute for these duties an internal tax which complies with the provisions of Article 95.

4. If the Commission finds that substitution for any customs duty of a fiscal nature meets with serious difficulties in a Member State, it shall authorize that State to retain the duty on condition that it shall abolish it not later than six years after the entry into force of this Treaty. Such authorization must be applied for before the end of the first year after the entry into force of this Treaty.

Section 2

Setting up of the common customs tariff

Article 18

The Member States declare their readiness to contribute to the development of international trade and the lowering of barriers to trade by entering into agreements designed, on a basis of reciprocity and mutual advantage, to reduce customs duties below the general level of which they could avail themselves as a result of the establishment of a customs union between them.

Article 19

1. Subject to the conditions and within the limits provided for hereinafter, duties in the common customs tariff shall be at the level of the arithmetical average of the duties applied in the four customs territories comprised in the Community.

2. The duties taken as the basis for calculating this average shall be those applied by Member States on 1 January 1957.

In the case of the Italian tariff, however, the duty applied shall be that without the temporary 10 % reduction. Furthermore, with respect to items on which the Italian tariff contains a conventional duty, this duty shall be substituted for the duty applied as defined above, provided that it does not exceed the latter by more than 10 %. Where the conventional duty exceeds the duty applied as defined above by more than 10 %, the latter duty plus 10 % shall be taken as the basis for calculating the arithmetical average.

With regard to the tariff headings in List A, the duties shown in that List shall, for the purpose of calculating the arithmetical average, be substituted for the duties applied.

3. The duties in the common customs tariff shall not exceed:

(a) 3 % for products within the tariff headings in List B;

(b) 10 % for products within the tariff headings in List C;

(c) 15 % for products within the tariff headings in List D;

(d) 25 % for products within the tariff headings in List E; where in respect of such products, the tariff of the Benelux countries contains a duty not exceeding 3 %, such duty shall, for the purpose of calculating the arithmetical average, be raised to 12 %.

4. List F prescribes the duties applicable to the products listed therein.

5. The Lists of tariff headings referred to in this Article and in Article 20 are set out in Annex I to this Treaty.

Article 20

The duties applicable to the products in List G shall be determined by negotiation between the Member States. Each Member State may add further products to this List to a value not exceeding 2 % of the total value of its imports from third countries in the course of the year 1956.

The Commission shall take all appropriate steps to ensure that such negotiations shall be undertaken before the end of the second year after the entry into force of this Treaty and be concluded before the end of the first stage.

If, for certain products, no agreement can be reached within these periods, the Council shall, on a proposal from the Commission, acting unanimously until the end of the second stage and by a qualified majority thereafter, determine the duties in the common customs tariff.

Article 21

1. Technical difficulties which may arise in applying Articles 19 and 20 shall be resolved, within two years of the entry into force of this Treaty, by directives issued by the Council acting by a qualified majority on a proposal from the Commission.

2. Before the end of the first stage, or at latest when the duties are determined, the Council shall, acting by a qualified majority on a proposal from the Commission, decide on any adjustments required in the interests of the internal consistency of the common customs tariff as a result of applying the rules set out in Articles 19 and 20, taking account in particular of the degree of processing undergone by the various goods to which the common tariff applies.

Article 22

The Commission shall, within two years of the entry into force of this Treaty, determine the extent to which the customs duties of a fiscal nature referred to in Article 17 (2) shall be taken into account in calculating the arithmetical average provided for in Article 19 (1). The Commission shall take account of any protective character which such duties may have.

Within six months of such determination, any Member State may request that the procedure provided for in Article 20 should be applied to the product in question, but in this event the percentage limit provided in that Article shall not be applicable to that State.

Article 23

1. For the purpose of the progressive introduction of the common customs tariff, Member States shall amend their tariffs applicable to third countries as follows:

(a) in the case of tariff headings on which the duties applied in practice on 1 January 1957 do not differ by more than 15 % in either direction from the duties in the common customs tariff, the latter duties shall be applied at the end of the fourth year after the entry into force of this Treaty;

(b) in any other case, each Member State shall, as from the same date, apply a duty reducing by 30 % the difference between the duty applied in practice on 1 January 1957 and the duty in the common customs tariff;

(c) at the end of the second stage this difference shall again be reduced by 30 %;

(d) in the case of tariff headings for which the duties in the common customs tariff are not yet available at the end of the first stage, each Member State shall, within six months of the Council's action in accordance with Article 20, apply such duties as would result from application of the rules contained in this paragraph.

2. Where a Member State has been granted an authorization under Article 17 (4), it need not, for as long as that authorization remains valid, apply the preceding provisions to the tariff headings to which the authorization applies. When such authorization expires, the Member

State concerned shall apply such duty as would have resulted from application of the rules contained in paragraph 1.

3. The common customs tariff shall be applied in its entirety by the end of the transitional period at the latest.

Article 24

Member States shall remain free to change their duties more rapidly than is provided for in Article 23 in order to bring them into line with the common customs tariff.

Article 25

1. If the Commission finds that the production in Member States of particular products contained in Lists B, C and D is insufficient to supply the demands of one of the Member States, and that such supply traditionally depends to a considerable extent on imports from third countries, the Council shall, acting by a qualified majority on a proposal from the Commission, grant the Member State concerned tariff quotas at a reduced rate of duty or duty free.

Such quotas may not exceed the limits beyond which the risk might arise of activities being transferred to the detriment of other Member States.

2. In the case of the products in List E, and of those in List G for which the rates of duty have been determined in accordance with the procedure provided for in the third paragraph of Article 20, the Commission shall, where a change in sources of supply or shortage of supplies within the Community is such as to entail harmful consequences for the processing industries of a Member State, at the request of that Member State, grant it tariff quotas at a reduced rate of duty or duty free.

Such quotas may not exceed the limits beyond which the risk might arise of activities being transferred to the detriment of other Member States.

3. In the case of the products listed in Annex II to this Treaty, the Commission may authorize any Member State to suspend, in whole or in part, collection of the duties applicable or may grant such Member State tariff quotas at a reduced rate of duty or duty free, provided that no serious disturbance of the market of the products concerned results therefrom.

4. The Commission shall periodically examine tariff quotas granted pursuant to this Article.

Article 26

The Commission may authorize any Member State encountering special difficulties to postpone the lowering or raising of duties provided for in Article 23 in respect of particular headings in its tariff.

Such authorization may only be granted for a limited period and in respect of tariff headings which, taken together, represent for such State not more than 5 % of the value of its imports from third countries in the course of the latest year for which statistical data are available.

Article 27

Before the end of the first stage, Member States shall, in so far as may be necessary, take steps to approximate their provisions laid down by law, regulation or administrative action in respect of customs matters. To this end, the Commission shall make all appropriate recommendations to Member States.

Article 28

Any autonomous alteration or suspension of duties in the common customs tariff shall be decided by the Council acting by a qualified majority on a proposal from the Commission.*

---

* Article as replaced by Article 16 (1) of the SEA.

In carrying out the tasks entrusted to it under this Section the Commission shall be guided by:

(a) the need to promote trade between Member States and third countries;

(b) developments in conditions of competition within the Community in so far as they lead to an improvement in the competitive capacity of undertakings;

(c) the requirements of the Community as regards the supply of raw materials and semi-finished goods; in this connection the Commission shall take care to avoid distorting conditions of competition between Member States in respect of finished goods;

(d) the need to avoid serious disturbances in the economies of Member States and to ensure rational development of production and an expansion of consumption within the Community.

CHAPTER 2

ELIMINATION OF QUANTITATIVE RESTRICTIONS BETWEEN MEMBER STATES

Article 30

Quantitative restrictions on imports and all measures having equivalent effect shall, without prejudice to the following provisions, be prohibited between Member States.

Article 31

Member States shall refrain from introducing between themselves any new quantitative restrictions or measures having equivalent effect.

This obligation shall, however, relate only to the degree of liberalization attained in pursuance of the decisions of the Council of the Organization for European Economic Cooperation of 14 January 1955. Member States shall supply the Commission, not later than six months after the entry into force of this Treaty, with lists of the products liberalized by them in pursuance of these decisions. These lists shall be consolidated between Member States.

Article 32

In their trade with one another Member States shall refrain from making more restrictive the quotas and measures having equivalent effect existing at the date of the entry into force of this Treaty.

These quotas shall be abolished by the end of the transitional period at the latest. During that period, they shall be progressively abolished in accordance with the following provisions.

Article 33

1. One year after the entry into force of this Treaty, each Member State shall convert any bilateral quotas open to any other Member States into global quotas open without discrimination to all other Member States.

On the same date, Member States shall increase the aggregate of the global quotas so established in such a manner as to bring about an increase of not less than 20% in their total value as compared with the preceding year. The global quota for each product, however, shall be increased by not less than 10%.

The quotas shall be increased annually in accordance with the same rules and in the same proportions in relation to the preceding year.

The fourth increase shall take place at the end of the fourth year after the entry into force of this Treaty; the fifth, one year after the beginning of the second stage.

2. Where, in the case of a product which has not been liberalized, the global quota does not amount to 3 % of the national production of the State concerned, a quota equal to not less than 3 % of such national production shall be introduced not later than one year after the entry into force of this Treaty. This quota shall be raised to 4 % at the end of the second year, and to 5 % at the end of the third. Thereafter, the Member State concerned shall increase the quota by not less than 15 % annually.

Where there is no such national production, the Commission shall take a decision establishing an appropriate quota.

3. At the end of the tenth year, each quota shall be equal to not less than 20 % of the national production.

4. If the Commission finds by means of a decision that during two successive years the imports of any product have been below the level of the quota opened, this global quota shall not be taken into account in calculating the total value of the global quotas. In such case, the Member State shall abolish quota restrictions on the product concerned.

5. In the case of quotas representing more than 20 % of the national production of the product concerned, the Council may, acting by a qualified majority on a proposal from the Commission, reduce the minimum percentage of 10 % laid down in paragraph 1. This alteration shall not, however, affect the obligation to increase the total value of global quotas by 20 % annually.

6. Member States which have exceeded their obligations as regards the degree of liberalization attained in pursuance of the decisions of the Council of the Organization for European Economic Cooperation of

14 January 1955 shall be entitled, when calculating the annual total increase of 20 % provided for in paragraph 1, to take into account the amount of imports liberalizd by autonomous action. Such calculation shall be submitted to the Commission for its prior approval.

7.   The Commission shall issue directives establishing the procedure and timetable in accordance with which Member States shall abolish, as between themselves, any measures in existence when this Treaty enters into force which have an effect equivalent to quotas.

8.   If the Commission finds that the application of the provisions of this Article, and in particular of the provisions concerning percentages, makes it impossible to ensure that the abolition of quotas provided for in the second paragraph of Article 32 is carried out progressively, the Council may, on a proposal from the Commission, acting unanimously during the first stage and by a qualified majority thereafter, amend the procedure laid down in this Article and may, in particular, increase the percentages fixed.

Article 34

1.   Quantitative restrictions on exports, and all measures having equivalent effect, shall be prohibited between Member States.

2.   Member States shall, by the end of the first stage at the latest, abolish all quantitative restrictions on exports and any measures having equivalent effect which are in existence when this Treaty enters into force.

Article 35

The Member States declare their readiness to abolish quantitative restrictions on imports from and exports to other Member States more rapidly than is provided for in the preceding Articles, if their general economic situation and the situation of the economic sector concerned so permit.

To this end, the Commission shall make recommendations to the Member States concerned.

Article 36

The provisions of Articles 30 to 34 shall not preclude prohibitions or restrictions on imports, exports or goods in transit justified on grounds of public morality, public policy or public security; the protection of health and life of humans, animals or plants; the protection of national treasures possessing artistic, historic or archaeological value; or the protection of industrial and commercial property. Such prohibitions or restrictions shall not, however, constitute a means of arbitrary discrimination or a disguised restriction on trade between Member States.

Article 37

1. Member States shall progressively adjust any State monopolies of a commercial character so as to ensure that when the transitional period has ended no discrimination regarding the conditions under which goods are procured and marketed exists between nationals of Member States.

The provisions of this Article shall apply to any body through which a Member State, in law or in fact, either directly or indirectly supervises, determines or appreciably influences imports or exports between Member States. These provisions shall likewise apply to monopolies delegated by the State to others.

2. Member States shall refrain from introducing any new measure which is contrary to the principles laid down in paragraph 1 or which restricts the scope of the Articles dealing with the abolition of customs duties and quantitative restrictions between Member States.

3. The timetable for the measures referred to in paragraph 1 shall be harmonized with the abolition of quantitative restrictions on the same products provided for in Articles 30 to 34.

If a product is subject to a State monopoly of a commercial character in only one or some Member States, the Commission may authorize the other Member States to apply protective measures until the adjustment provided for in paragraph 1 has been effected; the Commission shall determine the conditions and details of such measures.

4. If a State monopoly of a commercial character has rules which are designed to make it easier to dispose of agricultural products or obtain for them the best return, steps should be taken in applying the rules contained in this Article to ensure equivalent safeguards for the employment and standard of living of the producers concerned, account being taken of the adjustments that will be possible and the specialization that will be needed with the passage of time.

5. The obligations on Member States shall be binding only in so far as they are compatible with existing international agreements.

6. With effect from the first stage the Commission shall make recommendations as to the manner in which and the timetable according to which the adjustment provided for in this Article shall be carried out.

TITLE II

Agriculture

Article 38

1. The common market shall extend to agriculture and trade in agricultural products. 'Agricultural products' means the products of the soil, of stockfarming and of fisheries and products of first-stage processing directly related to these products.

2. Save as otherwise provided in Articles 39 to 46, the rules laid down for the establishment of the common market shall apply to agricultural products.

3. The products subject to the provisions of Articles 39 to 46 are listed in Annex II to this Treaty. Within two years of the entry into force of this Treaty, however, the Council shall, acting by a qualified majority on a proposal from the Commission, decide what products are to be added to this list.

4. The operation and development of the common market for agricultural products must be accompanied by the establishment of a common agricultural policy among the Member States.

Article 39

1. The objectives of the common agricultural policy shall be:

(a) to increase agricultural productivity by promoting technical progress and by ensuring the rational development of agricultural production and the optimum utilization of the factors of production, in particular labour;

(b) thus to ensure a fair standard of living for the agricultural community, in particular by increasing the individual earnings of persons engaged in agriculture;

(c) to stabilize markets;

(d) to assure the availability of supplies;

(e) to ensure that supplies reach consumers at reasonable prices.

2. In working out the common agricultural policy and the special methods for its application, account shall be taken of:

(a) the particular nature of agricultural activity, which results from the social structure of agriculture and from structural and natural disparities between the various agricultural regions;

(b) the need to effect the appropriate adjustments by degrees;

(c) the fact that in the Member States agriculture constitutes a sector closely linked with the economy as a whole.

Article 40

1. Member States shall develop the common agricultural policy by degrees during the transitional period and shall bring it into force by the end of that period at the latest.

2. In order to attain the objectives set out in Article 39 a common organization of agricultural markets shall be established.

This organization shall take one of the following forms, depending on the product concerned:

(a) common rules on competition;

(b) compulsory coordination of the various national market organizations;

(c) a European market organization.

3.   The common organization established in accordance with paragraph 2 may include all measures required to attain the objectives set out in Article 39, in particular regulation of prices, aids for the production and marketing of the various products, storage and carryover arrangements and common machinery for stabilizing imports or exports.

The common organization shall be limited to pursuit of the objectives set out in Article 39 and shall exclude any discrimination between producers or consumers within the Community.

Any common price policy shall be based on common criteria and uniform methods of calculation.

4.   In order to enable the common organization referred to in paragraph 2 to attain its objectives, one or more agricultural guidance and guarantee funds may be set up.

Article 41

To enable the objectives set out in Article 39 to be attained, provision may be made within the framework of the common agricultural policy for measures such as:

(a) an effective coordination of efforts in the spheres of vocational training, of research and of the dissemination of agricultural knowledge; this may include joint financing of projects or institutions;

(b) joint measures to promote consumption of certain products.

Article 42

The provisions of the Chapter relating to rules on competition shall apply to production of and trade in agricultural products only to the extent determined by the Council within the framework of Article 43 (2) and (3) and in accordance with the procedure laid down therein, account being taken of the objectives set out in Article 39.

The Council may, in particular, authorize the granting of aid:

(a) for the protection of enterprises handicapped by structural or natural conditions;

(b) within the framework of economic development programmes.

Article 43

1. In order to evolve the broad lines of a common agricultural policy, the Commission shall, immediately this Treaty enters into force, convene a conference of the Member States with a view to making a comparison of their agricultural policies, in particular by producing a statement of their resources and needs.

2. Having taken into account the work of the conference provided for in paragraph 1, after consulting the Economic and Social Committee and within two years of the entry into force of this Treaty, the Commission shall submit proposals for working out and implementing the common agricultural policy, including the replacement of the national organizations by one of the forms of common organization provided for in Article 40 (2), and for implementing the measures specified in this Title.

These proposals shall take account of the interdependence of the agricultural matters mentioned in this Title.

The Council shall, on a proposal from the Commission and after consulting the European Parliament, acting unanimously during the first two stages and by a qualified majority thereafter, make regulations, issue directives, or take decisions, without prejudice to any recommendations it may also make.

3.   The Council may, acting by a qualified majority and in accordance with paragraph 2, replace the national market organizations by the common organization provided for in Article 40 (2) if:

(a) the common organization offers Member States which are opposed to this measure and which have an organization of their own for the production in question equivalent safeguards for the employment and standard of living of the producers concerned, account being taken of the adjustments that will be possible and the specialization that will be needed with the passage of time;

(b) such an organization ensures conditions for trade within the Community similar to those existing in a national market.

4.   If a common organization for certain raw materials is established before a common organization exists for the corresponding processed products, such raw materials as are used for processed products intended for export to third countries may be imported from outside the Community.

Article 44

1.   In so far as progressive abolition of customs duties and quantitative restrictions between Member States may result in prices likely to jeopardize the attainment of the objectives set out in Article 39, each Member State shall, during the transitional period, be entitled to apply to particular products, in a non-discriminatory manner and in substitution for quotas and to such an extent as shall not impede the expansion of the volume of trade provided for in Article 45 (2), a system of minimum prices below which imports may be either:

— temporarily suspended or reduced; or

— allowed, but subjected to the condition that they are made at a price higher than the minimum price for the product concerned.

In the latter case the minimum prices shall not include customs duties.

2. Minimum prices shall neither cause a reduction of the trade existing between Member States when this Treaty enters into force nor form an obstacle to progressive expansion of this trade. Minimum prices shall not be applied so as to form an obstacle to the development of a natural preference between Member States.

3. As soon as this Treaty enters into force the Council shall, on a proposal from the Commission, determine objective criteria for the establishment of minimum price systems and for the fixing of such prices.

These criteria shall in particular take account of the average national production costs in the Member State applying the minimum price, of the position of the various undertakings concerned in relation to such average production costs, and of the need to promote both the progressive improvement of agricultural practice and the adjustments and specialization needed within the common market.

The Commission shall further propose a procedure for revising these criteria in order to allow for and speed up technical progress and to approximate prices progressively within the common market.

These criteria and the procedure for revising them shall be determined by the Council acting unanimously within three years of the entry into force of this Treaty.

4. Until the decision of the Council takes effect, Member States may fix minimum prices on condition that these are communicated be-

forehand to the Commission and to the other Member States so that they may submit their comments.

Once the Council has taken its decision, Member States shall fix minimum prices on the basis of the criteria determined as above.

The Council may, acting by a qualified majority on a proposal from the Commission, rectify any decisions taken by Member States which do not conform to the criteria defined above.

5. If it does not prove possible to determine the said objective criteria for certain products by the beginning of the third stage, the Council may, acting by a qualified majority on a proposal from the Commission, vary the minimum prices applied to these products.

6. At the end of the transitional period, a table of minimum prices still in force shall be drawn up. The Council shall, acting on a proposal from the Commission and by a majority of nine votes in accordance with the weighting laid down in the first subparagraph of Article 148 (2), determine the system to be applied within the framework of the common agricultural policy.

Article 45

1. Until national market organizations have been replaced by one of the forms of common organization referred to in Article 40 (2), trade in products in respect of which certain Member States:

— have arrangements designed to guarantee national producers a market for their products; and

— are in need of imports,

shall be developed by the conclusion of long-term agreements or contracts between importing and exporting Member States.

These agreements or contracts shall be directed towards the progressive abolition of any discrimination in the application of these arrangements to the various producers within the Community.

Such agreements or contracts shall be concluded during the first stage; account shall be taken of the principle or reciprocity.

2.   As regards quantities, these agreements or contracts shall be based on the average volume of trade between Member States in the products concerned during the three years before the entry into force of this Treaty and shall provide for an increase in the volume of trade within the limits of existing requirements, account being taken of traditional patterns of trade.

As regards prices, these agreements or contracts shall enable producers to dispose of the agreed quantities at prices which shall be progressively approximated to those paid to national producers on the domestic market of the purchasing country.

This approximation shall proceed as steadily as possible and shall be completed by the end of the transitional period at the latest.

Prices shall be negotiated between the parties concerned within the framework of directives issued by the Commission for the purpose of implementing the two preceding subparagraphs.

If the first stage is extended, these agreements or contracts shall continue to be carried out in accordance with the conditions applicable at the end of the fourth year after the entry into force of this Treaty, the obligation to increase quantities and to approximate prices being suspended until the transition to the second stage.

Member States shall avail themselves of any opportunity open to them under their legislation, particularly in respect of import policy, to ensure the conclusion and carrying out of these agreements or contracts.

3. To the extent that Member States require raw materials for the manufacture of products to be exported outside the Community in competition with products of third countries, the above agreements or contracts shall not form an obstacle to the importation of raw materials for this purpose from third countries. This provision shall not, however, apply if the Council unanimously decides to make provision for payments required to compensate for the higher price paid on goods imported for this purpose on the basis of these agreements or contracts in relation to the delivered price of the same goods purchased on the world market.

Article 46

Where in a Member State a product is subject to a national market organization or to internal rules having equivalent effect which affect the competitive position of similar production in another Member State, a countervailing charge shall be applied by Member States to imports of this product coming from the Member State where such organization or rules exist, unless that State applies a countervailing charge on export.

The Commission shall fix the amount of these charges at the level required to redress the balance; it may also authorize other measures, the conditions and details of which it shall determine.

Article 47

As to the functions to be performed by the Economic and Social Committee in pursuance of this Title, its agricultural section shall hold itself at the disposal of the Commission to prepare, in accordance with the provisions of Articles 197 and 198, the deliberations of the Committee.

TITLE III

Free movement of persons, services and capital

CHAPTER 1

WORKERS

Article 48

1. Freedom of movement for workers shall be secured within the Community by the end of the transitional period at the latest.

2. Such freedom of movement shall entail the abolition of any discrimination based on nationality between workers of the Member States as regards employment, remuneration and other conditions of work and employment.

3. It shall entail the right, subject to limitations justified on grounds of public policy, public security or public health:

(a) to accept offers of employment actually made;

(b) to move freely within the territory of Member States for this purpose;

(c) to stay in a Member State for the purpose of employment in accordance with the provisions governing the employment of nationals of that State laid down by law, regulation or administrative action;

(d) to remain in the territory of a Member State after having been employed in that State, subject to conditions which shall be embodied in implementing regulations to be drawn up by the Commission.

4. The provisions of this Article shall not apply to employment in the public service.

Article 49

As soon as this Treaty enters into force, the Council shall, acting by a qualified majority on a proposal from the Commission, in cooperation with the European Parliament and after consulting the Economic and Social Committee, issue directives or make regulations setting out the measures required to bring about, by progressive stages, freedom of movement for workers, as defined in Article 48, in particular:*

(a) by ensuring close cooperation between national employment services;

(b) by systematically and progressively abolishing those administrative procedures and practices and those qualifying periods in respect of eligibility for available employment, whether resulting from national legislation or from agreements previously concluded between Member States, the maintenance of which would form an obstacle to liberalization of the movement of workers;

(c) by systematically and progressively abolishing all such qualifying periods and other restrictions provided for either under national legislation or under agreements previously concluded between Member States as imposed on workers of other Member States conditions regarding the free choice of employment other than those imposed on workers of the State concerned;

(d) by setting up appropriate machinery to bring offers of employment into touch with applications for employment and to facilitate the achievement of a balance between supply and demand in the employment market in such a way as to avoid serious threats to the standard of living and level of employment in the various regions and industries.

---

* First sentence as amended by Article 6 (3) of the SEA.

Article 50

Member States shall, within the framework of a joint programme, encourage the exchange of young workers.

Article 51

The Council shall, acting unanimously on a proposal from the Commission, adopt such measures in the field of social security as are necessary to provide freedom of movement for workers; to this end, it shall make arrangements to secure for migrant workers and their dependants:

(a) aggregation, for the purpose of acquiring and retaining the right to benefit and of calculating the amount of benefit, of all periods taken into account under the laws of the several countries;

(b) payment of benefits to persons resident in the territories of Member States.

CHAPTER 2

RIGHT OF ESTABLISHMENT

Article 52

Within the framework of the provisions set out below, restrictions on the freedom of establishment of nationals of a Member State in the territory of another Member State shall be abolished by progressive stages in the course of the transitional period. Such progressive abolition shall also apply to restrictions on the setting up of agencies, branches or subsidiaries by nationals of any Member State established in the territory of any Member State.

Freedom of establishment shall include the right to take up and pursue activities as self-employed persons and to set up and manage undertakings, in particular companies or firms within the meaning of the second paragraph of Article 58, under the conditions laid down for its own nationals by the law of the country where such establishment is effected, subject to the provisions of the Chapter relating to capital.

Article 53

Member States shall not introduce any new restrictions on the right of establishment in their territories of nationals of other Member States, save as otherwise provided in this Treaty.

Article 54

1. Before the end of the first stage, the Council shall, acting unanimously from the Commission and after consulting the Economic and Social Committee and the European Parliament, draw up a general programme for the abolition of existing restrictions on freedom of establishment within the Community. The Commission shall submit its proposal to the Council during the first two years of the first stage.

The programme shall set out the general conditions under which freedom of establishment is to be attained in the case of each type of activity and in particular the stages by which it is to be attained.

2. In order to implement this general programme or, in the absence of such programme, in order to achieve a stage in attaining freedom of establishment as regards a particular activity, the Council shall, acting on a proposal from the Commission, in cooperation with the European Parliament and after consulting the Economic and Social Committee, issue directives, acting unanimously until the end of the first stage and by a qualified majority thereafter.*

---

* Paragraph 2 as amended by Article 6 (4) of the SEA.

3. The Council and the Commission shall carry out the duties devolving upon them under the preceding provisions, in particular:

(a) by according, as a general rule, priority treatment to activities where freedom of establishment makes a particularly valuable contribution to the development of production and trade;

(b) by ensuring close cooperation between the competent authorities in the Member States in order to ascertain the particular situation within the Community of the various activities concerned;

(c) by abolishing those administrative procedures and practices, whether resulting from national legislation or from agreements previously concluded between Member States, the maintenance of which would form an obstacle to freedom of establishment;

(d) by ensuring that workers of one Member State employed in the territory of another Member State may remain in that territory for the purpose of taking up activities therein as self-employed persons, where they satisfy the conditions which they would be required to satisfy if they were entering that State at the time when they intended to take up such activities;

(e) by enabling a national of one Member State to acquire and use land and buildings situated in the territory of another Member State, in so far as this does not conflict with the principles laid down in Article 39 (2);

(f) by effecting the progressive abolition of restrictions on freedom of establishment in every branch of activity under consideration, both as regards the conditions for setting up agencies, branches or subsidiaries in the territory of a Member State and as regards the subsidiaries in the territory of a Member State and as regards the conditions governing the entry of personnel belonging to the main establishment into managerial or supervisory posts in such agencies, branches or subsidiaries;

(g) by coordinating to the necessary extent the safeguards which, for the protection of the interests of members and others, are required by Member States of companies or firms within the meaning of the second paragraph of Article 58 with a view to making such safeguards equivalent throughout the Community;

(h) by satisfying themselves that the conditions of establishment are not distorted by aids granted by Member States.

Article 55

The provisions of this Chapter shall not apply, so far as any given Member State is concerned, to activities which in that State are connected, even occasionally, with the exercise of official authority.

The Council may, acting by a qualified majority on a proposal from the Commission, rule that the provisions of this Chapter shall not apply to certain activities.

Article 56

1. The provisions of this Chapter and measures taken in pursuance thereof shall not prejudice the applicability of provisions laid down by law, regulation or administrative action providing for special treatment for foreign nationals on grounds of public policy, public security or public health.

2. Before the end of the transitional period, the Council shall, acting unanimously on a proposal from the Commission and after consulting the European Parliament, issue directives for the coordination of the aforementioned provisions laid down by law, regulation or administrative action. After the end of the second stage, however, the Council shall, acting by a qualified majority on a proposal from the Commission and in cooperation with the European Parliament, issue directives for the coordination of such provisions as, in each Member State, are a matter for regulation or administrative action.*

------

* Second sentence of paragraph 2 as amended by Article 6 (5) of the SEA.

Article 57

1. In order to make it easier for persons to take up and pursue activities as self-employed persons, the Council shall, on a proposal from the Commission and in cooperation with the European Parliament, acting unanimously during the first stage and by a qualified majority thereafter, issue directives for the mutual recognition of diplomas, certificates and other evidence of formal qualifications.*

2. For the same purpose, the Council shall, before the end of the transitional period, acting on a proposal from the Commission and after consulting the European Parliament, issue directives for the coordination of the provisions laid down by law, regulation or administrative action in Member States concerning the taking up and pursuit of activities as self-employed persons. Unanimity shall be required for directives the implementation of which involves in at least one Member State amendment of the existing principles laid down by law governing the professions with respect to training and conditions of access for natural persons.** In other cases the Council shall act by a qualified majority, in cooperation with the European Parliament.***

3. In the case of the medical and allied and pharmaceutical professions, the progressive abolition of restrictions shall be dependent upon coordination of the conditions for their exercise in the various Member States.

Article 58

Companies or firms formed in accordance with the law of a Member State and having their registered office, central administration or principal place of business within the Community shall, for the purposes of this Chapter, be treated in the same way as natural persons who are nationals of Member States.

---

* Paragraph 1 as amended by Article 6 (6) of the SEA.
** Second sentence of paragraph 2 as amended by Article 16 (2) of the SEA.
*** Third sentence of paragraph 2 as amended by Article 6 (7) of the SEA.

'Companies or firms' means companies or firms constituted under civil or commercial law, including cooperative societies, and other legal persons governed by public or private law, save for those which are non-profit-making.

CHAPTER 3

SERVICES

Article 59

Within the framework of the provisions set out below, restrictions on freedom to provide services within the Community shall be progressively abolished during the transitional period in respect of nationals of Member States who are established in a State of the Community other than that of the person for whom the services are intended.

The Council may, acting by a qualified majority on a proposal from the Commission, extend the provisions of the Chapter to nationals of a third country who provide services and who are established within the Community.*

Article 60

Services shall be considered to be 'services' within the meaning of this Treaty where they are normally provided for remuneration, in so far as they are not governed by the provisions relating to freedom of movement for goods, capital and persons.

'Services' shall in particular include:

(a) activities of an industrial character;

(b) activities of a commercial character;

(c) activities of craftsmen;

(d) activities of the professions.

---

* Second paragraph as amended by Article 16 (3) of the SEA.

Without prejudice to the provisions of the Chapter relating to the right of establishment, the person providing a service may, in order to do so, temporarily pursue his activity in the State where the service is provided, under the same conditions as are imposed by that State on its own nationals.

Article 61

1.   Freedom to provide services in the field of transport shall be governed by the provisions of the Title relating to transport.

2.   The liberalization of banking and insurance services connected with movements of capital shall be effected in step with the progressive liberalization of movement of capital.

Article 62

Save as otherwise provided in this Treaty, Member States shall not introduce any new restrictions on the freedom to provide services which have in fact been attained at the date of the entry into force of this Treaty.

Article 63

1.   Before the end of the first stage, the Council shall, acting unanimously on a proposal from the Commission and after consulting the Economic and Social Committee and the European Parliament, draw up a general programme for the abolition of existing restrictions on freedom to provide services within the Community. The Commission shall submit its proposal to the Council during the first two years of the first stage.

The programme shall set out the general conditions under which and the stages by which each type of service is to be liberalized.

2.   In order to implement this general programme or, in the absence of such programme, in order to achieve a stage in the liberalization of a spe-

cific service, the Council shall, on a proposal from the Commission and after consulting the Economic and Social Committee and the European Parliament, issue directives acting unanimously until the end of the first stage and by a qualified majority thereafter.

3.   As regards the proposals and decisions referred to in paragraphs 1 and 2, priority shall as a general rule be given to those services which directly affect production costs or the liberalization of which helps to promote trade in goods.

Article 64

The Member States declare their readiness to undertake the liberalization of services beyond the extent required by the directives issued pursuant to Article 63 (2), if their general economic situation and the situation of the economic sector concerned so permit.

To this end, the Commission shall make recommendations to the Member States concerned.

Article 65

As long as restrictions on freedom to provide services have not been abolished, each Member State shall apply such restrictions without distinction on grounds of nationality or residence to all persons providing services within the meaning of the first paragraph of Article 59.

Article 66

The provisions of Articles 55 to 58 shall apply to the matters covered by this Chapter.

CHAPTER 4

CAPITAL

Article 67

1. During the transitional period and to the extent necessary to ensure the proper functioning of the common market, Member States shall progressively abolish between themselves all restrictions on the movement of capital belonging to persons resident in Member States and any discrimination based on the nationality or on the place of residence of the parties or on the place where such capital is invested.

2. Current payments connected with the movement of capital between Member States shall be freed from all restrictions by the end of the first stage at the latest.

Article 68

1. Member States shall, as regards the matters dealt with in this Chapter, be as liberal as possible in granting such exchange authorizations as are still necessary after the entry into force of this Treaty.

2. Where a Member State applies to the movements of capital liberalized in accordance with the provisions of this Chapter the domestic rules governing the capital market and the credit system, it shall do so in a non-discriminatory manner.

3. Loans for the direct or indirect financing of a Member State or its regional or local authorities shall not be issued or placed in other Member States unless the States concerned have reached agreement thereon. This provision shall not preclude the application of Article 22 of the Protocol on the Statute of the European Investment Bank.

Article 69

The Council shall, on a proposal from the Commission, which for this purpose shall consult the Monetary Committee provided for in Article 105, issue the necessary directives for the progressive implementation of the provisions of Article 67, acting unanimously during the first two stages and by a qualified majority thereafter.

Article 70

1. The Commission shall propose to the Council measures for the progressive coordination of the exchange policies of Member States in respect of the movement of capital between those States and third countries. For this purpose the Council shall issue directives, acting by a qualified majority. It shall endeavour to attain the highest possible degree of liberalization. Unanimity shall be required for measures which constitute a step back as regards the liberalization of capital movements.*

2. Where the measures taken in accordance with paragraph 1 do not permit the elimination of differences between the exchange rules of Member States and where such differences could lead persons resident in one of the Member States to use the freer transfer facilities within the Community which are provided for in Article 67 in order to evade the rules of one of the Member States concerning the movement of capital to or from third countries, that State may, after consulting the other Member States and the Commission, take appropriate measures to overcome these difficulties.

Should the Council find that these measures are restricting the free movement of capital within the Community to a greater extent than is required for the purpose of overcoming the difficulties, it may, acting by a qualified majority on a proposal from the Commission, decide that the State concerned shall amend or abolish these measures.

_____

* Paragraph 1, excepting the first sentence, as amended by Article 16 (4) of the SEA.

Article 71

Member States shall endeavour to avoid introducing within the Community any new exchange restrictions on the movement of capital and current payments connected with such movements, and shall endeavour not to make existing rules more restrictive.

They declare their readiness to go beyond the degree of liberalization of capital movements provided for in the preceding Articles in so far as their economic situation, in particular the situation of their balance of payments, so permits.

The Commission may, after consulting the Monetary Committee, make recommendations to Member States on this subject.

Article 72

Member States shall keep the Commission informed of any movements of capital to and from third countries which come to their knowledge. The Commission may deliver to Member States any opinions which it considers appropriate on this subject.

Article 73

1. If movements of capital lead to disturbances in the functioning of the capital market in any Member State, the Commission shall, after consulting the Monetary Committee, authorize that State to take protective measures in the field of capital movements, the conditions and details of which the Commission shall determine.

The Council may, acting by a qualified majority, revoke this authorization or amend the conditions or details thereof.

2. A Member State which is in difficulties may, however, on grounds of secrecy or urgency, take the measures mentioned above, where this proves

necessary, on its own initiative. The Commission and the other Member States shall be informed of such measures by the date of their entry into force at the latest. In this event the Commission may, after consulting the Monetary Committee, decide that the State concerned shall amend or abolish the measures.

Transport

Article 74

The objectives of this Treaty shall, in matters governed by this Title, be pursued by Member States within the framework of a common transport policy.

Article 75

1. For the purpose of implementing Article 74, and taking into account the distinctive features of transport, the Council shall, acting unanimously until the end of the second stage and by a qualified majority thereafter, lay down, on a proposal from the Commission and after consulting the Economic and Social Committee and the European Parliament:

(a) common rules applicable to international transport to or from the territory of a Member State or passing across the territory of one or more Member States;

(b) the conditions under which non-resident carriers may operate transport services within a Member State;

(c) any other appropriate provisions.

2. The provisions referred to in *(a)* and *(b)* of paragraph 1 shall be laid down during the transitional period.

3. By way of derogation from the procedure provided for in paragraph 1, where the application of provisions concerning the principles of the regulatory system for transport would be liable to have a serious effect on the standard of living and on employment in certain areas and on the operation of transport facilities, they shall be laid down by the Council acting unanimously. In so doing, the Council shall take into account the need for adaptation to the economic development which will result from establishing the common market.

Article 76

Until the provisions referred to in Article 75 (1) have been laid down, no Member State may, without the unanimous approval of the Council, make the various provisions governing the subject when this Treaty enters into force less favourable in their direct or indirect effect on carriers of other Member States as compared with carriers who are nationals of that State.

Article 77

Aids shall be compatible with this Treaty if they meet the needs of coordination of transport or if they represent reimbursement for the discharge of certain obligations inherent in the concept of a public service.

Article 78

Any measures taken within the framework of this Treaty in respect of transport rates and conditions shall take account of the economic circumstances of carriers.

Article 79

1. In the case of transport within the Community, discrimination which takes the form of carriers charging different rates and imposing different conditions for the carriage of the same goods over the same transport links on grounds of the country of origin or of destination of the goods in question, shall be abolished, at the latest, before the end of the second stage.

2. Paragraph 1 shall not prevent the Council from adopting other measures in pursuance of Article 75 (1).

3. Within two years of the entry into force of this Treaty, the Council shall, acting by a qualified majority on a proposal from the

Commission and after consulting the Economic and Social Committee, lay down rules for implementing the provisions of paragraph 1.

The Council may in particular lay down the provisions needed to enable the institutions of the Community to secure compliance with the rule laid down in paragraph 1 and to ensure that users benefit from it to the full.

4. The Commission shall, acting on its own initiative or on application by a Member State, investigate any cases of discrimination falling within paragraph 1 and, after consulting any Member State concerned, shall take the necessary decisions within the framework of the rules laid down in accordance with the provisions of paragraph 3.

Article 80

1. The imposition by a Member State, in respect of transport operations carried out within the Community, of rates and conditions involving any element of support or protection in the interest of one or more particular undertakings or industries shall be prohibited as from the beginning of the second stage, unless authorized by the Commission.

2. The Commission shall, acting on its own initiative or on application by a Member State, examine the rates and conditions referred to in paragraph 1, taking account in particular of the requirements of an appropriate regional economic policy, the needs of underdeveloped areas and the problems of areas seriously affected by political circumstances on the one hand, and of the effects of such rates and conditions on competition between the different modes of transport on the other.

After consulting each Member State concerned, the Commission shall take the necessary decisions.

3. The prohibition provided for in paragraph 1 shall not apply to tariffs fixed to meet competition.

Article 81

Charges or dues in respect of the crossing of frontiers which are charged by a carrier in addition to the transport rates shall not exceed a reasonable level after taking the costs actually incurred thereby into account.

Member States shall endeavour to reduce these costs progressively.

The Commission may make recommendations to Member States for the application of this Article.

Article 82

The provisions of this Title shall not form an obstacle to the application of measures taken in the Federal Republic of Germany to the extent that such measures are required in order to compensate for the economic disadvantages caused by the division of Germany to the economy of certain areas of the Federal Republic affected by that division.

Article 83

An Advisory Committee consisting of experts designated by the Governments of Member States, shall be attached to the Commission. The Commission, whenever it considers it desirable, shall consult the Committee on transport matters without prejudice to the powers of the transport section of the Economic and Social Committee.

Article 84

1. The provisions of this Title shall apply to transport by rail, road and inland waterway.

2. The Council may, acting by a qualified majority, decide whether, to what extent and by what procedure appropriate provisions may be laid down for sea and air transport.*

The procedural provisions of Article 75 (1) and (3) shall apply.**

---

* First subparagraph of paragraph 2 as amended by Article 16 (5) of the SEA
** Second subparagraph of paragraph 2 as amended by Article 16 (6) of the SEA.

PART THREE

POLICY OF THE COMMUNITY

TITLE I

Common rules

CHAPTER 1

RULES ON COMPETITION

Section 1

Rules applying to undertakings

Article 85

1. The following shall be prohibited as incompatible with the common market: all agreements between undertakings, decisions by associations of undertakings and concerted practices which may affect trade between Member States and which have as their object or effect the prevention, restriction or distortion of competition within the common market, and in particular those which:

(a) directly or indirectly fix purchase or selling prices or any other trading conditions;

(b) limit or control production, markets, technical development, or investment;

(c) share markets or sources of supply;

(d) apply dissimilar conditions to equivalent transactions with other trading parties, thereby placing them at a competitive disadvantage;

(e) make the conclusion of contracts subject to acceptance by the other parties of supplementary obligations which, by their nature or according to commercial usage, have no connection with the subject of such contracts.

2. Any agreements or decisions prohibited pursuant to this Article shall be automatically void.

3. The provisions of paragraph 1 may, however, be declared inapplicable in the case of:

— any agreement or category of agreements between undertakings;

— any decision or category of decisions by associations of undertakings;

— any concerted practice or category of concerted practices;

which contributes to improving the production or distribution of goods or to promoting technical or economic progress, while allowing consumers a fair share of the resulting benefit, and which does not:

(a) impose on the undertakings concerned restrictions which are not indispensable to the attainment of these objectives;

(b) afford such undertakings the possibility of eliminating competition in respect of a substantial part of the products in question.

Article 86

Any abuse by one or more undertakings of a dominant position within the common market or in a substantial part of it shall be prohibited as incompatible with the common market in so far as it may affect trade between Member States.

Such abuse may, in particular, consist in:

(a) directly or indirectly imposing unfair purchase or selling prices or other unfair trading conditions;

(b) limiting production, markets or technical development to the prejudice of consumers;

(c) applying dissimilar conditions to equivalent transactions with other trading parties, thereby placing them at a competitive disadvantage;

(d) making the conclusion of contracts subject to acceptance by the other parties of supplementary obligations which, by their nature or according to commercial usage, have no connection with the subject of such contracts.

Article 87

1. Within three years of the entry into force of this Treaty the Council shall, acting unanimously on a proposal from the Commission and after consulting the European Parliament, adopt any appropriate regulations or directives to give effect to the principles set out in Articles 85 and 86.

If such provisions have not been adopted within the period mentioned, they shall be laid down by the Council, acting by a qualified majority on a proposal from the Commission and after consulting the European Parliament.

2. The regulations or directives referred to in paragraph 1 shall be designed in particular:

(a) to ensure compliance with the prohibitions laid down in Article 85 (1) and in Article 86 by making provision for fines and periodic penalty payments;

(b) to lay down detailed rules for the application of Article 85 (3), taking into account the need to ensure effective supervision on the one hand, and to simplify administration to the greatest possible extent on the other;

(c) to define, if need be, in the various branches of the economy, the scope of the provisions of Articles 85 and 86;

(d) to define the respective functions of the Commission and of the Court of Justice in applying the provisions laid down in this paragraph;

(e) to determine the relationship between national laws and the provisions contained in this Section or adopted pursuant to this Article.

Article 88

Until the entry into force of the provisions adopted in pursuance of Article 87, the authorities in Member States shall rule on the admissibility of agreements, decisions and concerted practices and on abuse of a dominant position in the common market in accordance with the law of their country and with the provisions of Article 85, in particular paragraph 3, and of Article 86.

Article 89

1. Without prejudice to Article 88, the Commission shall, as soon as it takes up its duties, ensure the application of the principles laid down in Articles 85 and 86. On application by a Member State or on its own initiative, and in cooperation with the competent authorities in the Member States, who shall give it their assistance, the Commission shall investigate cases of suspected infringement of these principles. If it finds that there has been an infringement, it shall propose appropriate measures to bring it to an end.

2. If the infringement is not brought to an end, the Commission shall record such infringement of the principles in a reasoned decision. The Commission may publish its decision and authorize Member States to take the measures, the conditions and details of which it shall determine, needed to remedy the situation.

Article 90

1. In the case of public undertakings and undertakings to which Member States grant special or exclusive rights, Member States shall neither enact nor maintain in force any measure contrary to the rules contained in this Treaty, in particular to those rules provided for in Article 7 and Articles 85 to 94.

2. Undertakings entrusted with the operation of services of general economic interest or having the character of a revenue-producing monopoly shall be subject to the rules contained in this Treaty, in particular to the rules on competition, in so far as the application of such rules does not obstruct the performance, in law or in fact, of the particular tasks assigned to them. The development of trade must not be affected to such an extent as would be contrary to the interests of the Community.

3. The Commission shall ensure the application of the provisions of this Article and shall, where necessary, address appropriate directives or decisions to Member States.

Section 2

Dumping

Article 91

1. If during the transitional period, the Commission, on application by a Member State or by any other interested party, finds that dumping is being practised within the common market, it shall address recommendations to the person or persons with whom such practices originate for the purpose of putting an end to them.

Should the practices continue, the Commission shall authorize the injured Member State to take protective measures, the conditions and details of which the Commission shall determine.

2. As soon as this Treaty enters into force, products which originate in or are in free circulation in one Member State and which have been exported to another Member State shall, on reimportation, be admitted into the territory of the first-mentioned State free of all customs duties, quantitative restrictions or measures having equivalent effect. The Commission shall lay down appropriate rules for the application of this paragraph.

Section 3

Aids granted by States

Article 92

1.   Save as otherwise provided in this Treaty, any aid granted by a Member State or through State resources in any form whatsoever which distorts or threatens to distort competition by favouring certain undertakings or the production of certain goods shall, in so far as it affects trade between Member States, be incompatible with the common market.

2.   The following shall be compatible with the common market:

(a) aid having a social character, granted to individual consumers, provided that such aid is granted without discrimination related to the origin of the products concerned;

(b) aid to make good the damage caused by natural disasters or exceptional occurrences;

(c) aid granted to the economy of certain areas of the Federal Republic of Germany affected by the division of Germany, in so far as such aid is required in order to compensate for the economic disadvantages caused by that division.

3.   The following may be considered to be compatible with the common market:

(a) aid to promote the economic development of areas where the standard of living is abnormally low or where there is serious underemployment;

(b) aid to promote the execution of an important project of common European interest or to remedy a serious disturbance in the economy of a Member State;

(c) aid to facilitate the development of certain economic activities or of certain economic areas, where such aid does not adversely affect trading conditions to an extent contrary to the common interest. However, the aids granted to shipbuilding as of 1 January 1957 shall, in so far as they serve only to compensate for the absence of customs protection, be progressively reduced under the same conditions as apply to the elimination of customs duties, subject to the provisions of this Treaty concerning common commercial policy towards third countries;

(d) such other categories of aid as may be specified by decision of the Council acting by a qualified majority on a proposal from the Commission.

Article 93

1. The Commission shall, in cooperation with Member States, keep under constant review all systems of aid existing in those States. It shall propose to the latter any appropriate measures required by the progressive development or by the functioning of the common market.

2. If, after giving notice to the parties concerned to submit their comments, the Commission finds that aid granted by a State or through State resources is not compatible with the common market having regard to Article 92, or that such aid is being misused, it shall decide that the State concerned shall abolish or alter such aid within a period of time to be determined by the Commission.

If the State concerned does not comply with this decision within the prescribed time, the Commission or any other interested State may, in derogation from the provisions of Articles 169 and 170, refer the matter to the Court of Justice direct.

On application by a Member State, the Council, may, acting unanimously, decide that aid which that State is granting or intends to grant shall be considered to be compatible with the common market, in derogation from the provisions of Article 92 or from the regulations provided for in Article 94, if such a decision is justified by exceptional circumstances. If, as regards the aid in question, the Commission has already initiated the procedure provided for in the first subparagraph of this paragraph, the fact that the State concerned has made its application to the Council shall have the effect of suspending that procedure until the Council has made its attitude known.

If, however, the Council has not made its attitude known within three months of the said application being made, the Commission shall give its decision on the case.

3. The Commission shall be informed, in sufficient time to enable it to submit its comments, of any plans to grant or alter aid. If it considers that any such plan is not compatible with the common market having regard to Article 92, it shall without delay initiate the procedure provided for in paragraph 2. The Member State concerned shall not put its proposed measures into effect until this procedure has resulted in a final decision.

Article 94

The Council may, acting by a qualified majority on a proposal from the Commission, make any appropriate regulations for the application of Articles 92 and 93 and may in particular determine the conditions in which Article 93 (3) shall apply and the categories of aid exempted from this procedure.

CHAPTER 2

TAX PROVISIONS

Article 95

No Member State shall impose, directly or indirectly, on the products of other Member States any internal taxation of any kind in excess of that imposed directly or indirectly on similar domestic products.

Furthermore, no Member State shall impose on the products of other Member States any internal taxation of such a nature as to afford indirect protection to other products.

Member States shall, not later than at the beginning of the second stage, repeal or amend any provisions existing when this Treaty enters into force which conflict with the preceding rules.

Article 96

Where products are exported to the territory of any Member State, any repayment of internal taxation shall not exceed the internal taxation imposed on them whether directly or indirectly.

Article 97

Member States which levy a turnover tax calculated on a cumulative multi-stage tax system may, in the case of internal taxation imposed by them on imported products or of repayments allowed by them on exported products, establish average rates for products or groups of products, provided that there is no infringement of the principles laid down in Articles 95 and 96.

Where the average rates established by a Member State do not conform to these principles, the Commission shall address appropriate directives or decisions to the State concerned.

Article 98

In the case of charges other than turnover taxes, excise duties and other forms of indirect taxation, remissions and repayments in respect of exports to other Member States may not be granted and countervailing charges in respect of imports from Member States may not be imposed unless the measures contemplated have been previously approved for a limited period by the Council acting by a qualified majority on a proposal from the Commission.

Article 99*

The Council shall, acting unanimously on a proposal from the Commission and after consulting the European Parliament, adopt provisions for the harmonization of legislation concerning turnover taxes, excise duties and other forms of indirect taxation to the extent that such harmonization is necessary to ensure the establishment and the functioning of the internal market within the time-limit laid down in Article 8a.

CHAPTER 3

APPROXIMATION OF LAWS

Article 100

The Council shall, acting unanimously on a proposal from the Commission, issue directives for the approximation of such provisions laid down by law, regulation or administrative action in Member States as directly affect the establishment or functioning of the common market.

---

* Article as replaced by Article 17 of the SEA.

The European Parliament and the Economic and Social Committee shall be consulted in the case of directives whose implementation would, in one or more Member States, involve the amendment of legislation.

Article 100a*

1. By way of derogation from Article 100 and save where otherwise provided in this Treaty, the following provisions shall apply for the achievement of the objectives set out in Article 8a. The Council shall, acting by a qualified majority on a proposal from the Commission in cooperation with the European Parliament and after consulting the Economic and Social Committee, adopt the measures for the approximation of the provisions laid down by law, regulation or administrative action in Member States which have as their object the establishment and functioning of the internal market.

2. Paragraph 1 shall not apply to fiscal provisions, to those relating to the free movement of persons nor to those relating to the rights and interests of employed persons.

3. The Commission, in its proposals envisaged in paragraph 1 concerning health, safety, environmental protection and consumer protection, will take as a base a high level of protection.

4. If, after the adoption of a harmonization measure by the Council acting by a qualified majority, a Member State deems it necessary to apply national provisions on grounds of major needs referred to in Article 36, or relating to protection of the environment or the working environment, it shall notify the Commission of these provisions.

---

* Article added by Article 18 of the SEA.

The Commission shall confirm the provisions involved after having verified that they are not a means of arbitrary discrimination or a disguised restriction on trade between Member States.

By way of derogation from the procedure laid down in Articles 169 and 170, the Commission or any Member State may bring the matter directly before the Court of Justice if it considers that another Member State is making improper use of the powers provided for in this Article.

5. The harmonization measures referred to above shall, in appropriate cases, include a safeguard clause authorizing the Member States to take, for one or more of the non-economic reasons referred to in Article 36, provisional measures subject to a Community control procedure.

Article 100b*

1. During 1992, the Commission shall, together with each Member State, draw up an inventory of national laws, regulations and administrative provisions which fall under Article 100a and which have not been harmonized pursuant to that Article.

The Council, acting in accordance with the provisions of Article 100a, may decide that the provisions in force in a Member State must be recognized as being equivalent to those applied by another Member State.

2. The provisions of Article 100a (4) shall apply by analogy.

---

* Article added by Article 19 of the SEA.

3. The Commission shall draw up the inventory referred to in the first subparagraph of paragraph 1 and shall submit appropriate proposals in good time to allow the Council to act before the end of 1992.

Article 101

Where the Commission finds that a difference between the provisions laid down by law, regulation or administrative action in Member States is distorting the conditions of competition in the common market and that the resultant distortion needs to be eliminated, it shall consult the Member States concerned.

If such consultation does not result in an agreement eliminating the distortion in question, the Council shall, on a proposal from the Commission, acting unanimously during the first stage and by a qualified majority thereafter, issue the necessary directives. The Commission and the Council may take any other appropriate measures provided for in this Treaty.

Article 102

1. Where there is reason to fear that the adoption or amendment of a provision laid down by law, regulation or administrative action may cause distortion within the meaning of Article 101, a Member State desiring to proceed therewith shall consult the Commission. After consulting the Member States, the Commission shall recommend to the States concerned such measures as may be appropriate to avoid the distortion in question.

2. If a State desiring to introduce or amend its own provisions does not comply with the recommendation addressed to it by the Commission, other Member States shall not be required, in pursuance of Article 101, to amend their own provisions in order to eliminate such distortion. If the Member State which has ignored the recommendation of the Commission causes distortion detrimental only to itself, the provisions of Article 101 shall not apply.

TITLE II

Economic policy

CHAPTER 1*

COOPERATION IN ECONOMIC AND MONETARY POLICY (ECONOMIC AND MONETARY UNION)

Article 102a

1. In order to ensure the convergence of economic and monetary policies which is necessary for the further development of the Community, Member States shall cooperate in accordance with the objectives of Article 104. In so doing, they shall take account of the experience acquired in cooperation within the framework of the European Monetary System (EMS) and in developing the ECU, and shall respect existing powers in this field.

2. Insofar as further development in the field of economic and monetary policy necessitates institutional changes, the provisions of Article 236 shall be applicable. The Monetary Committee and the Committee of Governors of the Central Banks shall also be consulted regarding institutional changes in the monetary area.

CHAPTER 2**

CONJUNCTURAL POLICY

Article 103

1. Member States shall regard their conjunctural policies as a matter of

---

* Chapter as inserted in Title II of Part Three of the Treaty by Article 20 of the SEA.
** Renumbering of the Chapter as established by Article 20 (2) of the SEA.

common concern. They shall consult each other and the Commission on the measures to be taken in the light of the prevailing circumstances.

2.   Without prejudice to any other procedures provided for in this Treaty, the Council may, acting unanimously on a proposal from the Commission, decide upon the measures appropriate to the situation.

3.   Acting by a qualified majority on a proposal from the Commission, the Council shall, where required, issue any directives needed to give effect to the measures decided upon under paragraph 2.

4.   The procedures provided for in this Article shall also apply if any difficulty should arise in the supply of certain products.

CHAPTER 3*

BALANCE OF PAYMENTS

Article 104

Each Member State shall pursue the economic policy needed to ensure the equilibrium of its overall balance of payments and to maintain confidence in its currency, while taking care to ensure a high level of employment and a stable level of prices.

---

* Renumbering of the Chapter as established by Article 20 (2) of the SEA.

Article 105

1. In order to facilitate attainment of the objectives set out in Article 104, Member States shall coordinate their economic policies. They shall for this purpose provide for cooperation between their appropriate administrative departments and between their central banks.

The Commission shall submit to the Council recommendations on how to achieve such cooperation.

2. In order to promote coordination of the policies of Member States in the monetary field to the full extent needed for the functioning of the common market, a Monetary Committee with advisory status is hereby set up. It shall have the following tasks:

— to keep under review the monetary and financial situation of the Member States and of the Community and the general payments system of the Member States and to report regularly thereon to the Council and to the Commission;

— to deliver opinions at the request of the Council or of the Commission or on its own initiative, for submission to these institutions.

The Member States and the Commission shall each appoint two members of the Monetary Committee.

Article 106

1. Each Member State undertakes to authorize, in the currency of the Member State in which the creditor or the beneficiary resides, any payments connected with the movement of goods, services or capital, and any transfers of capital and earnings, to the extent that the movement of goods, services, capital and persons between Member States has been liberalized pursuant to this Treaty.

The Member States declare their readiness to undertake the liberalization of payments beyond the extent provided in the preceding subparagraph, in so far as their economic situation in general and the state of their balance of payments in particular so permit.

2.   In so far as movements of goods, services, and capital are limited only by restrictions on payments connected therewith, these restrictions shall be progressively abolished by applying, *mutatis mutandis,* the provisions of the Chapters relating to the abolition of quantitative restrictions, to the liberalization of services and to the free movement of capital.

3.   Member States undertake not to introduce between themselves any new restrictions on transfers connected with the invisible transactions listed in Annex III to this Treaty.

The progressive abolition of existing restrictions shall be effected in accordance with the provisions of Articles 63 to 65, in so far as such abolition is not governed by the provisions contained in paragraphs 1 and 2 or by the Chapter relating to the free movement of capital.

4.   If need be, Member States shall consult each other on the measures to be taken to enable the payments and transfers mentioned in this Article to be effected; such measures shall not prejudice the attainment of the objectives set out in this Chapter.

Article 107

1.   Each Member State shall treat its policy with regard to rates of exchange as a matter of common concern.

2.   If a Member State makes an alteration in its rate of exchange which is inconsistent with the objectives set out in Article 104 and which seriously distorts conditions of competition, the Commission may, after consulting the Monetary Committee, authorize other Member States to take for a strictly limited period the necessary measures, the conditions and details of which it shall determine, in order to counter the consequences of such alteration.

1. Where a Member State is in difficulties or is seriously threatened with difficulties as regards its balance of payments either as a result of an over-all disequilibrium in its balance of payments, or as a result of the type of currency at its disposal, and where such difficulties are liable in particular to jeopardize the functioning of the common market or the progressive implementation of the common commercial policy, the Commission shall immediately investigate the position of the State in question and the action which, making use of all the means at its disposal, that State has taken or may take in accordance with the provisions of Article 104. The Commission shall state what measures it recommends the State concerned to take.

If the action taken by a Member State and the measures suggested by the Commission do not prove sufficient to overcome the difficulties which have arisen or which threaten, the Commission shall, after consulting the Monetary Committee, recommend to the Council the granting of mutual assistance and appropriate methods therefor.

The Commission shall keep the Council regularly informed of the situation and of how it is developing.

2. The Council, acting by a qualified majority, shall grant such mutual assistance; it shall adopt directives or decisions laying down the conditions and details of such assistance, which may take such forms as:

(a) a concerted approach to or within any other international organizations to which Member States may have recourse;

(b) measures needed to avoid deflection of trade where the State which is in difficulties maintains or reintroduces quantitative restrictions against third countries;

(c) the granting of limited credits by other Member States, subject to their agreement.

During the transitional period, mutual assistance may also take the form of special reductions in customs duties or enlargements of quotas in order to facilitate an increase in imports from the State which is in difficulties, subject to the agreement of the States by which such measures would have to be taken.

3. If the mutual assistance recommended by the Commission is not granted by the Council or if the mutual assistance granted and the measures taken are insufficient, the Commission shall authorize the State which is in difficulties to take protective measures, the conditions and details of which the Commission shall determine.

Such authorization may be revoked and such conditions and details may be changed by the Council acting by a qualified majority.

Article 109

1. Where a sudden crisis in the balance of payments occurs and a decision within the meaning of Article 108 (2) is not immediately taken, the Member State concerned may, as a precaution, take the necessary protective measures. Such measures must cause the least possible disturbance in the functioning of the common market and must not be wider in scope than is strictly necessary to remedy the sudden difficulties which have arisen.

2. The Commission and the other Member States shall be informed of such protective measures not later than when they enter into force. The Commission may recommend to the Council the granting of mutual assistance under Article 108.

3. After the Commission has delivered an opinion and the Monetary Committee has been consulted, the Council may, acting by a qualified majority, decide that the State concerned shall amend, suspend or abolish the protective measures referred to above.

CHAPTER 4*

COMMERCIAL POLICY

Article 110

By establishing a customs union between themselves Member States aim to contribute, in the common interest, to the harmonious development of world trade, the progressive abolition of restrictions on international trade and the lowering of customs barriers.

The common commercial policy shall take into account the favourable effect which the abolition of customs duties between Member States may have on the increase in the competitive strength of undertakings in those States.

Article 111

The following provisions shall, without prejudice to Articles 115 and 116, apply during the transitional period:

1. Member States shall coordinate their trade relations with third countries so as to bring about, by the end of the transitional period, the conditions needed for implementing a common policy in the field of external trade.

The Commission shall submit to the Council proposals regarding the procedure for common action to be followed during the transitional period and regarding the achievement of uniformity in their commercial policies.

_____

* Renumbering of the Chapter as established by Article 20 (2) of the SEA.

2. The Commission shall submit to the Council recommendations for tariff negotiations with third countries in respect of the common customs tariff.

The Council shall authorize the Commission to open such negotiations.

The Commission shall conduct these negotiations in consultation with a special committee appointed by the Council to assist the Commission in this task and within the framework of such directives as the Council may issue to it.

3. In exercising the powers conferred upon it by this Article, the Council shall act unanimously during the first two stages and by a qualified majority thereafter.

4. Member States shall, in consultation with the Commission, take all necessary measures, particularly those designed to bring about an adjustment of tariff agreements in force with third countries, in order that the entry into force of the common customs tariff shall not be delayed.

5. Member States shall aim at securing as high a level of uniformity as possible between themselves as regards their liberalization lists in relation to third countries or groups of third countries. To this end, the Commission shall make all appropriate recommendations to Member States.

If Member States abolish or reduce quantitative restrictions in relation to third countries, they shall inform the Commission beforehand and shall accord the same treatment to other Member States.

Article 112

1. Without prejudice to obligations undertaken by them within the framework of other international organizations, Member States shall, before the end of the transitional period, progressively harmonize the systems whereby they grant aid for exports to third countries, to the extent necessary to ensure that competition between undertakings of the Community is not distorted.

On a proposal from the Commission, the Council, shall, acting unanimously until the end of the second stage and by a qualified majority thereafter, issue any directives needed for this purpose.

2. The preceding provisions shall not apply to such drawback of customs duties or charges having equivalent effect nor to such repayment of indirect taxation including turnover taxes, excise duties and other indirect taxes as is allowed when goods are exported from a Member State to a third country, in so far as such drawback or repayment does not exceed the amount imposed, directly or indirectly, on the products exported.

Article 113

1. After the transitional period has ended, the common commercial policy shall be based on uniform principles, particularly in regard to changes in tariff rates, the conclusion of tariff and trade agreements, the achievement of uniformity in measures of liberalization, export policy and measures to protect trade such as those to be taken in case of dumping or subsidies.

2. The Commission shall submit proposals to the Council for implementing the common commercial policy.

3. Where agreements with third countries need to be negotiated, the Commission shall make recommendations to the Council, which shall authorize the Commission to open the necessary negotiations.

The Commission shall conduct these negotiations in consultation with a special committee appointed by the Council to assist the Commission in this task and within the framework of such directives as the Council may issue to it.

4. In exercising the powers conferred upon it by this Article, the Council shall act by a qualified majority.

Article 114

The agreements referred to in Article 111 (2) and in Article 113 shall be concluded by the Council on behalf of the Community, acting unanimously during the first two stages and by a qualified majority thereafter.

Article 115

In order to ensure that the execution of measures of commercial policy taken in accordance with this Treaty by any Member State is not obstructed by deflection of trade, or where differences between such measures lead to economic difficulties in one or more of the Member States, the Commission shall recommend the methods for the requisite cooperation between Member States. Failing this, the Commission shall authorize Member States to take the necessary protective measures, the conditions and details of which it shall determine.

In case of urgency during the transitional period, Member States may themselves take the necessary measures and shall notify them to the other Member States and to the Commission, which may decide that the States concerned shall amend or abolish such measures.

In the selection of such measures, priority shall be given to those which cause the least disturbance to the functioning of the common market and which take into account the need to expedite, as far as possible, the introduction of the common customs tariff.

Article 116

From the end of the transitional period onwards, Member States shall, in respect of all matters of particular interest to the common market, proceed within the framework of international organizations of an economic character only by common action. To this end, the Commission shall submit to the Council, which shall act by a qualified majority, proposals concerning the scope and implementation of such common action.

During the transitional period, Member States shall consult each other for the purpose of concerting the action they take and adopting as far as possible a uniform attitude.

TITLE III

Social policy

CHAPTER 1

SOCIAL PROVISIONS

Article 117

Member States agree upon the need to promote improved working conditions and an improved standard of living for workers, so as to make possible their harmonization while the improvement is being maintained.

They believe that such a development will ensue not only from the functioning of the common market, which will favour the harmonization of social systems, but also from the procedures provided for in this Treaty and from the approximation of provisions laid down by law, regulation or administrative action.

Article 118

Without prejudice to the other provisions of this Treaty and in conformity with its general objectives, the Commission shall have the task of promoting close cooperation between Member States in the social field, particularly in matters relating to:

— employment;

— labour law and working conditions;

— basic and advanced vocational training;

— social security;

— prevention of occupational accidents and diseases;

— occupational hygiene;

— the right of association, and collective bargaining between employers and workers.

To this end, the Commission shall act in close contact with Member States by making studies, delivering opinions and arranging consultations both on problems arising at national level and on those of concern to international organizations.

Before delivering the opinions provided for in this Article, the Commission shall consult the Economic and Social Committee.

Article 118a*

1. Member States shall pay particular attention to encouraging improvements, especially in the working environment, as regards the health and safety of workers, and shall set as their objective the harmonization of conditions in this area, while maintaining the improvements made.

2. In order to help achieve the objective laid down in the first paragraph, the Council, acting by a qualified majority on a proposal from the Commission, in cooperation with the European Parliament and after consulting the Economic and Social Committee, shall adopt, by means of directives, minimum requirements for gradual implementation, having regard to the conditions and technical rules obtaining in each of the Member States.

Such directives shall avoid imposing administrative, financial and legal constraints in a way which would hold back the creation and development of small and medium-sized undertakings.

3. The provisions adopted pursuant to this Article shall not prevent any Member State from maintaining or introducing more stringent measures for the protection of working conditions compatible with this Treaty.

---

* Article added by Article 21 of the SEA.

Article 118b*

The Commission shall endeavour to develop the dialogue between management and labour at European level which could, if the two sides consider it desirable, lead to relations based on agreement.

Article 119

Each Member State shall during the first stage ensure and subsequently maintain the application of the principle that men and women should receive equal pay for equal work.

For the purpose of this Article, 'pay' means the ordinary basic or minimum wage or salary and any other consideration, whether in cash or in kind, which the worker receives, directly or indirectly, in respect of his employment from his employer.

Equal pay without discrimination based on sex means:

(a) that pay for the same work at piece rates shall be calculated on the basis of the same unit of measurement;

(b) that pay for work at time rates shall be the same for the same job.

Article 120

Member States shall endeavour to maintain the existing equivalence between paid holiday schemes.

Article 121

The Council may, acting unanimously and after consulting the Economic and Social Committee, assign to the Commission tasks in con-

---

* Article added by Article 22 of the SEA.

nection with the implementation of common measures, particularly as regards social security for the migrant workers referred to in Articles 48 to 51.

Article 122

The Commission shall include a separate chapter on social developments within the Community in its annual report to the European Parliament.

The European Parliament may invite the Commission to draw up reports on any particular problems concerning social conditions.

CHAPTER 2

THE EUROPEAN SOCIAL FUND

Article 123

In order to improve employment opportunities for workers in the common market and to contribute thereby to raising the standard of living, a European Social Fund is hereby established in accordance with the provisions set out below; it shall have the task of rendering the employment of workers easier and of increasing their geographical and occupational mobility within the Community.

Article 124

The Fund shall be administered by the Commission.

The Commission shall be assisted in this task by a Committee presided over by a member of the Commission and composed of representatives of Governments, trade unions and employers' organizations.

1. On application by a Member State the Fund shall, within the framework of the rules provided for in Article 127, meet 50 % of the expenditure incurred after the entry into force of this Treaty by that State or by a body governed by public law for the purposes of:

(a) ensuring productive re-employment of workers by means of:

— vocational retraining;

— resettlement allowances;

(b) granting aid for the benefit of workers whose employment is reduced or temporarily suspended, in whole or in part, as a result of the conversion of an undertaking to other production, in order that they may retain the same wage level pending their full re-employment.

2. Assistance granted by the Fund towards the cost of vocational retraining shall be granted only if the unemployed workers could not be found employment except in a new occupation and only if they have been in productive employment for at least six months in the occupation for which they have been retrained.

Assistance towards resettlement allowances shall be granted only if the unemployed workers have been caused to change their home within the Community and have been in productive employment for at least six months in their new place of residence.

Assistance for workers in the case of the conversion of an undertaking shall be granted only if:

(a) the workers concerned have again been fully employed in that undertaking for at least six months;

(b) the Government concerned has submitted a plan beforehand, drawn up by the undertaking in question, for that particular conversion and for financing it;

(c) the Commission has given its prior approval to the conversion plan.

Article 126

When the transitional period has ended, the Council, after receiving the opinion of the Commission and after consulting the Economic and Social Committee and the European Parliament, may:

(a) rule, by a qualified majority, that all or part of the assistance referred to in Article 125 shall no longer be granted; or

(b) unanimously determine what new tasks may be entrusted to the Fund within the framework of its terms of reference as laid down in Article 123.

Article 127

The Council shall, acting by a qualified majority on a proposal from the Commission and after consulting the Economic and Social Committee and the European Parliament, lay down the provisions required to implement Articles 124 to 126; in particular it shall determine in detail the conditions under which assistance shall be granted by the Fund in accordance with Article 125 and the classes of undertakings whose workers shall benefit from the assistance provided for in Article 125 (1) *(b)*.

Article 128

The Council shall, acting on a proposal from the Commission and after consulting the Economic and Social Committee, lay down general principles for implementing a common vocational training policy capable of contributing to the harmonious development both of the national economies and of the common market.

The European Investment Bank

Article 129

A European Investment Bank is hereby established; it shall have legal personality.

The members of the European Investment Bank shall be the Member States.

The Statute of the European Investment Bank is laid down in a Protocol annexed to this Treaty.

Article 130

The task of the European Investment Bank shall be to contribute, by having recourse to the capital market and utilizing its own resources, to the balanced and steady development of the common market in the interest of the Community. For this purpose the Bank shall, operating on a non-profit-making basis, grant loans and give guarantees which facilitate the financing of the following projects in all sectors of the economy:

(a) projects for developing less-developed regions;

(b) projects for modernizing or converting undertakings or for developing fresh activities called for by the progressive establishment of the common market, where these projects are of such a size or nature that they cannot be entirely financed by the various means available in the individual Member States;

(c) projects of common interest to several Member States which are of such a size or nature that they cannot be entirely financed by the various means available in the individual Member States.

Economic and social cohesion

---

* Title V consisting of Articles 130a, 130b, 130c, 130d and 130e as added to Part Three of the Treaty by Article 23 of the SEA.

Article 130a*

In order to promote its overall harmonious development, the Community shall develop and pursue its actions leading to the strengthening of its economic and social cohesion.

In particular the Community shall aim at reducing disparities between the various regions and the backwardness of the least-favoured regions.

Article 130b*

Member States shall conduct their economic policies, and shall coordinate them, in such a way as, in addition, to attain the objectives set out in Article 130a. The implementation of the common policies and of the internal market shall take into account the objectives set out in Article 130a and in Article 130c and shall contribute to their achievement. The Community shall support the achievement of these objectives by the action it takes through the structural Funds (European Agricultural Guidance and Guarantee Fund, Guidance Section, European Social Fund, European Regional Development Fund), the European Investment Bank and the other existing financial instruments.

Article 130c*

The European Regional Development Fund is intended to help redress the principal regional imbalances in the Community through participating in the development and structural adjustment of regions whose development is lagging behind and in the conversion of declining industrial regions.

---

* See footnote on p. 331.

Article 130d*

Once the Single European Act enters into force the Commission shall submit a comprehensive proposal to the Council, the purpose of which will be to make such amendments to the structure and operational rules of the existing structural Funds (European Agricultural Guidance and Guarantee Fund, Guidance Section, European Social Fund, European Regional Development Fund) as are necessary to clarify and rationalize their tasks in order to contribute to the achievement of the objectives set out in Article 130a and Article 130c, to increase their efficiency and to coordinate their activities between themselves and with the operations of the existing financial instruments. The Council shall act unanimously on this proposal within a period of one year, after consulting the European Parliament and the Economic and Social Committee.

Article 130e*

After adoption of the decision referred to in Article 130d, implementing decisions relating to the European Regional Development Fund shall be taken by the Council, acting by a qualified majority on a proposal from the Commission and in cooperation with the European Parliament.

With regard to the European Agricultural Guidance and Guarantee Fund, Guidance Section and the European Social Fund, Articles 43, 126 and 127 remain applicable respectively.

---

* See footnote on p. 331.

TITLE VI*

Research and technological development

---

* Title VI consisting of Articles 130f, 130g, 130h, 130i, 130k, 130l, 130m, 130n, 130o, 130p and 130q, as added to Part Three of the Treaty by Article 24 of the SEA.

Article 130f*

1. The Community's aim shall be to strengthen the scientific and technological basis of European industry and to encourage it to become more competitive at international level.

2. In order to achieve this, it shall encourage undertakings including small and medium-sized undertakings, research centres and universities in their research and technological development activities; it shall support their efforts to cooperate with one another, aiming, notably, at enabling undertakings to exploit the Community's internal market potential to the full, in particular through the opening up of national public contracts, the definition of common standards and the removal of legal and fiscal barriers to that cooperation.

3. In the achievement of these aims, special account shall be taken of the connection between the common research and technological development effort, the establishment of the internal market and the implementation of common policies, particularly as regards competition and trade.

Article 130g*

In pursuing these objectives the Community shall carry out the following activities, complementing the activities carried out in the Member States:

(a) implementation of research, technological development and demonstration programmes, by promoting cooperation with undertakings, research centres and universities;

---

* See footnote on p. 335.

(b) promotion of cooperation in the field of Community research, technological development, and demonstration with third countries and international organizations;

(c) dissemination and optimization of the results of activities in Community research, technological development, and demonstration;

(d) stimulation of the training and mobility of researchers in the Community.

Article 130h*

Member States shall, in liaison with the Commission, coordinate among themselves the policies and programmes carried out at national level. In close contact with the Member States, the Commission may take any useful initiative to promote such coordination.

Article 130i*

1. The Community shall adopt a multiannual framework programme setting out all its activities. The framework programme shall lay down the scientific and technical objectives, define their respective priorities, set out the main lines of the activities envisaged and fix the amount deemed necessary, the detailed rules for financial participation by the Community in the programme as a whole and the breakdown of this amount between the various activities envisaged.

2. The framework programme may be adapted or supplemented, as the situation changes.

---

* See footnote on p. 335.

Article 130k*

The framework programme shall be implemented through specific programmes developed within each activity. Each specific programme shall define the detailed rules for implementing it, fix its duration and provide for the means deemed necessary.

The Council shall define the detailed arrangements for the dissemination of knowledge resulting from the specific programmes.

Article 130l*

In implementing the multiannual framework programme, supplementary programmes may be decided on involving the participation of certain Member States only, which shall finance them subject to possible Community participation.

The Council shall adopt the rules applicable to supplementary programmes, particularly as regards the dissemination of knowledge and the access of other Member States.

Article 130m*

In implementing the multiannual framework programme, the Community may make provision, with the agreement of the Member States concerned, for participation in research and development programmes undertaken by several Member States, including participation in the structures created for the execution of those programmes.

---

* See footnote on p. 335.

Article 130n*

In implementing the multiannual framework programme, the Community may make provision for cooperation in Community research, technological development and demonstration with third countries or international organizations.

The detailed arrangements for such cooperation may be the subject of international agreements between the Community and the third parties concerned which shall be negotiated and concluded in accordance with Article 228.

Article 130o*

The Community may set up joint undertakings or any other structure necessary for the efficient execution of programmes of Community research, technological development and demonstration.

Article 130p*

1. The detailed arrangements for financing each programme, including any Community contribution, shall be established at the time of the adoption of the programme.

2. The amount of the Community's annual contribution shall be laid down under the budgetary procedure, without prejudice to other possible methods of Community financing. The estimated cost of the specific programmes must not in aggregate exceed the financial provision in the framework programme.

---

* See footnote on p. 335.

Article 130q*

1. The Council shall, acting unanimously on a proposal from the Commission and after consulting the European Parliament and the Economic and Social Committee, adopt the provisions referred to in Articles 130i and 130o.

2. The Council shall, acting by a qualified majority on a proposal from the Commission, after consulting the Economic and Social Committee, and in cooperation with the European Parliament, adopt the provisions referred to in Articles 130k, 130l, 130m, 130n and 130p (1). The adoption of these supplementary programmes shall also require the agreement of the Member States concerned.

---

* See footnote on p. 335.

TITLE VII*

Environment

---

* Title VII consisting of Articles 130r, 130s and 130t, as added to Part Three of the Treaty by Article 25 of the SEA.

Article 130r*

1. Action by the Community relating to the environment shall have the following objectives:

(i) to preserve, protect and improve the quality of the environment;

(ii) to contribute towards protecting human health;

(iii) to ensure a prudent and rational utilization of natural resources.

2. Action by the Community relating to the environment shall be based on the principles that preventive action should be taken, that environmental damage should as a priority be rectified at source, and that the polluter should pay. Environmental protection requirements shall be a component of the Community's other policies.

3. In preparing its action relating to the environment, the Community shall take account of:

(i) available scientific and technical data;

(ii) environmental conditions in the various regions of the Community;

(iii) the potential benefits and costs of action or of lack of action;

(iv) the economic and social development of the Community as a whole and the balanced development of its regions.

4. The Community shall take action relating to the environment to the extent to which the objectives referred to in paragraph 1 can be attained

---

* See footnote on p. 343.

better at Community level than at the level of the individual Member States. Without prejudice to certain measures of a Community nature, the Member States shall finance and implement the other measures.

5.   Within their respective spheres of competence, the Community and the Member States shall cooperate with third countries and with the relevant international organizations. The arrangements for Community cooperation may be the subject of agreements between the Community and the third parties concerned, which shall be negotiated and concluded in accordance with Article 228.

The previous paragraph shall be without prejudice to Member States' competence to negotiate in international bodies and to conclude international agreements.

Article 130s*

The Council, acting unanimously on a proposal from the Commission and after consulting the European Parliament and the Economic and Social Committee, shall decide what action is to be taken by the Community.

The Council shall, under the conditions laid down in the preceding subparagraph, define those matters on which decisions are to be taken by a qualified majority.

Article 130t*

The protective measures adopted in common pursuant to Article 130s shall not prevent any Member State from maintaining or introducing more stringent protective measures compatible with this Treaty.

---

* See footnote on p. 343.

PART FOUR

ASSOCIATION
OF THE OVERSEAS COUNTRIES
AND TERRITORIES

Article 131

The Member States agree to associate with the Community the non-European countries and territories which have special relations with Belgium, Denmark,* France, Italy, the Netherlands and the United Kingdom.** These countries and territories (hereinafter called the 'countries and territories') are listed in Annex IV to this Treaty.

The purpose of association shall be to promote the economic and social development of the countries and territories and to establish close economic relations between them and the Community as a whole.

In accordance with the principles set out in the Preamble to this Treaty, association shall serve primarily to further the interests and prosperity of the inhabitants of these countries and territories in order to lead them to the economic, social and cultural development to which they aspire.

Article 132

Association shall have the following objectives:

1. Member States shall apply to their trade with the countries and territories the same treatment as they accord each other pursuant to this Treaty.

2. Each country or territory shall apply to its trade with Member States and with the other countries and territories the same treatment as that which it applies to the European State with which it has special relations.

---

* The term 'Denmark' was added by Article 2 of the Greenland Treaty.

** First sentence, with the exception of the term 'Denmark', as amended by Article 24 (1) of the Act of Accession DK/IRL/UK in the version resulting from Article 13 of the AD AA DK/IRL/UK.

3.   The Member States shall contribute to the investments required for the progressive development of these countries and territories.

4.   For investments financed by the Community, participation in tenders and supplies shall be open on equal terms to all natural and legal persons who are nationals of a Member State or of one of the countries and territories.

5.   In relations between Member States and the countries and territories the right of establishment of nationals and companies or firms shall be regulated in accordance with the provisions and procedures laid down in the Chapter relating to the right of establishment and on a non-discriminatory basis, subject to any special provisions laid down pursuant to Article 136.

Article 133

1.   Customs duties on imports into the Member States of goods originating in the countries and territories shall be completely abolished in conformity with the progressive abolition of customs duties between Member States in accordance with the provisions of this Treaty.

2.   Customs duties on imports into each country or territory from Member States or from the other countries or territories shall be progressively abolished in accordance with the provisions of Articles 12, 13, 14, 15 and 17.

3.   The countries and territories may, however, levy customs duties which meet the needs of their development and industrialization or produce revenue for their budgets.

The duties referred to in the preceding subparagraph shall nevertheless be progressively reduced to the level of those imposed on imports of products from the Member State with which each country or territory has special relations. The percentages and the timetable of the reductions provided for under this Treaty shall apply to the difference between the duty imposed on a product coming from the Member State which has special relations with the country or territory concerned and the duty imposed on the same product coming from within the Community on entry into the importing country or territory.

4. Paragraph 2 shall not apply to countries and territories which, by reason of the particular international obligations by which they are bound, already apply a non-discriminatory customs tariff when this Treaty enters into force.

5. The introduction of or any change in customs duties imposed on goods imported into the countries and territories shall not, either in law or in fact, give rise to any direct or indirect discrimination between imports from the various Member States.

Article 134

If the level of the duties applicable to goods from a third country on entry into a country or territory is liable, when the provisions of Article 133 (1) have been applied, to cause deflections of trade to the detriment of any Member State, the latter may request the Commission to propose to the other Member States the measures needed to remedy the situation.

Article 135

Subject to the provisions relating to public health, public security or public policy, freedom of movement within Member States for workers from the countries and territories, and within the countries and territories for workers from Member States, shall be governed by agreements to be concluded subsequently with the unanimous approval of Member States.

Article 136

For an initial period of five years after the entry into force of this Treaty, the details of and procedure for the association of the countries and territories with the Community shall be determined by an Implementing Convention annexed to this Treaty.

Before the Convention referred to in the preceding paragraph expires, the Council shall, acting unanimously, lay down provisions for a further period, on the basis of the experience acquired and of the principles set out in this Treaty.

Article 136a*

The provisions of Articles 131 to 136 shall apply to Greenland, subject to the specific provisions for Greenland set out in the Protocol on special arrangements for Greenland, annexed to this Treaty.

---

* Article added by Article 3 of the Greenland Treaty.

PART FIVE

INSTITUTIONS OF THE COMMUNITY

TITLE I

Provisions governing the institutions

CHAPTER 1

THE INSTITUTIONS

Section 1

The European Parliament

Article 137

The European Parliament, which shall consist of representatives of the peoples of the States brought together in the Community, shall exercise the advisory and supervisory powers which are conferred upon it by this Treaty.

Article 138

(Paragraphs 1 and 2 lapsed on 17 July 1979 in accordance with Article 14 of the Act concerning the election of the representatives of the European Parliament)

[See Article 1 of that Act which reads as follows:

1. The representatives in the European Parliament of the peoples of the States brought together in the Community shall be elected by direct universal suffrage.]

[See Article 2 of that Act which reads as follows:

2. The number of representatives elected in each Member State is as follows:

Belgium	24
Denmark	16
Germany	81
Greece	24
Spain	60
France	81
Ireland	15
Italy	81
Luxembourg	6
Netherlands	25
Portugal	24
United Kingdom	81 .]*

3. The European Parliament shall draw up proposals for elections by direct universal suffrage in accordance with a uniform procedure in all Member States.**

The Council shall, acting unanimously, lay down the appropriate provisions, which it shall recommend to Member States for adoption in accordance with their respective constitutional requirements.

---

* Number of representatives as fixed by Article 10 of the Act of Accession ESP/PORT.

** See also Article 7 (1) and (2) of the Act concerning the election of the representatives of the European Parliament.

Article 139

The European Parliament shall hold an annual session. It shall meet, without requiring to be convened, on the second Tuesday in March.* **

The European Parliament may meet in extraordinary session at the request of a majority of its members or at the request of the Council or of the Commission.

Article 140

The European Parliament shall elect its President and its officers from among its members.

Members of the Commission may attend all meetings and shall, at their request, be heard on behalf of the Commission.

The Commission shall reply orally or in writing to questions put to it by the European Parliament or by its members.

The Council shall be heard by the European Parliament in accordance with the conditions laid down by the Council in its rules of procedure.

Article 141

Save as otherwise provided in this Treaty, the European Parliament shall act by an absolute majority of the votes cast.

The rules of procedure shall determine the quorum.

---

* First paragraph as amended by Article 27 (1) of the Merger Treaty.
** As regards the second sentence of this Article see also Article 10 (3) of the Act concerning the election of the representatives of the European Parliament.

Article 142

The European Parliament shall adopt its rules of procedure, acting by a majority of its members.

The proceedings of the European Parliament shall be published in the manner laid down in its rules of procedure.

Article 143

The European Parliament shall discuss in open session the annual general report submitted to it by the Commission.

Article 144

If a motion of censure on the activities of the Commission is tabled before it, the European Parliament shall not vote thereon until at least three days after the motion has been tabled and only by open vote.

If the motion of censure is carried by a two-third majority of the votes cast, representing a majority of the members of the European Parliament, the members of the Commission shall resign as a body. They shall continue to deal with current business until they are replaced in accordance with Article 158.

Section 2

The Council

Article 145

To ensure that the objectives set out in this Treaty are attained, the Council shall, in accordance with the provisions of this Treaty:

— ensure coordination of the general economic policies of the Member States;

— have power to take decisions.

— confer on the Commission, in the acts which the Council adopts, powers for the implementation of the rules which the Council lays down. The Council may impose certain requirements in respect of the exercise of these powers. The Council may also reserve the right, in specific cases, to exercise directly implementing powers itself. The procedures referred to above must be consonant with principles and rules to be laid down in advance by the Council, acting unanimously on a proposal from the Commission and after obtaining the Opinion of the European Parliament.*

Article 146

(Article repealed by Article 7 of the Merger Treaty)

[*See Article 2 of the Merger Treaty, which reads as follows:*

The Council shall consist of representatives of the Member States. Each Government shall delegate to it one of its members.

The office of President shall be held for a term of six months by each member of the Council in turn, in the following order of Member States:

— for a first cycle of six years: Belgium, Denmark, Germany, Greece, Spain, France, Ireland, Italy, Luxembourg, Netherlands, Portugal, United Kingdom,

---

* Third indent added by Article 10 of the SEA.

— for the following cycle of six years: Denmark, Belgium, Greece, Germany, France, Spain, Italy, Ireland, Netherlands, Luxembourg, United Kingdom, Portugal.]*

Article 147

(Article repealed by Article 7 of the Merger Treaty)

[*See Article 3 of the Merger Treaty, which reads as follows:*

The Council shall meet when convened by its President on his own initiative or at the request of one of its members or of the Commission.]

Article 148

1. Save as otherwise provided in this Treaty, the Council shall act by a majority of its members.

2. Where the Council is required to act by a qualified majority, the votes of its members shall be weighted as follows:

Belgium	5
Denmark	3
Germany	10
Greece	5
Spain	8
France	10
Ireland	3
Italy	10
Luxembourg	2
Netherlands	5
Portugal	5
United Kingdom	10

---

* Second paragraph as amended by Article 11 of the Act of Accession ESP/PORT.

For their adoption, acts of the Council shall require at least:

— fifty-four votes in favour where this Treaty requires them to be adopted on a proposal from the Commission,

— fifty-four votes in favour, cast by at least eight members, in other cases.*

3. Abstentions by members present in person or represented shall not prevent the adoption by the Council of acts which require unanimity.

*Article 149***

1. Where, in pursuance of this Treaty, the Council acts on a proposal from the Commission, unanimity shall be required for an act constituting an amendment to that proposal.

2. Where, in pursuance of this Treaty, the Council acts in cooperation with the European Parliament, the following procedure shall apply:

(a) The Council, acting by a qualified majority under the conditions of paragraph 1, on a proposal from the Commission and after obtaining the Opinion of the European Parliament, shall adopt a common position.

(b) The Council's common position shall be communicated to the European Parliament. The Council and the Commission shall inform the European Parliament fully of the reasons which led the Council to adopt its common position and also of the Commission's position.

If, within three months of such communication, the European Parliament approves this common position or has not taken a decision

---

 * Paragraph 2 as amended by Article 14 of the Act of Accession ESP./PORT.
** Article as replaced by Article 7 of the SEA.

within that period, the Council shall definitively adopt the act in question in accordance with the common position.

(c) The European Parliament may within the period of three months referred to in point *(b)*, by an absolute majority of its component members, propose amendments to the Council's common position. The European Parliament may also, by the same majority, reject the Council's common position. The result of the proceedings shall be transmitted to the Council and the Commission.

If the European Parliament has rejected the Council's common position, unanimity shall be required for the Council to act on a second reading.

(d) The Commission shall, within a period of one month, re-examine the proposal on the basis of which the Council adopted its common position, by taking into account the amendments proposed by the European Parliament.

The Commission shall forward to the Council, at the same time as its re-examined proposal, the amendments of the European Parliament which it has not accepted, and shall express its opinion on them. The Council may adopt these amendments unanimously.

(e) The Council, acting by a qualified majority, shall adopt the proposal as re-examined by the Commission.

Unanimity shall be required for the Council to amend the proposal as re-examined by the Commission.

(f) In the cases referred to in points *(c)*, *(d)* and *(e)*, the Council shall be required to act within a period of three months. If no decision is taken within this period, the Commission proposal shall be deemed not to have been adopted.

(g) The periods referred to in points *(b)* and *(f)* may be extended by a maximum of one month by common accord between the Council and the European Parliament.

3. As long as the Council has not acted, the Commission may alter its proposal at any time during the procedures mentioned in paragraphs 1 and 2.

Article 150

Where a vote is taken, any member of the Council may also act on behalf of not more than one other member.

Article 151

(Article repealed by Article 7 of the Merger Treaty)

[*See Articles 5 and 4 of the Merger Treaty, which read as follows:*

Article 5:

The Council shall adopt its rules of procedure.

Article 4:

A committee consisting of the Permanent Representatives of the Member States shall be responsible for preparing the work of the Council and for carrying out the tasks assigned to it by the Council.]

Article 152

The Council may request the Commission to undertake any studies the Council considers desirable for the attainment of the common objectives, and to submit to it any appropriate proposals.

Article 153

The Council shall, after receiving an opinion from the Commission, determine the rules governing the committees provided for in this Treaty.

Article 154

(Article repealed by Article 7 of the Merger Treaty)

[*See Article 6 of the Merger Treaty, which reads as follows:*

The Council shall, acting by a qualified majority, determine the salaries, allowances and pensions of the President and members of the Commission, and of the President, Judges, Advocates-General and Registrar of the Court of Justice. It shall also, again by a qualified majority, determine any payment to be made instead of remuneration.]

Section 3

The Commission

Article 155

In order to ensure the proper functioning and development of the common market, the Commission shall:

— ensure that the provisions of this Treaty and the measures taken by the institutions pursuant thereto are applied;

— formulate recommendations or deliver opinions on matters dealt with in this Treaty, if it expressly so provides or if the Commission considers it necessary;

— have its own power of decision and participate in the shaping of measures taken by the Council and by the European Parliament in the manner provided for in this Treaty;

— exercise the powers conferred on it by the Council for the implementation of the rules laid down by the latter.

Article 156

(Article repealed by Article 19 of the Merger Treaty)

[*See Article 18 of the Merger Treaty, which reads as follows:*

The Commission shall publish annually, not later than one month before the opening of the session of the European Parliament, a general report on the activities of the Communities.]

Article 157

(Article repealed by Article 19 of the Merger Treaty)

[*See Article 10 of the Merger Treaty, which reads as follows:*

1. The Commission shall consist of seventeen members, who shall be chosen on the grounds of their general competence and whose independence is beyond doubt.*

The number of members of the Commission may be altered by the Council, acting unanimously.

Only nationals of Member States may be members of the Commission.

The Commission must include at least one national of each of the Member States, but may not include more than two members having the nationality of the same State.

2. The members of the Commission shall, in the general interest of the Communities, be completely independent in the performance of their duties.

In the performance of these duties, they shall neither seek nor take instructions from any Government or from any other body.

They shall refrain from any action incompatible with their duties.

---

* First subparagraph of paragraph 1 as amended by Article 15 of the Act of Accession ESP/PORT.

Each Member State undertakes to respect this principle and not to seek to influence the members of the Commission in the performance of their tasks.

The members of the Commission may not, during their term of office, engage in any other occupation, whether gainful or not. When entering upon their duties they shall give a solemn undertaking that, both during and after their term of office, they will respect the obligations arising therefrom and in particular their duty to behave with integrity and discretion as regards the acceptance, after they have ceased to hold office, of certain appointments or benefits. In the event of any breach of these obligations, the Court of Justice may, on application by the Council or the Commission, rule that the member concerned be, according to the circumstances, either compulsorily retired in accordance with the provisions of Article 13* or deprived of his right to a pension or other benefits in its stead.]

Article 158

(Article repealed by Article 19 of the Merger Treaty)

[*See Article 11 of the Merger Treaty, which reads as follows:*

The members of the Commission shall be appointed by common accord of the Governments of the Member States.

Their term of office shall be four years. It shall be renewable.]

Article 159

(Article repealed by Article 19 of the Merger Treaty)

[*See Article 12 of the Merger Treaty, which reads as follows:*

Apart from normal replacement, or death, the duties of a member of the Commission shall end when he resigns or is compulsorily retired.

The vacancy thus caused shall be filled for the remainder of the member's term of office. The Council may, acting unanimously, decide that such a vacancy need not be filled.

---

* Article 13 of the Merger Treaty. See Article 160 below.

Save in the case of compulsory retirement under the provisions of Article 13,* members of the Commission shall remain in office until they have been replaced.]

Article 160

(Article repealed by Article 19 of the Merger Treaty)

[*See Article 13 of the Merger Treaty, which reads as follows:*

If any member of the Commission no longer fulfils the conditions required for the performance of his duties or if he has been guilty of serious misconduct, the Court of Justice may, on application by the Council or the Commission, compulsorily retire him.]

Article 161

(Article repealed by Article 19 of the Merger Treaty)

[*See Article 14 of the Merger Treaty, which reads as follows:*

The President and the six Vice-Presidents of the Commission shall be appointed from among its members for a term of two years in accordance with the same procedure as that laid down for the appointment of members of the Commission. Their appointments may be renewed.**

The Council, acting unanimously, may amend the provisions concerning Vice-Presidents.***

Save where the entire Commission is replaced, such appointments shall be made after the Commission has been consulted.

In the event of retirement or death, the President and the Vice-Presidents shall be replaced for the remainder of their term of office in accordance with the preceding provisions.]

---

* Article 13 of the Merger Treaty. See Article 160 below.

** First paragraph as amended by Article 16 of the Act of Accession ESP/PORT.

*** Second paragraph added by Article 16 of that Act.

Article 162

(Article repealed by Article 19 of the Merger Treaty)

[*See Articles 15 and 16 of the Merger Treaty, which read as follows:*

Article 15:

The Council and the Commission shall consult each other and shall settle by common accord their methods of cooperation.

Article 16:

The Commission shall adopt its rules of procedure so as to ensure that both it and its departments operate in accordance with the provisions of the Treaties establishing the European Coal and Steel Community, the European Economic Community and the European Atomic Energy Community, and of this Treaty. It shall ensure that these rules are published.]

Article 163

(Article repealed by Article 19 of the Merger Treaty)

[*See Article 17 of the Merger Treaty, which reads as follows:*

The Commission shall act by a majority of the number of members provided for in Article 10.*

A meeting of the Commission shall be valid only if the number of members laid down in its rules of procedure is present.]

---

* Article 10 of the Merger Treaty. See Article 157 above.

Section 4

The Court of Justice

Article 164

The Court of Justice shall ensure that in the interpretation and application of this Treaty the law is observed.

Article 165

The Court of Justice shall consist of thirteen Judges.*

The Court of Justice shall sit in plenary session. It may, however, form Chambers, each consisting of three or five Judges, either to undertake certain preparatory inquiries or to adjudicate on particular categories of cases in accordance with rules laid down for these purposes.

Whenever the Court of Justice hears cases brought before it by a Member State or by one of the institutions of the Community or, to the extent that the Chambers of the Court do not have the requisite jurisdiction under the Rules of Procedure, has to give preliminary rulings on questions submitted to it pursuant to Article 177, it shall sit in plenary session.**

Should the Court of Justice so request, the Council may, acting unanimously, increase the number of Judges and make the necessary adjustments to the second and third paragraphs of this Article and to the second paragraph of Article 167.

---

* First paragraph as amended by Article 17 of the Act of Accession ESP/PORT.

** Third paragraph as amended by Article 1 of the Council Decision of 26 November 1974 (*Official Journal of the European Communities*, No L 318, 28 November 1974).

Article 166

The Court of Justice shall be assisted by six Advocates-General.*

It shall be the duty of the Advocate-General, acting with complete impartiality and independence, to make, in open court, reasoned submissions on cases brought before the Court of Justice, in order to assist the Court in the performance of the task assigned to it in Article 164.

Should the Court of Justice so request, the Council may, acting unanimously, increase the number of Advocates-General and make the necessary adjustments to the third paragraph of Article 167.

Article 167

The Judges and Advocates-General shall be chosen from persons whose independence is beyond doubt and who possess the qualifications required for appointment to the highest judicial offices in their respective countries or who are jurisconsults of recognized competence; they shall be appointed by common accord of the Governments of the Member States for a term of six years.

Every three years there shall be a partial replacement of the Judges. Seven and six Judges shall be replaced alternately.**

Every three years there shall be a partial replacement of the Advocates-General. Three Advocates-General shall be replaced on each occasion.**

---

* First paragraph as amended by Article 18 of the Act of Accession ESP/PORT.
** Second and third paragraphs as amended by Article 19 of the Act of Accession ESP/PORT.

Retiring Judges and Advocates-General shall be eligible for reappointment.

The Judges shall elect the President of the Court of Justice from among their number for a term of three years. He may be re-elected.

Article 168

The Court of Justice shall appoint its Registrar and lay down the rules governing his service.

Article 168a*

1. At the request of the Court of Justice and after consulting the Commission and the European Parliament, the Council may, acting unanimously, attach to the Court of Justice a court with jurisdiction to hear and determine at first instance, subject to a right of appeal to the Court of Justice on points of law only and in accordance with the conditions laid down by the Statute, certain classes of action or proceeding brought by natural or legal persons. That court shall not be competent to hear and determine actions brought by Member States or by Community institutions or questions referred for a preliminary ruling under Article 177.

2. The Council, following the procedure laid down in paragraph 1, shall determine the composition of that court and adopt the necessary adjustments and additional provisions to the Statute of the Court of Justice. Unless the Council decides otherwise, the provisions of this Treaty relating to the Court of Justice, in particular the provisions of the Protocol on the Statute of the Court of Justice, shall apply to that court.

---

* Article added by Article 11 of the SEA.

3. The members of that court shall be chosen from persons whose independence is beyond doubt and who possess the ability required for appointment to judicial office; they shall be appointed by common accord of the Governments of the Member States for a term of six years. The membership shall be partially renewed every three years. Retiring members shall be eligible for reappointment.

4. That court shall establish its rules of procedure in agreement with the Court of Justice. Those rules shall require the unanimous approval of the Council.

Article 169

If the Commission considers that a Member State has failed to fulfil an obligation under this Treaty, it shall deliver a reasoned opinion on the matter after giving the State concerned the opportunity to submit its observations.

If the State concerned does not comply with the opinion within the period laid down by the Commission, the latter may bring the matter before the Court of Justice.

Article 170

A Member State which considers that another Member State has failed to fulfil an obligation under this Treaty may bring the matter before the Court of Justice.

Before a Member State brings an action against another Member State for an alleged infringement of an obligation under this Treaty, it shall bring the matter before the Commission.

The Commission shall deliver a reasoned opinion after each of the States concerned has been given the opportunity to submit its own case and its observations on the other party's case both orally and in writing.

If the Commission has not delivered an opinion within three months of the date on which the matter was brought before it, the absence of such opinion shall not prevent the matter from being brought before the Court of Justice.

Article 171

If the Court of Justice finds that a Member State has failed to fulfil an obligation under this Treaty, the State shall be required to take the necessary measures to comply with the judgment of the Court of Justice.

Article 172

Regulations made by the Council pursuant to the provisions of this Treaty may give the Court of Justice unlimited jurisdiction in regard to the penalties provided for in such regulations.

Article 173

The Court of Justice shall review the legality of acts of the Council and the Commission other than recommendations or opinions. It shall for this purpose have jurisdiction in actions brought by a Member State, the Council or the Commission on grounds of lack of competence, infringement of an essential procedural requirement, infringement of this Treaty or of any rule of law relating to its application, or misuse of powers.

Any natural or legal person may, under the same conditions, institute proceedings against a decision addressed to that person or against a decision which, although in the form of a regulation or a decision addressed to another person, is of direct and individual concern to the former.

The proceedings provided for in this Article shall be instituted within two months of the publication of the measure, or of its notification to the plaintiff, or, in the absence thereof, of the day on which it came to the knowledge of the latter, as the case may be.

Article 174

If the action is well founded, the Court of Justice shall declare the act concerned to be void.

In the case of a regulation, however, the Court of Justice shall, if it considers this necessary, state which of the effects of the regulation which it has declared void shall be considered as definitive.

Article 175

Should the Council or the Commission, in infringement of this Treaty, fail to act, the Member States and the other institutions of the Community may bring an action before the Court of Justice to have the infringement established.

The action shall be admissible only if the institution concerned has first been called upon to act. If, within two months of being so called upon, the institution concerned has not defined its position, the action may be brought within a further period of two months.

Any natural or legal person may, under the conditions laid down in the preceding paragraphs, complain to the Court of Justice that an institution of the Community has failed to address to that person any act other than a recommendation or an opinion.

Article 176

The institution whose act has been declared void or whose failure to act has been declared contrary to this Treaty shall be required to take the necessary measures to comply with the judgment of the Court of Justice.

This obligation shall not affect any obligation which may result from the application of the second paragraph of Article 215.

Article 177

The Court of Justice shall have jurisdiction to give preliminary rulings concerning:

(a) the interpretation of this Treaty;

(b) the validity and interpretation of acts of the institutions of the Community;

(c) the interpretation of the statutes of bodies established by an act of the Council, where those statutes so provide.

Where such a question is raised before any court or tribunal of a Member State, that court or tribunal may, if it considers that a decision on the question is necessary to enable it to give judgment, request the Court of Justice to give a ruling thereon.

Where any such question is raised in a case pending before a court or tribunal of a Member State, against whose decisions there is no judicial remedy under national law, that court or tribunal shall bring the matter before the Court of Justice.

Article 178

The Court of Justice shall have jurisdiction in disputes relating to compensation for damage provided for in the second paragraph of Article 215.

Article 179

The Court of Justice shall have jurisdiction in any dispute between the Community and its servants within the limits and under the conditions laid down in the Staff Regulations or the Conditions of Employment.

Article 180

The Court of Justice shall, within the limits hereinafter laid down, have jurisdiction in disputes concerning:

(a) the fulfilment by Member States of obligations under the Statute of the European Investment Bank. In this connection, the Board of Directors of the Bank shall enjoy the powers conferred upon the Commission by Article 169;

(b) measures adopted by the Board of Governors of the Bank. In this connection, any Member State, the Commission or the Board of Directors of the Bank may institute proceedings under the conditions laid down in Article 173;

(c) measures adopted by the Board of Directors of the Bank. Proceedings against such measures may be instituted only by Member States or by the Commission, under the conditions laid down in Article 173, and solely on the grounds of non-compliance with the procedure provided for in Article 21 (2), (5), (6) and (7) of the Statute of the Bank.

Article 181

The Court of Justice shall have jurisdiction to give judgment pursuant to any arbitration clause contained in a contract concluded by or on behalf of the Community, whether that contract be governed by public or private law.

Article 182

The Court of Justice shall have jurisdiction in any dispute between Member States which relates to the subject matter of this Treaty if the dispute is submitted to it under a special agreement between the parties.

Article 183

Save where jurisdiction is conferred on the Court of Justice by this Treaty, disputes to which the Community is a party shall not on that ground be excluded from the jurisdiction of the courts or tribunals of the Member States.

Article 184

Notwithstanding the expiry of the period laid down in the third paragraph of Article 173, any party may, in proceedings in which a regulation of the Council or of the Commission is in issue, plead the grounds specified in the first paragraph of Article 173, in order to invoke before the Court of Justice the inapplicability of that regulation.

Article 185

Actions brought before the Court of Justice shall not have suspensory effect. The Court of Justice may, however, if it considers that circumstances so require, order that application of the contested act be suspended.

Article 186

The Court of Justice may in any cases before it prescribe any necessary interim measures.

Article 187

The judgments of the Court of Justice shall be enforceable under the conditions laid down in Article 192.

Article 188

The Statute of the Court of Justice is laid down in a separate Protocol.

The Council may, acting unanimously at the request of the Court of Justice and after consulting the Commission and the European Parliament, amend the provisions of Title III of the Statute.*

The Court of Justice shall adopt its rules of procedure. These shall require the unanimous approval of the Council.

CHAPTER 2

PROVISIONS COMMON
TO SEVERAL INSTITUTIONS

Article 189

In order to carry out their task the Council and the Commission shall, in accordance with the provisions of this Treaty, make regulations, issue directives, take decisions, make recommendations or deliver opinions.

A regulation shall have general application. It shall be binding in its entirety and directly applicable in all Member States.

A directive shall be binding, as to the result to be achieved, upon each Member State to which it is addressed, but shall leave to the national authorities the choice of form and methods.

---

* Second paragraph as inserted by Article 12 of the SEA.

A decision shall be binding in its entirety upon those to whom it is addressed.

Recommendations and opinions shall have no binding force.

Article 190

Regulations, directives and decisions of the Council and of the Commission shall state the reasons on which they are based and shall refer to any proposals or opinions which were required to be obtained pursuant to this Treaty.

Article 191

Regulations shall be published in the Official Journal of the Community. They shall enter into force on the date specified in them or, in the absence thereof, on the twentieth day following their publication.

Directives and decisions shall be notified to those to whom they are addressed and shall take effect upon such notification.

Article 192

Decisions of the Council or of the Commission which impose a pecuniary obligation on persons other than States, shall be enforceable.

Enforcement shall be governed by the rules of civil procedure in force in the State in the territory of which it is carried out. The order for its enforcement shall be appended to the decision, without other formality than verification of the authenticity of the decision, by the national authority which the Government of each Member State shall designate for this purpose and shall make known to the Commission and to the Court of Justice.

When these formalities have been completed on application by the party concerned, the latter may proceed to enforcement in accordance with the national law, by bringing the matter directly before the competent authority.

Enforcement may be suspended only by a decision of the Court of Justice. However, the courts of the country concerned shall have jurisdiction over complaints that enforcement is being carried out in an irregular manner.

CHAPTER 3

THE ECONOMIC AND SOCIAL COMMITTEE

Article 193

An Economic and Social Committee is hereby established. It shall have advisory status.

The Committee shall consist of representatives of the various categories of economic and social activity, in particular, representatives of producers, farmers, carriers, workers, dealers, craftsmen, professional occupations and representatives of the general public.

Article 194

The number of members of the Committee shall be as follows:

Belgium	12
Denmark	9
Germany	24
Greece	12
Spain	21
France	24
Ireland	9
Italy	24

Luxembourg	6
Netherlands	12
Portugal	12
United Kingdom	24*

The members of the Committee shall be appointed by the Council, acting unanimously, for four years. Their appointments shall be renewable.

The members of the Committee shall be appointed in their personal capacity and may not be bound by any mandatory instructions.

Article 195

1. For the appointment of the members of the Committee, each Member State shall provide the Council with a list containing twice as many candidates as there are seats allotted to its nationals.

The composition of the Committee shall take account of the need to ensure adequate representation of the various categories of economic and social activity.

2. The Council shall consult the Commission. It may obtain the opinion of European bodies which are representative of the various economic and social sectors to which the activities of the Community are of concern.

Article 196

The Committee shall elect its chairman and officers from among its members for a term of two years.

It shall adopt its rules of procedure and shall submit them to the Council for its approval, which must be unanimous.

The Committee shall be convened by its chairman at the request of the Council or of the Commission.

---

* First paragraph as amended by Article 21 of the Act of Accession ESP/PORT.

Article 197

The Committee shall include specialized sections for the principal fields covered by this Treaty.

In particular, it shall contain an agricultural section and a transport section, which are the subject of special provisions in the Titles relating to agriculture and transport.

These specialized sections shall operate within the general terms of reference of the Committee. They may not be consulted independently of the Committee.

Sub-committees may also be established within the Committee to prepare on specific questions or in specific fields, draft opinions to be submitted to the Committee for its consideration.

The rules of procedure shall lay down the methods of composition and the terms of reference of the specialized sections and of the sub-committees.

Article 198

The Committee must be consulted by the Council or by the Commission where this Treaty so provides. The Committee may be consulted by these institutions in all cases in which they consider it appropriate.

The Council or the Commission shall, if it considers it necessary, set the Committee, for the submission of its opinion, a time limit which may not be less than ten days from the date which the chairman receives notification to this effect. Upon expiry of the time limit, the absence of an opinion shall not prevent further action.

The opinion of the Committee and that of the specialized section, together with a record of the proceedings, shall be forwarded to the Council and to the Commission.

TITLE II

Financial provisions

Article 199

All items of revenue and expenditure of the Community, including those relating to the European Social Fund, shall be included in estimates to be drawn up for each financial year and shall be shown in the budget.

The revenue and expenditure shown in the budget shall be in balance.

Article 200

1. The budget revenue shall include, irrespective of any other revenue, financial contributions of Member States on the following scale:

Netherlands	7.9
Germany	28
France	28
Italy	28
Luxembourg	0.2
Netherlands	7.9

2. The financial contributions of Member States to cover the expenditure of the European Social Fund, however, shall be determined on the following scale:

Belgium	8.8
Germany	32
France	32
Italy	20
Luxembourg	0.2
Netherlands	7

3. The scales may be modified by the Council, acting unanimously.

Article 201*

The Commission shall examine the conditions under which the financial contributions of Member States provided for in Article 200 could be replaced by the Community's own resources, in particular by revenue accruing from the common customs tariff when it has been finally introduced.

To this end, the Commission shall submit proposals to the Council.

After consulting the European Parliament on these proposals the Council may, acting unanimously, lay down the appropriate provisions, which it shall recommend to the Member States for adoption in accordance with their respective constitutional requirements.

Article 202

The expenditure shown in the budget shall be authorized for one financial year, unless the regulations made pursuant to Article 209 provide otherwise.

In accordance with conditions to be laid down pursuant to Article 209, any appropriations, other than those relating to staff expenditure, that are unexpended at the end of the financial year may be carried forward to the next financial year only.

Appropriations shall be classified under different chapters grouping items of expenditure according to their nature or purpose and subdivided, as far as may be necessary, in accordance with the regulations made pursuant to Article 209.

---

* EDITORIAL NOTE:
  The Council Decision on the Communities' system of own resources is reproduced on page 995 of this volume.

The expenditure of the European Parliament, the Council, the Commission and the Court of Justice shall be set out in separate parts of the budget, without prejudice to special arrangements for certain common items of expenditure.

Article 203* **

1. The financial year shall run from 1 January to 31 December.

2. Each institution of the Community shall, before 1 July, draw up estimates of its expenditure. The Commission shall consolidate these estimates in a preliminary draft budget. It shall attach thereto an opinion which may contain different estimates.

The preliminary draft budget shall contain an estimate of revenue and an estimate of expenditure.

3. The Commission shall place the preliminary draft budget before the Council not later than 1 September of the year preceding that in which the budget is to be implemented.

The Council shall consult the Commission and, where appropriate, the other institutions concerned whenever it intends to depart from the preliminary draft budget.

The Council, acting by a qualified majority, shall establish the draft budget and forward it to the European Parliament.

4. The draft budget shall be placed before the European Parliament not later than 5 October of the year preceding that in which the budget is to be implemented.

---

* Text as amended by Article 12 of the Treaty amending Certain Financial Provisions.

** EDITORIAL NOTE:
  The Joint Declaration by the European Parliament, the Council and the Commission, adopted on 30 June 1982, on various measures to improve the budgetary procedure, is reproduced on page 1103 of this volume.

The European Parliament shall have the right to amend the draft budget, acting by a majority of its members, and to propose to the Council, acting by an absolute majority of the votes cast, modifications to the draft budget relating to expenditure necessarily resulting from this Treaty or from acts adopted in accordance therewith.

If, within 45 days of the draft budget being placed before it, the European Parliament has given its approval, the budget shall stand as finally adopted. If within this period the European Parliament has not amended the draft budget nor proposed any modifications thereto, the budget shall be deemed to be finally adopted.

If within this period the European Parliament has adopted amendments or proposed modifications, the draft budget together with the amendments or proposed modifications shall be forwarded to the Council.

5. After discussing the draft budget with the Commission and, where appropriate, with the other institutions concerned, the Council shall act under the following conditions:

(a) The Council may, acting by a qualifed majority, modify any of the amendments adopted by the European Parliament;

(b) With regard to the proposed modifications:

— where a modification proposed by the European Parliament does not have the effect of increasing the total amount of the expenditure of an institution, owing in particular to the fact that the increase in expenditure which it would involve would be expressly compensated by one or more proposed modifications correspondingly reducing expenditure, the Council may, acting by a qualified majority, reject the proposed modification. In the absence of a decision to reject it, the proposed modification shall stand as accepted;

— where a modification proposed by the European Parliament has the effect of increasing the total amount of the expenditure of an institution, the Council may, acting by a qualified majority, accept this proposed modification. In the absence of a decision to accept it, the proposed modification shall stand as rejected;

— where, in pursuance of one of the two preceding subparagraphs, the Council has rejected a proposed modification, it may, acting by a qualified majority, either retain the amount shown in the draft budget or fix another amount.

The draft budget shall be modified on the basis of the proposed modifications accepted by the Council.

If, within 15 days of the draft being placed before it, the Council has not modified any of the amendments adopted by the European Parliament and if the modifications proposed by the latter have been accepted, the budget shall be deemed to be finally adopted. The Council shall inform the European Parliament that it has not modified any of the amendments and that the proposed modifications have been accepted.

If within this period the Council has modified one or more of the amendments adopted by the European Parliament or if the modifications proposed by the latter have been rejected or modified, the modified draft budget shall again be forwarded to the European Parliament. The Council shall inform the European Parliament of the results of its deliberations.

6. Within 15 days of the draft budget being placed before it, the European Parliament, which shall have been notified of the action taken on its proposed modifications, may, acting by a majority of its members and three-fifths of the votes cast, amend or reject the modifications to its amendments made by the Council and shall adopt the budget accordingly. If within this period the European Parliament has not acted, the budget shall be deemed to be finally adopted.

7. When the procedure provided for in this Article has been completed, the President of the European Parliament shall declare that the budget has been finally adopted.

8. However, the European Parliament, acting by a majority of its members and two-thirds of the votes cast, may, if there are important reasons, reject the draft budget and ask for a new draft to be submitted to it.

9. A maximum rate of increase in relation to the expenditure of the same type to be incurred during the current year shall be fixed annually for the total expenditure other than that necessarily resulting from this Treaty or from acts adopted in accordance therewith.

The Commission shall, after consulting the Economic Policy Committee, declare what this maximum rate is as it results from:

— the trend, in terms of volume, of the gross national product within the Community;

— the average variation in the budgets of the Member States;

and

— the trend of the cost of living during the preceding financial year.

The maximum rate shall be communicated, before 1 May, to all the institutions of the Community. The latter shall be required to conform to this during the budgetary procedure, subject to the provisions of the fourth and fifth subparagraphs of this paragraph.

If, in respect of expenditure other than that necessarily resulting from this Treaty or from acts adopted in accordance therewith, the actual rate of increase in the draft budget, established by the Council is over half the maximum rate, the European Parliament may, exercising its right of amendment, further increase the total amount of that expenditure to a limit not exceeding half the maximum rate.

Where the European Parliament, the Council or the Commission consider that the activities of the Communities require that the rate determined according to the procedure laid down in this paragraph should be exceeded, another rate may be fixed by agreement between the Council, acting by a qualified majority, and the European Parliament, acting by a majority of its members and three-fifths of the votes cast.

10. Each institution shall exercise the powers conferred upon it by this Article, with due regard for the provisions of the Treaty and for acts adopted in accordance therewith, in particular those relating to the Communities' own resources and to the balance between revenue and expenditure.

Article 204*

If at the beginning of a financial year, the budget has not yet been voted, a sum equivalent to not more than one-twelfth of the budget appropriations for the preceding financial year may be spent each month in respect of any chapter or other subdivision of the budget in accordance with the provisions of the Regulations made pursuant to Article 209; this arrangement shall not, however, have the effect of placing at the disposal of the Commission appropriations in excess of one-twelfth of those provided for in the draft budget in course of preparation.

The Council may, acting by a qualified majority, provided that the other conditions laid down in the first subparagraph are observed, authorize expenditure in excess of one-twelfth.

If the decision relates to expenditure which does not necessarily result from this Treaty or from acts adopted in accordance therewith, the Council shall forward it immediately to the European Parliament; within 30 days

---

* Text as amended by Article 13 of the Treaty amending Certain Financial Provisions.

the European Parliament, acting by a majority of its members and three-fifths of the votes cast, may adopt a different decision on the expenditure in excess of the one-twelfth referred to in the first subparagraph. This part of the decision of the Council shall be suspended until the European Parliament has taken its decision. If within the said period the European Parliament has not taken a decision which differs from the decision of the Council, the latter shall be deemed to be finally adopted.

The decisions referred to in the second and third subparagraphs shall lay down the necessary measures relating to resources to ensure application of this Article.

Article 205

The Commission shall implement the budget, in accordance with provisions of the regulations made pursuant to Article 209, on its own responsibility and within the limits of the appropriations.

The regulations shall lay down detailed rules for each institution concerning its part in effecting its own expenditure.

Within the budget, the Commission may, subject to the limits and conditions laid down in the regulations made pursuant to Article 209, transfer appropriations from one chapter to another or from one sub-division to another.

Article 205a*

The Commission shall submit annually to the Council and to the European Parliament the accounts of the preceding financial year relating to the implementation of the budget. The Commission shall also forward to them a financial statement of the assets and liabilities of the Community.

---

* Article added by Article 14 of the Treaty amending Certain Financial Provisions.

Article 206*

1. A Court of Auditors is hereby established.

2. The Court of Auditors shall consist of twelve members.**

3. The members of the Court of Auditors shall be chosen from among persons who belong or have belonged in their respective countries to external audit bodies or who are especially qualified for this office. Their independence must be beyond doubt.

4. The members of the Court of Auditors shall be appointed for a term of six years by the Council, acting unanimously after consulting the European Parliament.

However, when the first appointments are made, four members of the Court of Auditors, chosen by lot, shall be appointed for a term of office of four years only.

The members of the Court of Auditors shall be eligible for reappointment.

They shall elect the President of the Court of Auditors from among their number for a term of three years. The President may be re-elected.

5. The members of the Court of Auditors shall, in the general interest of the Community, be completely independent in the performance of their duties.

In the performance of these duties, they shall neither seek nor take instructions from any government or from any other body. They shall refrain from any action incompatible with their duties.

---

* Text, excepting paragraph 2, as amended by Article 15 of the Treaty amending Certain Financial Provisions.

** Paragraph 2 as amended by Article 20 of the Act of Accession ESP/PORT.

6. The members of the Court of Auditors may not, during their term of office, engage in any other occupation, whether gainful or not. When entering upon their duties they shall give a solemn undertaking that, both during and after their term of office, they will respect the obligations arising therefrom and in particular their duty to behave with integrity and discretion as regards the acceptance, after they have ceased to hold office, of certain appointments or benefits.

7. Apart from normal replacement, or death, the duties of a member of the Court of Auditors shall end when he resigns, or is compulsorily retired by a ruling of the Court of Justice pursuant to paragraph 8.

The vacancy thus caused shall be filled for the remainder of the member's term of office.

Save in the case of compulsory retirement, members of the Court of Auditors shall remain in office until they have been replaced.

8. A member of the Court of Auditors may be deprived of his office or of his right to a pension or other benefits in its stead only if the Court of Justice, at the request of the Court of Auditors, finds that he no longer fulfils the requisite conditions or meets the obligations arising from his office.

9. The Council, acting by a qualified majority, shall determine the conditions of employment of the President and the members of the Court of Auditors and in particular their salaries, allowances and pensions. It shall also, by the same majority, determine any payment to be made instead of remuneration.

10. The provisions of the Protocol on the Privileges and Immunities of the European Communities applicable to the Judges of the Court of Justice shall also apply to the members of the Court of Auditors.

Article 206a*

1. The Court of Auditors shall examine the accounts of all revenue and expenditure of the Community. It shall also examine the accounts of all revenue and expenditure of all bodies set up by the Community in so far as the relevant constituent instrument does not preclude such examination.

2. The Court of Auditors shall examine whether all revenue has been received and all expenditure incurred in a lawful and regular manner and whether the financial management has been sound.

The audit of revenue shall be carried out on the basis both of the amounts established as due and the amounts actually paid to the Community.

The audit of expenditure shall be carried out on the basis both of commitments undertaken and payments made.

These audits may be carried out before the closure of accounts for the financial year in question.

3. The audit shall be based on records and, if necessary, performed on the spot in the institutions of the Community and in the Member States. In the Member States the audit shall be carried out in liaison with the national audit bodies or, if these do not have the necessary powers, with the competent national departments. These bodies or departments shall inform the Court of Auditors whether they intend to take part in the audit.

The institutions of the Community and the national audit bodies or, if these do not have the necessary powers, the competent national departments, shall forward to the Court of Auditors, at its request, any document or information necessary to carry out its task.

---

* Article added by Article 16 of the Treaty amending Certain Financial Provisions.

4.   The Court of Auditors shall draw up an annual report after the close of each financial year. It shall be forwarded to the institutions of the Community and shall be published, together with the replies of these institutions to the observations of the Court of Auditors, in the *Official Journal of the European Communities*.

The Court of Auditors may also, at any time, submit observations on specific questions and deliver opinions at the request of one of the institutions of the Community.

It shall adopt its annual reports or opinions by a majority of its members.

It shall assist the European Parliament and the Council in exercising their powers of control over the implementation of the budget.

Article 206b*

The European Parliament, acting on a recommendation from the Council which shall act by a qualified majority, shall give a discharge to the Commission in respect of the implementation of the budget. To this end, the Council and the European Parliament in turn shall examine the accounts and the financial statement referred to in Article 205a and the annual report by the Court of Auditors together with the replies of the institutions under audit to the observations of the Court of Auditors.

Article 207

The budget shall be drawn up in the unit of account determined in accordance with the provisions of the regulations made pursuant to Article 209.

The financial contributions provided for in Article 200 (1) shall be placed at the disposal of the Community by the Member States in their national currencies.

---

* Article added by Article 17 of the Treaty amending Certain Financial Provisions.

The available balances of these contributions shall be deposited with the Treasuries of Member States or with bodies designated by them. While on deposit, such funds shall retain the value corresponding to the parity, at the date of deposit, in relation to the unit of account referred to in the first paragraph.

The balances may be invested on terms to be agreed between the Commission and the Member State concerned.

The regulations made pursuant to Article 209 shall lay down the technical conditions under which financial operations relating to the European Social Fund shall be carried out.

Article 208

The Commission may, provided it notifies the competent authorities of the Member States concerned, transfer into the currency of one of the Member States its holdings in the currency of another Member State, to the extent necessary to enable them to be used for purposes which come within the scope of this Treaty. The Commission shall as far as possible avoid making such transfers if it possesses cash or liquid assets in the currencies which it needs.

The Commission shall deal with each Member State through the authority designated by the State concerned. In carrying out financial operations the Commission shall employ the services of the bank of issue of the Member State concerned or of any other financial institution approved by that State.

Article 209*

The Council, acting unanimously on a proposal from the Commission and after consulting the European Parliament and obtaining the opinion of the Court of Auditors, shall:

---

* Text as amended by Article 18 of the Treaty amending Certain Financial Provisions.

(a) make Financial Regulations specifying in particular the procedure to be adopted for establishing and implementing the budget and for presenting and auditing accounts;

(b) determine the methods and procedure whereby the budget revenue provided under the arrangements relating to the Communities' own resources shall be made available to the Commission, and determine the measures to be applied, if need be, to meet cash requirements;

(c) lay down rules concerning the responsibility of authorizing officers and accounting officers and concerning appropriate arrangements for inspection.

PART SIX

GENERAL AND FINAL PROVISIONS

Article 210

The Community shall have legal personality.

Article 211

In each of the Member States, the Community shall enjoy the most extensive legal capacity accorded to legal persons under their laws; it may, in particular, acquire or dispose of movable and immovable property and may be a party to legal proceedings. To this end, the Community shall be represented by the Commission.

Article 212

(Article repealed by Article 24 of the Merger Treaty)

[*See Article 24 (1) of the Merger Treaty, which reads as follows:*

1. The officials and other servants of the European Coal and Steel Community, the European Economic Community and the European Atomic Energy Community shall, at the date of entry into force of this Treaty, become officials and other servants of the European Communities and form part of the single administration of those Communities.

The Council shall, acting by a qualified majority on a proposal from the Commission and after consulting the other institutions concerned, lay down the Staff Regulations of officials of the European Communities and the Conditions of Employment of other servants of those Communities.]

Article 213

The Commission may, within the limits and under conditions laid down by the Council in accordance with the provisions of this Treaty, collect any information and carry out any checks required for the performance of the tasks entrusted to it.

Article 214

The members of the institutions of the Community, the members of committees, and the officials and other servants of the Community shall be required, even after their duties have ceased, not to disclose information of the kind covered by the obligation of professional secrecy, in particular information about undertakings, their business relations or their cost components.

Article 215

The contractual liability of the Community shall be governed by the law applicable to the contract in question.

In the case of non-contractual liability, the Community shall, in accordance with the general principles common to the laws of the Member States, make good any damage caused by its institutions or by its servants in the performance of their duties.

The personal liability of its servants towards the Community shall be governed by the provisions laid down in their Staff Regulations or in the Conditions of Employment applicable to them.

Article 216

The seat of the institutions of the Community shall be determined by common accord of the Governments of the Member States.

Article 217

The rules governing the languages of the institutions of the Community shall, without prejudice to the provisions contained in the rules of procedure of the Court of Justice, be determined by the Council, acting unanimously.

Article 218

(Article repealed by the second paragraph of Article 28 of the Merger Treaty)

[*See the first paragraph of Article 28 of the Merger Treaty, which reads as follows:*

The European Communities shall enjoy in the territories of the Member States such privileges and immunities as are necessary for the performance of their tasks, under the conditions laid down in the Protocol annexed to this Treaty. The same shall apply to the European Investment Bank.]

Article 219

Member States undertake not to submit a dispute concerning the interpretation or application of this Treaty to any method of settlement other than those provided for therein.

Article 220

Member States shall, so far as is necessary, enter into negotiations with each other with a view to securing for the benefit of their nationals:

— the protection of persons and the enjoyment and protection of rights under the same conditions as those accorded by each State to its own nationals;

— the abolition of double taxation within the Community;

— the mutual recognition of companies or firms within the meaning of the second paragraph of Article 48, the retention of legal personality in the event of transfer of their seat from one country to another, and the possibility of mergers between companies or firms governed by the laws of different countries;

— the simplification of formalities governing the reciprocal recognition and enforcement of judgments of courts or tribunals and of arbitration awards.

Article 221

Within three years of the entry into force of this Treaty, Member States shall accord nationals of the other Member States the same treatment as their own nationals as regards participation in the capital of companies or firms within the meaning of Article 58, without prejudice to the application of the other provisions of this Treaty.

Article 222

This Treaty shall in no way prejudice the rules in Member States governing the system of property ownership.

Article 223

1. The provisions of this Treaty shall not preclude the application of the following rules:

(a) No Member State shall be obliged to supply information the disclosure of which it considers contrary to the essential interests of its security;

(b) Any Member State may take such measures as it considers necessary for the protection of the essential interests of its security which are connected with the production of or trade in arms, munitions and war material; such measures shall not adversely affect the conditions of competition in the common market regarding products which are not intended for specifically military purposes.

2.　During the first year after the entry into force of this Treaty, the Council shall, acting unanimously, draw up a list of products to which the provisions of paragraph 1 *(b)* shall apply.

3.　The Council may, acting unanimously on a proposal from the Commission, make changes in this list.

Article 224

Member States shall consult each other with a view to taking together the steps needed to prevent the functioning of the common market being affected by measures which a Member State may be called upon to take in the event of serious internal disturbances affecting the maintenance of law and order, in the event of war, serious international tension constituting a threat of war, or in order to carry out obligations it has accepted for the purpose of maintaining peace and international security.

Article 225

If measures taken in the circumstances referred to in Articles 223 and 224 have the effect of distorting the conditions of competition in the common market, the Commission shall, together with the State concerned, examine how these measures can be adjusted to the rules laid down in this Treaty.

By way of derogation from the procedure laid down in Articles 169 and 170, the Commission or any Member State may bring the matter directly before the Court of Justice if it considers that another Member State is making improper use of the powers provided for in Articles 223 and 224. The Court of Justice shall give its ruling *in camera*.

Article 226

1. If, during the transitional period, difficulties arise which are serious and liable to persist in any sector of the economy or which could bring about serious deterioration in the economic situation of a given area, a Member State may apply for authorization to take protective measures in order to rectify the situation and adjust the sector concerned to the economomy of the common market.

2. On application by the State concerned, the Commission shall, by emergency procedure, determine without delay the protective measures which it considers necessary, specifying the circumstances and the manner in which they are to be put into effect.

3. The measures authorized under paragraph 2 may involve derogations from the rules of this Treaty, to such an extent and for such periods as are strictly necessary in order to attain the objectives referred to in paragraph 1. Priority shall be given to such measures as will least disturb the functioning of the common market.

Article 227

1. This Treaty shall apply to the Kingdom of Belgium, the Kingdom of Denmark, the Federal Republic of Germany, the Hellenic Republic, the Kingdom of Spain, the French Republic, Ireland, the Italian Republic, the Grand Duchy of Luxembourg, the Kingdom of the Netherlands, the Portuguese Republic and the United Kingdom of Great Britain and Northern Ireland.*

---

* Paragraph (1) as amended by Article 24 of the Act of Accession ESP/PORT.

2. With regard to Algeria and the French overseas departments, the general and particular provisions of this Treaty relating to:

— the free movement of goods;

— agriculture, save for Article 40 (4);

— the liberalization of services;

— the rules on competition;

— the protective measures provided for in Articles 108, 109 and 226;

— the institutions,

shall apply as soon as this Treaty enters into force.

The conditions under which the other provisions of this Treaty are to apply shall be determined, within two years of the entry into force of this Treaty, by decisions of the Council, acting unanimously on a proposal from the Commission.

The institutions of the Community will, within the framework of the procedures provided for in this Treaty, in particular Article 226, take care that the economic and social development of these areas is made possible.

3. The special arrangements for association set out in Part Four of this Treaty shall apply to the overseas countries and territories listed in Annex IV to this Treaty.

This Treaty shall not apply to those overseas countries and territories having special relations with the United Kingdom of Great Britain and Northern Ireland which are not included in the aforementioned list.*

4. The provisions of this Treaty shall apply to the European territories for whose external relations a Member State is responsible.

---

* Second subparagraph of paragraph 3 added by Article 26 (2) of the Act of Accession DK/IRL/ UK.

5. * Notwithstanding the preceding paragraphs:

(a) This Treaty shall not apply to the Faeroe Islands. The Government of the Kingdom of Denmark may, however, give notice, by a declaration deposited by 31 December 1975 at the latest with the Government of the Italian Republic, which shall transmit a certified copy thereof to each of the Governments of the other Member States, that this Treaty shall apply to those Islands. In that event, this Treaty shall apply to those Islands from the first day of the second month following the deposit of the declaration.

(b) This Treaty shall not apply to the Sovereign Base Areas of the United Kingdom of Great Britain and Northern Ireland in Cyprus.

(c) This Treaty shall apply to the Channel Islands and the Isle of Man only to the extent necessary to ensure the implementation of the arrangements for those islands set out in the Treaty concerning the accession of new Member States to the European Economic Community and to the European Atomic Energy Community signed on 22 January 1972.**

Article 228

1. Where this Treaty provides for the conclusion of agreements between the Community and one or more States or an international organization, such agreements shall be negotiated by the Commission. Subject to the powers vested in the Commission in this field, such agreements shall be concluded by the Council, after consulting the European Parliament where required by this Treaty.

The Council, the Commission or a Member State may obtain before-hand the opinion of the Court of Justice as to whether an agreement envis-

---

* Paragraph 5 added by Article 26 (3) of the Act of Accession DK/IRL/UK, modified by Article 15 (2) of the AD AA DK/IRL/UK.
** See Volume II of this edition.

aged is compatible with the provisions of this Treaty. Where the opinion of the Court of Justice is adverse, the agreement may enter into force only in accordance with Article 236.

2.   Agreements concluded under these conditions shall be binding on the institutions of the Community and on Member States.

Article 229

It shall be for the Commission to ensure the maintenance of all appropriate relations with the organs of the United Nations, of its specialized agencies and of the General Agreement on Tariffs and Trade.

The Commission shall also maintain such relations as are appropriate with all international organizations.

Article 230

The Community shall establish all appropriate forms of cooperation with the Council of Europe.

Article 231

The Community shall establish close cooperation with the Organization for European Economic Cooperation, the details to be determined by common accord.

Article 232

1.   The provisions of this Treaty shall not affect the provisions of the Treaty establishing the European Coal and Steel Community, in particular as regards the rights and obligations of Member States, the powers of the institutions of that Community and the rules laid down by that Treaty for the functioning of the common market in coal and steel.

2.   The provisions of this Treaty shall not derogate from those of the Treaty establishing the European Atomic Energy Community.

Article 233

The provisions of this Treaty shall not preclude the existence or completion of regional unions between Belgium and Luxembourg, or between Belgium, Luxembourg and the Netherlands, to the extent that the objectives of these regional unions are not attained by application of this Treaty.

Article 234

The rights and obligations arising from agreements concluded before the entry into force of this Treaty between one or more Member States on the one hand, and one or more third countries on the other, shall not be affected by the provisions of this Treaty.

To the extent that such agreements are not compatible with this Treaty, the Member State or States concerned shall take all appropriate steps to eliminate the incompatibilities established. Member States shall, where necessary, assist each other to this end and shall, where appropriate, adopt a common attitude.

In applying the agreements referred to in the first paragraph, Member States shall take into account the fact that the advantages accorded under this Treaty by each Member State form an integral part of the establishment of the Community and are thereby inseparably linked with the creation of common institutions, the conferring of powers upon them and the granting of the same advantages by all the other Member States.

Article 235

If action by the Community should prove necessary to attain, in the course of the operation of the common market, one of the objectives of the Community and this Treaty has not provided the necessary powers, the Council shall, acting unanimously on a proposal from the Commission and after consulting the European Parliament, take the appropriate measures.

Article 236

The Government of any Member State or the Commission may submit to the Council proposals for the amendment of this Treaty.

If the Council, after consulting the European Parliament and, where appropriate, the Commission, delivers an opinion in favour of calling a conference of representatives of the Governments of the Member States, the conference shall be convened by the President of the Council for the purpose of determining by common accord the amendments to be made to this Treaty.

The amendments shall enter into force after being ratified by all the Member States in accordance with their respective constitutional requirements.

Article 237

Any European State may apply to become a member of the Community. It shall address its application to the Council, which shall act unanimously after consulting the Commission and after receiving the assent of the European Parliament which shall act by an absolute majority of its component members.*

The conditions of admission and the adjustments to this Treaty necessitated thereby shall be the subject of an agreement between the Member States and the applicant State. This agreement shall be submitted for ratification by all the Contracting States in accordance with their respective constitutional requirements.

Article 238

The Community may conclude with a third State, a union of States or an international organization agreements establishing an association involving reciprocal rights and obligations, common action and special procedures.

---

* First paragraph as replaced by Article 8 of the SEA.

These agreements shall be concluded by the Council, acting unanimously and after receiving the assent of the European Parliament which shall act by an absolute majority of its component members.*

Where such agreements call for amendments to this Treaty, these amendments shall first be adopted in accordance with the procedure laid down in Article 236.

Article 239

The Protocols annexed to this Treaty by common accord of the Member States shall form an integral part thereof.

Article 240

This Treaty is concluded for an unlimited period.

---

* Second paragraph as replaced by Article 9 of the SEA.

Setting up of the institutions

Article 241

The Council shall meet within one month of the entry into force of this Treaty.

Article 242

The Council shall, within three months of its first meeting, take all appropriate measures to constitute the Economic and Social Committee.

Article 243

The Assembly* shall meet within two months of the first meeting of the Council, having been convened by the President of the Council, in order to elect its officers and draw up its rules of procedure. Pending the election of its officers, the oldest member shall take the chair.

Article 244

The Court of Justice shall take up its duties as soon as its members have been appointed. Its first President shall be appointed for three years in the same manner as its members.

The Court of Justice shall adopt its rules of procedure within three months of taking up its duties.

---

* EDITORIAL NOTE:
  Notwithstanding the provisions of Article 3 of the SEA, and for historical reasons, the term 'Assembly' has not been replaced by the terms 'European Parliament'.

No matter may be brought before the Court of Justice until its rules of procedure have been published. The time within which an action must be brought shall run only from the date of this publication.

Upon his appointment, the President of the Court of Justice shall exercise the powers conferred upon him by this Treaty.

Article 245

The Commission shall take up its duties and assume the responsibilities conferred upon it by this Treaty as soon as its members have been appointed.

Upon taking up its duties, the Commission shall undertake the studies and arrange the contacts needed for making an overall survey of the economic situation of the Community.

Article 246

1. The first financial year shall run from the date on which this Treaty enters into force until 31 December following. Should this Treaty, however, enter into force during the second half of the year, the first financial year shall run until 31 December of the following year.

2. Until the budget for the first financial year has been established, Member States shall make the Community interest-free advances which shall be deducted from their financial contributions to the implementation of the budget.

3. Until the Staff Regulations of officials and the Conditions of Employment of other servants of the Community provided for in Article 212 have been laid down, each institution shall recruit the Staff it needs and to this end conclude contracts of limited duration.

Each institution shall examine together with the Council any question concerning the number, remuneration and distribution of posts.

Final provisions

Article 247

This Treaty shall be ratified by the High Contracting Parties in accordance with their respective constitutional requirements. The instruments of ratification shall be deposited with the Government of the Italian Republic.

This Treaty shall enter into force on the first day of the month following the deposit of the instrument of ratification by the last signatory State to take this step. If, however, such deposit is made less than fifteen days before the beginning of the following month, this Treaty shall not enter into force until the first day of the second month after the date of such deposit.

Article 248

This Treaty, drawn up in a single original in the Dutch, French, German and Italian languages, all four texts being equally authentic, shall be deposited in the archives of the Government of the Italian Republic, which shall transmit a certified copy to each of the Governments of the other signatory States.

IN WITNESS WHEREOF, the undersigned Plenipotentiaries have signed this Treaty.

Done at Rome this twenty-fifth day of March in the year one thousand nine hundred and fifty-seven.

P. H. SPAAK	J. Ch. SNOY ET D'OPPUERS
ADENAUER	HALLSTEIN
PINEAU	M. FAURE
Antonio SEGNI	Gaetano MARTINO
BECH	Lambert SCHAUS
J. LUNS	J. LINTHORST HOMAN

Annexes

ANNEX I

LISTS A to G

referred to in Articles 19 and 20 of this Treaty

LIST A

List of tariff headings in respect of which the rates of duty
listed in column 3 below are to be taken into account in
calculating the arithmetical average

— 1 — No in the Brussels Nomenclature	— 2 — Description of products	— 3 — Duty (in %) to be taken into account for France
ex 15.10	Acid oils from refining	18
15.11	Glycerol and glycerol lyes:	
	Crude	6
	Purified	10
19.04	Tapioca and sago; tapioca and sago substitutes obtained from potato or other starches	45
ex 28.28	Vanadic pentoxide	15
ex 28.37	Neutral sodium sulphite	20
ex 28.52	Cerium chlorides; cerium sulphates	20
ex 29.01	Aromatic hydrocarbons: Xylenes:	
	Mixed isomers	20

— 1 — No in the Brussels Nomenclature	— 2 — Description of products	— 3 — Duty (in %) to be taken into account for France
ex 29.01	Orthoxylene, metaxylene, paraxylene	25
	Styrene monomer	20
	Isopropylbenzene (cumene)	25
ex 29.02	Dichloromethane	20
	Vinylidene chloride monomer	25
ex 29.03	Tolueneparasulphonyl chloride	15
ex 29.15	Dimethyl terephthalate	30
ex 29.22	Ethylenediamine and its salts	20
ex 29.23	Cyclic amino-aldehydes, cyclic amino-ketones and amino-quinones, their halogenated, sulphonated, nitrated or nitrosated derivatives, and their salts and esters	25
ex 29.25	Homoveratrylamine	25
29.28	Diazo, azo- and azoxy-compounds	25
ex 29.31	Disulphide of chlorinated benzyl	25
ex 29.44	Antibiotics (other than penicillin, streptomycin, chloramphenicol and their salts, and aureomycin	15
ex 30.02	Foot-and-mouth vaccines, strains of micro-organisms for their manufacture; antisera and vaccines against swine fever	15

— 1 — No in the Brussels Nomenclature	— 2 — Description of products	— 3 — Duty (in %) to be taken into account for France
ex 30.03	Sarkomycin	18
ex 31.02	Mineral or chemical fertilizers, nitrogenous, composite	20
ex 31.03	Mineral or chemical fertilizers, phosphatic:	
	Single:	
	Superphosphates:	
	Of bone	10
	Other	12
	Mixed	7
ex 31.04	Mineral or chemical fertilizers, potassic, mixed	7
ex 31.05	Other fertilizers, including both composite and complex fertilizers:	
	Phosphor nitrates and ammonium-potassium phosphates	10
	Other fertilizers, excluding dissolved organic fertilizers	7
	Fertilizers in tablets, lozenges and similar prepared forms or in packings of a gross weight not exceeding ten kilograms	15
ex 32.07	Natural magnetite, finely ground, of a kind used for pigments, intended exclusively for cleaning coal	25

— 1 — No in the Brussels Nomenclature	— 2 — Description of products	— 3 — Duty (in %) to be taken into account for France
ex 37.02	Film in rolls, sensitized, unexposed, perforated:	
	For monochrome pictures (positives), imported in packages containing three units not separately utilizable, to form the base for a polychrome film	20
	For polychrome pictures exceeding 100 metres in length	20
ex 39.02	Polyvinylidene chloride; polyvinyl butyral in sheets	30
ex 39.03	Cellulose esters, excluding nitrates and acetates	20
	Plastic materials with a basis of cellulose esters (other than nitrates and acetates)	15
	Plastic materials with a basis of ethers or other chemical derivatives of cellulose	30
ex 39.06	Alginic acid, its salts and esters, dry	20
ex 48.01	Paper and paperboard, machine-made:	
	Kraft paper and kraft paperboard	25
	Other, continuously made, consisting of two or more layers, with kraft paper inside	25

— 1 — No in the Brussels Nomenclature	— 2 — Description of products	— 3 — Duty (in %) to be taken into account for France
48.04	Composite paper or paperboard (made by sticking flat layers together with an adhesive), not surface-coated or impregnated, whether or not internally reinforced, in rolls or sheets	25
ex 48.05	Paper and paperboard, corrugated	25
	Kraft paper and kraft paperboard, creped or crinkled	25
ex 48.07	Kraft paper and kraft paperboard, adhesive	25
ex 51.01	Yarn of man-made (regenerated) fibres (continuous), single, without twist or with a twist of less than 400 turns	20
ex 55.05	Cotton yarn, multiple, other than fancy yarn, unbleached, measuring 337 500 metres or more per kilogram in the single yarn	20
ex 57.07	Yarn of coir	18
ex 58.01	Carpets, carpeting and rugs, knotted, of silk, of silk waste other than noil, of man-made (synthetic) fibres, of yarn falling within heading No 52.01, of metal thread, of wool or of fine animal hair	80
ex 59.04	Multiple yarn of coir	18
ex 71.04	Dust and powder of diamonds	10

—1— No in the Brussels Nomenclature	—2— Description of products	—3— Duty (in %) to be taken into account for France
ex 84.10	Pump housings or bodies, of steel other than stainless steel or of light metals or their alloys, for aircraft piston engines	15
ex 84.11	Pump or compressor housings or bodies, of steel other than stainless steel or of light metals or their alloys, for aircraft piston engines	15
ex 84.37	Machines for making plain or figured tulle, and lace	10
	Embroidery machines, other than thread drawing and binding machines (machines for making open-work embroidery)	10
ex 84.38	Auxiliary machinery for use with machines for making plain or figured tulle, and lace:	
	Slide-lifting machines	10
	Jacquards	18
	Auxiliary machinery for use with embroidery machines:	
	Automatic machines	18

— 1 — No in the Brussels Nomenclature	— 2 — Description of products	— 3 — Duty (in %) to be taken into account for France
ex 84.38	Card punching machines, card reproducing machines, control machines, spool-winders	10
	Parts and accessories for machines for making plain or figured tulle, and lace, and for auxiliary machinery for such machines:	
	Slides, bobbins, combs, slide bars and ribs of combs for flat machines, battens (their plates and blades), complete bobbins and parts of battens and bobbins for circular machines	10
	Parts and accessories for embroidery machines and for auxiliary machinery for such machines:	
	Shuttles, shuttle-boxes including their plates; clips	10
ex 84.59	Coil-winders for winding conductor-wires and insulating or protecting tapes for the manufacture of electric coils and windings	23

— 1 — No in the Brussels Nomenclature	— 2 — Description of products	— 3 — Duty (in %) to be taken into account for France
ex 84.59	Starters, direct drive or inertia, for aircraft	25
ex 84.63	Crankshafts for aircraft piston engines	10
ex 85.08	Starter motors for aircraft	20
	Ignition magnetos, including magneto-dynamos for aircraft	25
88.01	Balloons and airships	25
ex 88.03	Parts of balloons and airships	25
88.04	Parachutes and parts thereof and accessories thereto	12
88.05	Catapults and similar aircraft launching gear, and parts thereof	15
	Ground flying trainers and parts thereof	20
ex 90.14	Instruments for air navigation	18
ex 92.10	Mechanisms and keyboards (containing not less than 85 notes) for pianos	30

LIST B

List of tariff headings in respect of which the rates of duty in
the common customs tariff may not exceed 3 %

— 1 — No in the Brussels Nomenclature	— 2 — Description of products
CHAPTER 5	
05.01	
05.02	
05.03	
05.05	
05.06	
ex 05.07	Feathers, skins and other parts of birds with their feathers or down, unworked (excluding bed feathers or down, unworked)
05.09 to 05.12	
ex 05.13	Natural sponges, raw
CHAPTER 13	
13.01	
13.02	
CHAPTER 14	
14.01 to 14.05	
CHAPTER 25	
25.02	

CHAPTER 25
(cont'd)

ex 25.04   Natural graphite, not put up for retail sale

25.05

25.06

ex 25.07   Clay (other than kaolin), andalusite and kyanite, whether or not calcined, but not including expanded clays falling within heading No 68.07; mullite; chamotte and dinas earths

ex 25.08   Chalk, not put up for retail sale

ex 25.09   Earth colours, not calcined or mixed; natural micaceous iron oxides

25.10

25.11

ex 25.12   Infusorial earths, siliceous fossil meals and similar siliceous earths (for example, kieselguhr, tripolite or diatomite) of an apparent density of 1 or less, whether or not calcined, not put up for retail sale

ex 25.13   Pumice stone, emery, natural corundum and other natural abrasives, not put up for retail sale

25.14

ex 25.17   Flint; crushed or broken stone, macadam and tarred macadam, pebbles and gravel, of a kind commonly used for road metalling, for railway or other ballast or for concrete aggregates; shingle

— 1 — No in the Brussels Nomenclature	— 2 — Description of products

CHAPTER 25
(cont'd)

ex 25.18   Dolomite, including dolomite not further worked than roughly split, roughly squared or squared by sawing

25.20

25.21

25.24

25.25

25.26

ex 25.27   Natural steatite, including natural steatite not further worked than roughly split, roughly squared or squared by sawing; talc other than in packings of a net weight not exceeding one kilogram

25.28

25.29

25.31

25.32

CHAPTER 26

ex 26.01   Metallic ores and concentrates other than lead ores, zinc ores and products within the province of the European Coal and Steel Community; roasted iron pyrites

26.02

ex 26.03   Ash and residues (other than from the manufacture of iron or steel), containing metals or metallic compounds other than those containing zinc

26.04

— 1 — No in the Brussels Nomenclature	— 2 — Description of products
CHAPTER 27	
27.03	
ex 27.04	Coke and semi-coke of coal, for the manufacture of electrodes, and coke of peat
27.05	
27.05 (bis)	
27.06	
ex 27.13	Ozokerite, lignite wax and peat wax, crude
27.15	
27.17	
CHAPTER 31	
31.01	
ex 31.02	Natural sodium nitrate
CHAPTER 40	
40.01	
40.03	
40.04	
CHAPTER 41	
41.09	
CHAPTER 43	
43.01	
CHAPTER 44	
44.01	

— 1 — No in the Brussels Nomenclature	— 2 — Description of products

CHAPTER 47

   47.02

CHAPTER 50

   50.01

CHAPTER 53

   53.01

   53.02

   53.03

   53.05

CHAPTER 55

   ex 55.02   Cotton linters, other than raw

   55.04

CHAPTER 57

   57.04

CHAPTER 63

   63.02

CHAPTER 70

   ex 70.01   Waste glass (cullet)

CHAPTER 71

   ex 71.01   Pearls, unworked

CHAPTER 71
(cont'd)

   ex 71.02   Precious and semi-precious stones, unworked

     71.04

     71.11

CHAPTER 77

   ex 77.04   Beryllium, unwrought

LIST C

List of tariff headings in respect of which the rates of duty in
the common customs tariff may not exceed 10 %

— 1 — No in the Brussels Nomenclature	— 2 — Description of products
CHAPTER 5	
ex 05.07	Feathers, skins and other parts of birds with their feathers or down, other than unworked
05.14	
CHAPTER 13	
ex 13.03	Vegetable saps and extracts; agar-agar and other natural mucilages and thickeners extracted from vegetable materials (excluding pectin)
CHAPTER 15	
ex 15.04	Fats and oils, of fish and marine mammals, whether or not refined (excluding whale oil)
15.05	
15.06	
15.09	
15.11	
15.14	
CHAPTER 25	
ex 25.09	Earth colours, calcined or mixed

CHAPTER 25
(cont'd)

ex 25.15   Marble, travertine, ecaussine and other calcareous monumental and building stone of an apparent density of 2.5 or more and alabaster, not further worked than squared by sawing, of a thickness not exceeding 25 centimetres

ex 25.16   Granite, porphyry, basalt, sandstone and other monumental and building stone, not further worked than squared by sawing, of a thickness not exceeding 25 centimetres

ex 25.17   Granules, chippings and powder of stones falling within heading No 25.15 or 25.16

ex 25.18   Dolomite, calcined or agglomerated (including tarred dolomite)

25.22

25.23

CHAPTER 27

ex 27.07   Oils and other products of the distillation of high temperature coal tar, and other oils and products as defined in Note 2 to this Chapter, excluding phenols, cresols and xylenols

27.08

ex 27.13   Ozokerite, lignite wax and peat wax, other than crude

ex 27.14   Petroleum bitumen and other petroleum and shale oil residues, excluding petroleum coke

27.16

440

— 1 — No in the Brussels Nomenclature	— 2 — Description of products

CHAPTER 30

ex 30.01   Organo-therapeutic glands or other organs, dried, whether or not powdered

CHAPTER 32

ex 32.01   Tanning extracts of vegetable origin, other than extracts of wattle (mimosa) and of quebracho

32.02

32.03

32.04

CHAPTER 33

ex 33.01   Essential oils (terpeneless or not), concretes and absolutes, other than those of citrus fruit; resinoids

33.02

33.03

33.04

CHAPTER 38

38.01

38.02

38.04

38.05

38.06

ex 38.07   Gum spirits of turpentine; sulphate turpentine, crude; crude dipentene

— 1 — No in the Brussels Nomenclature	— 2 — Description of products

CHAPTER 38
(cont'd)

    38.08

    38.10

CHAPTER 40

    40.05

    ex 40.07   Textile thread covered or impregnated with vulcanized rubber

    40.15

CHAPTER 41

    41.02

    ex 41.03   Sheep and lamb skin leather, further prepared than tanned

    ex 41.04   Goat and kid skin leather, further prepared than tanned

    41.05

    41.06

    41.07

    41.10

CHAPTER 43

    43.02

CHAPTER 44

    44.06
    to
    44.13

— 1 — No in the Brussels Nomenclature	— 2 — Description of products
CHAPTER 44 *(cont'd)*	
44.16	
44.17	
44.18	
CHAPTER 48	
ex 48.01	Newsprint in rolls
CHAPTER 50	
50.06	
50.08	
CHAPTER 52	
52.01	
CHAPTER 53	
53.06 to 53.09	
CHAPTER 54	
54.03	
CHAPTER 55	
55.05	

CHAPTER 57

ex 57.05   Yarn of true hemp, not put up for retail sale

ex 57.06   Yarn of jute, not put up for retail sale

ex 57.07   Yarn of other vegetable textile fibres, not put up for retail sale

ex 57.08   Paper yarn, not put up for retail sale

CHAPTER 68

68.01

68.03

68.08

ex 68.10   Building materials of plastering material

ex 68.11   Building materials of cement (including slag cement), of concrete or of artificial stone (including granulated marble agglomerated with cement), reinforced or not

ex 68.12   Building materials of asbestos-cement, of cellulose fibre-cement or the like

ex 68.13   Fabricated asbestos; mixtures with a basis of asbestos and mixtures with a basis of asbestos and magnesium carbonate

CHAPTER 69

69.01

69.02

69.04

69.05

CHAPTER 70

ex 70.01   Glass in the mass (excluding optical glass)

70.02

70.03

70.04

70.05

70.06

70.16

CHAPTER 71

ex 71.05   Silver, unwrought

ex 71.06   Rolled silver, unworked

ex 71.07   Gold, unwrought

ex 71.08   Rolled gold on base metal or silver, unworked

ex 71.09   Platinum and other metals of the platinum group, un-wrought

ex 71.10   Rolled platinum or other platinum group metals, on base metal or precious metal, unworked

CHAPTER 73

73.04

73.05

ex 73.07   Blooms, billets, slabs and sheet bars (including tin-plate bars), of iron or steel (other than products within the province of the European Coal and Steel Community); pieces roughly shaped by forging, of iron or steel

CHAPTER 73
(cont'd)

ex 73.10 Bars and rods (including wire rod), of iron or steel, hot-rolled, forged, extruded, cold-formed or cold-finished (including precision-made); hollow mining drill steel (other than products within the province of the European Coal and Steel Community)

ex 73.11 Angles, shapes and sections, of iron or steel, hot-rolled, forged, extruded, cold-formed or cold-finished; sheet piling of iron or steel, whether or not drilled, punched or made from assembled elements (other than products within the province of the European Coal and Steel Community)

ex 73.12 Hoop and strip, of iron or steel, hot-rolled or cold-rolled (other than products within the province of the European Coal and Steel Community)

ex 73.13 Sheets and plates, of iron or steel, hot-rolled or cold-rolled (other than products within the province of the European Coal and Steel Community)

73.14

ex 73.15 Alloy steel and high carbon steel in the forms mentioned in headings Nos 73.06 to 73.14 (other than products within the province of the European Coal and Steel Community)

CHAPTER 74

74.03

74.04

CHAPTER 74
(cont'd)

ex 74.05   Copper foil, whether or not embossed, cut to shape, perforated, coated or printed, other than that backed with reinforcing material

ex 74.06   Copper powder (other than impalpable powder)

CHAPTER 75

75.02

75.03

ex 75.05   Electro-plating anodes, of nickel, unwrought, produced by casting

CHAPTER 76

76.02

76.03

ex 76.04   Aluminium foil, whether or not embossed, cut to shape, perforated, coated or printed, other than that backed with reinforcing material

ex 76.05   Aluminium powder (other than impalpable powder)

CHAPTER 77

ex 77.02   Wrought bars, rods, angles, shapes and sections, of magnesium; magnesium wire; wrought plates, sheets and strip, of magnesium; magnesium foil; raspings and shavings of uniform size; magnesium powder (other than impalpable powder)

ex 77.04   Wrought bars, rods, angles, shapes and sections, of beryllium; beryllium wire; wrought plates, sheets and strip, of beryllium, beryllium foil

— 1 — No in the Brussels Nomenclature	— 2 — Description of products

CHAPTER 78

78.02

78.03

ex 78.04   Leadfoil, whether or not embossed, cut to shape, perforated, coated or printed, other than that backed with reinforcing material

CHAPTER 79

79.02

79.03

CHAPTER 80

80.02

80.03

ex 80.04   Tin foil, whether or not embossed, cut to shape, perforated, coated or printed, other than that backed with reinforcing material

CHAPTER 81

ex 81.01   Wrought bars, rods, angles, shapes and sections, of tungsten (wolfram); wrought plates sheets and strip, of tungsten (wolfram); tungsten (wolfram) foil; wire and filament of tungsten (wolfram)

ex 81.02   Wrought bars, rods, angles, shapes and sections, of molybdenum; wrought plates, sheets and strip, of molybdenum; molybdenum foil; wire and filament of molybdenum

CHAPTER 81
(cont'd)

ex 81.03   Wrought bars. rods, angles, shapes and sections, of tantalum; wrought plates, sheets and strip, of tantalum; tantalum foil; wire and filament of tantalum

ex 81.04   Wrought bars, rods, angles shapes and sections of other base metals; wrought plates, sheets and strip, of other base metals; foil, wire and filament, of other base metals

CHAPTER 93

ex 93.06   Stocks and other wooden parts for guns

CHAPTER 95

ex 95.01
to
ex 95.07   Roughly shaped carving material, that is to say, plates, sheets, rods, tubes and similar forms, not polished or otherwise worked

CHAPTER 98

ex 98.11   Roughly shaped blocks of wood or root, for the manufacture of pipes

LIST D

List of tariff headings in respect of which the rates of duty
in the common customs tariff may not exceed 15 %

— 1 — No in the Brussels Nomenclature	— 2 — Description of products
CHAPTER 28	*Inorganic chemicals; organic and inorganic compounds of precious metals, of rare earth metals, of radioactive elements and of isotopes*
ex 28.01	Halogens (excluding iodine, crude and bromine)
ex 28.04	Hydrogen, rare gases and other metalloids and non-metals (excluding selenium and phosphorus)
28.05 to 28.10	
ex 28.11	Arsenic trioxide; acid of arsenic
28.13 to 28.22	
28.24	
28.26 to 28.31	
ex 28.32	Chlorates (excluding sodium chlorate and potassium chlorate and perchlorates)
ex 28.34	Oxyiodides and periodates
28.35 to 28.45	
28.47 to 28.58	

LIST E

List of tariff headings in respect of which the rates of duty
in the common customs tariff may not exceed 25 %

— 1 — No in the Brussels Nomenclature	— 2 — Description of products
CHAPTER 29	*Organic chemicals*
ex 29.01	Hydrocarbons (excluding naphthalene)
29.02	
29.03	
ex 29.04	Acyclic alcohols and their halogenated, sulphonated, nitrated or nitrosated derivatives (excluding butyl and isobutyl alcohols)
29.05	
ex 29.06	Phenols (excluding phenol, cresols and xylenols) and phenol-alcohols
29.07 to 29.45	
CHAPTER 32	
32.05	
32.06	
CHAPTER 39	
39.01 to 39.06	

LIST F

List of tariff headings in respect of which the rates of duty in the common customs tariff have been determined by common accord

— 1 — No in the Brussels Nomenclature	— 2 — Description of products	— 3 — Common customs tariff (*ad valorem* rate in %)
ex 01.01	Live horses for slaughter	11
ex 01.02	Live animals of the bovine species (other than pure-bred breeding animals)[1]	16
ex 01.03	Live swine (other than pure-bred breeding animals)[1]	16
ex 02.01	Meat and edible offal, fresh, chilled or frozen:	
	Of horses	16
	Of bovine animals[1]	20
	Of swine[1]	20
02.02	Dead poultry (that is to say, fowls, ducks, geese, turkeys and guinea fowls) and edible offal thereof (except liver), fresh, chilled or frozen	18
ex 02.06	Horsemeat, salted or dried	16
ex 03.01	Freshwater fish, fresh (live or dead), chilled or frozen:	
	Trout and other salmonidae	16
	Other	10

---

[1] Domestic species only.

452

— 1 — No in the Brussels Nomenclature	— 2 — Description of products	— 3 — Common customs tariff (*ad valorem* rate in %)
ex 03.03	Crustaceans and molluscs, whether in shell or not, fresh (live or dead), chilled, frozen, salted, in brine or dried; crustaceans, in shell, simply boiled in water:	
	Crawfish and lobsters	25
	Crabs, shrimps and prawns	18
	Oysters	18
04.03	Butter	24
ex 04.05	Birds' eggs in shell, fresh or preserved:	
	From 16/2 to 31/8	12
	From 1/9 to 15/2	15
04.06	Natural honey	30
ex 05.07	Bed feathers and down, unworked	0
05.08	Bones and horn-cores, unworked, defatted, simply prepared but not cut to shape, treated with acid or degelatinized; powder and waste of these products	0
ex 06.03	Cut flowers and flower buds of a kind suitable for bouquets or for ornamental purposes, fresh:	
	From 1/6 to 31/10	24
	From 1/11 to 31/5	20

— 1 —	— 2 —	— 3 —
No in the Brussels Nomenclature	Description of products	Common customs tariff (*ad valorem* rate in %)

ex 07.01	Vegetables, fresh or chilled:	
	Onions, shallots, garlic	12
	New potatoes:	
	From 1/1 to 15/5	15
	From 16/5 to 30/6	21
	Other[1]	
07.04	Dried, dehydrated or evaporated vegetables, whole, cut, sliced, broken or in powder, but not further prepared:	
	Onions	20
	Other	16
ex 07.05	Dried leguminous vegetables, shelled, whether or not skinned or split:	
	Peas and beans	10
ex 08.01	Bananas, fresh	20
08.02	Citrus fruit, fresh or dried:	
	Oranges:	
	From 15/3 to 30/9	15
	Outside this period	20
	Mandarins and clementines	20
	Lemons	8
	Grapefruit	12
	Other	16

---

[1] The rate is normally fixed at the level of the arithmetical average. This may be adjusted, as necessary, by fixing seasonal rates within the framework of the agricultural policy of the Community.

— 1 — No in the Brussels Nomenclature	— 2 — Description of products	— 3 — Common customs tariff (*ad valorem* rage in %)
ex 08.04	Grapes, fresh:	
	From 1/11 to 14/7	18
	From 15/7 to 31/10	22
08.06	Apples, pears and quinces, fresh[1]	8
08.07	Stone fruit, fresh:	
	Apricots	25
	Other[1]	
ex 08.12	Prunes	18
ex 09.01	Raw coffee	16
10.01 to 10.07	Cereals[2]	
ex 11.01	Wheat flour[2]	
12.01	Oil seeds and oleaginous fruits, whole or broken	0

---

[1] The rate is normally fixed at the level of the arithmetical average. This may be adjusted, as necessary, by fixing seasonal rates within the framework of the agricultural policy of the Community.

[2] (a) The rates of duty on cereals and wheat flour in the common customs tariff shall be equal to the arithmetical average of the rates in the national tariffs.

(b) Until the treatment to be applied within the framework of the measures provided for in Article 40 (2) has been determined, Member States may, by way of derogation from Article 23, suspend the collection of duties on these products.

(c) Should the production or processing of cereals or wheat flour in any Member State be seriously threatened or prejudiced by the suspension of duties in another Member State, the Member States concerned shall enter into negotiations with each other. Should these negotiations fail to produce results, the Commission may authorize the injured State to take appropriate measures, to be implemented as determined by the Commission, in so far as the difference in cost is not compensated for by the existence of an internal organization of the market in cereals in the Member State suspending the duties.

— 1 — No in the Brussels Nomenclature	— 2 — Description of products	— 3 — Common customs tariff (*ad valorem* rate in %)
ex 12.03	Seeds of a kind used for sowing (other than beet seed)	10
12.06	Hop cones and lupulin	12
15.15	Beeswax and other insect waxes, whether or not coloured:	
	Raw	0
	Other	10
15.16	Vegetable waxes, whether or not coloured:	
	Raw	0
	Other	8
ex 16.04	Prepared or preserved fish:	
	Salmonidae	20
ex 16.05	Crustaceans, prepared or preserved	20
17.01	Beet sugar and cane sugar, solid	80
18.01	Cocoa beans, whole or broken, raw or roasted	9
18.02	Cocoa shells, husks, skins and waste	9
19.02	Preparations of flour, starch or malt extract, of a kind used as infant food or for dietetic or culinary purposes, containing less than 50 per cent by weight of cocoa	25
ex 20.02	Sauerkraut	20
21.07	Food preparations not elsewhere specified or included	25

— 1 — No in the Brussels Nomenclature	— 2 — Description of products	— 3 — Common customs tariff (*ad valorem* rate in %)
22.04	Grape must, in fermentation or with fermentation arrested otherwise than by the addition of alcohol	40
23.01	Flours and meals, unfit for human consumption:	
	Of meat and offal; greaves	4
	Of fish, crustaceans or molluscs	5
24.01	Unmanufactured tobacco; tobacco refuse	30
ex 25.07	Kaolin, sillimanite	0
ex 25.15	Marble, including marble not further worked than roughly split, roughly squared or squared by sawing, of a thickness exceeding 25 centimetres	0
ex 25.16	Granite, porphyry, basalt, sandstone and other monumental and building stone, including such stone not further worked than roughly split, roughly squared or squared by sawing, of a thickness exceeding 25 centimetres	0
25.19	Natural magnesium carbonate (magnesite), whether or not calcined, other than magnesium oxide	0
ex 25.27	Talc put up in packings of a net weight not exceeding one kilogram	8
ex 27.07	Phenols, cresols and xylenols, crude	3
27.09	Petroleum and shale oils, crude	0

— 1 — No in the Brussels Nomenclature	— 2 — Description of products	— 3 — Common customs tariff (*ad valorem* rate in %)
ex 27.14	Petroleum coke	0
28.03	Carbon, including carbon black, anthracene black, acetylene black and lamp black	5
ex 28.04	Phosphorus	15
	Selenium	0
28.23	Iron oxides and hydroxides, including earth colours containing 70 per cent or more by weight of combined iron evaluated as Fe_2O_3	10
28.25	Titanium oxides	15
ex 28.32	Sodium and potassium chlorates	10
ex 29.01	Aromatic hydrocarbons Naphthalene	8
ex 29.04	*tert*-butyl alcohol	8
ex 32.07	Titanium white	15
ex 33.01	Essential oils (terpeneless or not), concretes and absolutes, of citrus fruit	12
34.04	Artificial waxes (including water-soluble waxes); prepared waxes, not emulsified or containing solvents	12
ex 40.07	Vulcanized rubber thread and cord, whether or not textile covered	15

— 1 — No in the Brussels Nomenclature	— 2 — Description of products	— 3 — Common customs tariff (*ad valorem* rate in %)
41.01	Raw hides and skins (fresh, salted, dried, pickled or limed), whether or not split, including sheepskins in the wool	0
ex 41.03	Sheep and lamb skin leather, not further prepared than tanned:	
	Of Indian crossbred sheep and goats	0
	Other	6
ex 41.04	Goat and kid skin leather, not further prepared than tanned:	
	Of Indian goats	0
	Other	7
41.08	Patent leather and metallized leather	12
44.14	Veneer sheets and sheets for plywood (sawn, sliced or peeled), of a thickness not exceeding five millimetres, whether or not reinforced with paper or fabric	10
44.15	Plywood, blockboard, laminboard, battenboard and veneered panels, whether or not containing any material other than wood; inlaid wood and wood marquetry	15
53.04	Waste of sheep's or lambs' wool or of other animal hair (fine or coarse), pulled or garnetted (including pulled or garnetted rags)	0

— 1 — No in the Brussels Nomenclature	— 2 — Description of products	— 3 — Common customs tariff (*ad valorem* rate in %)
54.01	Flax, raw or processed but not spun; flax tow and waste (including pulled or garnetted rags)	0
54.02	Ramie, raw or processed but not spun; ramie noils and waste (including pulled or garnetted rags)	0
55.01	Cotton, not carded or combed	0
ex 55.02	Cotton linters, raw	0
55.03	Cotton waste (including pulled or garnetted rags), not carded or combed	0
57.01	True hemp *(Cannabis sativa)*, raw or processed but not spun; tow and waste of true hemp (including pulled or garnetted rags or ropes)	0
57.02	Manila hemp (abaca) *(Musa textilis)*, raw or processed but not spun; tow and waste of manila hemp (including pulled or garnetted rags or ropes)	0
57.03	Jute, raw or processed but not spun; tow and waste of jute (including pulled or garnetted rags or ropes)	0
74.01	Copper matte; unwrought copper (refined or not); copper waste and scrap	0

— 1 — No in the Brussels Nomenclature	— 2 — Description of products	— 3 — Common customs tariff (*ad valorem* rate in %)
74.02	Master alloys	0
75.01	Nickel mattes, nickel speiss and other intermediate products of nickel metallurgy; unwrought nickel (excluding electroplating anodes); nickel waste and scrap	0
80.01	Unwrought tin, tin waste and scrap	0
ex 85.08	Sparking plugs	18

LIST G

List of tariff headings in respect of which the rates of ducty in the common customs tariff are to be negotiated between the Member States

— 1 — No in the Brussels Nomenclature	— 2 — Description of products
ex 03.01	Saltwater fish, fresh (live or dead), chilled or frozen
03.02	Fish, salted, in brine, dried or smoked
04.04	Cheese and curd
11.02	Cereal groats and cereal meal; other worked cereal grains (for example, rolled, flaked, polished, pearled or kibbled, but not further prepared), except husked, glazed, polished or broken rice; germ of cereals, whole, rolled, flaked or ground
11.07	Malt, roasted or not
ex 15.01	Lard and other rendered pig fat
15.02	Unrendered fats of bovine cattle, sheep or goats; tallow (including 'premier jus') produced from those fats
15.03	Lard stearin, oleostearin and tallow stearin; lard oil, oleo-oil and tallow oil, not emulsified or mixed or prepared in any way
ex 15.04	Whale oil, whether or not refined
15.07	Fixed vegetable oils, fluid or solid, crude, refined or purified
15.12	Animal or vegetable fats and oils, hydrogenated, whether or not refined, but not further prepared
18.03	Cocoa paste (in bulk or in block), whether or not defatted

— 1 —	— 2 —
No in the Brussels Nomenclature	Description of products

18.04   Cocoa butter (fat or oil)

18.05   Cocoa powder, unsweetened

18.06   Chocolate and other food preparations containing cocoa

19.07   Bread, ships' biscuits and other ordinary bakers' wares, not containing sugar, honey, eggs, fats, cheese or fruit

19.08   Pastry, biscuits, cakes and other fine bakers' wares, whether or not containing cocoa in any proportion

21.02   Extracts, essences or concentrates, of coffee, tea or maté; preparations with a basis of those extracts, essences or concentrates

22.05   Wine of fresh grapes; grape must with fermentation arrested by the addition of alcohol

22.08   Ethyl alcohol or neutral spirits, undenatured, of a strength of 80 degrees or higher; denatured spirits (including ethyl alcohol and neutral spirits) of any strength

22.09   Spirits (other than those of heading No 22.08); liqueurs and other spirituous beverages; compound alcoholic preparations (known as 'concentrated extracts') for the manufacture of beverages

25.01   Common salt (including rock salt, sea salt and table salt); pure sodium chloride; salt liquors, sea water

— 1 — No in the Brussels Nomenclature	— 2 — Description of products
25.03	Sulphur of all kinds, other than sublimed sulphur, precipitated sulphur and colloidal sulphur
25.30	Crude, natural borates and concentrates thereof (calcined or not), but not including borates separated from natural brine; crude natural boric acid containing not more than 85 per cent of H_3BO_3 calculated on the dry weight
ex 26.01	Lead ores and zinc ores
ex 26.03	Ash and residues, containing zinc
27.10	Petroleum and shale oils, other than crude; preparations not elsewhere specified or included, containing not less than 70 per cent by weight of petroleum or shale oils, these oils being the basic constituents of the preparations
27.11	Petroleum gases and other gaseous hydrocarbons
27.12	Petroleum jelly
ex 27.13	Paraffin wax, micro-crystalline wax, slack wax and other mineral wax, whether or not coloured, except ozokerite, lignite wax and peat wax
ex 28.01	Iodine, crude, and bromine
28.02	Sulphur, sublimed or precipitated; colloidal sulphur
ex 28.11	Arsenic pentoxide
28.12	Boric oxide and boric acid
28.33	Bromides, oxybromides, bromates and perbromates, and hypobromites
ex 28.34	Iodides and iodates

— 1 — No in the Brussels Nomenclature	— 2 — Description of products
28.46	Borates and perborates
ex 29.04	Butyl and isobutyl alcohols (other than *tert*-butyl alcohol)
ex 29.06	Phenol, cresols and xylenols
ex 32.01	Extracts of quebracho and of wattle (mimosa)
40.02	Synthetic rubbers, including synthetic latex, whether or not stabilized; factice derived from oils
44.03	Wood in the rough, whether or not stripped of its bark or merely roughed down
44.04	Wood, roughly squared or half-squared, but not further manufactured
44.05	Wood sawn lengthwise, sliced or peeled, but not further prepared, of a thickness exceeding 5 millimetres
45.01	Natural cork, unworked, crushed, granulated or ground; waste cork
45.02	Natural cork in blocks, plates, sheets or strips (including cubes or square slabs, cut to size for corks or stoppers)
47.01	Pulp derived by mechanical or chemical means from any fibrous vegetable mineral
50.02	Raw silk (not thrown)
50.03	Silk waste (including cocoons unsuitable for reeling, silk noils and pulled or garnetted rags)
50.04	Silk yarn, other than yarn of noil or other waste silk, not put up for retail sale

— 1 — No in the Brussels Nomenclature	— 2 — Description of products
50.05	Yarn spun from silk waste other than noil, not put up for retail sale
ex 62.03	Used sacks and bags, of jute, of a kind used for the packing of goods
ex 70.19	Glass beads, imitation pearls, imitation precious and semi-precious stones, imitation synthetic stones and similar fancy or decorative glass smallwares
ex 73.02	Ferro-alloys (other than high carbon ferro-manganese)
76.01	Unwrought aluminium; aluminium waste and scrap[1]
77.01	Unwrought magnesium; magnesium waste (excluding shavings of uniform size) and scrap[1]
78.01	Unwrought lead (including argentiferous lead); lead waste and scrap[1]
79.01	Zinc pelter; unwrought zinc; zinc waste and scrap[1]
ex 81.01	Tungsten (wolfram) unwrought, in powder[1]
ex 81.02	Molybdenum, unwrought[1]
ex 81.03	Tantalum, unwrought[1]
ex 81.04	Other base metals, unwrought[1]
ex 84.06	Engines for motor vehicles, flying machines and ships, boats and other vessels, and parts of such engines
ex 84.08	Reaction engines, and parts and accessories thereof

---

[1] The rates of duty applicable to semi-finished products are to be reviewed in the light of the rate fixed for the unwrought metal, in accordance with the procedure laid down in Article 21 (2) of this Treaty.

84.45	Machine-tools for working metal or metallic carbides, not being machines falling within heading Nos 84.49 or 84.50
84.48	Accessories and parts suitable for use solely or principally with the machines falling within headings Nos 84.45 to 84.47, including work and tool holders, self-opening die-heads, dividing heads and other appliances for machine-tools; tool holders for the mechanical hand tools of headings Nos 82.04, 84.49 or 85.05
ex 84.63	Transmission components for engines of motor vehicles
87.06	Parts and accessories of the motor vehicles falling within headings Nos 87.01, 87.02 or 87.03
88.02	Flying machines, gliders and kites; rotochutes
ex 88.03	Parts of flying machines, gliders and kites

ANNEX II

LIST

referred to in Article 38 of this Treaty

— 1 — No in the Brussels Nomenclature	— 2 — Description of products
CHAPTER 1	*Live animals*
CHAPTER 2	*Meat and edible meat offal*
CHAPTER 3	*Fish, crustaceans and molluscs*
CHAPTER 4	*Dairy produce; birds' eggs; natural honey*
CHAPTER 5	
05.04	Guts, bladders and stomachs of animals (other than fish), whole and pieces thereof
05.15	Animal products not elsewhere specified or included; dead animals of Chapter 1 or Chapter 3, unfit for human consumption
CHAPTER 6	*Live trees and other plants; bulbs, roots and the like; cut flowers and ornamental foliage*
CHAPTER 7	*Edible vegetables and certain roots and tubers*

CHAPTER 15
(cont'd)

15.07 Fixed vegetable oils, fluid or solid, crude, refined or purified

15.12 Animal or vegetable fats and oils, hydrogenated, whether or not refined, but not further prepared

15.13 Margarine, imitation lard and other prepared edible fats

15.17 Residues resulting from the treatment of fatty substances or animal or vegetable waxes

CHAPTER 16 *Preparations of meat, of fish, of crustaceans or molluscs*

CHAPTER 17

17.01 Beet sugar and cane sugar, solid

17.02 Other sugars; sugar syrups; artificial honey (whether or not mixed with natural honey); caramel

17.03 Molasses, whether or not decolourized

17.05 * Flavoured or coloured sugars, syrups and molasses, but not including fruit juices containing added sugar in any proportion.

---

* Heading added by Article 1 of Regulation No 7a of the Council of European Economic Community, of 18 December 1959 (*Official Journal of the European Communities*, No 7, 30 January 1961, p. 71 – Special edition (English edition) 1959-1962, p. 68).

CHAPTER 18

18.01   Cocoa beans, whole or broken, raw or roasted

18.02   Cocoa shells, husks, skins and waste

CHAPTER 20   *Preparations of vegetables, fruit or other parts of plants*

CHAPTER 22

22.04   Grape must, in fermentation or with fermentation arrested otherwise than by the addition of alcohol

22.05   Wine of fresh grapes; grape must with fermentation arrested by the addition of alcohol

22.07   Other fermented beverages (for example, cider, perry and mead)

ex 22.08*
ex 22.09*   Ethyl alcohol or neutral spirits, whether or not denatured, of any strength, obtained from agricultural products listed in Annex II to the Treaty, excluding liqueurs and other spirituous beverages and compound alcoholic preparations (known as 'concentrated extracts') for the manufacture of beverages

ex 22.10*   Vinegar and substitutes for vinegar

---

* Heading added by Article 1 of Regulation No 7a of the Council of the European Community, of 18 December 1959 (*Official Journal of the European Communities,* No 7, 30 January 1961, p. 71 – Special edition (English edition) 1959-1962, p. 68).

CHAPTER 23 *Residues and waste from the food industries; prepared animal fodder*

CHAPTER 24

24.01 Unmanufactured tobacco, tobacco refuse

CHAPTER 45

45.01 Natural cork, unworked, crushed, granulated or ground; waste cork

CHAPTER 54

54.01 Flax, raw or processed but not spun; flax tow and waste (including pulled or garnetted rags)

CHAPTER 57

57.01 True hemp *(Cannabis sativa),* raw or processed but not spun; tow and waste of true hemp (including pulled or garnetted rags or ropes)

LIST OF INVISIBLE TRANSACTIONS

referred to in Article 106 of this Treaty

— Maritime freights, including chartering, harbour expenses, disbursements for fishing vessels, etc.

— Inland waterway freights, including chartering.

— Road transport: passengers and freights, including chartering.

— Air transport: passengers and freights, including chartering.

> Payment by passengers of international air tickets and excess luggage charges; payment of international air freight charges and chartered flights.

> Receipts from the sale of international air tickets, excess luggage charges, international air freight charges, and chargered flights.

— For all means of maritime transport: harbour services (bunkering and provisioning, maintenance, repairs, expenses for crews, etc.).

For all means of inland waterway transport: harbour services (bunkering and provisioning, maintenance and minor repairs of equipment, expenses for crews, etc.).

For all means of commercial road transport: fuel, oil, minor repairs, garaging, expenses for drivers and crews, etc.

For all means of air transport: operating costs and general overheads, including repairs to aircraft and to air transport equipment.

— Warehousing and storage charges, customs clearance.

— Customs duties and fees.

— Transit charges.

— Repair and assembly charges.

Processing, finishing, processing of work under contract, and other services of the same nature.

— Repair of ships.

Repair of means of transport other than ships and aircraft.

— Technical assistance (assistance relating to the production and distribution of goods and services at all stages, given over a period limited according to the specific purpose of such assistance, and including e.g. advice or visits by experts, preparation of plans and blueprints, supervision of manufacture, market research, training of personnel).

— Commission and brokerage.

Profits arising out of transit operations or sales of transhipment.

Banking commissions and charges.

Representation expenses.

— Advertising by all media.

— Business travel.

— Participation by subsidiary companies and branches in overhead expenses of parent companies situated abroad and vice-versa.

— Contracting (construction and maintenance of buildings, roads,

476

bridges, ports, etc. carried out by specialized firms, and, generally, at fixed prices after open tender).

— Differences, margins and deposits due in respect of operations on commodity terminal markets in conformity with normal bona fide commercial practice.

— Tourism.

— Travel for private reasons (education).

— Travel for private reasons (health).

— Travel for private reasons (family).

— Subscriptions to newspapers, periodicals, books, musical publications.

  Newspapers, periodicals, books, musical publications and records.

— Printed films, commercial, documentary, educational, etc. (rentals, dues, subscriptions, reproduction and synchronization fees, etc.).

— Membership fees.

— Current maintenance and repair of private property abroad.

— Government expenditure (official representation abroad, contributions to international organizations).

— Taxes, court expenses, registration fees for patents and trade marks.

  Claims for damages.

  Refunds in the case of cancellation of contracts and refunds of uncalled-for payments.

  Fines.

— Periodical settlements in connection with public transport and postal, telegraphic and telephone services.

— Exchange authorizations granted to own or foreign national emigrating.

Exchange authorization granted to own or foreign nationals returning to their country of origin.

— Salaries and wages (of frontier or seasonal workers and of other non-residents, without prejudice to the right of a country to regulate terms of employment of foreign nationals).

— Emigrants' remittances (without prejudice to the right of a country to regulate immigration).

— Fees.

— Dividends and shares in profits.

— Interest on debentures, mortgages, etc.

— Rent.

— Contractual amortization (with the exception of transfers in connection with amortization having the character either of anticipated repayments or of the discharge of accumulated arrears).

— Profits from business activity.

— Authors' royalties.

Patents, designs, trade marks and inventions (the assignment and licensing of patent rights, designs, trade marks and inventions, whether or not legally protected, and transfers arising out of such assignment or licensing).

— Consular receipts.

— Pensions and other income of a similar nature.

Maintenance payments resulting from a legal obligation or from a decision of a court and financial assistance in cases of hardship.

Transfers by instalments of assets deposited in one member country by persons residing in another member country whose personal income in that country is not sufficient to cover their living expenses.

— Transactions and transfers in connection with direct insurance.

— Transactions and transfers in connection with reinsurance and retrocession.

— Opening and reimbursement of commercial or industrial credits.

— Transfers of minor amounts abroad.

— Charges for documentation of all kinds incurred on their own account by authorized dealers in foreign exchange.

— Sports prizes and racing earnings.

— Inheritances.

— Dowries.

ANNEX IV

OVERSEAS COUNTRIES AND TERRITORIES

to which the provisions of Part IV of this Treaty apply[1, 2, 3]

French West Africa: Senegal, French Sudan, French Guinea, Ivory Coast, Dahomey, Mauritania, Niger and Upper Volta;[4]

EDITORIAL NOTES:

[1] As amended by
  — Article 1 of the Convention of 13 November 1962 amending the Treaty establishing the European Economic Community, (*Official Journal of the European Communities*, No 150, 1 October 1964, p. 2414) and
  — Article 24 (2) of the Act of Accession DK/IRL/UK, modified by Article 13 of the AD AA DK/IRL/UK,
  — The Treaty of 13 March 1984 amending, with regard to Greenland, the Treaties establishing the European Communities (*Official Journal of the European Communities*, No L 29, 1 February 1985).

[2] Council Decision 86/283/EEC of 30 June 1986 on the association of the overseas countries and territories with the European Economic Community (*Official Journal of the European Communities*, No L 175, 1 July 1986) contains a list of overseas countries and territories to which the provisions of Part Four of the Treaty apply.

[3] The provisions of Part Four of the Treaty applied to Surinam, by virtue of a Supplementary Act of the Kingdom of the Netherlands to complete its instruments of ratification, from 1 September 1962 to 16 July 1976.

[4] The provisions of Part Four of the Treaty no longer apply to these countries and territories, which have become independent and whose names may have been changed.
  The relations between the European Economic Community and certain African States and Madagascar were the subject of the Conventions of Association signed at Yaoundé on 20 July 1963 and 29 July 1969. The relations with certain African, Caribbean and Pacific States were subsequently the subject of:
  — the ACP-EEC Convention of Lomé, signed on 28 February 1975 (*Official Journal of the European Communities*, No L 25, 30 January 1976), which entered into force on 1 April 1976,
  — the Second ACP-EEC Convention, signed at Lomé on 31 October 1979 (*Official Journal of the European Communities*, No L 347, 22 December 1980), which entered into force on 1 January 1981,
  — the Third ACP-EEC Convention, signed at Lomé on 8 December 1984 (*Official Journal of the European Communities*, No L 86, 31 March 1986), which entered into force on 1 May 1986.

French Equatorial Africa: Middle Congo, Ubangi-Shari, Chad and Gabon;[1]

Saint Pierre and Miquelon,[2] the Comoro Archipelago,[3] Madagascar[1] and dependencies,[1] French Somaliland,[1] New Caledonia and dependencies, French Settlements in Oceania,[4] Southern and Antarctic Territories;[5]

The autonomous Republic of Togoland;[1]

The trust territory of the Cameroons under French administration;[1]

The Belgian Congo and Ruanda-Urundi;[1]

The trust territory of Somaliland under Italian administration;[1]

Netherlands New Guinea;[1]

The Netherlands Antilles;[6]

Anglo-French Condominium of the New Hebrides;[1]

EDITORIAL NOTES:

[1] See footnote 4 on the previous page.

[2] Has become a French overseas department.

[3] The provisions of Part Four of the Treaty no longer apply to this Archipelago, except for the territorial collectivity of Mayotte which has remained on the list of overseas countries and territories (see footnote 2 on the previous page).

[4] New name: Overseas territory of French Polynesia,
Overseas territory of the Wallis and Futuna Islands.

[5] New name: French Southern and Antarctic Territories.

[6] New name: Overseas countries of the Kingdom of the Netherlands:
— Aruba
— the Netherlands Antilles
— Bonaire,
— Curaçao,
— Saba,
— Sint Eustatius,
— Sint Maarten.

The Bahamas;[1]

Bermuda;[2]

Brunei;[3]

Associated States in the Caribbean: Antigua, Dominica, Grenada, St Lucia, St Vincent, St Christopher, Nevis, Anguilla;[4]

British Honduras;[1]

Cayman Islands;

Falkland Islands and Dependencies;[5]

Gilbert and Ellice Islands;[1]

Central and Southern Line Islands;[2]

British Solomon Islands;[1]

Turks and Caicos Islands;

British Virgin Islands;

Montserrat;

EDITORIAL NOTES:

[1] See footnote 4 on the first page of this Annex.

[2] These territories are not included in the overseas countries and territories covered by Council Decision 86/283/EEC of 30 June 1986 (see footnote 2 on the first page of this Annex).

[3] The provisions of Part Four of the Treaty no longer apply to this territory, which became independent on 31 December 1983.

[4] The associated States, as a constitutional group, no longer exist. All the component territories have become independent, except Anguilla, to which the provisions of Part Four of the Treaty continue to apply.

[5] The dependencies of the Falkland Islands changed their name to South Georgia and the South Sandwich Islands on 3 October 1985 on ceasing to be dependencies of the Falkland Islands.

Pitcairn;

St Helena and Dependencies;

The Seychelles;[1]

British Antarctic Territory;

British Indian Ocean Territory;

Greenland.[2]

---

[1] See footnote 4 on the first page of this Annex.

[2] Entry added by Article 4 of the Greenland Treaty.

II — PROTOCOLS

Protocol
on the Statute of
the European Investment Bank

THE HIGH CONTRACTING PARTIES,

DESIRING to lay down the Statute of the European Investment Bank provided for in Article 129 of this Treaty,

HAVE AGREED upon the following provisions, which shall be annexed to this Treaty:

Article 1

The European Investment Bank established by Article 129 of this Treaty (hereinafter called the 'Bank') is hereby constituted; it shall perform its functions and carry on its activities in accordance with the provisions of this Treaty and of this Statute.

The seat of the Bank shall be determined by common accord of the Governments of the Member States.

Article 2

The task of the Bank shall be that defined in Article 130 of this Treaty.

Article 3*

In accordance with Article 129 of this Treaty, the following shall be members of the Bank:

— the Kingdom of Belgium;

— the Kingdom of Denmark;

— the Federal Republic of Germany;

— the Hellenic Republic;

— the Kingdom of Spain;

---

* Text as replaced by Article 1 of Protocol No 1 annexed to the Act of Accession ESP/PORT.

— the French Republic;

— Ireland;

— the Italian Republic;

— the Grand Duchy of Luxembourg;

— the Kingdom of the Netherlands;

— the Portuguese Republic;

— the United Kingdom of Great Britain and Northern Ireland.

Article 4

1. The capital of the Bank shall be twenty-eight thousand eight hundred million ECU, subscribed by the Member States as follows:

Germany	5 508 725 000
France	5 508 725 000
Italy	5 508 725 000
United Kingdom	5 508 725 000
Spain	2 024 928 000
Belgium	1 526 980 000
Netherlands	1 526 980 000
Denmark	773 154 000
Greece	414 190 000
Portugal	266 922 000
Ireland	193 288 000
Luxembourg	38 658 000*

The unit of account shall be defined as being the ECU used by the European Communities.** The Board of Governors, acting unanimously

---

* First subparagraph of paragraph 1 as replaced by Article 2 of Protocol No 1 annexed to the Act of Accession ESP/PORT.

** Second subparagraph of paragraph 1 as amended by the Decision of the Board of Governors of 13 May 1981 (*Official Journal of the European Communities*, No L 311, 30 October 1981).

on a proposal from the Board of Directors, may alter the definition of the unit of account.*

The Member States shall be liable only up to the amount of their share of the capital subscribed and not paid up.

2. The admission of a new member shall entail an increase in the subscribed capital corresponding to the capital brought in by the new member.

3. The Board of Governors may, acting unanimously, decide to increase the subscribed capital.

4. The share of a member in the subscribed capital may not be transferred, pledged or attached.

Article 5

1. The subscribed capital shall be paid in by Member States to the extent of 9.01367457 % on average of the amounts laid down in Article 4 (1).**

2. In the event of an increase in the subscribed capital, the Board of Governors, acting unanimously, shall fix the percentage to be paid up and the arrangements for payment.***

3. The Board of Directors may require payment of the balance of the

---

* Second subparagraph of paragraph 1 as supplemented by Article 1 of the Treaty amending the Protocol on the Statute of the Bank.

** Paragraph 1 as replaced by Article 3 of Protocol No 1 annexed to the Act of Accession ESP/PORT.

*** Paragraph 2 as replaced by Article 3 of Protocol No 1 annexed to the Act of Accession DK/IRL/UK.

subscribed capital, to such extent as may be required for the Bank to meet its obligations towards those who have made loans to it.

Each Member State shall make this payment in proportion to its share of the subscribed capital in the currencies required by the Bank to meet these obligations.*

Article 6

1. The Board of Governors may, acting by a qualified majority on a proposal from the Board of Directors, decide that Member States shall grant the Bank special interest-bearing loans if and to the extent that the Bank requires such loans to finance specific projects and the Board of Directors shows that the Bank is unable to obtain the necessary funds on the capital markets on terms appropriate to the nature and purpose of the projects to be financed.

2. Special loans may not be called for until the beginning of the fourth year after the entry into force of this Treaty. They shall not exceed 400 million units of account in the aggregate or 100 million units of account per annum.

3. The term of special loans shall be related to the term of the loans or guarantees which the Bank proposes to grant by means of the special loans; it shall not exceed twenty years. The Board of Governors may, acting by a qualified majority on a proposal from the Board of Directors, decide upon the prior repayment of special loans.

4. Special loans shall bear interest at 4 % per annum, unless the Board of Governors, taking into account the trend and level of interest rates on the capital markets, decides to fix a different rate.

----

* Paragraph 3 as replaced by Article 3 of Protocol No 1 annexed to the Act of Accession DK/IRL/UK.

5.   Special loans shall be granted by Member States in proportion to their share in the subscribed capital; payment shall be made in national currency within six months of such loans being called for.

6.   Should the Bank go into liquidation, special loans granted by Member States shall be repaid only after the other debts of the Bank have been settled.

Article 7*

1.   Should the value of the currency of a Member State in relation to the unit of account defined in Article 4 be reduced, that State shall adjust the amount of its capital share paid in in its own currency in proportion to the change in value by making a supplementary payment to the Bank.

2.   Should the value of the currency of a Member State in relation to the unit of account defined in Article 4 be increased, the Bank shall adjust the amount of the capital share paid in by that State in its own currency in proportion to the change in value by making a repayment to that State.

3.   For the purpose of this Article, the value of the currency of a Member State in relation to the unit of account, defined in Article 4, shall correspond to the rate for converting the unit of account into this currency and vice versa based on market rates.

4.   The Board of Governors, acting unanimously on a proposal from the

---

* Article as amended by Article 3 of Protocol No 1 annexed to the Act of Accession GR.

Board of Directors, may alter the method of converting sums expressed in units of account into national currencies and vice versa.

Furthermore, acting unanimously on a proposal from the Board of Directors, it may define the method for adjusting the capital referred to in paragraphs 1 and 2 of this Article; adjustment payments must be made at least once a year.

Article 8

The Bank shall be directed and managed by a Board of Governors, a Board of Directors and a Management Committee.

Article 9

1. The Board of Governors shall consist of the Ministers designated by the Member States.

2. The Board of Governors shall lay down general directives for the credit policy of the Bank, with particular reference to the objectives to be pursued as progress is made in the attainment of the common market.

The Board of Governors shall ensure that these directives are implemented.

3. The Board of Governors shall in addition:

(a) decide whether to increase the subscribed capital in accordance with Article 4 (3) and Article 5 (2);*

---

* Subparagraphs (a) and (c) as amended by Article 4 of Protocol No 1 annexed to the Act of Accession DK/IRL/UK.

(b) exercise the powers provided in Article 6 in respect of special loans;

(c) exercise the powers provided in Articles 11 and 13 in respect of the appointment and the compulsory retirement of the members of the Board of Directors and of the Management Committee, and those powers provided in the second subparagraph of Article 13 (1);*

(d) authorize the derogation provided for in Article 18 (1);

(e) approve the annual report of the Board of Directors;

(f) approve the annual balance sheet and profit and loss account;

(g) exercise the powers and functions provided in Articles 4, 7, 14, 17, 26 and 27;**

(h) approve the rules of procedure of the Bank.

4. Within the framework of this Treaty and this Statute, the Board of Governors shall be competent to take, acting unanimously, any decisions concerning the suspension of the operations of the Bank and, should the event arise, its liquidation.

Article 10***

Save as otherwise provided in this Statute, decisions of the Board of Governors shall be taken by a majority of its members. This majority must

---

* Subparagraphs *(a)* and *(c)* as amended by Article 4 of Protocol No 1 annexed to the Act of Accession DK/IRL/UK.
** Subparagraph *(g)* as amended by Article 3 of the Treaty amending the Protocol on the Statute of the Bank.
*** Article as amended by Article 4 of Protocol No 1 annexed to the Act of Accession ESP/PORT.

represent at least 45 % of the subscribed capital. Voting by the Board of Governors shall be in accordance with the provisions of Article 148 of this Treaty.

Article 11

1. The Board of Directors shall have sole power to take decisions in respect of granting loans and guarantees and raising loans; it shall fix the interest rates on loans granted and the commission on guarantees; it shall see that the Bank is properly run; it shall ensure that the Bank is managed in accordance with the provisions of this Treaty and of this Statute and with the general directives laid down by the Board of Governors.

At the end of the financial year the Board of Directors shall submit a report to the Board of Governors and shall publish it when approved.

2. The Board of Directors shall consist of 22 directors and 12 alternates.*

The directors shall be appointed by the Board of Governors for five years as shown below:

— three directors nominated by the Federal Republic of Germany,

— three directors nominated by the French Republic,

— three directors nominated by the Italian Republic,

— three directors nominated by the United Kingdom of Great Britain and Northern Ireland,

— two directors nominated by the Kingdom of Spain,

---

* First, second and third subparagraphs of paragraph 2 as amended by Article 5 of Protocol No 1 annexed to the Act of Accession ESP/PORT.

- one director nominated by the Kingdom of Belgium,

- one director nominated by the Kingdom of Denmark,

- one director nominated by the Hellenic Republic,

- one director nominated by Ireland,

- one director nominated by the Grand Duchy of Luxembourg,

- one director nominated by the Kingdom of the Netherlands,

- one director nominated by the Portuguese Republic,

- one director nominated by the Commission.*

The alternates shall be appointed by the Board of Governors for five years as shown below:

- two alternates nominated by the Federal Republic of Germany,

- two alternates nominated by the French Republic,

- two alternates nominated by the Italian Republic,

- two alternates nominated by the United Kingdom of Great Britain and Northern Ireland,

- one alternate nominated by common accord of the Kingdom of Denmark, the Hellenic Republic and Ireland,

- one alternate nominated by common accord of the Benelux countries,

- one alternate nominated by common accord of the Kingdom of Spain and the Portuguese Republic,

- one alternate nominated by the Commission.*

---

* First, second and third subparagraphs of paragraph 2 as amended by Article 5 of Protocol No 1 annexed to the Act of Accession ESP/PORT.

The appointments of the directors and the alternates shall be renewable.*

Alternates may take part in the meetings of the Board of Directors. Alternates nominated by a State, or by common accord of several States, or by the Commission, may replace directors nominated by that State, by one of those States or by the Commission respectively. Alternates shall have no right of vote except where they replace one director or more than one director or where they have been delegated for this purpose in accordance with Article 12 (1).*

The President of the Management Committee or, in his absence, one of the Vice-Presidents, shall preside over meetings of the Board of Directors but shall not vote.

Members of the Board of Directors shall be chosen from persons whose independence and competence are beyond doubt; they shall be responsible only to the Bank.

3.   A director may be compulsorily retired by the Board of Governors only if he no longer fulfils the conditions required for the performance of his duties; the Board must act by a qualified majority.

If the annual report is not approved, the Board of Directors shall resign.

4.   Any vacancy arising as a result of death, voluntary resignation, compulsory retirement or collective resignation shall be filled in accordance with paragraph 2. A member shall be replaced for the remainder of his term of office, save where the entire Board of Directors is being replaced.

---

* Fourth and fifth subparagraphs of paragraph 2 as amended by Article 6 of Protocol No 1 annexed to the Act of Accession DK/IRL/UK in the version resulting from Article 37 of the AD AA DK/IRL/UK.

5. The Board of Governors shall determine the remuneration of members of the Board of Directors. The Board of Governors shall, acting unanimously, lay down what activities are incompatible with the duties of a director or an alternate.

Article 12

1. Each director shall have one vote on the Board of Directors. He may delegate his vote in all cases, according to procedures to be laid down in the rules of procedure of the Bank.*

2. Save as otherwise provided in this Statute, decisions of the Board of Directors shall be taken by a simple majority of the members entitled to vote. A qualified majority shall require fifteen votes in favour.** The rules of procedure of the Bank shall lay down how many members of the Board of Directors constitute the quorum needed for the adoption of decisions.

Article 13

1. The Management Committee shall consist of a President and six Vice-Presidents appointed for a period of six years by the Board of Governors on a proposal from the Board of Directors. Their appointments shall be renewable.***

The Board of Governors, acting unanimously, may vary the number of members on the Management Committee.****

2. On a proposal from the Board of Directors adopted by a qualified ma-

---

* Paragraph 1 as amended by Article 7 of Protocol No 1 annexed to the Act of Accession DK/IRL/UK.

** Second sentence of paragraph 2 as amended by Article 6 of Protocol No 1 annexed to the Act of Accession ESP/PORT.

*** First subparagraph of paragraph 1 as amended by Article 7 of Protocol No 1 annexed to the Act of Accession ESP/PORT.

**** Second subparagraph of paragraph 1 as amended by Article 9 of Protocol No 1 annexed to the Act of Accession DK/IRL/UK.

jority, the Board of Governors may, acting in its turn by a qualified majority, compulsorily retire a member of the Management Committee.

3. The Management Committee shall be responsible for the current business of the Bank, under the authority of the President and the supervision of the Board of Directors.

It shall prepare the decisions of the Board of Directors, in particular decisions on the raising of loans and the granting of loans and guarantees; it shall ensure that these decisions are implemented.

4. The Management Committee shall act by a majority when delivering opinions on proposals for raising loans or granting loans and guarantees.

5. The Board of Governors shall determine the remuneration of members of the Management Committee and shall lay down what activities are incompatible with their duties.

6. The President or, if he is prevented, a Vice-President shall represent the Bank in judicial and other matters.

7. The officials and other employees of the Bank shall be under the authority of the President. They shall be engaged and discharged by him. In the selection of staff, account shall be taken not only of personal ability and qualifications but also of an equitable representation of nationals of Member States.

8. The Management Committee and the staff of the Bank shall be responsible only to the Bank and shall be completely independent in the performance of their duties.

Article 14

1. A Committee consisting of three members, appointed on the grounds of their competence by the Board of Governors, shall annually verify that the operations of the Bank have been conducted and its books kept in a proper manner.

2. The Committee shall confirm that the balance sheet and profit and loss account are in agreement with the accounts and faithfully reflect the position of the Bank in respect of its assets and liabilities.

Article 15

The Bank shall deal with each Member State through the authority designated by that State. In the conduct of financial operations the Bank shall have recourse to the bank of issue of the Member State concerned or to other financial institutions approved by that State.

Article 16

1. The Bank shall cooperate with all international organizations active in fields similar to its own.

2. The Bank shall seek to establish all appropriate contacts in the interests of cooperation with banking and financial institutions in the countries to which its operations extend.

Article 17

At the request of a Member State or of the Commission, or on its own initiative, the Board of Governors shall, in accordance with the same provisions as governed their adoption, interpret or supplement the directives laid down by it under Article 9 of this Statute.

Article 18

1. Within the framework of the task set out in Article 130 of this Treaty, the Bank shall grant loans to its members or to private or public undertakings for investment projects to be carried out in the European territories of Member States, to the extent that funds are not available from other sources on reasonable terms.

However, by way of derogation authorized by the Board of Governors, acting unanimously on a proposal from the Board of Directors, the Bank may grant loans for investment projects to be carried out, in whole or in part, outside the European territories of Member States.

2.   As far as possible, loans shall be granted only on condition that other sources of finance are also used.

3.   When granting a loan to an undertaking or to a body other than a Member State, the Bank shall make the loan conditional either on a guarantee from the Member State in whose territory the project will be carried out or on other adequate guarantees.

4.   The Bank may guarantee loans contracted by public or private undertakings or other bodies for the purpose of carrying out projects provided for in Article 130 of this Treaty.

5.   The aggregate amount outstanding at any time of loans and guarantees granted by the Bank shall not exceed 250 % of its subscribed capital.

6.   The Bank shall protect itself against exchange risks by including in contracts for loans and guarantees such clauses as it considers appropriate.

Article 19

1.   Interest rates on loans to be granted by the Bank and commission on guarantees shall be adjusted to conditions prevailing on the capital market and shall be calculated in such a way that the income therefrom shall enable the Bank to meet its obligations, to cover its expenses and to build up a reserve fund as provided for in Article 24.

2.   The Bank shall not grant any reduction in interest rates. Where a reduction in the interest rate appears desirable in view of the nature of the

project to be financed, the Member State concerned or some other agency may grant aid towards the payment of interest to the extent that this is compatible with Article 92 of this Treaty.

Article 20

In its loan and guarantee operations, the Bank shall observe the following principles:

1. It shall ensure that its funds are employed as rationally as possible in the interests of the Community.

It may grant loans or guarantees only:

(a) where, in the case of projects carried out by undertakings in the production sector, interest and amortization payments are covered out of operating profits or, in other cases, either by a commitment entered into by the State in which the project is carried out or by some other means; and

(b) where the execution of the project contributes to an increase in economic productivity in general and promotes the attainment of the common market.

2. It shall neither acquire any interest in an undertaking nor assume any responsibility in its management unless this is required to safeguard the rights of the Bank in ensuring recovery of funds lent.

3. It may dispose of its claims on the capital market and may, to this end, require its debtors to issue bonds or other securities.

4. Neither the Bank nor the Member States shall impose conditions requiring funds lent by the Bank to be spent within a specified Member State.

5. The Bank may make its loans conditional on international invitations to tender being arranged.

6. The Bank shall not finance, in whole or in part, any project opposed by the Member State in whose territory it is to be carried out.

Article 21

1. Applications for loans or guarantees may be made to the Bank either through the Commission or through the Member State in whose territory the projcet will be carried out. An undertaking may also apply direct to the Bank for a loan or guarantee.

2. Applications made through the Commission shall be submitted for an opinion to the Member State in whose territory the project will be carried out. Applications made through a Member State shall be submitted to the Commission for an opinion. Applications made direct by an undertaking shall be submitted to the Member State concerned and to the Commission.

The Member State concerned and the Commission shall deliver their opinions within two months. If no reply is received within this period, the Bank may assume that there is no objection to the project in question.

3. The Board of Directors shall rule on applications for loans or guarantees submitted to it by the Management Committee.

4. The Management Committee shall examine whether applications for loans or guarantees submitted to it comply with the provisions of this Statute, in particular with Article 20. Where the Management Committee is in favour of granting the loan or guarantee, it shall submit the draft contract to the Board of Directors; the Committee may make its favourable opinion subject to such conditions as it considers essential. Where the Management Committee is against granting the loan or guarantee, it shall submit the relevant documents together with its opinion to the Board of Directors.

5. Where the Management Committee delivers an unfavourable opinion, the Board of Directors may not grant the loan or guarantee concerned unless its decision is unanimous.

6. Where the Commission delivers an unfavourable opinion, the Board of Directors may not grant the loan or guarantee concerned unless its decision is unanimous, the director nominated by the Commission abstaining.

7. Where both the Management Committee and the Commission deliver an unfavourable opinion, the Board of Directors may not grant the loan or guarantee.

Article 22

1. The Bank shall borrow on the international capital markets the funds necessary for the performance of its tasks.

2. The Bank may borrow on the capital market of a Member State either in accordance with the legal provisions applying to internal issues or, if there are no such provisions in a Member State, after the Bank and the Member State concerned have conferred together and reached agreement on the proposed loan.

The competent authorities in the Member State concerned may refuse to give their assent only if there is reason to fear serious disturbances on the capital market of that State.

Article 23

1. The Bank may employ any available funds which it does not immediately require to meet its obligations in the following ways:

(a) it may invest on the money markets;

(b) it may, subject to the provisions of Article 20 (2), buy and sell securities issued by itself or by those who have borrowed from it;

(c) it may carry out any other financial operation linked with its objectives.

2.   Without prejudice to the provisions of Article 25, the Bank shall not, in managing its investments, engage in any currency arbitrage not directly required to carry out its lending operations or fulfil commitments arising out of loans raised or guarantees granted by it.

3.   The Bank shall, in the fields covered by this Article, act in agreement with the competent authorities or with the bank of issue of the Member State concerned.

Article 24

1.   A reserve fund of up to 10 % of the subscribed capital shall be built up progressively. If the state of the liabilities of the Bank should so justify, the Board of Directors may decide to set aside additional reserves. Until such time as the reserve fund has been fully built up, it shall be fed by:

(a) interest received on loans granted by the Bank out of sums to be paid up by the Member States pursuant to Article 5;

(b) interest received on loans granted by the Bank out of funds derived from repayment of the loans referred to in *(a);*

to the extent that this income is not required to meet the obligations of the Bank or to cover its expenses.

2.   The resources of the reserve fund shall be so invested as to be available at any time to meet the purpose of the fund.

Article 25

1.   The Bank shall at all times be entitled to transfer its assets in the currency of one Member State into the currency of another Member State in

order to carry out financial operations corresponding to the task set out in Article 130 of this Treaty, taking into account the provisions of Article 23 of this Statute. The Bank shall, as far as possible, avoid making such transfers if it has cash or liquid assets in the currency required.

2. The Bank may not convert its assets in the currency of a Member State into the currency of a third country without the agreement of the Member State concerned.

3. The Bank may freely dispose of that part of its capital which is paid up in gold or convertible currency and of any currency borrowed on markets outside the Community.

4. The Member States undertake to make available to the debtors of the Bank the currency needed to repay the capital and pay the interest on loans or commission on guarantees granted by the Bank for projects to be carried out in their territory.

Article 26

If a Member State fails to meet the obligations of membership arising from this Statute, in particular the obligation to pay its share of the subscribed capital, to grant its special loans or to service its borrowings, the granting of loans or guarantees to that Member State or its nationals may be suspended by a decision of the Board of Governors, acting by a qualified majority.

Such decision shall not release either the State or its nationals from their obligations towards the Bank.

Article 27

1. If the Board of Governors decides to suspend the operations of the Bank, all its activities shall cease forthwith, except those required to ensure

the due realization, protection and preservation of its assets and the settlement of its liabilities.

2. In the event of liquidation, the Board of Governors shall appoint the liquidators and give them instructions for carrying out the liquidation.

Article 28

1. In each of the Member States, the Bank shall enjoy the most extensive legal capacity accorded to legal persons under their laws; it may, in particular, acquire or dispose of movable or immovable property and may be a party to legal proceedings.

(Second subparagraph repealed by the second paragraph of Article 28 of the Merger Treaty)

[*See the first paragraph of Article 28 of the Merger Treaty, which reads as follows:*

The European Communities shall enjoy in the territories of the Member States such privileges and immunities as are necessary for the performance of their tasks, under the conditions laid down in the Protocol annexed to this Treaty. The same shall apply to the European Investment Bank.]

2. The property of the Bank shall be exempt from all forms of requisition or expropriation.

Article 29

Disputes between the Bank on the one hand, and its creditors, debtors or any other person on the other, shall be decided by the competent national courts, save where jurisdiction has been conferred on the Court of Justice.

The Bank shall have an address for service in each Member State. It may, however, in any contract, specify a particular address for service or provide for arbitration.

The property and assets of the Bank shall not be liable to attachment or to seizure by way of execution except by decision of a court.

Done at Rome this twenty-fifth day of March in the year one thousand nine hundred and fifty-seven.

P. H. SPAAK	J. Ch. SNOY ET D'OPPUERS
ADENAUER	HALLSTEIN
PINEAU	M. FAURE
Antonio SEGNI	Gaetano MARTINO
BECH	Lambert SCHAUS
J. LUNS	J. LINTHORST HOMAN

Protocol
on German internal trade
and connected problems

THE HIGH CONTRACTING PARTIES,

CONSIDERING the conditions at present existing by reason of the division of Germany,

HAVE AGREED upon the following provisions, which shall be annexed to this Treaty:

1. Since trade between the German territories subject to the Basic Law for the Federal Republic of Germany and the German territories in which the Basic Law does not apply is a part of German internal trade, the application of this Treaty in Germany requires no change in the treatment currently accorded this trade.

2. Each Member State shall inform the other Member States and the Commission of any agreements relating to trade with the German territories in which the Basic Law for the Federal Republic of Germany does not apply, and of any implementing provisions. Each Member State shall ensure that the implementation of such agreements does not conflict with the principles of the common market and shall in particular take appropriate measures to avoid harming the economies of the other Member States.

3. Each Member State may take appropriate measures to prevent any difficulties arising for it from trade between another Member State and the German territories in which the Basic Law for the Federal Republic of Germany does not apply.

Done at Rome this twenty-fifth day of March in the year one thousand nine hundred and fifty-seven.

P. H. SPAAK	J. Ch. SNOY ET D'OPPUERS
ADENAUER	HALLSTEIN
PINEAU	M. FAURE
Antonio SEGNI	Gaetano MARTINO
BECH	Lambert SCHAUS
J. LUNS	J. LINTHORST HOMAN

Protocol
on certain provisions
relating to France

THE HIGH CONTRACTING PARTIES,

DESIRING to settle in accordance with the general objectives of this Treaty certain particular problems existing at the present time,

HAVE AGREED upon the following provisions, which shall be annexed to this Treaty:

I — Charges and aids

1. The Commission and the Council shall annually examine the system of aid to exports and of special charges on imports in force in the franc area.

The French Government shall, at the time of this examination, make known the measures it proposes to take to reduce and rationalize the level of the aids and charges.

It shall also inform the Council and the Commission of any new charges which it intends to introduce as a result of further liberalization and of any adjustments to the aids and charges which it intends to make within the limit of the maximum rate of charge in force on 1 January 1957. These various measures may be discussed within those institutions.

2. If it considers that the lack of uniformity is prejudicial to certain sectors of industry in other Member States, the Council may, acting by a qualified majority on a proposal from the Commission, request the French Government to take certain measures to standardize the charges and aids in each of the following three categories; raw materials, semi-finished products and finished products. If the French Government does not take such measures, the Council shall, again by a qualified majority, authorize the other Member States to take protective measures, the conditions and details of which it shall determine.

3.   Where the balance of current payments of the franc area has remained in equilibrium for more than one year, and where its monetary reserves have reached a level which is to be considered satisfactory, in particular as regards the volume of its external trade, the Council may, acting by a qualified majority on a proposal from the Commission, decide that the French Government must abolish the system of charges and aids.

If the Commission and the French Government do not agree on the question whether the level of the monetary reserves of the franc area can be considered satisfactory, they shall refer the matter for an opinion to a person or body chosen by common accord as arbitrator. In the event of disagreement, the arbitrator shall be designated by the President of the Court of Justice.

If it is decided that the system of charges and aids must be abolished, this shall be done in such a manner as to avoid risk of disturbance to the equilibrium of the balance of payments; it may, in particular, be done progressively. Once the system has been abolished, the provisions of this Treaty shall apply in their entirety.

The expression 'balance of current payments' shall have the meaning given to it by international organizations and by the International Monetary Fund; it shall comprise the trade balance and the invisible transactions which have the character of income or services.

II — Payment for overtime

1.   The Member States consider that the establishment of the common market will result, by the end of the first stage, in a situation in

which the basic number of hours beyond which overtime is paid for and the average rate of additional payment for overtime in industry will correspond to the average obtaining in France in 1956.

2. If this situation does not come about by the end of the first stage, the Commission shall authorize France to take, in respect of the sectors of industry affected by disparities in the method of payment for overtime, protective measures, the conditions and details of which the Commission shall determine, unless, during this stage, the average increase in the wage level in the same sectors of industry in other Member States, by comparison with the average for 1956, exceeds the increase which has occurred in France by a percentage fixed by the Commission with the approval of the Council acting by a qualified majority.

Done at Rome this twenty-fifth day of March in the year one thousand nine hundred and fifty-seven.

P. H. SPAAK	J. Ch. SNOY ET D'OPPUERS
ADENAUER	HALLSTEIN
PINEAU	M. FAURE
Antonio SEGNI	Gaetano MARTINO
BECH	Lambert SCHAUS
J. LUNS	J. LINTHORST HOMAN

Protocol on Italy

THE HIGH CONTRACTING PARTIES,

DESIRING to settle certain particular problems relating to Italy,

HAVE AGREED upon the following provisions, which shall be annexed to this Treaty:

THE MEMBER STATES OF THE COMMUNITY

TAKE NOTE of the fact that the Italian Government is carrying out a ten-year programme of economic expansion designed to rectify the disequilibria in the structure of the Italian economy, in particular by providing an infrastructure for the less developed areas in southern Italy and in the Italian islands and by creating new jobs in order to eliminate unemployment;

RECALL that the principles and objectives of this programme of the Italian Government have been considered and approved by organizations for international cooperation of which the Member States are members;

RECOGNIZE that it is in their common interest that the objectives of the Italian programme should be attained;

AGREE, in order to facilitate the accomplishment of this task by the Italian Government, to recommend to the institutions of the Community that they should employ all the methods and procedures provided in this Treaty and, in particular, make appropriate use of the resources of the European Investment Bank and the European Social Fund;

ARE OF THE OPINION that the institutions of the Community should, in applying this Treaty, take account of the sustained effort to be made by the Italian economy in the coming years and of the desirability of avoiding dangerous stresses in particular within the balance of payments or the level of employment, which might jeopardize the application of this Treaty in Italy;

RECOGNIZE that in the event of Articles 108 and 109 being applied it will be necessary to take care that any measures required of the Italian Government do not prejudice the completion of its programme for economic expansion and for raising the standard of living of the population.

Done at Rome this twenty-fifth day of March in the year one thousand nine hundred and fifty-seven.

P. H. SPAAK	J. Ch. SNOY ET D'OPPUERS
ADENAUER	HALLSTEIN
PINEAU	M. FAURE
Antonio SEGNI	Gaetano MARTINO
BECH	Lambert SCHAUS
J. LUNS	J. LINTHORST HOMAN

Protocol

on

the Grand Duchy of Luxembourg

THE HIGH CONTRACTING PARTIES,

DESIRING to settle certain particular problems relating to the Grand Duchy of Luxembourg,

HAVE AGREED upon the following provisions, which shall be annexed to this Treaty:

Article 1

1. By reason of the special position of its agriculture, the Grand Duchy of Luxembourg is hereby authorized to maintain quantitative restrictions on imports of the products included in the list annexed to the Decision of the Contracting Parties to the General Agreement on Tariffs and Trade of 3 December 1955 concerning the agriculture of Luxembourg.

Belgium, Luxembourg and the Netherlands shall apply the system provided for in the third paragraph of Article 6 of the Convention on the Economic Union of Belgium and Luxembourg of 25 July 1921.

2. The Grand Duchy of Luxembourg shall take all measures of a structural, technical or economic nature that will make possible the progressive integration of its agriculture in the common market. The Commission may make recommendations to the Grand Duchy concerning the measures to be taken.

At the end of the transitional period the Council shall, acting by a qualified majority on a proposal from the Commission, decide to what extent the derogations accorded the Grand Duchy of Luxembourg shall be maintained, altered or terminated.

Any Member State concerned may appeal against this decision to an arbitration board appointed in accordance with Article 8 (4) of this Treaty.

Article 2

When framing the regulations on freedom of movement for workers provided for in Article 48 (3) of this Treaty, the Commission shall take account, as regards the Grand Duchy of Luxembourg, of the special demographic situation in that country.

Done at Rome this twenty-fifth day of March in the year one thousand nine hundred and fifty-seven.

P. H. SPAAK	J. Ch. SNOY ET D'OPPUERS
ADENAUER	HALLSTEIN
PINEAU	M. FAURE
Antonio SEGNI	Gaetano MARTINO
BECH	Lambert SCHAUS
J. LUNS	J. LINTHORST HOMAN

Protocol
on goods originating in
and coming from certain countries
and enjoying special treatment
when imported into a Member State

THE HIGH CONTRACTING PARTIES

DESIRING to define in greater detail the application of this Treaty to certain goods originating in and coming from certain countries and enjoying special treatment when imported into a Member State,

HAVE AGREED upon the following provisions, which shall be annexed to this Treaty:

1. The application of the Treaty establishing the European Economic Community shall not require any alteration in the customs treatment applicable, at the time of the entry into force of this Treaty, to imports:

(a) into the Benelux countries of goods originating in and coming from Surinam* or the Netherlands Antilles;**

(b) into France of goods originating in and coming from Morocco, Tunisia, the Republic of Vietnam, Cambodia or Laos. This shall also apply to the French Settlements in the Condominium of the New Hebrides;***

(c) into Italy of goods originating in and coming from Libya or the Trust Territory of Somaliland currently under Italian administration.****

---

  * This provisions of Part Four of the Treaty were applied to Surinam, by virtue of a Supplementary Act of the Kingdom of the Netherlands to complete its instrument of ratification, from 1 September 1962 to 16 July 1976.
  ** In accordance with Article 1 of the Convention of 13 November 1962 amending the Treaty establishing the European Economic Community (*Official Journal of the European Communities,* No 150, 1 October 1964, p. 2414), the protocol no longer applies to the Netherlands Antilles.
  *** See Annex IV of the Treaty, p. 481 *et seq.* of this volume.
  **** These two countries have become independent.

2. Goods imported into a Member State and benefiting from the treatment referred to above shall not be considered to be in free circulation in that State within the meaning of Article 10 of this Treaty when re-exported to another Member State.

3. Before the end of the first year after the entry into force of this Treaty, Member States shall communicate to the Commission and to the other Member States their rules governing the special treatment referred to in this Protocol, together with a list of the goods entitled to such treatment.

They shall also inform the Commission and the other Member States of any changes subsequently made in those lists or in the treatment.

4. The Commission shall ensure that the application of these rules cannot be prejudicial to other Member States; to this end it may take any appropriate measures as regards relations between Member States.

Done at Rome this twenty-fifth day of March in the year one thousand nine hundred and fifty-seven.

P. H. Spaak	J. Ch. Snoy et d'Oppuers
Adenauer	Hallstein
Pineau	M. Faure
Antonio Segni	Gaetano Martino
Bech	Lambert Schaus
J. Luns	J. Linthorst Homan

Protocol
on the treatment to be applied to
products within the province of
the European
Coal and Steel Community
in respect of Algeria
and the Overseas Departments
of the French Republic

THE HIGH CONTRACTING PARTIES,

CONSCIOUS of the fact that the provisions of this Treaty relating to Algeria and the overseas departments of the French Republic raise the problem of the treatment to be applied, in respect of Algeria and those departments, to products covered by the Treaty establishing the European Coal and Steel Community.

DESIRING to seek an appropriate solution in harmony with the principles of the two Treaties,

UNDERTAKE to settle this problem in a spirit of mutual cooperation within the shortest possible time and not later than the first revision of the Treaty establishing the European Coal and Steel Community.

Done at Rome this twenty-fifth day of March in the year one thousand nine hundred and fifty-seven.

P. H. SPAAK	J. Ch. SNOY ET D'OPPUERS
ADENAUER	HALLSTEIN
PINEAU	M. FAURE
Antonio SEGNI	Gaetano MARTINO
BECH	Lambert SCHAUS
J. LUNS	J. LINTHORST HOMAN

Protocol
on mineral oils
and certain of their derivatives

Have agreed upon the following provisions, which shall be annexed to this Treaty:

1. Each Member State may, for a period of six years after this Treaty enters into force, maintain in regard to other Member States and third countries the customs duties and charges having equivalent effect applied to products falling within headings Nos 27.09, 27.10, 27.11, 27.12 and ex 27.13 (paraffin wax, microcrystalline wax, slack wax and scale wax) of the Brussels Nomenclature on 1 January 1957 or, if lower, on the date when this Treaty enters into force. The duty to be maintained on crude oils shall not, however, be such as to result in an increase of more than 5 % in the difference existing on 1 January 1957 between the duties on crude oils and those on the derivatives referred to above. Where no such difference exists, any difference subsequently introduced shall not exceed 5 % of the duty which applied on 1 January 1957 to products falling within heading No 27.09. If, before the end of this period of six years, a reduction is made in the customs duties or charges having equivalent effect in respect of products falling within heading No 27.09, a corresponding reduction shall be made in any customs duties or charges having equivalent effect imposed on the other products referred to above.

At the end of this period, the duties maintained in accordance with the preceding subparagraph shall be completely abolished in respect of other Member States. At the same time, the common customs tariff shall be applicable to third countries.

2. Any aids to the production of mineral oils falling within heading No 27.09 of the Brussels Nomenclature shall, where such aids prove necessary in order to bring the price of crude oils down to the world market price cif European port of a Member State, be governed by Article 92 (3) *(c)* of this Treaty. The Commission shall, during the first two stages, make use of the powers provided under Article 93 only to the extent required to prevent such aids being misused.

Done at Rome this twenty-fifth day of March in the year one thousand nine hundred and fifty-seven.

P. H. Spaak	J. Ch. Snoy et d'Oppuers
Adenauer	Hallstein
Pineau	M. Faure
Antonio Segni	Gaetano Martino
Bech	Lambert Schaus
J. Luns	J. Linthorst Homan

Protocol
on the application of the Treaty
establishing
the European Economic Community
to the non-European parts
of the Kingdom of the Netherlands

THE HIGH CONTRACTING PARTIES,

ANXIOUS, at the time of signature of the Treaty establishing the European Economic Community, to define the scope of the provisions of Article 227 of this Treaty in respect of the Kingdom of the Netherlands,

HAVE AGREED upon the following provisions, which shall be annexed to this Treaty:

The Government of the Kingdom of the Netherlands, by reason of the constitutional structure of the Kingdom resulting from the Statute of 29 December 1954, shall, by way of derogation from Article 227, be entitled to ratify the Treaty on behalf of the Kingdom in Europe and Netherlands New Guinea only.

Done at Rome this twenty-fifth day of March in the year one thousand nine hundred and fifty-seven.

P. H. SPAAK	J. Ch. SNOY ET D'OPPUERS
ADENAUER	HALLSTEIN
PINEAU	M. FAURE
Antonio SEGNI	Gaetano MARTINO
BECH	Lambert SCHAUS
J. LUNS	J. LINTHORST HOMAN

Protocol
on the Statute of the
Court of Justice of the
European Economic Community

THE HIGH CONTRACTING PARTIES TO THE TREATY ESTABLISHING THE EUROPEAN ECONOMIC COMMUNITY,

DESIRING to lay down the Statute of the Court provided for in Article 188 of this Treaty,

HAVE DESIGNATED as their Plenipotentiaries for this purpose:

HIS MAJESTY THE KING OF THE BELGIANS:

Baron J. Ch. SNOY ET D'OPPUERS, Secretary-General of the Ministry of Economic Affairs, Head of the Belgian Delegation to the Intergovernmental Conference;

THE PRESIDENT OF THE FEDERAL REPUBLIC OF GERMANY:

Professor Dr Carl Friedrich OPHÜLS, Ambassador of the Federal Republic of Germany, Head of the German Delegation to the Intergovernmental Conference;

THE PRESIDENT OF THE FRENCH REPUBLIC:

Mr Robert MARJOLIN, Professor of Law, Deputy Head of the French Delegation to the Intergovernmental Conference;

THE PRESIDENT OF THE ITALIAN REPUBLIC:

Mr V. BADINI CONFALONIERI, Under-Secretary of State in the Ministry of Foreign Affairs, Head of the Italian Delegation to the Intergovernmental Conference;

HER ROYAL HIGHNESS THE GRAND DUCHESS OF LUXEMBOURG:

Mr Lambert SCHAUS, Ambassador of the Grand Duchy of Luxembourg, Head of the Luxembourg Delegation to the Intergovernmental Conference;

HER MAJESTY THE QUEEN OF THE NETHERLANDS:

Mr J. LINTHORST HOMAN, Head of the Netherlands Delegation to the Intergovernmental Conference;

WHO, having exchanged their Full Powers, found in good and due form,

HAVE AGREED upon the following provisions, which shall be annexed to the Treaty establishing the European Economic Community.

Article 1

The Court established by Article 4 of this Treaty shall be constituted and shall function in accordance with the provisions of this Treaty and of this Statute.

TITLE I

JUDGES AND ADVOCATES-GENERAL

Article 2

Before taking up his duties each Judge shall, in open court, take an oath to perform his duties impartially and conscientiously and to preserve the secrecy of the deliberations of the Court.

Article 3

The Judges shall be immune from legal proceedings. After they have ceased to hold office, they shall continue to enjoy immunity in respect of acts performed by them in their official capacity including words spoken or written.

The Court, sitting in plenary session, may waive the immunity.

Where immunity has been waived and criminal proceedings are instituted against a Judge, he shall be tried, in any of the Member States, only by the Court competent to judge the members of the highest national judiciary.

Article 4

The Judges may not hold any political or administrative office.

They may not engage in any occupation, whether gainful or not, unless exemption is exceptionally granted by the Council.

When taking up their duties, they shall give a solemn undertaking that, both during and after their term of office, they will respect the obligations arising therefrom, in particular the duty to behave with integrity and discretion as regards the acceptance, after they have ceased to hold office, of certain appointments or benefits.

Any doubt on this point shall be settled by decision of the Court.

Article 5

Apart from normal replacement, or death, the duties of a Judge shall end when he resigns.

Where a Judge resigns, his letter of resignation shall be addressed to the President of the Court for transmission to the President of the Council. Upon this notification a vacancy shall arise on the bench.

Save where Article 6 applies, a Judge shall continue to hold office until his successor takes up his duties.

Article 6

A Judge may be deprived of his office or of his right to a pension or other benefits in its stead only if, in the unanimous opinion of the Judges and Advocates-General of the Court, he no longer fulfils the requisite conditions or meets the obligations arising from his office. The Judge concerned shall not take part in any such deliberations.

The Registrar of the Court shall communicate the decision of the Court to the President of the European Parliament and to the President of the Commission and shall notify it to the President of the Council.

In the case of a decision depriving a Judge of his office, a vacancy shall arise on the bench upon this latter notification.

Article 7

A Judge who is to replace a member of the Court whose term of office has not expired shall be appointed for the remainder of his predecessor's term.

Article 8

The provisions of Articles 2 to 7 shall apply to the Advocates-General.

TITLE II

ORGANIZATION

Article 9

The registrar shall take an oath before the Court to perform his duties impartially and conscientiously and to preserve the secrecy of the deliberations of the Court.

Article 10

The Court shall arrange for replacement of the Registrar on occasions when he is prevented from attending the Court.

Article 11

Officials and other servants shall be attached to the Court to enable it to function. They shall be responsible to the Registrar under the authority of the President.

Article 12

On a proposal from the Court, the Council may, acting unanimously, provide for the appointment of Assistant Rapporteurs and lay down the rules governing their service. The Assistant Rapporteurs may be required, under conditions laid down in the rules of procedure, to participate in preparatory inquiries in cases pending before the Court and to cooperate with the Judge who acts as Rapporteur.

The Assistant Rapporteurs shall be chosen from persons whose independence is beyond doubt and who possess the necessary legal qualifications; they shall be appointed by the Council. They shall take an oath before the Court to perform their duties impartially and conscientiously and to preserve the secrecy of the deliberations of the Court.

Article 13

The Judges, the Advocates-General and the Registrar shall be required to reside at the place where the Court has its seat.

Article 14

The Court shall remain permanently in session. The duration of the judicial vacations shall be determined by the Court with due regard to the needs of its business.

Article 15*

Decisions of the Court shall be valid only when an uneven number of its members is sitting in the deliberations. Decisions of the full Court shall be valid if seven members are sitting. Decisions of the Chambers shall be valid only if three Judges are sitting; in the event of one of the Judges of a Chamber being prevented from attending, a Judge of another Chamber may be called upon to sit in accordance with conditions laid down in the rules of procedure.

Article 16

No Judge or Advocate-General may take part in the disposal of any case in which he has previously taken part as agent or adviser or has acted for one of the parties, or in which he has been called upon to pronounce as a Member of a court or tribunal, of a commission of inquiry or in any other capacity.

If, for some special reason, any Judge or Advocate-General considers that he should not take part in the judgment or examination of a

---

* Text as amended by Article 20 of the Act of Accession DK/IRL/UK.

particular case, he shall so inform the President. If, for some special reason, the President considers that any Judge or Advocate-General should not sit or make submissions in a particular case, he shall notify him accordingly.

Any difficulty arising as to the application of this Article shall be settled by decision of the Court.

A party may not apply for a change in the composition of the Court or of one of its Chambers on the grounds of either the nationality of a Judge or the absence from the Court or from the Chamber of a Judge of the nationality of that party.

TITLE III

PROCEDURE

Article 17

The States and the institutions of the Community shall be represented before the Court by an agent appointed for each case; the agent may be assisted by an adviser or by a lawyer entitled to practise before a court of a Member State.

Other parties must be represented by a lawyer entitled to practise before a court of a Member State.

Such agents, advisers and lawyers shall, when they appear before the Court, enjoy the rights and immunities necessary to the independent exercise of their duties, under conditions laid down in the rules of procedure.

As regards such advisers and lawyers who appear before it, the Court shall have the powers normally accorded to courts of law, under conditions laid down in the rules of procedure.

University teachers being nationals of a Member State whose law accords them a right of audience shall have the same rights before the Court as are accorded by this Article to lawyers entitled to practise before a court of a Member State.

Article 18

The procedure before the Court shall consist of two parts: written and oral.

The written procedure shall consist of the communication to the parties and to the institutions of the Community whose decisions are in dispute, of applications, statements of case, defences and observations, and of replies, if any, as well as of all papers and documents in support or of certified copies of them.

Communications shall be made by the Registrar in the order and within the time laid down in the rules of procedure.

The oral procedure shall consist of the reading of the report presented by a Judge acting as Rapporteur, the hearing by the Court of agents, advisers and lawyers entitled to practise before a court of a Member State and of the submissions of the Advocate-General, as well as the hearing, if any, of witnesses and experts.

Article 19

A case shall be brought before the Court by a written application addressed to the Registrar. The application shall contain the applicant's name and permanent address and the description of the signatory, the name of the party against whom the application is made, the subject matter of the dispute, the submissions and a brief statement of the grounds on which the application is based.

The application shall be accompanied, where appropriate, by the measure the annulment of which is sought or, in the circumstances referred to in Article 175 of this Treaty, by documentary evidence of the date on which an institution was, in accordance with that Article, requested to act. If the documents are not submitted with the application, the Registrar shall ask the party concerned to produce them within a reasonable period, but in that event the rights of the party shall not lapse even if such documents are produced after the time limit for bringing proceedings.

Article 20

In the cases governed by Article 177 of this Treaty, the decision of the court or tribunal of a Member State which suspends its proceedings and refers a case to the Court shall be notified to the Court by the court or tribunal concerned. The decision shall then be notified by the Registrar of the Court to the parties, to the Member States and to the Commission, and also to the Council if the act the validity or interpretation of which is in dispute originates from the Council.

Within two months of this notification, the parties, the Member State, the Commission and, where appropriate, the Council, shall be entitled to submit statements of case or written observations to the Court.

Article 21

The Court may require the parties to produce all documents and to supply all information which the Court considers desirable. Formal note shall be taken of any refusal.

The Court may also require the Member States and institutions not being parties to the case to supply all information which the Court considers necessary for the proceedings.

Article 22

The Court may at any time entrust any individual, body, authority, committee or other organization it chooses with the task of giving an expert opinion.

Article 23

Witnesses may be heard under conditions laid down in the rules of procedure.

Article 24

With respect to defaulting witnesses the Court shall have the powers generally granted to courts and tribunals and may impose pecuniary penalties under conditions laid down in the rules of procedure.

Article 25

Witnesses and experts may be heard on oath taken in the form laid down in the rules of procedure or in the manner laid down by the law of the country of the witness or expert.

Article 26

The Court may order that a witness or expert be heard by the judicial authority of his place of permanent residence.

The order shall be sent for implementation to the competent judicial authority under conditions laid down in the rules of procedure. The documents drawn up in compliance with the letters rogatory shall be returned to the Court under the same conditions.

The Court shall defray the expenses, without prejudice to the right to charge them, where appropriate, to the parties.

Article 27

A Member State shall treat any violation of an oath by a witness or expert in the same manner as if the offence had been committed before one of its courts with jurisdiction in civil proceedings. At the instance of the Court, the Member State concerned shall prosecute the offender before its competent court.

Article 28

The hearing in court shall be public, unless the Court, of its own motion or on application by the parties, decides otherwise for serious reasons.

Article 29

During the hearings the Court may examine the experts, the witnesses and the parties themselves. The latter, however, may address the Court only through their representatives.

Article 30

Minutes shall be made of each hearing and signed by the President and the Registrar.

Article 31

The case list shall be established by the President.

Article 32

The deliberations of the Court shall be and shall remain secret.

Article 33

Judgments shall state the reasons on which they are based. They shall contain the names of the Judges who took part in the deliberations.

Article 34

Judgments shall be signed by the President and the Registrar. They shall be read in open court.

Article 35

The Court shall adjudicate upon costs.

Article 36

The President of the Court may, by way of summary procedure, which may, in so far as necessary, differ from some of the rules contained in this Statute and which shall be laid down in the rules of procedure, adjudicate upon applications to suspend execution, as provided for in Article 185 of this Treaty, or to prescribe interim measures in pursuance of Article 186, or to suspend enforcement in accordance with the last paragraph of Article 192.

Should the President be prevented from attending, his place shall be taken by another Judge under conditions laid down in the rules of procedure.

The ruling of the President or of the Judge replacing him shall be provisional and shall in no way prejudice the decision of the Court on the substance of the case.

Article 37

Member States and institutions of the Community may intervene in cases before the Court.

The same right shall be open to any other person establishing an interest in the result of any case submitted to the Court, save in cases between Member States, between institutions of the Community or between Member States and institutions of the Community.

Submissions made in an application to intervene shall be limited to supporting the submissions of one of the parties.

Article 38

Where the defending party, after having been duly summoned, fails to file written submissions in defence, judgment shall be given against that party by default. An objection may be lodged against the judgment within one month of it being notified. The objection shall not have the effect of staying enforcement of the judgment by default unless the Court decides otherwise.

Article 39

Member States, institutions of the Community and any other natural or legal persons may, in cases and under conditions to be determined by the rules of procedure, institute third-party proceedings to contest a judgment rendered without their being heard, where the judgment is prejudicial to their rights.

Article 40

If the meaning or scope of a judgment is in doubt, the Court shall construe it on application by any party or any institution of the Community establishing an interest therein.

Article 41

An application for revision of a judgment may be made to the Court only on discovery of a fact which is of such a nature as to be a decisive factor, and which, when the judgment was given, was unknown to the Court and to the party claiming the revision.

The revision shall be opened by a judgment of the Court expressly recording the existence of a new fact, recognizing that it is of such a character as to lay the case open to revision and declaring the application admissible on this ground.

No application for revision may be made after the lapse of ten years from the date of the judgment.

Article 42

Periods of grace based on considerations of distance shall be determined by the rules of procedure.

No right shall be prejudiced in consequence of the expiry of a time limit if the party concerned proves the existence of unforeseeable circumstances or of *force majeure*.

Article 43

Proceedings against the Community in matters arising from non-contractual liability shall be barred after a period of five years from the occurrence of the event giving rise thereto. The period of limitation shall be interrupted if proceedings are instituted before the Court or if prior to such proceedings an application is made by the aggrieved party to the relevant institution of the Community. In the latter event the proceedings must be instituted within the period of two months provided for in Article 173; the provisions of the second paragraph of Article 175 shall apply where appropriate.

Article 44

The rules of procedure of the Court provided for in Article 188 of this Treaty shall contain, apart from the provisions contemplated by this Statute, any other provisions necessary for applying and, where required, supplementing it.

Article 45

The Council may, acting unanimously, make such further adjustments to the provisions of this Statute as may be required by reason of measures taken by the Council in accordance with the last paragraph of Article 165 of this Treaty.

Article 46

Immediately after the oath has been taken, the President of the Council shall proceed to choose by lot the Judges and the Advocates-General whose terms of office are to expire at the end of the first three years in accordance with the second and third paragraphs of Article 167 of this Treaty.

IN WITNESS WHEREOF, the undersigned Plenipotentiaries have signed this Protocol.

Done at Brussels this seventeenth day of April in the year one thousand nine hundred and fifty-seven.

J. Ch. SNOY ET D'OPPUERS

C. F. OPHÜLS

Robert MARJOLIN

Vittorio BADINI

Lambert SCHAUS

J. LINTHORST HOMAN

Protocol
concerning imports
into the European Economic Community
of petroleum products refined
in the Netherlands Antilles*

* Added by Article 2 of the Convention of 13 November 1962 amending the Treaty establishing the European Economic Community (*Official Journal of the European Communities*, No 150, 1 October 1964).

THE HIGH CONTRACTING PARTIES,

BEING DESIROUS of giving fuller details about the system of trade applicable to imports into the European Economic Community of petroleum products refined in the Netherlands Antilles,

HAVE AGREED on the following provisions to be appended to that Treaty:

Article 1

This Protocol is applicable to petroleum products coming under the Brussels Nomenclature numbers 27.10, 27.11, 27.12, ex 27.13 (paraffin wax, petroleum or shale wax and paraffin residues) and 27.14, imported for use in Member States.

Article 2

Member States shall undertake to grant to petroleum products refined in the Netherlands Antilles the tariff preferences resulting from the association of the latter with the Community, under the conditions provided for in this Protocol. These provisions shall hold good whatever may be the rules of origin applied by the Member States.

Article 3

1. When the Commission, at the request of a Member State or on its own initiative, establishes that imports into the Community of petroleum products refined in the Netherlands Antilles under the system provided for in Article 2 above are giving rise to real difficulties on the market

of one or more Member States, it shall decide that customs duties on the said imports shall be introduced, increased or re-introduced by the Member States in question, to such an extent and for such a period as may be necessary to meet that situation. The rates of the customs duties thus introduced, increased or re-introduced may not exceed the customs duties applicable to third countries for these same products.

2. The provisions of paragraph 1 can in any case be applied when imports into the Community of petroleum products refined in the Netherlands Antilles reach two million metric tonnes a year.

3. The Council shall be informed of decisions taken by the Commission in pursuance of paragraphs 1 and 2, including those directed at rejecting the request of a Member State. The Council shall, at the request of any Member State, assume responsibility for the matter and may at any time amend or revoke them by a decision taken by a qualified majority.

Article 4

1. If a Member State considers that imports of petroleum products refined in the Netherlands Antilles, made either directly or through another Member State under the system provided for in Article 2 above, are giving rise to real difficulties on its market and that immediate action is necessary to meet them, it may on its own initiative decide to apply customs duties to such imports, the rate of which may not exceed those of the customs duties applicable to third countries in respect of the same products. It shall notify its decision to the Commission which shall decide within one month whether the measures taken by the State should be maintained or must be amended or cancelled. The provisions of Article 3 (3) shall be applicable to such decision of the Commission.

2. When the quantities of petroleum products refined in the Netherlands Antilles imported either directly or through another Member State,

under the system provided for in Article 2 above, into a Member State or States of the EEC exceed during a calendar year the tonnage shown in the Annex to this Protocol, the measures taken in pursuance of paragraph 1 by that or those Member States for the current year shall be considered to be justified; the Commission shall, after assuring itself that the tonnage fixed has been reached, formally record the measures taken. In such a case the other Member States shall abstain from formally placing the matter before the Council.

Article 5

If the Community decides to apply quantitative restrictions to petroleum products, no matter whence they are imported, these restrictions may also be applied to imports of such products from the Netherlands Antilles. In such a case preferential treatment shall be granted to the Netherlands Antilles as compared with third countries.

Article 6

1. The provisions of Articles 2 to 5 shall be reviewed by the Council, by unanimous decision, after consulting the European Parliament and the Commission, when a common definition of origin for petroleum products from third countries and associated countries is adopted, or when decisions are taken within the framework of a common commercial policy for the products in question or when a common energy policy is established.

2. When such revision is made, however, equivalent preferences must in any case be maintained in favour of the Netherlands Antilles in a suitable form and for a minimum quantity of 2½ million metric tonnes of petroleum products.

3. The Community's commitments in regard to equivalent preferences as mentioned in paragraph 2 of this Article may, if necessary, be broken down country by country taking into account the tonnage indicated in the Annex to this Protocol.

Article 7

For the implementation of this Protocol, the Commission is responsible for following the pattern of imports into the Member States of petroleum products refined in the Netherlands Antilles. Member States shall communicate to the Commission, which shall see that it is circulated, all useful information to that end in accordance with the administrative conditions recommended by it.

IN WITNESS WHEREOF the undersigned plenipotentiaries have placed their signatures below this Protocol.

H. FAYAT	E. SCHAUS
R. LAHR	H. R. VAN HOUTEN
J.-M. BOEGNER	W. F. M. LAMPE
C. RUSSO	

Done at Brussels, the thirteenth day of November, one thousand nine hundred and sixty-two.

Annex to the Protocol

For the implementation of Article 4 (2) of the Protocol concerning imports into the European Economic Community of petroleum products refined in the Netherlands Antilles, the High Contracting Parties have decided that the quantity of 2 million metric tonnes of petroleum products from the Antilles shall be allocated among the Member States as follows:

Germany	625 000 metric tonnes
Belgo/Luxembourg Economic Union	200 000 metric tonnes
France	75 000 metric tonnes
Italy	100 000 metric tonnes
Netherlands	1 000 000 metric tonnes

Protocol*
on special arrangements for Greenland

---

* Article 3 of the Greenland Treaty provides that this Protocol, attached to the latter Treaty, shall be annexed to the Treaty establishing the European Economic Community (*Official Journal of the European Communities*, No L 29, 1 February 1985).

Article 1

1.   The treatment on import into the Community of products subject to the common organization of the market in fishery products, originating in Greenland, shall, while complying with the mechanisms of the common market organization, involve exemption from customs duties and charges having equivalent effect and the absence of quantitative restrictions or measures having equivalent effect if the possibilities for access to Greenland fishing zones granted to the Community pursuant to an agreement between the Community and the authority responsible for Greenland are satisfactory to the Community.

2.   All measures relating to the import arrangements for such products, including those relating to the adoption of such measures, shall be adopted in accordance with the procedure laid down in Article 43 of the Treaty establishing the European Economic Community.

Article 2

The Commission shall make proposals to the Council, which shall act by a qualified majority, for the transitional measures which it considers necessary, by reason of the entry into force of the new arrangements, with regard to the maintenance of rights acquired by natural or legal persons during the period when Greenland was part of the Community and the regularization of the situation with regard to financial assistance granted by the Community to Greenland during that period.

Article 3

The following text shall be added to Annex I to the Council Decision of 16 December 1980 on the association of the overseas countries and territories with the European Economic Community:

   '6.   Distinct community of the Kingdom of Denmark:

        — Greenland.'

III — IMPLEMENTING CONVENTION
ON THE
ASSOCIATION OF THE OVERSEAS COUNTRIES
AND TERRITORIES
WITH THE COMMUNITY*

---

* EDITORIAL NOTE:
This Implementing Convention, which was concluded for a period of five years, expired on 31 December 1962. See also footnote 4 of the editorial notes on p. 481 of this volume.

1. TEXT
OF THE IMPLEMENTING CONVENTION

THE HIGH CONTRACTING PARTIES,

DESIRING to enter into the Implementing Convention provided for in Article 136 of this Treaty,

HAVE AGREED upon the following provisions, which shall be annexed to this Treaty:

Article 1

The Member States shall, under the conditions laid down below, participate in measures which will promote the social and economic development of the countries and territories listed in Annex IV to this Treaty, by supplementing the efforts made by the authorities responsible for those countries and territories.

For this purpose, a Development Fund for the Overseas Countries and Territories is hereby established, into which the Member States shall, over a period of five years, pay the annual contributions set out in Annex A to this Convention.

The Fund shall be administered by the Commission.

Article 2

The authorities responsible for the countries and territories shall, in agreement with the local authorities or with the representatives of the peoples of the countries and territories concerned, submit to the Commission the social or economic projects for which financing by the Community is requested.

Article 3

The Commission shall draw up annually general programmes for allocation to the different classes of project of the funds made available in accordance with Annex B to this Convention.

The general programmes shall contain projects for financing:

(a) certain social institutions, in particular hospitals, teaching or technical research establishments and institutions for vocational guidance and advancement among the peoples concerned;

(b) economic investments which are in the public interest and are directly connected with the implementation of a programme containing specific productive development projects.

Article 4

At the beginning of each financial year the Council shall, acting by a qualified majority after consulting the Commission, determine what funds will be devoted to financing:

(a) the social institutions referred to in Article 3 *(a);*

(b) the economic investments in the public interest referred to in Article 3 *(b).*

The decision of the Council shall aim at a rational geographical distribution of the funds made available.

Article 5

1. The Commission shall determine how the funds made available under Article 4 *(a)* shall be allocated according to the various requests received for the financing of social institutions.

2. The Commission shall draw up proposals for financing the economic investment projects which it is considering under Article 4 *(b)*.

It shall submit these proposals to the Council.

If, within one month, no Member State requests that the Council examine the proposals, they shall be deemed to be approved.

If the Council examines the proposals, it shall act by a qualified majority within two months.

3. Any funds not allocated during any one year shall be carried forward to the following years.

4. The funds allocated shall be made available to the authorities responsible for carrying out the work concerned. The Commission shall ensure that such funds are used for the purposes which have been decided upon, and are expended to the best economic advantage.

Article 6

Within six months of the entry into force of this Treaty, the Council shall, acting by a qualified majority on a proposal from the Commission, lay down rules for the collection and transfer of financial contributions, for budgeting and for the administration of the resources of the Development Fund.

Article 7

The qualified majority referred to in Articles 4, 5 and 6 shall be 67 votes. Member States shall have the following number of votes:

Belgium .... 11 votes

Germany .... 33 votes

France	33 votes
Italy	11 votes
Luxembourg	1 vote
Netherlands	11 votes

Article 8

The right of establishment shall, in each country or territory, be progressively extended to nationals, companies or firms of Member States other than the State which has special relations with the country or territory concerned. During the first year in which this Convention is applied, the manner in which this is to be effected shall be so determined by the Council, acting by a qualified majority on a proposal from the Commission, as to ensure the progressive abolition during the transitional period of any discrimination.

Article 9

The customs treatment to be applied to trade between Member States and the countries and territories shall be that provided for in Articles 133 and 134 of this Treaty.

Article 10

For the duration of this Convention, Member States shall apply to their trade with the countries and territories those provisions of the Chapter of this Treaty relating to the elimination of quantitative restrictions between Member States which they apply to trade with one another during the same period.

Article 11

1. In each country or territory where import quotas exist, one year after this Convention enters into force, the quotas open to States other than the State with which such country or territory has special relations shall be converted into global quotas open without discrimination to the other Member States. As from the same date, these quotas shall be increased annually in accordance with Article 32 and Article 33 (1), (2), (4), (5), (6) and (7) of this Treaty.

2. Where, in the case of a product which has not been liberalized, the global quota does not amount to 7 % of total imports into a country or territory, a quota equal to 7 % of such imports shall be introduced not later than one year after the entry into force of this Convention, and shall be increased annually in accordance with paragraph 1.

3. Where, in the case of certain products, no quota has been opened for imports into a country or territory, the Commission shall, by means of a decision, determine the manner in which the quotas to be offered to other Member States shall be opened and increased.

Article 12

Where import quotas established by Member States cover both imports from a State having special relations with a country or territory and imports from the country or territory concerned, the share of imports from the countries and territories shall be the subject of a global quota based on import statistics. Any such quota shall be established during the first year in which this Convention is in force and shall be increased as provided for in Article 10.

Article 13

The provisions of Article 10 shall not preclude prohibitions or restrictions on imports, exports or goods in transit justified on grounds of public morality; public policy or public security; the protection of health and life of humans, animals or plants; the protection of national treasures possessing artistic, historic or archaeological value; or the protection of industrial and commercial property. Such prohibitions or restrictions shall not, however, constitute a means of arbitrary discrimination or a disguised restriction on trade.

Article 14

After the date of expiry of this Convention and until provisions covering association for a further period have been adopted, quotas for imports into the countries and territories on the one hand, and into the Member States on the other, of products originating in the countries and territories shall remain at the level set for the fifth year. The arrangements in respect of the right of establishment in force at the end of the fifth year shall also be maintained.

Article 15

1. Tariff quotas for imports from third countries of raw coffee into Italy and the Benelux countries, and of bananas into the Federal Republic of Germany, shall be introduced in accordance with the Protocols annexed to this Convention.

2. If this Convention expires before the conclusion of a new agreement, the Member States shall, pending such new agreement, enjoy tariff quotas for bananas, cocoa beans and raw coffee at the rates of duty applying at the beginning of the second stage; such quotas shall be equal to the volume of imports from third countries in the course of the latest year for which statistics are available.

Such quotas shall, where appropriate, be increased in proportion to the increase in consumption within the importing countries.

3. Member States enjoying tariff quotas at the rates of duty applied when this Treaty enters into force under the Protocols relating to imports of raw coffee and bananas from third countries may require that, instead of the treatment provided for in paragraph 2, the tariff quotas for these products be maintained at the level reached at the date of expiry of this Convention.

Such quotas shall, where appropriate, be increased as provided in paragraph 2.

4. The Commission shall, at the request of the States concerned, determine the size of the tariff quotas referred to in the preceding paragraphs.

Article 16

The provisions contained in Articles 1 to 8 of this Convention shall apply to Algeria and the French overseas departments.

Article 17

Without prejudice to cases in which the provisions of Articles 14 and 15 apply, this Convention is concluded for a period of five years.

Done at Rome this twenty-fifth day of March in the year one thousand nine hundred and fifty-seven.

P. H. SPAAK	J. Ch. SNOY ET D'OPPUERS
ADENAUER	HALLSTEIN
PINEAU	M. FAURE
Antonio SEGNI	Gaetano MARTINO
BECH	Lambert SCHAUS
J. LUNS	J. LINTHORST HOMAN

Annex A referred to in Article 1 of this Convention

Percentages Countries	1st year 10%	2nd year 12.5%	3rd year 16.5%	4th year 22.5%	5th year 38.5%	Total 100%
			MILLIONS OF EPU UNITS OF ACCOUNT			
Belgium	7	8.75	11.55	15.75	26.95	70
Germany	20	25	33	45	77	200
France	20	25	33	45	77	200
Italy	4	5	6.60	9	15.40	40
Luxembourg	0.125	0.15625	0.20625	0.28125	0.48125	1.25
Netherlands	7	8.75	11.55	15.75	26.95	70

Annex B referred to in Article 3 of this Convention

Percentages Overseas countries and territories of	1st year 10%	2nd year 12.5%	3rd year 16.5%	4th year 22.5%	5th year 38.5%	Total 100%
			MILLIONS OF EPU UNITS OF ACCOUNT			
Belgium	3	3.75	4.95	6.75	11.55	30
France	51.125	63.906	84.356	115.031	196.832	511.25
Italy	0.5	0.625	0.825	1.125	1.925	5
Netherlands	3.5	4.375	5.775	7.875	13.475	35

2. PROTOCOLS

Protocol
on the tariff quota
for imports of bananas

(ex 08.01 of the Brussels Nomenclature)

THE HIGH CONTRACTING PARTIES,

HAVE AGREED upon the following provisions, which shall be annexed to this Convention:

1. From the first approximation of external duties provided for in Article 23 (1) *(b)* of this Treaty until the end of the second stage, the Federal Republic of Germany shall enjoy an annual duty-free import quota equal to 90 % of the quantities imported in 1956, less the quantities coming from the countries and territories referred to in Article 131 of this Treaty.

2. From the end of the second stage until the end of the third stage, the quota shall be 80 % of the quantity defined above.

3. The annual quotas determined in paragraphs 1 and 2 shall be increased by 50 % of the difference between the total quantities imported during each preceding year and the quantities imported in 1956.

If total imports decrease in comparison with those for 1956, the annual quotas provided for above shall not exceed 90 % of the imports for each preceding year during the period referred to in paragraph 1, or 80 % of the imports for each preceding year during the period referred to in paragraph 2.

4. As soon as the common customs tariff applies in its entirety, the quota shall be 75 % of the imports for 1956. This quota shall be increased as provided in the first subparagraph of paragraph 3.

If imports have decreased in comparison with those for 1956, the annual quota provided for above shall not exceed 75 % of the imports for each preceding year.

Any decision to abolish or amend this quota shall be taken by the Council, acting by a qualified majority on a proposal from the Commission.

5. The figure for imports for 1956, less imports from the countries and territories referred to in Article 131 of this Treaty, which in accordance with the above provisions is to serve as the basis for calculating quotas, is 290 000 metric tons.

6. If the countries and territories are unable to supply in full the quantities requested by the Federal Republic of Germany, the Member States concerned declare their readiness to agree to a corresponding increase in the German tariff quota.

Done in Rome this twenty-fifth day of March in the year one thousand nine hundred and fifty-seven.

P. H. SPAAK	J. Ch. SNOY ET D'OPPUERS
ADENAUER	HALLSTEIN
PINEAU	M. FAURE
Antonio SEGNI	Gaetano MARTINO
BECH	Lambert SCHAUS
J. LUNS	J. LINTHORST HOMAN

At the time of signature of this Protocol, the Plenipotentiary of the Federal Republic of Germany made, on behalf of his Government, the following declaration, of which the other Plenipotentiaries took note:

The Federal Republic of Germany declares its readiness to support any measures that may be taken by German private interests to encourage sales of bananas from the associated overseas countries and territories within the Federal Republic.

For this purpose, negotiations shall be started as soon as possible between business circles in the various countries concerned in the supply and sale of bananas.

Protocol
on the tariff quota
for imports of raw coffee

(ex 09.01 of the Brussels Nomenclature)

The High Contracting Parties

Have agreed upon the following provisions, which shall be annexed to this Convention:

A. Italy

During the first period of association of the overseas countries and territories with the Community and after the first change in customs duties in accordance with Article 23 of this Treaty, raw coffee imported from third countries into the territory of Italy, within an annual quota equal to the total imports into Italy of raw coffee from third countries in 1956, shall be subject to the customs duties applicable at the date of entry into force of this Treaty.

From the sixth year after the entry into force of this Treaty until the end of the second stage, the initial quota provided for in the preceding paragraph shall be reduced by 20%.

From the beginning of the third stage and throughout that stage, the quota shall be 50% of the initial quota.

For four years after the end of the transitional period, customs duties on raw coffee imported into Italy may, up to an amount not exceeding 20% of the initial quota, continue to be charged at the rate applied in that country at the date of entry into force of this Treaty.

The Commission shall examine whether the percentage and the period provided for in the preceding paragraph are justified.

The provisions of this Treaty shall apply to any quantities imported in excess of the quotas provided for above.

B. The Benelux countries

From the beginning of the second stage and throughout that stage, raw coffee imported from third countries into the territories of the Benelux countries may continue to be imported free of customs duty, up to a tonnage of 85 % of the total quantity of raw coffee imported during the last year for which statistics are available.

From the beginning of the third stage and throughout that stage, the duty-free imports referred to in the preceding paragraph shall be reduced to 50 % of the total tonnage of raw coffee imported during the last year for which statistics are available.

The provisions of this Treaty shall apply to any quantities imported in excess of the quotas provided for above.

Done at Rome this twenty-fifth day of March in the year one thousand nine hundred and fifty-seven.

P. H. SPAAK	J. Ch. SNOY ET D'OPPUERS
ADENAUER	HALLSTEIN
PINEAU	M. FAURE
Antonio SEGNI	Gaetano MARTINO
BECH	Lambert SCHAUS
J. LUNS	J. LINTHORST HOMAN

IV — FINAL ACT

THE INTERGOVERNMENTAL CONFERENCE ON THE COMMON MARKET AND EURATOM, convened in Venice on 29 May 1956 by the Ministers for Foreign Affairs of the Kingdom of Belgium, the Federal Republic of Germany, the French Republic, the Italian Republic, the Grand Duchy of Luxembourg and the Kingdom of the Netherlands, having continued its deliberations in Brussels and having, on concluding them, met in Rome on 25 March 1957, has adopted the following texts:

I

1. THE TREATY establishing the European Economic Community, and the Annexes thereto,

2. The Protocol on the Statute of the European Investment Bank,

3. The Protocol on German internal trade and connected problems,

4. The Protocol on certain provisions relating to France,

5. The Protocol on Italy.

6. The Protocol on the Grand Duchy of Luxembourg,

7. The Protocol on goods originating in and coming from certain countries and enjoying special treatment when imported into a Member State,

8. The Protocol on the treatment to be applied to products within the province of the European Coal and Steel Community in respect of Algeria and the Overseas Departments of the French Republic,

9. The Protocol on mineral oils and certain of their derivatives,

10. The Protocol on the application of the Treaty establishing the European Economic Community to the non-European parts of the Kingdom of the Netherlands,

11. The Implementing Convention on the association of the overseas countries and territories with the Community, and the Annexes thereto,

12. The Protocol on the tariff quota for imports of bananas,

13. The Protocol on the tariff quota for imports of raw coffee.

II

1. THE TREATY establishing the European Atomic Energy Community, and the Annexes thereto,

2. The Protocol on the application of the Treaty establishing the European Atomic Energy Community to the non-European parts of the Kingdom of the Netherlands.

III

THE CONVENTION on certain institutions common to the European Communities.

At the time of signature of these texts, the Conference adopted the declarations listed below and annexed to this Act:

1. A joint declaration on cooperation with the Member States of international organizations,

2. A joint declaration on Berlin,

3. A declaration of intent on the association of the independent countries of the Franc area with the European Economic Community,

4. A declaration of intent on the association of the Kingdom of Libya with the European Economic Community,

5. A declaration of intent on the Trust Territory of Somaliland currently under the administration of the Italian Republic,

6. A declaration of intent on the association of Surinam and the Netherlands Antilles with the European Economic Community.

The Conference further took note of the declarations listed below and annexed to this Act:

1. A declaration by the Government of the Federal Republic of Germany on the definition of the expression 'German national',

2. A declaration by the Government of the Federal Republic of Germany on the application of the Treaties to Berlin,

3. A declaration by the Government of the French Republic on applications for patents covering information to be kept secret for defence reasons.

Finally, the Conference decided to draw up at a later date:

1. The Protocol on the Statute of the Court of Justice of the European Economic Community,

2. The Protocol on the privileges and immunities of the European Economic Community,

3. The Protocol on the Statute of the Court of Justice of the European Atomic Energy Community,

4. The Protocol on the privileges and immunities of the European Atomic Community.

Protocols 1 and 2 shall be annexed to the Treaty establishing the European Economic Community; Protocols 3 and 4 shall be annexed to the Treaty establishing the European Atomic Energy Community.

IN WITNESS WHEREOF, the undersigned plenipotentiaries have signed this Final Act.

Done at Rome this twenty-fifth day of March in the year one thousand nine hundred and fifty-seven.

P. H. SPAAK	J. Ch. SNOY ET D'OPPUERS
ADENAUER	HALLSTEIN
PINEAU	M. FAURE
Antonio SEGNI	Gaetano MARTINO
BECH	Lambert SCHAUS
J. LUNS	J. LINTHORST HOMAN

JOINT DECLARATION

on

cooperation with the States
members of international organizations

THE GOVERNMENTS OF THE KINGDOM OF BELGIUM, THE FEDERAL REPUBLIC OF GERMANY, THE FRENCH REPUBLIC, THE ITALIAN REPUBLIC, THE GRAND DUCHY OF LUXEMBOURG AND THE KINGDOM OF THE NETHERLANDS,

AT THE TIME of signature of the Treaties establishing the European Economic Community and the European Atomic Energy Community,

CONSCIOUS of the responsibilities which they are assuming for the future of Europe by combining their markets, bringing their economies closer together and laying down the principles and details of a common policy in this field;

RECOGNIZING that, by setting up a customs union and working closely together on the peaceful development of nuclear energy, they will be ensuring economic and social progress and thus contributing not only to their own prosperity but also to that of other countries,

ANXIOUS that these countries should share in the prospects of expansion afforded thereby,

DECLARE THEIR READINESS to conclude, as soon as these Treaties enter into force, agreements with other countries, particularly within the framework of the international organizations to which they belong, in order to attain these objectives of common interest and to ensure the harmonious development of trade in general.

JOINT DECLARATION

on

Berlin

THE GOVERNMENTS OF THE KINGDOM OF BELGIUM, THE FEDERAL REPUBLIC OF GERMANY, THE FRENCH REPUBLIC, THE ITALIAN REPUBLIC, THE GRAND DUCHY OF LUXEMBOURG AND THE KINGDOM OF THE NETHERLANDS,

HAVING REGARD to the special position of Berlin and the need to afford it the support of the free world,

ANXIOUS to confirm their solidarity with the people of Berlin,

WILL USE THEIR GOOD OFFICES within the Community in order that all necessary measures may be taken to ease the economic and social situation of Berlin, to promote its development and to ensure its economic stability.

DECLARATION OF INTENT

on the

association of the independent countries of the Franc Area

with the European Economic Community

THE GOVERNMENTS OF THE KINGDOM OF BELGIUM, THE FEDERAL RE-
PUBLIC OF GERMANY, THE FRENCH REPUBLIC, THE ITALIAN REPUBLIC,
THE GRAND DUCHY OF LUXEMBOURG AND THE KINGDOM OF THE NETH-
ERLANDS,

TAKING INTO CONSIDERATION the economic, financial and monetary
agreements and conventions concluded between France and the other independent countries of the Franc Area,

ANXIOUS to maintain and intensify the traditional trade flows between
the Member States of the European Economic Community and these independent countries and to contribute to the economic and social development of the latter.

DECLARE THEIR READINESS, as soon as this Treaty enters into force, to
propose to these countries the opening of negotiations with a view to concluding conventions for economic association with the Community.

DECLARATION OF INTENT

on the

association of the Kingdom of Libya
with the European Economic Community

THE GOVERNMENTS OF THE KINGDOM OF BELGIUM, THE FEDERAL REPUBLIC OF GERMANY, THE FRENCH REPUBLIC, THE ITALIAN REPUBLIC, THE GRAND DUCHY OF LUXEMBOURG AND THE KINGDOM OF THE NETHERLANDS,

TAKING INTO CONSIDERATION the economic links between Italy and the Kingdom of Libya,

ANXIOUS to maintain and intensify the traditional trade flows between the Member States of the Community and the Kingdom of Libya, and to contribute to the economic and social development of Libya,

DECLARE THEIR READINESS, as soon as this Treaty enters into force, to propose to the Kingdom of Libya the opening of negotiations with a view to concluding conventions for economic association with the Community.

DECLARATION OF INTENT

on

the Trust Territory of Somaliland*
currently under the administration of the Italian Republic

THE GOVERNMENTS OF THE KINGDOM OF BELGIUM, THE FEDERAL REPUBLIC OF GERMANY, THE FRENCH REPUBLIC, THE ITALIAN REPUBLIC, THE GRAND DUCHY OF LUXEMBOURG AND THE KINGDOM OF THE NETHERLANDS,

ANXIOUS, at the time of signature of the Treaty establishing the European Economic Community, to define the exact scope of Articles 131 and 227 of this Treaty, in view of the fact that under Article 24 of the Trusteeship Agreement with respect to the Trust Territory of Somaliland the Italian administration of that territory will end on 2 December 1960,

HAVE AGREED to give the authorities who will after that date be responsible for the external relations of Somaliland the option of confirming the association of that Territory with the Community, and declare their readiness to propose, if need be, to these authorities the opening of negotiations with a view to concluding conventions for economic association with the Community.

EDITORIAL NOTE:
* The country has become independent.

DECLARATION OF INTENT

on the

association of Surinam and the Netherlands Antilles

with the European Economic Community

THE GOVERNMENTS OF THE KINGDOM OF BELGIUM, THE FEDERAL REPUBLIC OF GERMANY, THE FRENCH REPUBLIC, THE ITALIAN REPUBLIC, THE GRAND DUCHY OF LUXEMBOURG AND THE KINGDOM OF THE NETHERLANDS,

TAKING INTO CONSIDERATION the close ties which unite the several parts of the Kingdom of the Netherlands,

ANXIOUS to maintain and intensify the traditional trade flows between the Member States of the European Economic Community on the one hand and Surinam and the Netherlands Antilles on the other, and to contribute to the economic and social development of these countries,

DECLARE THEIR READINESS, as soon as this Treaty enters into force, to open negotiations at the request of the Kingdom of the Netherlands, with a view to concluding conventions for the economic association of Surinam and the Netherlands Antilles with the Community.

DECLARATION BY THE GOVERNMENT
OF THE FEDERAL REPUBLIC OF GERMANY

on

the definition of the expression 'German national'

At the time of signature of the Treaty establishing the European Economic Community and the Treaty establishing the European Atomic Energy Community, the Government of the Federal Republic of Germany makes the following declaration:

'All Germans as defined in the Basic Law for the Federal Republic of Germany shall be considered nationals of the Federal Republic of Germany.'

DECLARATION BY THE GOVERNMENT
OF THE FEDERAL REPUBLIC OF GERMANY

on

the application of the Treaties to Berlin

The Government of the Federal Republic of Germany reserves the right to declare, when depositing its instruments of ratification, that the Treaty establishing the European Economic Community and the Treaty establishing the European Atomic Energy Community shall equally apply to *Land* Berlin.

DECLARATION BY THE GOVERNMENT
OF THE FRENCH REPUBLIC

on

applications for patents

covering information to be kept secret for defence reasons

THE GOVERNMENT OF THE FRENCH REPUBLIC,

TAKING INTO ACCOUNT the provisions of Articles 17 and 25 (2) of the Treaty establishing the European Atomic Energy Community,

DECLARES ITS READINESS to take such administrative measures and to propose to the French Parliament such legislative measures as may be necessary to ensure that, as soon as this Treaty enters into force, applications for patents covering secret information result, following the normal procedure, in the grant of patents subject to temporary prohibition of publication.

Treaty
establishing
the European Atomic Energy
Community

E
A
E
C

Contents

---

* The Protocol on the Privileges and Immunities of the European Atomic Energy Community has
been repealed by the second paragraph of Article 28 of the Merger Treaty; see Protocol on the
Privileges and Immunities of the European Communities (p. 853).

I — TEXT OF THE TREATY

His Majesty the King of the Belgians, the President of the Federal Republic of Germany, the President of the French Republic, the President of the Italian Republic, Her Royal Highness the Grand Duchess of Luxembourg, Her Majesty the Queen of the Netherlands,

Recognizing that nuclear energy represents an essential resource for the development and invigoration of industry and will permit the advancement of the cause of peace,

Convinced that only a joint effort undertaken without delay can offer the prospect of achievements commensurate with the creative capacities of their countries,

Resolved to create the conditions necessary for the development of a powerful nuclear industry which will provide extensive energy resources, lead to the modernization of technical processes and contribute, through its many other applications, to the prosperity of their peoples,

Anxious to create the conditions of safety necessary to eliminate hazards to the life and health of the public,

Desiring to associate other countries with their work and to cooperate with international organizations concerned with the peaceful development of atomic energy,

Have decided to create a European Atomic Energy Community (Euratom) and to this end have designated as their Plenipotentiaries:

HIS MAJESTY THE KING OF THE BELGIANS:

Mr Paul-Henri SPAAK, Minister for Foreign Affairs,
Baron J. Ch. SNOY ET D'OPPUERS, Secretary-General of the Ministry of
Economic Affairs, Head of the Belgian Delegation to the Intergovern-
mental Conference;

THE PRESIDENT OF THE FEDERAL REPUBLIC OF GERMANY:

Dr Konrad ADENAUER, Federal Chancellor,
Professor Dr Walter HALLSTEIN, State Secretary of the Federal Foreign
Office;

THE PRESIDENT OF THE FRENCH REPUBLIC:

Mr Christian PINEAU, Minister for Foreign Affairs,
Mr Maurice FAURE, Under-Secretary of State for Foreign Affairs;

THE PRESIDENT OF THE ITALIAN REPUBLIC:

Mr Antonio SEGNI, President of the Council of Ministers,
Professor Gaetano MARTINO, Minister for Foreign Affairs;

HER ROYAL HIGHNESS THE GRAND DUCHESS OF LUXEMBOURG:

Mr Joseph BECH, President of the Government, Minister for Foreign
Affairs,
Mr Lambert SCHAUS, Ambassador, Head of the Luxembourg Delega-
tion to the Intergovernmental Conference;

HER MAJESTY THE QUEEN OF THE NETHERLANDS:

Mr Joseph LUNS, Minister for Foreign Affairs,
Mr J. LINTHORST HOMAN, Head of the Netherlands Delegation to the
Intergovernmental Conference;

WHO, having exchanged their Full Powers, found in good and due
form, have agreed as follows.

TITLE ONE

The tasks of the Community

Article 1

By this Treaty the HIGH CONTRACTING PARTIES establish among themselves a EUROPEAN ATOMIC ENERGY COMMUNITY (EURATOM).

It shall be the task of the Community to contribute to the raising of the standard of living in the Member States and to the development of relations with the other countries by creating the conditions necessary for the speedy establishment and growth of nuclear industries.

Article 2

In order to perform its task, the Community shall, as provided in this Treaty:

(a) promote research and ensure the dissemination of technical information;

(b) establish uniform safety standards to protect the health of workers and of the general public and ensure that they are applied;

(c) facilitate investment and ensure, particularly by encouraging ventures on the part of undertakings, the establishment of the basic installations necessary for the development of nuclear energy in the Community;

(d) ensure that all users in the Community receive a regular and equitable supply of ores and nuclear fuels;

(e) make certain, by appropriate supervision, that nuclear materials are not diverted to purposes other than those for which they are intended;

(f) exercise the right of ownership conferred upon it with respect to special fissile materials;

(g) ensure wide commercial outlets and access to the best technical facilities by the creation of a common market in specialized materials and equipment, by the free movement of capital for investment in the field of nuclear energy and by freedom of employment for specialists within the Community;

(h) establish with other countries and international organizations such relations as will foster progress in the peaceful uses of nuclear energy.

Article 3

1. The tasks entrusted to the Community shall be carried out by the following institutions:

— a EUROPEAN PARLIAMENT,
— a COUNCIL,
— a COMMISSION,
— a COURT OF JUSTICE.

Each institution shall act within the limits of the powers conferred upon it by this Treaty.

2. The Council and the Commission shall be assisted by an *Economic and Social Committee* acting in an advisory capacity.

3. The audit shall be carried out by a Court of Auditors acting within the limits of the powers conferred upon it by this Treaty.*

---

* Third paragraph added under Article 19 of the Treaty amending Certain Financial Provisions.

TITLE TWO

Provisions for the encouragement of progress in the field of nuclear energy

CHAPTER I

PROMOTION OF RESEARCH

Article 4

1. The Commission shall be responsible for promoting and facilitating nuclear research in the Member States and for complementing it by carrying out a Community research and training programme.

2. The activity of the Commission in this respect shall be carried out within the fields listed in Annex I to this Treaty.

This list may be amended by the Council, acting by a qualified majority on a proposal from the Commission. The latter shall consult the Scientific and Technical Committee established under Article 134.

Article 5

For purposes of coordinating and complementing research undertaken in Member States, the Commission shall, either by a specific request addressed to a given recipient and conveyed to the Government concerned, or by a general published request, call upon Member States, persons or undertakings to communicate to it their programmes relating to the research which it specifies in the request.

After giving those concerned full opportunity to comment, the Commission may deliver a reasoned opinion on each of the programmes communicated to it. The Commission shall deliver such an opinion if the State, person or undertaking which has communicated the programme so requests.

By such opinions the Commission shall discourage unnecessary duplication and shall direct research towards sectors which are insufficiently explored. The Commission may not publish these programmes without the consent of the State, person or undertaking which has communicated them.

The Commission shall publish at regular intervals a list of those sectors of nuclear research which it considers to be insufficiently explored.

The Commission may bring together representatives of public and private research centres as well as any experts engaged in research in the same or related fields for mutual consultation and exchanges of information.

Article 6

To encourage the carrying out of research programmes communicated to it the Commission may:

(a) provide financial assistance within the framework of research contracts, without, however, offering subsidies;

(b) supply, either free of charge or against payment, for carrying out such programmes, any source materials or special fissile materials which it has available;

(c) place installations, equipment or expert assistance at the disposal of Member States, persons or undertakings, either free of charge or against payment;

(d) promote joint financing by the Member States, persons or undertakings concerned.

Article 7

Community research and training programmes shall be determined by the Council, acting unanimously on a proposal from the Commission, which shall consult the Scientific and Technical Committee.

These programmes shall be drawn up for a period of not more than five years.

The funds required for carrying out these programmes shall be included each year in the research and investment budget of the Community.

The Commission shall ensure that these programmes are carried out and shall submit an annual report thereon to the Council.

The Commission shall keep the Economic and Social Committee informed of the broad outlines of Community research and training programmes.

Article 8

1. After consulting the Scientific and Technical Committee, the Commission shall establish a Joint Nuclear Research Centre.

This Centre shall ensure that the research programmes and other tasks assigned to it by the Commission are carried out.

It shall also ensure that a uniform nuclear terminology and a standard system of measurements are established.

It shall set up a central bureau for nuclear measurements.

2. The activities of the Centre may, for geographical or functional reasons, be carried out in separate establishments.

Article 9

1. After obtaining the opinion of the Economic and Social Committee the Commission may, within the framework of the Joint Nuclear Research Centre, set up schools for the training of specialists, particularly in the fields of prospecting for minerals, the production of high-purity nuclear materials, the processing of irradiated fuels, nuclear engineering, health and safety and the production and use of radioisotopes.

The Commission shall determine the details of such training.

2. An institution of university status shall be established; the way in which it will function shall be determined by the Council, acting by a qualified majority on a proposal from the Commission.

Article 10

The Commission may, by contract, entrust the carrying out of certain parts of the Community research programme to Member States, persons or undertakings, or to third countries, international organizations or nationals of third countries.

Article 11

The Commission shall publish the research programmes referred to in Articles 7, 8 and 10, and also regular progress reports on their implementation.

CHAPTER II

DISSEMINATION OF INFORMATION

Section I

Information over which the Community has power of disposal

Article 12

Member States, persons or undertakings shall have the right, on application to the Commission, to obtain non-exclusive licences under patents, provisionally protected patent rights, utility models or patent applications owned by the Community, where they are able to make effective use of the inventions covered thereby.

Under the same conditions, the Commission shall grant sub-licences under patents, provisionally protected patent rights, utility models or patent applications, where the Community holds contractual licences conferring power to do so.

The Commission shall grant such licences or sub-licences on terms to be agreed with the licensees and shall furnish all the information required for their use. These terms shall relate in particular to suitable remuneration and, where appropriate, to the right of the licensee to grant sub-licences to third parties and to the obligation to treat the information as a trade secret.

Failing agreement on the terms referred to in the third paragraph, the licensees may bring the matter before the Court of Justice so that appropriate terms may be fixed.

Article 13

The Commission shall communicate to Member States, persons and undertakings information acquired by the Community which is not covered by the provisions of Article 12, whether such information is derived from its own research programme or communicated to the Commission with authority to make free use of it.

The Commission may, however, make the disclosure of such information conditional on its being treated as confidential and not passed on to third parties.

The Commission may not disclose information which has been acquired subject to restrictions on its use or dissemination — such as information known as classified information — unless it ensures compliance with these restrictions.

S e c t i o n I I

Other information

(a) Dissemination by amicable agreement

Article 14

The Commission shall endeavour, by amicable agreement, to secure both the communication of information which is of use to the Community in the attainment of its objectives and the granting of licences under patents, provisionally protected patent rights, utility models or patent applications covering such information.

Article 15

The Commission shall establish a procedure by which Member States, persons and undertakings may use it as an intermediary for exchanging provisional or final results of their research, in so far as these results have not been acquired by the Community under research contracts awarded by the Commission.

This procedure must be such as to ensure the confidential nature of the exchange. The results communicated may, however, be transmitted by the Commission to the Joint Nuclear Research Centre for documentation purposes; this shall not entail any right of use to which the communicating party has not agreed.

(b) Compulsory communication to the Commission

Article 16

1. As soon as an application for a patent or a utility model relating to a specifically nuclear subject is filed with a Member State, that State shall ask the applicant to agree that the contents of the application be communicated to the Commission forthwith.

If the applicant agrees, this communication shall be made within three months of the date of filing the application. If the applicant does not agree, the Member State shall, within the same period, notify the Commission of the existence of the application.

The Commission may require a Member State to communicate the contents of an application of whose existence it has been notified.

The Commission shall make any such request within two months of the date of notification. Any extension of this period shall entail a corresponding extension of the period referred to in the sixth subparagraph of this paragraph.

On receiving such a request from the Commission, the Member State shall again ask the applicant to agree to communication of the contents of the application. If the applicant agrees, communication shall be made forthwith.

If the applicant does not agree, the Member State shall nevertheless be required to make this communication to the Commission within eighteen months of the date on which the application was filed.

2.   Member States shall inform the Commission, within eighteen months of the filing date, of the existence of any as yet unpublished application for a patent or utility model which seems to them, *prima facie,* to deal with a subject which, although not specifically nuclear, is direclty connected with and essential to the development of nuclear energy in the Community.

If the Commission so requests, the contents of the application shall be communicated to it within two months.

3.   In order that publication may take place as soon as possible, Member States shall reduce to a minimum the time taken to process applications for patents or utility models relating to subjects referred to in paragraphs 1 and 2 concerning which a request has been made by the Commission.

4.   The Commission shall treat the above-mentioned communications as confidential. They may only be made for documentation purposes. The Commission may, however, make use of the inventions communicated to it, either with the consent of the applicant or in accordance with Articles 17 to 23.

5. The provisions of this Article shall not apply when an agreement concluded with a third State or an international organization precludes communication.

*(c) Grant of licences by arbitration
or under compulsory powers*

Article 17

1. Failing amicable agreement, non-exclusive licences may be granted either by arbitration or under compulsory powers in accordance with Articles 18 to 23:

(a) to the Community or to Joint Undertakings accorded this right under Article 48 in respect of patents, provisionally protected patent rights or utility models relating to inventions directly connected with nuclear research, where the granting of such licences is necessary for the continuance of their own research or indispensable to the operation of their installations.

If the Commission so requests, such licences shall include the right to authorize third parties to make use of the invention, where they are carrying out work for or orders placed by the Community or Joint Undertakings;

(b) to persons or undertakings which have applied to the Commission for them in respect of patents, provisionally protected patent rights or utility models relating to inventions directly connected with and essential to the development of nuclear energy in the Community, provided that all the following conditions are fulfilled:

(i) At least four years have elapsed since the filing of the patent application, save in the case of an invention relating to a specifically nuclear subject;

(ii) The requirements arising out of the development of nuclear energy, in the Commission's conception of such development, in the territory of a Member State where an invention is protected, are not being met with regard to that invention;

(iii) The proprietor, having been called upon to meet such requirements either himself or through his licensees, has not complied with this request;

(iv) The persons or undertakings applying for licences are in a position to meet such requirements effectively by making use of the invention.

Member States may not, in order to meet such requirements, take any coercive measures provided for in their national legislation which will limit the protection accorded to the invention, save at the prior request of the Commission.

2. A non-exclusive licence may not be granted as provided for in paragraph 1 where the proprietor can establish the existence of legitimate reasons, in particular that he has not had sufficient time at his disposal.

3. The granting of a licence pursuant to paragraph 1 shall confer a right to full compensation, the amount of which shall be agreed between the proprietor of the patent, provisionally protected patent right or utility model and the licensee.

4. The provisions of this Article shall not affect those of the Paris Convention for the Protection of Industrial Property.

Article 18

An Arbitration Committee is hereby established for the purposes provided for in this Section. The Council shall appoint the members and lay down the rules of procedure of this Committee, acting on a proposal from the Court of Justice.

An appeal, having suspensory effect, may be brought by the parties before the Court of Justice against a decision of the Arbitration Committee within one month of notification thereof. The Court of Justice shall confine its examination to the formal validity of the decision and to the interpretation of the provisions of this Treaty by the Arbitration Committee.

The final decisions of the Arbitration Committee shall have the force of *res judicata* between the parties concerned. They shall be enforceable as provided in Article 164.

Article 19

Where, failing amicable agreement, the Commission intends to secure the granting of licences in one of the cases provided for in Article 17, it shall give notice of its intention to the proprietor of the patent, provisionally protected patent right, utility model or patent application, and shall specify in such notice the name of the applicant for and the scope of the licence.

Article 20

The proprietor may, within one month of receipt of the notice referred to in Article 19, propose to the Commission and, where appropriate, to the applicant that they conclude a special agreement to refer the matter to the Arbitration Committee.

Should the Commission or the applicant refuse to enter into such an agreement, the Commission shall not require the Member State or its appropriate authorities to grant the licence or cause it to be granted.

If, when the matter is referred to it under a special agreement, the Arbitration Committee finds that the request from the Commission complies with the provisions of Article 17, it shall give a reasoned decision containing a grant of the licence to the applicant and laying down the terms of the licence and the remuneration therefor, to the extent that the parties have not reached agreement on these points.

Article 21

If the proprietor does not propose that the matter be referred to the Arbitration Committee, the Commission may call upon the Member State concerned or its appropriate authorities to grant the licence or cause it to be granted.

If, having heard the proprietor's case, the Member State, or its appropriate authorities, considers that the conditions of Article 17 have not been complied with, it shall notify the Commission of its refusal to grant the licence or to cause it to be granted.

If it refuses to grant the licence or to cause it to be granted, or if, within four months of the date of the request, no information is forthcoming with regard to the granting of the licence, the Commission shall have two months in which to bring the matter before the Court of Justice.

The proprietor must be heard in the proceedings before the Court of Justice.

If the judgment of the Court of Justice establishes that the conditions of Article 17 have been complied with, the Member State concerned, or its appropriate authorities, shall take such measures as enforcement of that judgment may require.

Article 22

1. If the proprietor of the patent, provisionally protected patent right or utility model and the licensee fail to agree on the amount of compensation, the parties concerned may conclude a special agreement to refer the matter to the Arbitration Committee.

By doing so, the parties waive the right to institute any proceedings other than those provided for in Article 18.

2. If the licensee refuses to conclude a special agreement, the licence he has been granted shall be deemed void.

If the proprietor refuses to conclude a special agreement, the compensation referred to in this Article shall be determined by the appropriate national authorities.

Article 23

After the lapse of one year, the decisions of the Arbitration Committee or the appropriate national authorities may, if there are new facts to justify it, be revised with respect to the terms of the licence.

Such revision shall be a matter for the body which gave the decision.

Section III

Security provisions

Article 24

Information which the Community acquires as a result of carrying out its research programme, and the disclosure of which is liable to harm the defence interests of one or more Member States, shall be subject to a security system in accordance with the following provisions.

1. The Council shall, acting on a proposal from the Commission, adopt security regulations which, account being taken of the provisions of this Article, lay down the various security gradings to be applied and the security measures appropriate to each grading.

2. Where the Commission considers that the disclosure of certain information is liable to harm the defence interests of one or more Member States, it shall provisionally apply to that information the security grading required in that case by the security regulations.

It shall communicate such information forthwith to the Member States, which shall provisionally ensure its security in the same manner.

Member States shall inform the Commission within three months whether they wish to maintain the grading provisionally applied, substitute another or declassify the information.

Upon the expiry of this period, the highest grading of those requested shall be applied. The Commission shall notify the Member States accordingly.

At the request of the Commission or of a Member State, the Council may, acting unanimously, at any time apply another grading or declassify the information. The Council shall obtain the opinion of the Commission before taking any action on a request from a Member State.

3. The provisions of Articles 12 and 13 shall not apply to information subject to a security grading.

Nevertheless, provided that the appropriate security measures are observed,

(a) the information referred to in Articles 12 and 13 may be communicated by the Commission:

> (i) to a Joint Undertaking;
>
> (ii) to a person or undertaking other than a Joint Undertaking, through the Member State in whose territory that person or undertaking operates;

(b) the information referred to in Article 13 may be communicated by a Member State to a person or to an undertaking other than a Joint

Undertaking, operating in the territory of that State, provided that the Commission is notified of this communication;

(c) each Member State has, however, the right to require the Commission to grant a licence under Article 12 to meet the needs of that State or those of a person or undertaking operating in its territory.

Article 25

1. A Member State notifying the existence or communicating the contents of an application for a patent or utility model relating to a subject specified in Article 16 (1) or (2) shall, where appropriate, draw attention to the need to apply a given security grading for defence reasons, at the same time stating the probable duration of such grading.

The Commission shall pass on to the other Member States all communications received in accordance with the preceding sub-paragraph. The Commission and the Member States shall take those measures which, under the security regulations, correspond to the grading required by the State of origin.

2. The Commission may also pass on these communications to Joint Undertakings or, through a Member State, to a person or to an undertaking other than a Joint Undertaking operating in the territory of that State.

Inventions which are the subject of applications referred to in paragraph 1 may be used only with the consent of the applicant or in accordance with Articles 17 to 23.

The communications and, where appropriate, the use referred to in this paragraph shall be subject to the measures which, under the security regulations, correspond to the security grading required by the State of origin.

The communications shall in all cases be subject to the consent of the State of origin. Consent to communication and use may be withheld only for defence reasons.

3. At the request of the Commission or of a Member State, the Council may, acting unanimously, at any time apply another grading or declassify the information. The Council shall obtain the opinion of the Commission before taking any action on a request from a Member State.

Article 26

1. Where information covered by patents, patent applications, provision-ally protected patent rights, utility models or applications for utility models has been classified in accordance with Articles 24 and 25, the States which have applied for such classification may not refuse to allow corresponding applications to be filed in the other Member States.

Each Member State shall take the necessary measures to maintain the security of such rights and applications in accordance with the procedure laid down in its own laws and regulations.

2. No applications relating to information classified in accordance with Article 24 may be filed outside the Member States except with the unani-mous consent of the latter. Should Member States fail to make known their attitude, their consent shall be deemed to have been obtained on the expiry of six months from the date on which the information was com-municated to the Member States by the Commission.

Article 27

Compensation for any damage suffered by the applicant as a result of classification for defence reasons shall be governed by the provisions of the national laws of the Member States and shall be the responsibility of the State which applied for such classification or which either obtained the upgrading or extension of the classification or caused the filing of applications outside the Community to be prohibited.

Where several Member States have either obtained the upgrading or extension of the classification or caused the filing of applications outside the Community to be prohibited, they shall be jointly responsible for making good any damage arising out of their action.

The Community may not claim any compensation under this Article.

Section IV

Special provisions

Article 28

Where, as a result of their communication to the Commission, unpublished applications for patents or utility models, or patents or utility models classified for defence reasons, are improperly used or come to the knowledge of an unauthorized person, the Community shall make good the damage suffered by the party concerned.

Without prejudice to its own rights against the person responsible for the damage, the Community shall, to the extent that it has made good such damage, acquire any rights of action enjoyed by those concerned against third parties. This shall not affect the right of the Community to take action against the person responsible for the damage in accordance with the general provisions in force.

Article 29

Where an agreement or contract for the exchange of scientific or industrial information in the nuclear field between a Member State, a person or an undertaking on the one hand, and a third State, an international organization or a national of a third State on the other, requires, on either part, the signature of a State acting in its sovereign capacity, it shall be concluded by the Commission.

Subject to the provisions of Articles 103 and 104, the Commission may, however, on such conditions as it considers appropriate, authorize a Member State, a person or an undertaking to conclude such agreements.

CHAPTER III

HEALTH AND SAFETY

Article 30

Basic standards shall be laid down within the Community for the protection of the health of workers and the general public against the dangers arising from ionizing radiations.

The expression 'basic standards' means:

(a) maximum permissible doses compatible with adequate safety;

(b) maximum permissible levels of exposure and contamination;

(c) the fundamental principles governing the health surveillance of workers.

Article 31

The basic standards shall be worked out by the Commission after it has obtained the opinion of a group of persons appointed by the Scientific and Technical Committee from among scientific experts, and in particular public health experts, in the Member States. The Commission shall obtain the opinion of the Economic and Social Committee on these basic standards.

After consulting the European Parliament the Council shall, on a proposal from the Commission, which shall forward to it the opinions obtained from these Committees, establish the basic standards; the Council shall act by a qualified majority.

Article 32

At the request of the Commission or of a Member State, the basic standards may be revised or supplemented in accordance with the procedure laid down in Article 31.

The Commission shall examine any request made by a Member State.

Article 33

Each Member State shall lay down the appropriate provisions, whether by legislation, regulation or administrative action, to ensure compliance with the basic standards which have been established and shall take the necessary measures with regard to teaching, education and vocational training.

The Commission shall make appropriate recommendations for harmonizing the provisions applicable in this field in the Member States.

To this end, the Member States shall communicate to the Commission the provisions applicable at the date of entry into force of this Treaty and any subsequent draft provisions of the same kind.

Any recommendations the Commission may wish to issue with regard to such draft provisions shall be made within three months of the date on which such draft provisions are communicated.

Article 34

Any Member State in whose territories particularly dangerous experiments are to take place shall take additional health and safety measures, on which it shall first obtain the opinion of the Commission.

The assent of the Commission shall be required where the effects of such experiments are liable to affect the territories of other Member States.

Article 35

Each Member State shall establish the facilities necessary to carry out continuous monitoring of the level of radioactivity in the air, water and soil and to ensure compliance with the basic standards.

The Commission shall have the right of access to such facilities; it may verify their operation and efficiency.

Article 36

The appropriate authorities shall periodically communicate information on the checks referred to in Article 35 to the Commission so that it is kept informed of the level of radioactivity to which the public is exposed.

Article 37

Each Member State shall provide the Commission with such general data relating to any plan for the disposal of radioactive waste in whatever form as will make it possible to determine whether the implementation of such plan is liable to result in the radioactive contamination of the water, soil or airspace of another Member State.

The Commission shall deliver its opinion within six months, after consulting the group of experts referred to in Article 31.

Article 38

The Commission shall make recommendations to the Member States with regard to the level of radioactivity in the air, water and soil.

In cases of urgency, the Commission shall issue a directive requiring the Member State concerned to take, within a period laid down by the Commission, all necessary measures to prevent infringement of the basic standards and to ensure compliance with regulations.

Should the State in question fail to comply with the Commission directive within the period laid down, the Commission or any Member State concerned may forthwith, by way of derogation from Articles 141 and 142, bring the matter before the Court of Justice.

Article 39

The Commission shall set up within the framework of the Joint Nuclear Research Centre, as soon as the latter has been established, a health and safety documentation and study section.

This section shall in particular have the task of collecting the documentation and information referred to in Articles 33, 36 and 37 and of assisting the Commission in carrying out the tasks assigned to it by this Chapter.

CHAPTER IV

INVESTMENT

Article 40

In order to stimulate action by persons and undertakings and to facilitate coordinated development of their investment in the nuclear field, the Commission shall periodically publish illustrative programmes indicating in particular nuclear energy production targets and all the types of investment required for their attainment.

The Commission shall obtain the opinion of the Economic and Social Committee on such programmes before their publication.

Article 41

Persons and undertakings engaged in the industrial activities listed in Annex II to this Treaty shall communicate to the Commission investment projects relating to new installations and also to replacements or conversions which fulfil the criteria as to type and size laid down by the Council on a proposal from the Commission.

The list of industrial activities referred to above may be altered by the Council, acting by a qualified majority on a proposal from the Commission, which shall first obtain the opinion of the Economic and Social Committee.

Article 42

The projects referred to in Article 41 shall be communicated to the Commission and, for information purposes, to the Member State concerned not later than three months before the first contracts are concluded with the suppliers or, if the work is to be carried out by the undertaking with its own resources, three months before the work begins.

The Council may, acting on a proposal from the Commission, alter this time limit.

Article 43

The Commission shall discuss with the persons or undertakings all aspects of investment projects which relate to the objectives of this Treaty.

It shall communicate its views to the Member State concerned.

Article 44

The Commission may, with the consent of the Member States, persons and undertakings concerned, publish any investment projects communicated to it.

CHAPTER V

JOINT UNDERTAKINGS

Article 45

Undertakings which are of fundamental importance to the development of the nuclear industry in the Community may be established as Joint Undertakings within the meaning of this Treaty, in accordance with the following Articles.

Article 46

1. Every project for establishing a Joint Undertaking, whether originating from the Commission, a Member State or any other quarter, shall be the subject of an inquiry by the Commission.

For this purpose, the Commission shall obtain the views of Member States and of any public or private body which in its opinion can usefully advise it.

2. The Commission shall forward to the Council any project for establishing a Joint Undertaking, together with its reasoned opinion.

If the Commission delivers a favourable opinion on the need for the proposed Joint Undertaking, it shall submit proposals to the Council concerning:

(a) location;

(b) statutes;

(c) the scale of and timetable for financing;

(d) possible participation by the Community in the financing of the Joint Undertaking;

(e) possible participation by a third State, an international organization or a national of a third State in the financing or management of the Joint Undertaking;

(f) the conferring of any or all of the advantages listed in Annex III to this Treaty.

The Commission shall attach a detailed report on the project as a whole.

Article 47

The Council may, when the matter has been submitted to it by the Commission, request the latter to supply such further information or to undertake such further inquiries as the Council may consider necessary.

If the Council, acting by a qualified majority, considers that a project forwarded by the Commission with an unfavourable opinion should nevertheless be carried out, the Commission shall submit to the Council the proposals and the detailed report referred to in Article 46.

Where the opinion of the Commission is favourable or in the case referred to in the preceding paragraph, the Council shall act by a qualified majority on each of the proposals from the Commission.

The Council shall, however, act unanimously in respect of:

(a) participation by the Community in the financing of the Joint Undertaking;

(b) participation by a third State, an international organization or a national of a third State in the financing or management of the Joint Undertaking.

Article 48

The Council may, acting unanimously on a proposal from the Commission, make applicable to each Joint Undertaking any or all of the advantages listed in Annex III to this Treaty; each Member State shall for its part ensure that these advantages are conferred.

The Council may, in accordance with the same procedure, lay down the conditions governing the conferment of these advantages.

Article 49

Joint Undertakings shall be established by Council decision.

Each Joint Undertaking shall have legal personality.

In each of the Member States, it shall enjoy the most extensive legal capacity accorded to legal persons under their respective national laws; it may, in particular, acquire or dispose of movable and immovable property and may be a party to legal proceedings.

Save as otherwise provided in this Treaty or in its own statutes, each Joint Undertaking shall be governed by the rules applying to industrial or commercial undertakings; its statutes may make subsidiary reference to the national laws of the Member States.

Save where jurisdiction is conferred upon the Court of Justice by this Treaty, disputes in which Joint Undertakings are concerned shall be determined by the appropriate national courts or tribunals.

Article 50

The statutes of Joint Undertakings shall be amended, where necessary, in accordance with the special provisions which they contain for this purpose.

Such amendments shall not, however, enter into force until they have been approved by the Council, acting in accordance with the procedure laid down in Article 47 on a proposal from the Commission.

Article 51

The Commission shall be responsible for carrying out all decisions of the Council relating to the establishment of Joint Undertakings until the bodies responsible for the operation of such Undertakings have been set up.

CHAPTER VI

SUPPLIES

Article 52

1. The supply of ores, source materials and special fissile materials shall be ensured, in accordance with the provisions of this Chapter, by means of a common supply policy on the principle of equal access to sources of supply.

2. For this purpose and under the conditions laid down in this Chapter:

(a) all practices designed to secure a privileged position for certain users shall be prohibited;

(b) an Agency is hereby established; it shall have a right of option on ores, source materials and special fissile materials produced in the territories of Member States and an exclusive right to conclude contracts relating to the supply of ores, source materials and special fissile materials coming from inside the Community or from outside.

The Agency may not discriminate in any way between users on grounds of the use which they intend to make of the supplies requested unless such use is unlawful or is found to be contrary to the conditions imposed by suppliers outside the Community on the consignment in question.

Section I

The Agency

Article 53

The Agency shall be under the supervision of the Commission, which shall issue directives to it, possess a right of veto over its decisions and appoint its Director-General and Deputy Director-General.

Any act, whether implied or expressed, performed by the Agency in the exercise of its right of option or of its exclusive right to conclude supply contracts, may be referred by the parties concerned to the Commission, which shall give a decision thereon within one month.

Article 54

The Agency shall have legal personality and financial autonomy.

The Council shall lay down the statutes of the Agency, acting by a qualified majority on a proposal from the Commission.

The statutes may be amended in accordance with the same procedure.

The statutes shall determine the Agency's capital and the terms upon which it is to be subscribed. The major part of the capital shall always belong to the Community and to the Member States. The contributions to the capital shall be determined by common accord of the Member States.

The rules for the commercial management of the activities of the Agency shall be laid down in the statutes. The latter may provide for a charge on transactions to defray the operating expenses of the Agency.

Article 55

The Member States shall communicate or cause to be communicated to the Agency all the information necessary to enable it to exercise its right of option and its exclusive right to conclude supply contracts.

Article 56

The Member States shall be responsible for ensuring that the Agency may operate freely in their territories.

They may establish one or more bodies having authority to represent, in relations with the Agency, producers and users in the non-European territories under their jurisdiction.

Section II

Ores, source materials and special fissile materials coming

from inside the Community

Article 57

1. The right of option of the Agency shall cover:

(a) the acquisition of rights to use and consume materials owned by the Community under the provisions of Chapter VIII;

(b) the acquisition of the right of ownership in all other cases.

2. The Agency shall exercise its right of option by concluding contracts with producers of ores, source materials and special fissile materials.

Subject to Articles 58, 62 and 63, every producer shall offer to the Agency the ores, source materials or special fissile materials which he produces within the territories of Member States before they are used, transferred or stored.

655

Article 58

Where a producer carries out several stages of production from extraction of the ore up to and including production of the metal, he may offer the product to the Agency at whichever stage of production he chooses.

The same shall apply to two or more connected undertakings, where the connection has been duly communicated to the Commission and discussed with it in accordance with the procedures laid down in Articles 43 and 44.

Article 59

If the Agency does not exercise its right of option on the whole or any part of the output of a producer, the latter

(a) may, either by using his own resources or under contract, process or cause to be processed the ores, source materials or special fissile materials, provided that he offers to the Agency the product of such processing;

(b) shall be authorized by a decision of the Commission to dispose of his available production outside the Community, provided that the terms he offers are not more favourable than those previously offered to the Agency. However, special fissile materials may be exported only through the Agency and in accordance with the provisions of Article 62.

The Commission may not grant such authorization if the recipients of the supplies fail to satisfy it that the general interests of the Community will be safeguarded or if the terms and conditions of such contracts are contrary to the objectives of this Treaty.

Article 60

Potential users shall periodically inform the Agency of the supplies they require, specifying the quantities, the physical and chemical nature, the place of origin, the intended use, delivery dates and price terms, which are to form the terms and conditions of the supply contract which they wish to conclude.

Similarly, producers shall inform the Agency of offers which they are able to make, stating all the specifications, and in particular the duration of contracts, required to enable their production programmes to be drawn up. Such contracts shall be of not more than ten year's duration save with the agreement of the Commission.

The Agency shall inform all potential users of the offers and of the volume of applications which it has received and shall call upon them to place their orders by a specified time limit.

When the Agency has received all such orders, it shall make known the terms on which it can meet them.

If the Agency cannot meet in their entirety all the orders received, it shall, subject to the provisions of Articles 68 and 69, share out the supplies proportionately among the orders relating to each offer.

Agency rules, which shall require approval by the Commission, shall determine the manner in which demand is to be balanced against supply.

Article 61

The Agency shall meet all orders unless prevented from so doing by legal or material obstacles.

When concluding a contract, the Agency may, while complying with the provisions of Article 52, require users to make appropriate advance payments either as security or to assist in meeting the Agency's own long-term commitments to producers where these are essential to carrying out the order.

Article 62

1. The Agency shall exercise its right of option on special fissile materials produced in the territories of Member States in order

(a) to meet demand from users within the Community in accordance with Article 60; or

(b) to store such materials itself; or

(c) to export such materials with the authorization of the Commission which shall comply with the second subparagraph of Article 59 *(b)*.

2. Nevertheless, while continuing to be subject to the provisions of Chapter VII, such materials and any fertile wastes shall be left in the possession of the producer, so that he may

(a) store them with the authorization of the Agency; or

(b) use them within the limits of his own requirements; or

(c) make them available to undertakings in the Community, within the limits of their requirements, where for carrying out a programme duly communicated to the Commission, these undertakings have with the producer a direct connection which has neither the aim nor the effect of limiting production, technical development or investment or of improperly creating inequalities between users in the Community.

3. The provisions of Article 89 (1) *(a)* shall apply to special fissile materials which are produced in the territories of Member States and on which the Agency has not exercised its right of option.

Article 63

Ores, source materials and special fissile materials produced by Joint Undertakings shall be allotted to users in accordance with the rules laid down in the statutes or agreements of such Undertakings.

Section III

Ores, source materials and special fissile materials coming from outside the Community

Article 64

The Agency, acting where appropriate within the framework of agreements concluded between the Community and a third State or an international organization, shall subject to the exceptions provided for in this Treaty, have the exclusive right to enter into agreements or contracts whose principal aim is the supply of ores, source materials or special fissile materials coming from outside the Community.

Article 65

Article 60 shall apply applications from users and to contracts between users and the Agency relating to the supply of ores, source materials or special fissile materials coming from outside the Community.

The Agency may, however, decide on the geographical origin of supplies provided that conditions which are at least as favourable as those specified in the order are thereby secured for the user.

Article 66

Should the Commission find, on application by the users concerned, that the Agency is not in a position to deliver within a reasonable period of time all or part of the supplies ordered, or that it can only do so at excessively high prices, the users shall have the right to conclude directly contracts relating to supplies from outside the Community, provided that such contracts meet in essential respects the requirements specified in their orders.

This right shall be granted for a period of one year; it may be extended if the situation which justified its granting continues.

Users who avail themselves of the right provided for in this Article shall communicate to the Commission the direct contracts which they propose to conclude. The Commission may, within one month, object to the conclusion of such contracts if they are contrary to the objectives of this Treaty.

S e c t i o n   I V

Prices

Article 67

Save where exceptions are provided for in this Treaty, prices shall be determined as a result of balancing supply against demand as provided in Article 60; the national regulations of the Member States shall not contravene such provisions.

Article 68

Pricing practices designed to secure a privileged position for certain users in violation of the principle of equal access laid down in the provisions of this Chapter shall be prohibited.

If the Agency finds that any such practices are being employed it shall report them to the Commission.

The Commission may, if it accepts the findings, set the prices of the offers in issue at a level compatible with the principle of equal access.

Article 69

The Council may fix prices, acting unanimously on a proposal from the Commission.

When the Agency lays down, in pursuance of Article 60, the terms on which orders can be met, it may propose to the users who have placed orders that prices be equalized.

Section V

Provisions relating to supply policy

Article 70

Within the limits set by the budget of the Community, the Commission may, on such conditions as it shall determine, give financial support to prospecting programmes in the territories of Member States.

The Commission may make recommendations to the Member States with a view to the development of prospecting for and exploitation of mineral deposits.

The Member States shall submit annually to the Commission a report on the development of prospecting and production, on probable reserves and on investment in mining which has been made or is planned in their territories. The reports shall be submitted to the Council, together with an opinion from the Commission which shall state in particular what action has been taken by Member States on recommendations made to them under the preceding paragraph.

If, when the matter has been submitted to it by the Commission, the Council finds by a qualified majority that, although the prospects for extraction appear economically justified on a long-term basis, prospecting activities and the expansion of mining operations continue to be markedly inadequate, the Member State concerned shall, for as long as it has failed to remedy this situation, be deemed to have waived, both for itself and for its nationals, the right of equal access to other sources of supply within the Community.

Article 71

The Commission shall make all appropriate recommendations to Member States with regard to revenue or mining regulations.

Article 72

The Agency may, from material available inside or outside the Community, build up the necessary commercial stocks to facilitate supplies to or normal deliveries by the Community.

The Commission may, where necessary, decide to build up emergency stocks. The method of financing such stocks shall be approved by the Council, acting by a qualified majority on a proposal from the Commission.

Section VI

Special provisions

Article 73

Where an agreement or contract between a Member State, a person or an undertaking on the one hand, and a third State, an international organization or a national of a third State on the other, provides *inter alia* for delivery of products which come within the province of the Agency, the prior consent of the Commission shall be required for the conclusion or renewal of that agreement or contract, as far as delivery of the products is concerned.

Article 74

The Commission may exempt from the provisions of this Chapter the transfer, import or export of small quantities of ores, source materials or special fissile materials such as are normally used in research.

The Agency shall be notified of every transfer, import or export operation effected by virtue of this provision.

Article 75

The provisions of this Chapter shall not apply to commitments relating to the processing, conversion or shaping of ores, source materials or special fissile materials and entered into,

(a) by several persons or undertakings, where the material is to return to the original person or undertaking after being processed, converted or shaped; or

(b) by a person or undertaking and an international organization or a national of a third State, where the material is processed, converted or shaped outside the Community and then returned to the original person or undertaking; or

(c) by a person or undertaking and an international organization or a national of a third State, where the material is processed, converted or shaped inside the Community and is then returned either to the original organization or national or to any other consignee likewise outside the Community designated by such organization or national.

The persons and undertakings concerned shall, however, notify the Agency of the existence of such commitments and, as soon as the contracts are signed, of the quantities of material involved in the movements. The Commission may prevent the commitments referred to in subparagraph *(b)* from being undertaken if it considers that the conversion or shaping cannot be carried out efficiently and safely and without the loss of material to the detriment of the Community.

The materials to which such commitments relate shall be subject in the territories of the Member States to the safeguards laid down in Chapter VII. The provisions of Chapter VIII shall not, however, be applicable to special fissile materials covered by the commitments referred to in subparagraph *(c)*.

Article 76

On the initiative of a Member State or of the Commission, and particularly if unforeseen circumstances create a situation of general shortage, the Council may, acting unanimously on a proposal from the Commission and after consulting the European Parliament, amend the provisions of this Chapter. The Commission shall inquire into any request made by a Member State.

Seven years after the entry into force of this Treaty, the Council may confirm these provisions in their entirety. Failing confirmation, new provisions relating to the subject matter of this Chapter shall be adopted in accordance with the procedure laid down in the preceding paragraph.

CHAPTER VII

SAFEGUARDS

Article 77

In accordance with the provisions of this Chapter, the Commission shall satisfy itself that, in the territories of Member States,

(a) ores, source materials and special fissile materials are not diverted from their intended uses as declared by the users;

(b) the provisions relating to supply and any particular safeguarding obligations assumed by the Community under an agreement concluded with a third State or an international organization are complied with.

Article 78

Anyone setting up or operating an installation for the production, separation or other use of source materials or special fissile materials or for the processing of irradiated nuclear fuels shall declare to the

665

Commission the basic technical characteristics of the installations, to the extent that knowledge of these characteristics is necessary for the attainment of the objectives set out in Article 77.

The Commission must approve the techniques to be used for the chemical processing of irradiated materials, to the extent necessary to attain the objectives set out in Article 77.

Article 79

The Commission shall require that operating records be kept and produced in order to permit accounting for ores, source materials and special fissile materials used or produced. The same requirement shall apply in the case of the transport of source materials and special fissile materials.

Those subject to such requirements shall notify the authorities of the Member State concerned of any communications they make to the Commission pursuant to Article 78 and to the first paragraph of this Article.

The nature and the extent of the requirements referred to in the first paragraph of this Article shall be defined in a regulation made by the Commission and approved by the Council.

Article 80

The Commission may require that any excess special fissile materials recovered or obtained as by-products and not actually being used or ready for use shall be deposited with the Agency or in other stores which are or can be supervised by the Commission.

Special fissile materials deposited in this way must be returned forthwith to those concerned at their request.

The Commission may send inspectors into the territories of Member States. Before sending an inspector on his first assignment in the territory of a Member State, the Commission shall consult the State concerned; such consultation shall suffice to cover all future assignments of this inspector.

On presentation of a document establishing their authority, inspectors shall at all times have access to all places and data and to all persons who, by reason of their occupation, deal with materials, equipment or installations subject to the safeguards provided for in this Chapter, to the extent necessary in order to apply such safeguards to ores, source materials and special fissile materials and to ensure compliance with the provisions of Article 77. Should the State concerned so request, inspectors appointed by the Commission shall be accompanied by respresentatives of the authorities of that State; however, the inspectors shall not thereby be delayed or otherwise impeded in the performance of their duties.

If the carrying out of an inspection is opposed, the Commission shall apply to the President of the Court of Justice for an order to ensure that the inspection be carried out compulsorily. The President of the Court of Justice shall give a decision within three days.

If there is danger in delay, the Commission may itself issue a written order, in the form of a decision, to proceed with the inspection. This order shall be submitted without delay to the President of the Court of Justice for subsequent approval.

After the order or decision has been issued, the authorities of the State concerned shall ensure that the inspectors have access to the places specified in the order or decision.

Article 82

Inspectors shall be recruited by the Commission.

They shall be responsible for obtaining and verifying the records referred to in Article 79. They shall report any infringement to the Commission.

The Commission may issue a directive calling upon the Member State concerned to take, by a time limit set by the Commission, all measures necessary to bring such infringement to an end; it shall inform the Council thereof.

If the Member State does not comply with the Commission directive by the time limit set, the Commission or any Member State concerned may, in derogation from Articles 141 and 142, refer the matter to the Court of Justice direct.

Article 83

1. In the event of an infringement on the part of persons or undertakings of the obligations imposed on them by this Chapter, the Commission may impose sanctions on such persons or undertakings.

These sanctions shall be in order of severity:

(a) a warning;

(b) the withdrawal of special benefits such as financial or technical assistance;

(c) the placing of the undertaking for a period not exceeding four months under the administration of a person or board appointed by common accord of the Commission and the State having jurisdiction over the undertaking;

(d) total or partial withdrawal of source materials or special fissile materials.

2. Decisions taken by the Commission in implementation of paragraph 1 and requiring the surrender of materials shall be enforceable.

They may be enforced in the territories of Member States in accordance with Article 164.

By way of derogation from Article 157, appeals brought before the Court of Justice against decisions of the Commission which impose any of the sanctions provided for in paragraph 1 shall have suspensory effect. The Court of Justice may, however, on application by the Commission or by any Member State concerned, order that the decision be enforced forthwith.

There shall be an appropriate legal procedure to ensure the protection of interests that have been prejudiced.

3. The Commission may make any recommendations to Member States concerning laws or regulations which are designed to ensure compliance in their territories with the obligations arising under this Chapter.

4. Member States shall ensure that sanctions are enforced and, where necessary, that the infringements are remedied by those committing them.

Article 84

In the application of the safeguards, no discrimination shall be made on grounds of the use for which ores, source materials and special fissile materials are intended.

The scope of and procedure for the safeguards and the powers of the bodies responsible for their application shall be confined to the attainment of the objectives set out in this Chapter.

The safeguards may not extend to materials intended to meet defence requirements which are in the course of being specially processed for this purpose or which, after being so processed, are, in accordance with an operational plan, placed or stored in a military establishment.

Article 85

Where new circumstances so require, the procedures for applying the safeguards laid down in this Chapter may, at the request of a Member State or of the Commission, be adapted by the Council, acting unanimously on a proposal from the Commission and after consulting the European Parliament. The Commission shall examine any such request made by a Member State.

CHAPTER VIII

PROPERTY OWNERSHIP

Article 86

Special fissile materials shall be the property of the Community.

The Community's right of ownership shall extend to all special fissile materials which are produced or imported by a Member State, a person or an undertaking and are subject to the safeguards provided for in Chapter VII.

Article 87

Member States, persons or undertakings shall have the unlimited right of use and consumption of special fissile materials which have properly come into their possession, subject to the obligations imposed on them by this Treaty, in particular those relating to safeguards, the right of option conferred on the Agency and health and safety.

Article 88

The Agency shall keep a special account in the name of the Community, called 'Special Fissile Materials Financial Account'.

Article 89

1. In the Special Fissile Materials Financial Account:

(a) the value of special fissile materials left in the possession of or put at the disposal of a Member State, person or undertaking shall be credited to the Community and debited to that Member State, person or undertaking;

(b) the value of special fissile materials which are produced or imported by a Member State, person or undertaking and become the property of the Community shall be debited to the Community and credited to that Member State, person or undertaking. A similar entry shall be made when a Member State, person or undertaking restores to the Community special fissile materials previously left in the possession of or put at the disposal of that State, person or undertaking.

2. Variations in value affecting the quantities of special fissile material shall be expressed for accounting purposes in such a way as not to give rise to any loss or gain to the Community. Any loss or gain shall be borne by or accrue to the holder.

3.   Balances arising from the transactions referred to above shall become payable forthwith upon the request of the creditor.

4.   Where the Agency undertakes transactions for its own account, it shall, for the purposes of this Chapter, be deemed to be an undertaking.

Article 90

Where new circumstances so require, the provisions of this Chapter relating to the Community's right of ownership may, at the request of a Member State or of the Commission, be adjusted by the Council, acting unanimously on a proposal from the Commission and after consulting the European Parliament. The Commission shall examine any such request made by a Member State.

Article 91

The system of ownership applicable to all objects, materials and assets which are not vested in the Community under this Chapter shall be determined by the law of each Member State.

CHAPTER IX

THE NUCLEAR COMMON MARKET

Article 92

The provisions of this Chapter shall apply to the goods and products specified in the Lists forming Annex IV to this Treaty.

These Lists may, at the request of the Commission or of a Member State, be amended by the Council, acting on a proposal from the Commission.

Article 93

Member States shall abolish between themselves, one year after the entry into force of this Treaty, all customs duties on imports and exports or charges having equivalent effect, and all quantitative restrictions on imports and exports, in respect of:

(a) products in List A[1] and A[2];

(b) products in List B if subject to a common customs tariff and accompanied by a certificate issued by the Commission stating that they are intended to be used for nuclear purposes.

Non-European territories under the jurisdiction of a Member State may, however, continue to levy import and export duties or charges having equivalent effect where they are of an exclusively fiscal nature. The rates of such duties and charges and the system governing them shall not give rise to any discrimination between that State and the other Member States.

Article 94

The Member States shall set up a common customs tariff in accordance with the following provisions:

(a) With regard to products specified in List A[1], the common customs tariff shall be fixed at the level of the lowest tariff in force in any Member State on 1 January 1957;

(b) With regard to products specified in List A[2], the Commission shall take all appropriate measures to ensure that negotiations between Member States shall begin within three months of the entry into force of this Treaty. If, on some of these products, no agreement can be reached with-

in one year of the entry into force of this Treaty, the Council shall, acting by a qualified majority on a proposal from the Commission, determine the applicable duties in the common customs tariff;

(c) The common customs tariff on the products specified in Lists A^1 and A^2 shall be applied from the end of the first year following the entry into force of this Treaty.

Article 95

The Council may, acting unanimously on a proposal from the Commission, decide on the earlier application of the duties in the common customs tariff on products in List B where such a measure would tend to contribute to the development of nuclear energy in the Community.

Article 96

The Member States shall abolish all restrictions based on nationality affecting the right of nationals of any Member State to take skilled employment in the field of nuclear energy, subject to the limitations resulting from the basic requirements of public policy, public security or public health.

After consulting the European Parliament, the Council may, acting by a qualified majority on a proposal from the Commission, which shall first request the opinion of the Economic and Social Committee, issue directives for the application of this Article.

Article 97

No restrictions based on nationality may be applied to natural or legal persons, whether public or private, under the jurisdiction of a Member State, where they desire to participate in the construction of nuclear installations of a scientific or industrial nature in the Community.

Article 98

Member States shall take all measures necessary to facilitate the conclusion of insurance contracts covering nuclear risks.

Within two years of the entry into force of this Treaty, the Council, acting by a qualified majority on a proposal from the Commission, which shall first request the opinion of the Economic and Social Committee, shall, after consulting the European Parliament, issue directives for the application of this Article.

Article 99

The Commission may make any recommendations for facilitating movements of capital intended to finance the industrial activities listed in Annex II to this Treaty.

Article 100

Each Member State undertakes to authorize, in the currency of the Member State in which the creditor or the beneficiary resides, any payments connected with the movement of goods, services or capital, and any transfers of capital and earnings, to the extent that the movement of goods, services, capital and persons between Member States has been liberalized pursuant to this Treaty.

CHAPTER X

EXTERNAL RELATIONS

Article 101

The Community may, within the limits of its powers and jurisdiction, enter into obligations by concluding agreements or contracts with a third State, an international organization or a national of a third State.

Such agreements or contracts shall be negotiated by the Commission in accordance with the directives of the Council: they shall be concluded by the Commission with the approval of the Council, which shall act by a qualified majority.

Agreements or contracts whose implementation does not require action by the Council and can be effected within the limits of the relevant budget shall, however, be negotiated and concluded solely by the Commission; the Commission shall keep the Council informed.

Article 102

Agreements or contracts concluded with a third State, an international organization or a national of a third State to which, in addition to the Community, one or more Member States are parties, shall not enter into force until the Commission has been notified by all the Member States concerned that those agreements or contracts have become applicable in accordance with the provisions of their respective national laws.

Article 103

Member States shall communicate to the Commission draft agreements or contracts with a third State, an international organization or a national of a third State to the extent that such agreements or contracts concern matters within the purview of this Treaty.

If a draft agreement or contract contains clauses which impede the application of this Treaty, the Commission shall, within one month of receipt of such communication, make its comments known to the State concerned.

The State shall not conclude the proposed agreement or contract until it has satisfied the objections of the Commission or complied with a ruling by the Court of Justice, adjudicating urgently upon an application from the State, on the compatibility of the proposed clauses with the provisions of this Treaty. An application may be made to the Court of Justice at any time after the State has received the comments of the Commission.

Article 104

No person or undertaking concluding or renewing an agreement or contract with a third State, an international organization or a national of a third State after the entry into force of this Treaty may invoke that agreement or contract in order to evade the obligations imposed by this Treaty.

Each Member State shall take such measures as it considers necessary in order to communicate to the Commission, at the request of the latter, all information relating to agreements or contracts concluded after the entry into force of this Treaty, within the purview thereof, by a person or undertaking with a third State, an international organization or a national of a third State. The Commission may require such communication only for the purpose of verifying that such agreements or contracts do not contain clauses impeding the implementation of this Treaty.

On application by the Commission, the Court of Justice shall give a ruling on the compatibility of such agreements or contracts with the provisions of this Treaty.

Article 105

The provisions of this Treaty shall not be invoked so as to prevent the implementation of agreements or contracts concluded before its entry into force by a Member State, a person or an undertaking with a third State, an international organization or a national of a third State where such agreements or contracts have been communicated to the Commission not later than 30 days after the entry into force of this Treaty.

Agreements or contracts concluded between the signature and the entry into force of this Treaty by a person or an undertaking with a third State, an international organization or a national of a third State shall not, however, be invoked as grounds for failure to implement this Treaty if, in the opinion of the Court of Justice, ruling on an application from the Commission, one of the decisive reasons on the part of either of the parties in concluding the agreement or contract was an intention to evade the provisions of this Treaty.

Article 106

Member States which, before the entry into force of this Treaty, have concluded agreements with third States providing for cooperation in the field of nuclear energy shall be required to undertake jointly with the Commission the necessary negotiations with these third States in order to ensure that the rights and obligations arising out of such agreements shall as far as possible be assumed by the Community.

Any new agreement ensuing from such negotiations shall require the consent of the Member State or States signatory to the agreements referred to above and the approval of the Council, which shall act by a qualified majority.

Provisions governing the institutions

CHAPTER I

THE INSTITUTIONS OF THE COMMUNITY

Section I

The European Parliament

Article 107

The European Parliament, which shall consist of representatives of the peoples of the States brought together in the Community, shall exercise the advisory and supervisory powers which are conferred upon it by this Treaty.

Article 108

(Paragraphs 1 and 2 lapsed on 17 July 1979 in accordance with Article 14 of the Act concerning the election of the representatives of the European Parliament)

[*See Article 1 of that Act which reads as follows:*

1. The representatives in the European Parliament of the peoples of the States brought together in the Community shall be elected by direct universal suffrage.]

[See Article 2 of that Act which reads as follows:

2. The number of representatives elected in each Member State is as follows:

Belgium	24
Denmark	16
Germany	81
Greece	24
Spain	60
France	81
Ireland	15
Italy	81
Luxembourg	6
Netherlands	25
Portugal	24
United Kingdom	81].*

3. The European Parliament shall draw up proposals for elections by direct universal suffrage in accordance with a uniform procedure in all Member States.**

The Council shall, acting unanimously, lay down the appropriate provisions, which it shall recommend to Member States for adoption in accordance with their respective constitutional requirements.

---

* Number of representatives as fixed by Article 10 of the Act of Accession ESP/PORT.
** In this connection, see also Article 7 (1) and (2) of the Act concerning the election of the representatives of the European Parliament.

Article 109

The European Parliament shall hold an annual session. It shall meet, without requiring to be convened, on the second Tuesday in March.* **

The European Parliament may meet in extraordinary session at the request of a majority of its members or at the request of the Council or of the Commission.

Article 110

The European Parliament shall elect its President and its officers from among its members.

Members of the Commission may attend all meetings and shall, at their request, be heard on behalf of the Commission.

The Commission shall reply orally or in writing to questions put to it by the European Parliament or by its members.

The Council shall be heard by the European Parliament in accordance with the conditions laid down by the Council in its rules of procedure.

Article 111

Save as otherwise provided in this Treaty, the European Parliament shall act by an absolute majority of the votes cast.

The rules of procedure shall determine the quorum.

Article 112

The European Parliament shall adopt its rules of procedure, acting by a majority of its members.

---

* First paragraph as amended by Article 27 (1) of the Merger Treaty.

** For the second sentence of this paragraph, see also Article 10 (3) of the Act concerning the election of the representatives of the European Parliament.

The proceedings of the European Parliament shall be published in the manner laid down in its rules of procedure.

Article 113

The European Parliament shall discuss in open session the annual general report submitted to it by the Commission.

Article 114

If a motion of censure on the activities of the Commission is tabled before it, the European Parliament shall not vote thereon until at least three days after the motion has been tabled and only by open vote.

If the motion of censure is carried by a two-thirds majority of the votes cast, representing a majority of the members of the European Parliament, the members of the Commission shall resign as a body. They shall continue to deal with current business until they are replaced in accordance with Article 127.

Section II

The Council

Article 115

The Council shall carry out its duties and exercise its powers of decision in accordance with the provisions of this Treaty.

It shall take all measures within its powers to coordinate the actions of the Member States and of the Community.

Article 116

(Article repealed by Article 7 of the Merger Treaty)

[*See Article 2 of the Merger Teaty, which reads as follows:*

The Council shall consist of representatives of the Member States. Each Government shall delegate to it one of its members.

The office of President shall be held in turn by each Member State in the Council for a term of six months, in the following order of Member States:

— for a first cycle of six years: Belgium, Denmark, Germany, Greece, Spain, France, Ireland, Italy, Luxembourg, Netherlands, Portugal, United Kingdom,

— for the following cycle of six years: Denmark, Belgium, Greece, Germany, France, Spain, Italy, Ireland, Netherlands, Luxembourg, United Kingdom, Portugal].*

Article 117

(Article repealed by Article 7 of the Merger Treaty)

[*See Article 3 of the Merger Treaty, which reads as follows:*

The Council shall meet when convened by its President on his own initiative or at the request of one of its members or of the Commission.]

Article 118

1. Save as otherwise provided in this Treaty, the Council shall act by a majority of its members.

---

* Second paragraph as amended by Article 11 of the Act of Accession ESP/PORT.

2. Where the Council is required to act by a qualified majority, the votes of its members shall be weighted as follows:

Belgium	5
Denmark	3
Germany	10
Greece	5
Spain	8
France	10
Ireland	3
Italy	10
Luxembourg	2
Netherlands	5
Portugal	5
United Kingdom	10

For their adoption, acts of the Council shall require at least:

— fifty-four votes in favour where this Treaty requires them to be adopted on a proposal from the Commission,

— fifty-four votes in favour, cast by at least eight members, in other cases.*

3. Abstentions by members present in person or represented shall not prevent the adoption by the Council of acts which require unanimity.

Article 119

Where, in pursuance of this Treaty, the Council acts on a proposal from the Commission, unanimity shall be required for an act constituting an amendment to that proposal.

As long as the Council has not acted, the Commission may alter its original proposal, in particular where the European Parliament has been consulted on that proposal.

---

* Paragraph 2 as amended by Article 14 of the Act of Accession ESP/PORT.

Article 120

Where a vote is taken, any member of the Council may also act on behalf of not more than one other member.

Article 121

(Article repealed by Article 7 of the Merger Treaty)

[*See Articles 5 and 4 of the Merger Treaty, which read as follows:*

Article 5:

The Council shall adopt its rules of procedure.

Article 4:

A committee consisting of the Permanent Representatives of the Member States shall be responsible for preparing the work of the Council and for carrying out the tasks assigned to it by the Council.]

Article 122

The Council may request the Commission to undertake any studies which the Council considers desirable for the attainment of the common objectives and to submit to it any appropriate proposals.

Article 123

(Article repealed by Article 7 of the Merger Treaty)

[*See Article 6 of the Merger Treaty, which reads as follows:*

The Council shall, acting by a qualified majority, determine the salaries, allowances and pensions of the President and members of the Commission, and of the President, Judges, Advocates-General and Registrar of the Court of Justice. It shall also, again by a qualified majority, determine any payment to be made instead of remuneration.]

Section III

The Commission

Article 124

In order to ensure the development of nuclear energy within the Community, the Commission shall:

— ensure that the provisions of this Treaty and the measures taken by the institutions pursuant thereto are applied;

— formulate recommendations or deliver opinions in the fields covered by this Treaty, if the Treaty expressly so provides or if the Commission considers it necessary;

— have its own power of decision and participate in the shaping of measures taken by the Council and by the European Parliament in the manner provided for in this Treaty;

— exercise the powers conferred on it by the Council for the implementation of the rules laid down by the latter.

Article 125

(Article repealed by Article 19 of the Merger Treaty)

[*See Article 18 of the Merger Treaty, which reads as follows:*

The Commission shall publish annually, not later than one month before the opening of the session of the European Parliament, a general report on the activities of the Communities.]

Article 126

(Article repealed by Article 19 of the Merger Treaty)

[*See Article 10 of the Merger Treaty, which reads as follows:*

1. The Commission shall consist of 17 members, who shall

be chosen on the grounds of their general competence and whose independence is beyond doubt.*

The number of members of the Commission may be altered by the Council, acting unanimously.

Only nationals of Member States may be members of the Commission.

The Commission must include at least one national of each of the Member States, but may not include more than two members having the nationality of the same State.

2. The members of the Commission shall, in the general interest of the Communities, be completely independent in the performance of their duties.

In the performance of these duties, they shall neither seek nor take instructions from any Government or from any other body. They shall refrain from any action incompatible with their duties. Each Member State undertakes to respect this principle and not to seek to influence the members of the Commission in the performance of their tasks.

The members of the Commission may not, during their term of office, engage in any other occupation, whether gainful or not. When entering upon their duties they shall give a solemn undertaking that, both during and after their term of office, they will respect the obligations arising therefrom and in particular their duty to behave with integrity and discretion as regards the acceptance, after they have ceased to hold office, of certain appointments or benefits. In the event of any breach of these obligations, the Court of Justice may, on application by the Council or the Commission, rule that the member concerned be, according to the circumstances, either com-

---

* First subparagraph of paragraph 1 as amended by Article 15 of the Act of Accession ESP/PORT.

pulsorily retired in accordance with the provisions of Article 13* or deprived of his right to a pension or other benefits in its stead.]

Article 127

(Article repealed by Article 19 of the Merger Treaty)

[*See Article 11 of the Merger Treaty, which reads as follows:*

The members of the Commission shall be appointed by common accord of the Governments of the Member States.

Their term of office shall be four years. It shall be renewable.]

Article 128

(Article repealed by Article 19 of the Merger Treaty)

[*See Article 12 of the Merger Treaty, which reads as follows:*

Apart from normal replacement, or death, the duties of a member of the Commission shall end when he resigns or is compulsorily retired.

The vacancy thus caused shall be filled for the remainder of the member's term of office. The Council may, acting unanimously, decide that such a vacancy need not be filled.

Save in the case of compulsory retirement under the provisions of Article 13,* members of the Commission shall remain in office until they have been replaced.]

Article 129

(Article repealed by Article 19 of the Merger Treaty)

[*See Article 13 of the Merger Treaty, which reads as follows:*

If any member of the Commission no longer fulfils the conditions required for the performance of his duties or if he has been

---

* Article 13 of the Merger Treaty. See Article 129 below.

guilty of serious misconduct, the Court of Justice may, on application by the Council or the Commission, compulsorily retire him.]

Article 130

(Article repealed by Article 19 of the Merger Treaty)
[*See Article 14 of the Merger Treaty, which reads as follows:*

The President and the six Vice-Presidents of the Commission shall be appointed from among its members for a term of two years in accordance with the same procedure as that laid down for the appointment of members of the Commission. Their appointments may be renewed.*

The Council, acting unanimously, may amend the provisions concerning Vice-Presidents.**

Save where the entire Commission is replaced, such appointments shall be made after the Commission has been consulted.

In the event of retirement or death, the President and the Vice-Presidents shall be replaced for the remainder of their term of office in accordance with the preceding provisions.]

Article 131

(Article repealed by Article 19 of the Merger Treaty)
[*See Articles 15 and 16 of the Merger Treaty, which read as follows:*
Article 15:

The Council and the Commission shall consult each other and shall settle by common accord their methods of cooperation.
Article 16

The Commission shall adopt its rules of procedure so as to ensure that both it and its departments operate in accordance with the provisions of the Treaties establishing the European Coal and Steel

---

* First paragraph as amended by Article 16 of the Act of Accession ESP/PORT.
** Second paragraph as added by Article 16 of the said Act.

Community, the European Economic Community and the European Atomic Energy Community, and of this Treaty. It shall ensure that these rules are published.]

Article 132

(Article repealed by Article 19 of the Merger Treaty)

[*See Article 17 of the Merger Treaty, which reads as follows:*

The Commission shall act by a majority of the number of members provided for in Article 10.*

A meeting of the Commission shall be valid only if the number of members laid down in its rules of procedure is present.]

Article 133**

Article 134

1. A Scientific and Technical Committee is hereby set up; it shall be attached to the Commission and shall have advisory status.

The Committee must be consulted where this Treaty so provides. The Committee may be consulted in all cases in which the Commission considers this appropriate.

2. The Committee shall consist of 33 members, appointed by the Council after consultation with the Commission.***

The members of the Committee shall be appointed in their personal capacity for five years. Their appointment shall be renewable. They shall not be bound by any mandatory instructions.

The Scientific and Technical Committee shall each year elect its chairman and officers from among its members.

---

* Article 10 of the Merger Treaty. See Article 126 above.

** Article repealed by Article 19 of the Merger Treaty.

*** First subparagraph of paragraph 2 as amended by Article 23 of the Act of Accession ESP/PORT.

Article 135

The Commission may undertake any consultations and establish any study groups necessary to the performance of its tasks.

Section IV

The Court of Justice

Article 136

The Court of Justice shall ensure that in the interpretation and application of this Treaty the law is observed.

Article 137

The Court of Justice shall consist of 13 Judges.*

The Court of Justice shall sit in plenary session. It may, however, form Chambers, each consisting of three or five Judges, either to undertake certain preparatory inquiries or to adjudicate on particular categories of cases in accordance with rules laid down for these purposes.

Whenever the Court of Justice hears cases brought before it by a Member State or by one of the institutions of the Community or, to the extent that the Chambers of the Court do not have the requisite jurisdiction under the Rules of Procedure, has to give preliminary rulings on questions submitted to it pursuant to Article 150, it shall sit in plenary session.**

---

* First paragraph as amended by Article 17 of the Act of Accession ESP/PORT.
** Third paragraph as amended by Article 1 of the Council Decision of 26 November 1974 *(Official Journal of the European Communities*, No L 318, 28 November 1974).

Should the Court of Justice so request, the Council may, acting unanimously, increase the number of Judges and make the necessary adjustments to the second and third paragraphs of this Article and to the second paragraph of Article 139.

Article 138

The Court of Justice shall be assisted by six Advocates-General.*

It shall be the duty of the Advocate-General, acting with complete impartiality and independence, to make, in open court, reasoned submissions on cases brought before the Court of Justice, in order to assist the Court in the performance of the task assigned to it in Article 136.

Should the Court of Justice so request, the Council may, acting unanimously, increase the number of Advocates-General and make the necessary adjustments to the third paragraph of Article 139.

Article 139

The Judges and Advocates-General shall be chosen from persons whose independence is beyond doubt and who possess the qualifications required for appointment to the highest judicial offices in their respective countries or who are jurisconsults of recognised competence; they shall be appointed by common accord of the Governments of the Member States for a term of six years.

Every three years there shall be a partial replacement of the Judges. Seven and six Judges shall be replaced alternately.**

---

* First paragraph as amended by Article 18 of the Act of Accession ESP/PORT.
** Second paragraph as amended by Article 19 of the Act of Accession ESP/PORT.

Every three years there shall be a partial replacement of the Advocates-General. Three Advocates-General shall be replaced on each occasion.*

Retiring Judges and Advocates-General shall be eligible for reappointment.

The Judges shall elect the President of the Court of Justice from among their number for a term of three years. He may be re-elected.

Article 140

The Court of Justice shall appoint its Registrar and lay down the rules governing his service.

Article 140a**

1. At the request of the Court of Justice and after consulting the Commission and the European Parliament, the Council may, acting unanimously, attach to the Court of Justice a court with jurisdiction to hear and determine at first instance, subject to a right of appeal to the Court of Justice on points of law only and in accordance with the conditions laid down by the Statute, certain classes of action or proceeding brought by natural or legal persons. That court shall not be competent to hear and determine actions brought by Member States or by Community institutions or questions referred for a preliminary ruling under Article 150.

2. The Council, following the procedure laid down in paragraph 1, shall determine the composition of that court and adopt the necessary adjustments and additional provisions to the Statute of the Court of Justice. Unless the Council decides otherwise, the provisions of this Treaty relating to

---

* Third paragraph as amended by Article 19 of the Act of Accession ESP/PORT.
** Article added by Article 26 of the SEA.

the Court of Justice, in particular the provisions of the Protocol on the Statute of the Court of Justice, shall apply to that court.

3. The members of that court shall be chosen from persons whose independence is beyond doubt and who possess the ability required for appointment to judicial office; they shall be appointed by common accord of the Governments of the Member States for a term of six years. The membership shall be partially renewed every three years. Retiring members shall be eligible for reappointment.

4. That court shall establish its rules of procedure in agreement with the Court of Justice. Those rules shall require the unanimous approval of the Council.

Article 141

If the Commission considers that a Member State has failed to fulfil an obligation under this Treaty, it shall deliver a reasoned opinion on the matter after giving the State concerned the opportunity to submit its observations.

If the State concerned does not comply with the opinion within the period laid down by the Commission, the latter may bring the matter before the Court of Justice.

Article 142

A Member State which considers that another Member State has failed to fulfil an obligation under this Treaty may bring the matter before the Court of Justice.

Before a Member State brings an action against another Member State for an alleged infringement of an obligation under this Treaty, it shall bring the matter before the Commission.

The Commission shall deliver a reasoned opinion after each of the States concerned has been given the opportunity to submit its own case and its observations on the other party's case both orally and in writing.

If the Commission has not delivered an opinion within three months of the date on which the matter was brought before it, the absence of such opinion shall not prevent the matter from being brought before the Court of Justice.

Article 143

If the Court of Justice finds that a Member State has failed to fulfil an obligation under this Treaty, the State shall be required to take the necessary measures to comply with the judgment of the Court of Justice.

Article 144

The Court of Justice shall have unlimited jurisdiction in:

(a) proceedings instituted under Article 12 to have the appropriate terms fixed for the granting by the Commission of licences or sub-licences;

(b) proceedings instituted by persons or undertakings against sanctions imposed on them by the Commission under Article 83.

If the Commission considers that a person or undertaking has committed an infringement of this Treaty to which the provisions of Article 83 do not apply, it shall call upon the Member State having jurisdiction over that person or undertaking to cause sanctions to be imposed in respect of the infringement in accordance with its national law.

If the State concerned does not comply with such a request within the period laid down by the Commission, the latter may bring an action before the Court of Justice to have the infringement of which the person or undertaking is accused established.

Article 146

The Court of Justice shall review the legality of acts of the Council and the Commission other than recommendations or opinions. It shall for this purpose have jurisdiction in actions brought by a Member State, the Council or the Commission on grounds of lack of competence, infringement of an essential procedural requirement, infringement of this Treaty or of any rule of law relating to its application, or misuse of powers.

Any natural or legal person may, under the same conditions, institute proceedings against a decision addressed to that person or against a decision which, although in the form of a regulation or a decision addressed to another person, is of direct and individual concern to the former.

The proceedings provided for in this Article shall be instituted within two months of the publication of the measure, or of its notification to the plaintiff, or, in the absence thereof, of the day on which it came to the knowledge of the latter, as the case may be.

Article 147

If the action is well founded, the Court of Justice shall declare the act concerned to be void.

In the case of a regulation, however, the Court of Justice shall, if it considers this necessary, state which of the effects of the regulation which it has declared void shall be considered as definitive.

Article 148

Should the Council or the Commission, in infringement of this Treaty, fail to act, the Member States and the other institutions of the Community may bring an action before the Court of Justice to have the infringement established.

The action shall be admissible only if the institution concerned has first been called upon to act. If, within two months of being so called upon, the institution concerned has not defined its position, the action may be brought within a further period of two months.

Any natural or legal person may, under the conditions laid down in the preceding paragraphs, complain to the Court of Justice that an institution of the Community has failed to address to that person any act other than a recommendation or an opinion.

Article 149

The institution whose act has been declared void or whose failure to act has been declared contrary to this Treaty shall be required to take the necessary measures to comply with the judgment of the Court of Justice.

This obligation shall not affect any obligation which may result from the application of the second paragraph of Article 188.

Article 150

The Court of Justice shall have jurisdiction to give preliminary rulings concerning:

(a) the interpretation of this Treaty;

(b) the validity and interpretation of acts of the institutions of the Community;

(c) the interpretation of the statutes of bodies established by an act of the Council, save where those statutes provide otherwise.

Where such a question is raised before any court or tribunal of a Member State, that court or tribunal may, if it considers that a decision on the question is necessary to enable it to give judgment, request the Court of Justice to give a ruling thereon.

Where any such question is raised in a case pending before a court or tribunal of a Member State, against whose decisions there is no judicial remedy under national law, that court or tribunal shall bring the matter before the Court of Justice.

Article 151

The Court of Justice shall have jurisdiction in disputes relating to the compensation for damage provided for in the second paragraph of Article 188.

Article 152

The Court of Justice shall have jurisdiction in any dispute between the Community and its servants within the limits and under the conditions laid down in the Staff Regulations or the Conditions of Employment.

Article 153

The Court of Justice shall have jurisdiction to give judgment pursuant to any arbitration clause contained in a contract concluded by or on behalf of the Community, whether that contract be governed by public or private law.

Article 154

The Court of Justice shall have jurisdiction in any dispute between Member States which relates to the subject matter of this Treaty if the dispute is submitted to it under a special agreement between the parties.

Article 155

Save where jurisdiction is conferred on the Court of Justice by this Treaty, disputes to which the Community is a party shall not on that ground be excluded from the jurisdiction of the courts or tribunals of the Member States.

Article 156

Notwithstanding the expiry of the period laid down in the third paragraph of Article 146, any party may, in proceedings in which a regulation of the Council or of the Commission is in issue, plead the grounds specified in the first paragraph of Article 146, in order to invoke before the Court of Justice the inapplicability of that regulation.

Article 157

Save as otherwise provided in this Treaty, actions brought before the Court of Justice shall not have suspensory effect. The Court of Justice may, however, if it considers that circumstances so require, order that application of the contested act be suspended.

Article 158

The Court of Justice may in any cases before it prescribe any necessary interim measures.

Article 159

The judgments of the Court of Justice shall be enforceable under the conditions laid down in Article 164.

Article 160

The Statute of the Court of Justice is laid down in a separate Protocol.

The Council may, acting unanimously at the request of the Court of Justice and after consulting the Commission and the European Parliament, amend the provisions of Title III of the Statute.*

The Court of Justice shall adopt its rules of procedure. These shall require the unanimous approval of the Council.

CHAPTER II

PROVISIONS COMMON TO SEVERAL INSTITUTIONS

Article 161

In order to carry out their task the Council and the Commission shall, in accordance with the provisions of this Treaty, make regulations, issue directives, take decisions, make recommendations or deliver opinions.

A regulation shall have general application. It shall be binding in its entirety and directly applicable in all Member States.

---

* Second paragraph inserted by Article 27 of the SEA.

A directive shall be binding, as to the result to be achieved, upon each Member State to which it is addressed, but shall leave to the national authorities the choice of form and methods.

A decision shall be binding in its entirety upon those to whom it is addressed.

Recommendations and opinions shall have no binding force.

Article 162

Regulations, directives and decisions of the Council and of the Commission shall state the reasons on which they are based and shall refer to any proposals or opinions which were required to be obtained pursuant to this Treaty.

Article 163

Regulations shall be published in the Official Journal of the Community. They shall enter into force on the date specified in them or, in the absence thereof, on the twentieth day following their publication.

Directives and decisions shall be notified to those to whom they are addressed and shall take effect upon such notification.

Article 164

Enforcement shall be governed by the rules of civil procedure in force in the State in the territory of which it is carried out. The order for its enforcement shall be appended to the decision, without other formality than verification of the authenticity of the decision, by the national authority which the Government of each Member State shall designate for this purpose and shall make known to the Commission, to the Court of Justice and to the Arbitration Committee set up by Article 18.

When these formalities have been completed on application by the party concerned, the latter may proceed to enforcement in accordance with the national law, by bringing the matter directly before the competent authority.

Enforcement may be suspended only by a decision of the Court of Justice. However, the courts of the country concerned shall have jurisdiction over complaints that enforcement is being carried out in an irregular manner.

CHAPTER III

THE ECONOMIC AND SOCIAL COMMITTEE

Article 165

An Economic and Social Committee is hereby established. It shall have advisory status.

The Committee shall consist of representatives of the various categories of economic and social activity.

Article 166

The number of members of the Committee shall be as follows:

Belgium	12
Denmark	9
Germany	24
Greece	12
Spain	21
France	24
Ireland	9
Italy	24
Luxembourg	6
Netherlands	12
Portugal	12
United Kingdom	24 *

---

* First paragraph as amended by Article 21 of the Act of Accession ESP/PORT.

The members of the Committee shall be appointed by the Council, acting unanimously, for four years. Their appointments shall be renewable.

The members of the Committee shall be appointed in their personal capacity and may not be bound by any mandatory instructions.

Article 167

1. For the appointment of the members of the Committee, each Member State shall provide the Council with a list containing twice as many candidates as there are seats allotted to its nationals.

The composition of the Committee shall take account of the need to ensure adequate representation of the various categories of economic and social activity.

2. The Council shall consult the Commission. It may obtain the opinion of European bodies which are representative of the various economic and social sectors to which the activities of the Community are of concern.

Article 168

The Committee shall elect its chairman and officers from among its members for a term of two years.

It shall adopt its rules of procedure and shall submit them to the Council for its approval, which must be unanimous.

The Committee shall be convened by its chairman at the request of the Council or of the Commission.

Article 169

The Committee may be divided into specialized sections.

These specialized sections shall operate within the general terms of reference of the Committee. They may not be consulted independently of the Committee.

Subcommittees may also be established within the Committee to prepare, on specific questions or in specific fields, draft opinions to be submitted to the Committee for its consideration.

The rules of procedure shall lay down the methods of composition and the terms of reference of the specialized sections and of the subcommittees.

Article 170

The Committee must be consulted by the Council or by the Commission where this Treaty so provides. The Committee may be consulted by these institutions in all cases in which they consider it appropriate.

The Council or the Commission shall, if it considers it necessary, set the Committee, for the submission of its opinion, a time limit which may not be less than 10 days from the date on which the chairman receives notification to this effect. Upon expiry of the time limit, the absence of an opinion shall not prevent further action.

The opinion of the Committee and that of the specialized section, together with a record of the proceedings, shall be forwarded to the Council and to the Commission.

TITLE FOUR

Financial provisions

Article 171

1.   Estimates shall be drawn up for each financial year of all revenue and expenditure of the Community, other than those of the Agency and the Joint Undertakings, and such revenue and expenditure shall be shown either in the operating budget or in the research and investment budget.

The revenue and expenditure shown in each budget shall be in balance.

2.   The revenue and expenditure of the Agency, which shall operate in accordance with commercial principles, shall be budgeted for in a special account.

The manner of estimating, implementing and auditing such revenue and expenditure shall be laid down, with due regard to the statutes of the Agency, in financial regulations made pursuant to Article 183.

3.   The estimates of revenue and expenditure, together with the operating accounts and the balance sheets of the Joint Undertakings for each financial year, shall be placed before the Commission, the Council and the European Parliament in accordance with the statutes of those Undertakings.

Article 172

1.   The operating budget revenue shall include, irrespective of any other current revenue, financial contributions of Member States on the following scale:

Belgium	7.9
Germany	28
France	28
Italy	28
Luxembourg	0.2
Netherlands	7.9

2. The research and investment budget revenue shall include, irrespective of any other resources, financial contributions of Member States on the following scale:

Belgium	9.9
Germany	30
France	30
Italy	23
Luxembourg	0.2
Netherlands	6.9

3. The scales may be modified by the Council, acting unanimously.

4. Loans for the financing of research or investment shall be raised on terms fixed by the Council in the manner provided for in Article 177 (5).

The Community may borrow on the capital market of a Member State, either in accordance with the legal provisions applying to internal issues, or, if there are no such provisions in a Member State, after the Member State concerned and the Commission have conferred together and have reached agreement upon the proposed loan.

The competent authorities of the Member State concerned may refuse to give their assent only if there is reason to fear serious disturbances on the capital market of that State.

Article 173*

The financial contributions of Member States provided for in Article 172 may be replaced in whole or in part by the proceeds of levies collected by the Community in Member States.

---

* EDITORIAL NOTE:
The Council Decision on the Community's system of own resources is reproduced on page 995 of this volume.

To this end, the Commission shall submit to the Council proposals concerning the assessment of such levies, the method of fixing their rate and the procedure for their collection.

After consulting the European Parliament on these proposals the Council may, acting unanimously, lay down the appropriate provisions, which it shall recommend to the Member States for adoption in accordance with their respective constitutional requirements.

Article 174

1. The expenditure shown in the operating budget shall include in particular:

(a) administrative expenditure;

(b) expenditure relating to safeguards and to health and safety.

2. The expenditure shown in the research and investment budget shall include in particular:

(a) expenditure relating to the implementation of the Community research programme;

(b) any participation in the capital of the Agency and in its investment expenditure;

(c) expenditure relating to the equipment of training establishments;

(d) any participation in Joint Undertakings or in certain joint operations.

Article 175

The expenditure shown in the operating budget shall be authorized for one financial year, unless the regulations made pursuant to Article 183 provide otherwise.

In accordance with conditions to be laid down pursuant to Article 183, any appropriations, other than those relating to staff expenditure, that are unexpended at the end of the financial year may be carried forward to the next financial year only.

Appropriations to cover expenditure shall be classified under different chapters grouping items of expenditure according to their nature or purpose and subdivided, as far as may be necessary, in accordance with the regulations made pursuant to Article 183.

The expenditure of the European Parliament, the Council, the Commission and the Court of Justice shall be set out in separate parts of the budget, without prejudice to special arrangements for certain common items of expenditure.

Article 176

1. Subject to the limits resulting from programmes or decisions involving expenditure which, in pursuance of this Treaty, require the unanimous approval of the Council, allocations for research and investment expenditure shall include:

(a) commitment appropriations, covering a series of items which constitute a separate unit and form a coherent whole;

(b) payment appropriations which represent the maximum amount payable each year in respect of the commitments entered into under subparagraph *(a)*.

2. The schedule of due dates for commitments and payments shall be annexed to the corresponding draft budget proposed by the Commission.

3. Appropriations for research and investment shall be classified under different chapters grouping items of expenditure according to their nature or purpose and subdivided, as far as may be necessary, in accordance with the regulations made pursuant to Article 183.

4. Unused payment authorizations shall be carried forward to the next financial year by decision of the Commission, unless the Council decides otherwise.

Article 177* **

1. The financial year shall run from 1 January to 31 December.

Within the meaning of this Article, 'budget' shall include the operating budget and the research and investment budget.

2. Each institution of the Community shall, before 1 July, draw up estimates of its expenditure. The Commission shall consolidate these estmates in a preliminary draft budget. It shall attach thereto an opinion which may contain different estimates.

The preliminary draft budget shall include an estimate of revenue and an estimate of expenditure.

3. The Commission shall place the preliminary draft budget before the Council not later than 1 September of the year preceding that in which the budget is to be implemented.

The Council shall consult the Commission and, where appropriate, the other institutions concerned whenever it intends to depart from the preliminary draft budget.

The Council shall, acting by a qualified majority, establish the draft budget and forward it to the European Parliament.

4. The draft budget shall be placed before the European Parliament not later than 5 October of the year preceding that in which the budget is to be implemented.

---

* Text as amended by Article 20 of the Treaty amending Certain Financial Provisions.
** EDITORIAL NOTE:
   The Joint Declaration by the European Parliament, the Council and the Commission, adopted on 30 June 1982, on various measures to improve the budgetary procedure is reproduced on page 1103 of this volume.

The European Parliament shall have the right to amend the draft budget acting by a majority of its members, and to propose to the Council, acting by an absolute majority of the votes cast, modifications to the draft budget relating to expenditure necessarily resulting from this Treaty or from acts adopted in accordance therewith.

If, within 45 days of the draft budget being placed before it, the European Parliament has given its approval, the budget shall stand as finally adopted. If within this period the European Parliament has not amended the draft budget or proposed any modifications thereto, the budget shall be deemed to be finally adopted.

If within this period the European Parliament has adopted amendments or proposed modifications, the draft budget together with the amendments or proposed modifications shall be forwarded to the Council.

5. After discussing the draft budget with the Commission and, where appropriate, with the other institutions concerned, the Council shall act under the following conditions:

(a) the Council may, acting by a qualified majority, modify any of the amendments adopted by the European Parliament;

(b) with regard to the proposed modifications:

— where a modification proposed by the European Parliament does not have the effect of increasing the total amount of the expenditure of an institution, owing in particular to the fact that the increase in expenditure which it would involve would be expressly compensated by one or more proposed modifications correspondingly reducing expenditure, the Council may, acting by a qualified majority, reject the proposed modification. In the absence of a decision to reject it, the proposed modification shall stand as accepted,

— where a modification proposed by the European Parliament has the effect of increasing the total amount of the expenditure of an institution, the Council may, acting by a qualified majority, accept this proposed

716

modification. In the absence of a decision to accept it, the proposed modification shall stand as rejected,

— where, in pursuance of the two preceding subparagraphs, the Council has rejected a proposed modification, it may, acting by a qualified majority, either retain the amount shown in the draft budget or fix another amount.

The draft shall be modified on the basis of the proposed modifications accepted by the Council.

If, within 15 days of the draft budget being placed before it, the Council has not modified any of the amendments adopted by the European Parliament and if the modifications proposed by the latter have been accepted, the budget shall be deemed to be finally adopted. The Council shall inform the European Parliament that it has not modified any of the amendments and that the proposed modifications have been accepted.

If within this period the Council has modified one or more of the amendments adopted by the European Parliament or if the modifications proposed by the latter have been rejected or modified, the modified draft budget shall again be forwarded to the European Parliament. The Council shall inform the European Parliament of the results of its deliberations.

6. Within 15 days of the draft budget being placed before it, the European Parliament, which shall have been notified of the action taken on its proposed modifications may, acting by a majority of its members and three-fifths of the votes cast, amend or reject the modifications to its amendments made by the Council and shall adopt the budget accordingly. If within this period the European Parliament has not acted, the budget shall be deemed to be finally adopted.

7. When the procedure provided for in this Article has been completed, the President of the European Parliament shall declare that the budget has been finally adopted.

8. However, the European Parliament, acting by a majority of its members and two-thirds of the votes cast may, if there are important reasons, reject the draft budget and ask for a new draft to be submitted to it.

9. A maximum rate of increase in relation to the expenditure of the same type to be incurred during the current year shall be fixed annually for the total expenditure other than that necessarily resulting from this Treaty or from acts adopted in accordance therewith.

The Commission shall, after consulting the Economic Policy Committee, declare what this maximum rate is, as it results from:

— the trend in terms of volume, of the gross national product within the Community,

— the average variation in the budgets of the Member States,

and

— the trend of the cost of living during the preceding financial year.

The maximum rate shall be communicated, before 1 May, to all the institutions of the Community. The latter shall be required to conform to this during the budgetary procedure, subject to the provisions of the fourth and fifth subparagraphs of this paragraph.

If, in respect of expenditure other than that necessarily resulting from this Treaty or from acts adopted in accordance therewith, the actual rate of increase in the draft budget established by the Council is over half the maximum rate, the European Parliament may, exercising its right of amendment, further increase the total amount of that expenditure to a limit not exceeding half the maximum rate.

Where the European Parliament, the Council or the Commission considers that the activities of the Communities require that the rate determined according to the procedure laid down in this paragraph should be exceeded, another rate may be fixed by agreement between the Council, acting by a qualified majority, and the European Parliament, acting by a majority of its members and three-fifths of the votes cast.

10. Each institution shall exercise the powers conferred upon it by this Article, with due regard for the provisions of the Treaty and for acts adopted in accordance therewith, in particular those relating to the Communities' own resources and to the balance between revenue and expenditure.

Article 178*

If, at the beginning of a financial year, the budget has not yet been voted, a sum equivalent to not more than one-twelfth of the budget appropriations for the preceding financial year may be spent each month in respect of any chapter or other subdivision of the budget in accordance with the provisions of the Regulations made pursuant to Article 183; this arrangement shall not, however, have the effect of placing at the disposal of the Commission appropriations in excess of one-twelfth of those provided for in the draft budget in the course of preparation.

The Council may, acting by a qualified majority, provided that the other conditions laid down in the first subparagraph are observed, authorize expenditure in excess of one-twelfth.

If the decision relates to expenditure which does not necessarily result from this Treaty or from acts adopted in accordance therewith, the Council shall forward it immediately to the European Parliament; within 30 days the European Parliament, acting by a majority of its members and three-fifths of the votes cast, may adopt a different decision on the expenditure

---

* Text as amended by Article 21 of the Treaty amending Certain Financial Provisions.

in excess of the one-twelfth referred to in the first subparagraph. This part of the decision of the Council shall be suspended until the European Parliament has taken its decision. If, within this period, the European Parliament has not taken a decision which differs from the decision of the Council, the latter shall be deemed to be finally adopted.

The decisions referred to in the second and third subparagraphs shall lay down the necessary measures relating to resources to ensure application of this Article.

Article 179

The Commission shall implement the budgets, in accordance with the provisions of the regulations made pursuant to Article 183, on its own responsibility and within the limits of the appropriations.

The regulations shall lay down detailed rules for each institution concerning its part in effecting its own expenditure.

Within the budgets, the Commission may, subject to the limits and conditions laid down in the regulations made pursuant to Article 183, transfer appropriations from one chapter to another or from one subdivision to another.

Article 179a*

The Commission shall submit annually to the Council and to the European Parliament the accounts of the preceding financial year relating

---

* Article added by Article 22 of the Treaty amending Certain Financial Provisions.

to the implementation of the budget. The Commission shall also forward to them a financial statement of the assets and liabilities of the Community.

Article 180*

1. A Court of Auditors is hereby established,

2. The Court of Auditors shall consist of 12 members.**

3. The members of the Court of Auditors shall be chosen from among persons who belong or have belonged in their respective countries to external audit bodies or who are especially qualified for this office. Their independence must be beyond doubt.

4. The members of the Court of Auditors shall be appointed for a term of six years by the Council, acting unanimously after consulting the European Parliament.

However, when the first appointments are made, four members of the Court of Auditors, chosen by lot, shall be appointed for a term of office of four years only.

The members of the Court of Auditors shall be eligible for reappointment.

They shall elect the President of the Court of Auditors from among their number for a term of three years. The President may be re-elected.

5. The members of the Court of Auditors shall, in the general interest of the Community, be completely independent in the performance of their duties.

In the performance of these duties, they shall neither seek nor take in-

---

* Text, with the exception of paragraph 2, as amended by Article 23 of the Treaty amending Certain Financial Provisions.
** Paragraph 2 as amended by Article 20 of the Act of Accession ESP/PORT.

structions from any government, or from any other body. They shall refrain from any action incompatible with their duties.

6. The members of the Court of Auditors may not, during their term of office, engage in any other occupation, whether gainful or not. When entering upon their duties they shall give a solemn undertaking that, both during and after their term of office, they will respect the obligations arising therefrom and in particular their duty to behave with integrity and discretion as regards the acceptance, after they have ceased to hold office, of certain appointments or benefits.

7. Apart from normal replacement, or death, the duties of a member of the Court of Auditors shall end when he resigns, or is compulsorily retired by a ruling of the Court of Justice pursuant to paragraph 8.

The vacancy thus caused shall be filled for the remainder of the member's term of office.

Save in the case of compulsory retirement under the provisions of paragraph 8, members of the Court of Auditors shall remain in office until they have been replaced.

8. A member of the Court of Auditors may be deprived of his office or of his right to a pension or other benefits in its stead only if the Court of Justice, at the request of the Court of Auditors, finds that he no longer fulfils the requisite conditions or meets the obligations arising from his office.

9. The Council, acting by a qualified majority, shall determine the conditions of employment of the President and the members of the Court of Auditors and in particular their salaries, allowances and pensions. It shall also, by the same majority, determine any payment to be made instead of remuneration.

10. The provisions of the Protocol on the Privileges and Immunities of the European Communities applicable to the Judges of the Court of Justice shall also apply to the members of the Court of Auditors.

Article 180a*

1. The Court of Auditors shall examine accounts of all revenue and expenditure of the Community. It shall also examine the accounts of all revenue and expenditure of all bodies set up by the Community in so far as the relevant constituent instrument does not preclude such examination.

2. The Court of Auditors shall examine whether all revenue has been received and all expenditure incurred in a lawful and regular manner and whether the financial management has been sound.

The audit of revenue shall be carried out on the basis both of the amounts established as due and the amounts actually paid to the Communities.

The audit of expenditure shall be carried out on the basis both of commitments undertaken and payments made.

These audits may be carried out before the closure of accounts for the financial year in question.

3. The audit shall be based on records and, if necessary, performed on the spot in the institutions of the Community and in the Member States. In the Member States the audit shall be carried out in liaison with the national audit bodies or, if these do not have the necessary powers, with the competent national departments. These bodies or departments shall inform the Court of Auditors whether they intend to take part in the audit.

The institutions of the Community and the national audit bodies or, if the latter do not have the necessary powers, the competent national departments, shall forward to the Court of Auditors, at its request, any document or information necessary to carry out its task.

---

* Article added by Article 24 of the Treaty amending Certain Financial Provisions.

4. The Court of Auditors shall draw up an annual report after the close of each financial year. It shall be forwarded to the institutions of the Community and shall be published together with the replies of these institutions to the observations of the Court for Auditors, in the *Official Journal of the European Communities*.

The Court of Auditors may also, at any time, submit observations on specific questions and deliver opinions at the request of one of the institutions of the Community.

It shall adopt its annual reports or opinions by a majority of its members.

It shall assist the European Parliament and the Council in exercising their powers of control over the implementation of the budget.

*Article 180b**

The European Parliament, acting on a recommendation from the Council which shall act by a qualified majority, shall give a discharge to the Commission in respect of the implementation of the budget. To this end, the Council and the European Parliament in turn shall examine the accounts and the financial statement referred to in Article 179a, and the annual report by the Court of Auditors together with the replies of the institutions under audit to the observations of the Court of Auditors.

Article 181

The budgets and the account provided for in Article 171 (1) and (2) shall be drawn up in the unit of account determined in accordance with the provisions of the financial regulations made pursuant to Article 183.

---

* Article added by Article 25 of the Treaty amending Certain Financial Provisions.

The financial contributions provided for in Article 172 shall be placed at the disposal of the Community by the Member States in their national currencies.

The available balances of these contributions shall be deposited with the Treasuries of Member States or with bodies designated by them. While on deposit, such funds shall retain the value corresponding to the parity, at the date of deposit, in relation to the unit of account referred to in the first paragraph.

The balances may be invested on terms to be agreed between the Commission and the Member State concerned.

Article 182

1. The Commission may, provided it notifies the competent authorities of the Member States concerned, transfer into the currency of one of the Member States its holdings of currency of another Member State, to the extent necessary to enable them to be used for purposes which come within the scope of this Treaty. The Commission shall as far as possible avoid making such transfers if it possesses cash or liquid assets in the currencies which it needs.

2. The Commission shall deal with each Member State through the authority designated by the State concerned. In carrying out financial operations the Commission shall employ the services of the bank of issue of the Member State concerned or any other financial institutions approved by that State.

3. As regards expenditure which the Community has to incur in the currencies of third countries, the Commission shall, before the budgets are finally adopted, submit to the Council a programme indicating anticipated revenue and expenditure in the different currencies.

This programme shall be approved by the Council, acting by a qualified majority. It may be modified in the course of the financial year in accordance with the same procedure.

4. Member States shall provide the Commission with the currency of third countries needed for the expenditure shown in the programme provided for in paragraph 3 according to the scales laid down in Article 172. Amounts collected by the Commission in the currency of third countries shall be transferred to Member States in accordance with the same scales.

5. The Commission may freely make use of any amounts in the currency of third countries derived from loans it has raised in such countries.

6. The Council may, acting unanimously on a proposal from the Commission apply, in whole or in part, to the Agency and to Joint Undertakings the exchange arrangements provided for in the preceding paragraphs, and, where appropriate, adapt these arrangements to their operational requirements.

Article 183*

The Council, acting unanimously on a proposal from the Commission and after consulting the European Parliament and obtaining the opinion of the Court of Auditors, shall:

(a) make Financial Regulations specifying in particular the procedure to be adopted for establishing and implementing the budget and for presenting and auditing accounts;

(b) determine the methods and procedure whereby the budget revenue provided for under the arrangements relating to the Communities' own re-

---

* Text as amended by Article 26 of the Treaty amending Certain Financial Provisions.

sources shall be made available to the Commission, and determine the measures to be applied, if need be, to meet cash requirements;

(c) lay down rules concerning the responsibility of authorizing officers and accounting officers and concerning appropriate arrangements for inspection.

TITLE FIVE

General provisions

Article 184

The Community shall have legal personality.

Article 185

In each of the Member States, the Community shall enjoy the most extensive legal capacity accorded to legal persons under their laws; it may, in particular, acquire or dispose of movable and immovable property and may be a party to legal proceedings. To this end, the Community shall be represented by the Commission.

Article 186

(Article repealed by Article 24 (2) of the Merger Treaty)

[*See Article 24 (1) of the Merger Treaty which reads as follows:*

1. The officials and other servants of the European Coal and Steel Community, the European Economic Community and the European Atomic Energy Community shall, at the date of entry into force of this Treaty, become officials and other servants of the European Communities and form part of the single administration of these Communities.

The Council shall, acting by a qualified majority on a proposal from the Commission and after consulting the other institutions concerned, lay down the Staff Regulations of officials of the European Communities and the Conditions of Employment of other servants of these Communities.]

Article 187

The Commission may, within the limits and under the conditions laid down by the Council in accordance with the provisions of this Treaty, collect any information and carry out any checks required for the performance of the tasks entrusted to it.

Article 188

The contractual liability of the Community shall be governed by the law applicable to the contract in question.

In the case of non-contractual liability, the Community shall, in accordance with the general principles common to the laws of the Member States, make good any damage caused by its institutions or by its servants in the performance of their duties.

The personal liability of its servants towards the Community shall be governed by the provisions laid down in the Staff Regulations or in the Conditions of Employment applicable to them.

Article 189

The seat of the institutions of the Community shall be determined by common accord of the Governments of the Member States.

Article 190

The rules governing the languages of the institutions of the Community shall, without prejudice to the provisions contained in the rules of procedure of the Court of Justice, be determined by the Council, acting unanimously.

Article 191

(Article repealed by the second paragraph of Article 28 of the Merger Treaty)

[*See the first paragraph of Article 28 of the Merger Treaty which reads as follows:*

The European Communities shall enjoy in the territories of the Member States such privileges and immunities as are necessary for the performance of their tasks, under the conditions laid down in the Protocol annexed to this Treaty. The same shall apply to the European Investment Bank.]

Article 192

Member States shall take all appropriate measures, whether general or particular, to ensure fulfilment of the obligations arising out of this Treaty or resulting from action taken by the institutions of the Community. They shall facilitate the achievement of the Community's tasks.

They shall abstain from any measure which could jeopardize the attainment of the objectives of this Treaty.

Article 193

Member States undertake not to submit a dispute concerning the interpretation or application of this Treaty to any method of settlement other than those provided for therein.

1. The members of the institutions of the Community, the members of committees, the officials and other servants of the Community and any other persons who by reason of their duties or their public or private relations with the institutions or installations of the Community or with Joint Undertakings are called upon to acquire or obtain cognizance of any facts, information, knowledge, documents or objects which are subject to a security system in accordance with provisions laid down by a Member State or by an institution of the Community, shall be required, even after such duties or relations have ceased, to keep them secret from any unauthorized person and from the general public.

Each Member State shall treat any infringement of this obligation as an act prejudicial to its rules on secrecy and as one falling, both as to merits and jurisdiction, within the scope of its laws relating to acts prejudicial to the security of the State or to disclosure of professional secrets. Such Member State shall, at the request of any Member State concerned or of the Commission, prosecute anyone within its jurisdiction who commits such an infringement.

2. Each Member State shall communicate to the Commission all provisions regulating within its territories the classification and secrecy of information, knowledge, documents or objects covered by this Treaty.

The Commission shall ensure that these provisions are communicated to the other Member States.

Each Member State shall take all appropriate measures to facilitate the gradual establishment of as uniform and comprehensive a security system as possible. The Commission may, after consulting the Member States concerned, make recommendations for this purpose.

3. The institutions of the Community, their installations and also the Joint Undertakings shall be required to apply the rules of the security system in force in the territory in which each of them is situated.

4. Any authorization granted either by an institution of the Community or by a Member State to a person carrying out his activities within the field covered by this Treaty to have access to facts, information, documents or objects covered by this Treaty which are subject to a security system, shall be recognized by every other institution and every other Member State.

5. The provisions of this Article shall not prevent application of special provisions resulting from agreements concluded between a Member State and a third State or an international organization.

Article 195

The institutions of the Community, the Agency and the Joint Undertakings shall, in applying this Treaty, comply with the conditions of access to ores, source materials and special fissile materials laid down in national rules and regulations made for reasons of public policy or public health.

Article 196

For the purposes of this Treaty, save as otherwise provided therein:

(a) 'person' means any natural person who pursues all or any of his activities in the territories of Member States within the field specified in the relevant chapter of this Treaty;

(b) 'undertaking' means any undertaking or institution which pursues all or any of its activities in the territories of Member States within the field specified in the relevant Chapter of this Treaty, whatever its public or private legal status.

Article 197

For the purposes of this Treaty:

1. 'Special fissile materials' means plutonium-239; uranium-233; uranium enriched in uranium-235 or uranium-233; and any substance containing one or more of the foregoing isotopes and such other fissile materials as may be specified by the Council, acting by a qualified majority on a proposal from the Commission; the expression 'special fissile materials' does not, however, include source materials.

2. 'Uranium enriched in uranium-235 or uranium-233' means uranium containing uranium-235 or uranium-233 or both in an amount such that the abundance ratio of the sum of these isotopes to isotope 238 is greater than the ratio of isotope 235 to isotope 238 occurring in nature.

3. Source materials' means uranium containing the mixture of isotopes occurring in nature; uranium whose content in uranium-235 is less than the normal; thorium; any of the foregoing in the form of metal, alloy, chemical compound or concentrate; any other substance containing one or more of the foregoing in such a concentration as shall be specified by the Council, acting by a qualified majority on a proposal from the Commission.

4. 'Ores' means any ore containing, in such average concentration as shall be specified by the Council acting by a qualified majority on a proposal from the Commission, substances from which the source materials defined above may be obtained by the appropriate chemical and physical processing.

Article 198

Save as otherwise provided, this Treaty shall apply to the European territories of Member States and to non-European territories under their jurisdiction.

It shall also apply to the European territories for whose external relations a Member State is responsible.

* Notwithstanding the previous paragraphs:

(a) This Treaty shall not apply to the Faroe Islands. The Government of the Kingdom of Denmark may, however, give notice, by a declaration deposited by 31 December 1975 at the latest, with the Government of the Italian Republic, which shall transmit a certified copy thereof to each of the Governments of the other Member States, that this Treaty shall apply to those islands. In that event, this Treaty shall apply to those islands from the first day of the second month following the deposit of the declaration.

This Treaty shall not apply to Greenland.**

(b) This Treaty shall not apply to the Sovereign Base Areas of the United Kingdom of Great Britain and Northern Ireland in Cyprus.

(c) This Treaty shall not apply to those overseas countries and territories having special relations with the United Kingdom of Great Britain and Northern Ireland which are not listed in Annex IV to the Treaty establishing the European Economic Community.

(d) This Treaty shall apply to the Channel Islands and the Isle of Man only to the extent necessary to ensure the implementation of the arrangements for those islands set out in the Treaty concerning the accession of New Member States to the European Economic Community and to the European Atomic Energy Community signed on 22 January 1972.***

---

* Third paragraph, with the exception of the second subparagraph of point (a), added by Article 27 of the Act of Accession DK/IRL/UK, modified by Article 16 of the AD AA DK/IRL/UK.

** Subparagraph added by Article 5 of the Greenland Treaty.

*** See Volume II of this edition.

Article 199

It shall be for the Commission to ensure the maintenance of all appropriate relations with the organs of the United Nations, of its specialized agencies and of the General Agreement on Tariffs and Trade.

The Commission shall also maintain such relations as are appropriate with all international organizations.

Article 200

The Community shall establish all appropriate forms of cooperation with the Council of Europe.

Article 201

The Community shall establish close cooperation with the Organization for European Economic Cooperation, the details to be determined by common accord.

Article 202

The provisions of this Treaty shall not preclude the existence or completion of regional unions between Belgium and Luxembourg, or between Belgium, Luxembourg and the Netherlands, to the extent that the objectives of these regional unions are not attained by application of this Treaty.

Article 203

If action by the Community should prove necessary to attain one of the objectives of the Community and this Treaty has not provided the necessary powers, the Council shall, acting unanimously on a proposal from the Commission and after consulting the European Parliament, take the appropriate measures.

Article 204

The Government of any Member State or the Commission may submit to the Council proposals for amendment of this Treaty.

If the Council, after consulting the European Parliament and, where appropriate, the Commission, delivers an opinion in favour of calling a conference of representatives of the Governments of the Member States, the conference shall be convened by the President of the Council for the purpose of determining by common accord the amendments to be made to this Treaty.

The amendments shall enter into force after being ratified by all the Member States in accordance with their respective constitutional requirements.

Article 205

Any European State may apply to become a member of the Community. It shall address its application to the Council, which shall act unanimously after obtaining the opinion of the Commission.

The conditions of admission and the adjustments to this Treaty necessitated thereby shall be the subject of an agreement between the Member States and the applicant State. This agreement shall be submitted for ratification by all the Contracting States in accordance with their respective constitutional requirements.

Article 206

The Community may conclude with a third State, a union of States or an international organization agreements establishing an association involving reciprocal rights and obligations, common action and special procedures.

These agreements shall be concluded by the Council, acting unanimously after consulting the European Parliament.

Where such agreements call for amendments to this Treaty, these amendments shall first be adopted in accordance with the procedure laid down in Article 204.

Article 207

The Protocols annexed to this Treaty by common accord of the Member States shall form an integral part thereof.

Article 208

This Treaty is concluded for an unlimited period.

TITLE SIX

Provisions relating to the initial period

Section I

Setting up of the institutions

Article 209

The Council shall meet within one month of the entry into force of this Treaty.

Article 210

The Council shall, within three months of its first meeting, take all appropriate measures to constitute the Economic and Social Committee.

Article 211

The Assembly* shall meet within two months of the first meeting of the Council, having been convened by the President of the Council, in order to elect its officers and draw up its rules of procedure. Pending the election of its officers, the oldest member shall take the chair.

Article 212

The Court of Justice shall take up its duties as soon as its members have been appointed. Its first President shall be appointed for three years in the same manner as its members.

EDITORIAL NOTE:
* Notwithstanding the provisions of Article 3 of the SEA, and for historical reasons, the term 'Assembly' has not been replaced by the terms 'European Parliament'.

The Court of Justice shall adopt its rules of procedure within three months of taking up its duties.

No matter may be brought before the Court of Justice until its rules of procedure have been published. The time within which an action must be brought shall run only from the date of this publication.

Upon his appointment, the President of the Court of Justice shall exercise the powers conferred upon him by this Treaty.

Article 213

The Commission shall take up its duties and assume the responsibilities conferred upon it by this Treaty as soon as its members have been appointed.

Upon taking up its duties, the Commission shall undertake the studies and arrange the contacts with Member States, undertakings, workers and consumers needed for making an overall survey of the situation of nuclear industries in the Community. The Commission shall submit a report on this subject to the European Parliament within six months.

Article 214

1.   The first financial year shall run from the date when this Treaty enters into force until 31 December following. Should this Treaty, however, enter into force during the second half of the year, the first financial year shall run until 31 December of the following year.

2.   Until the budgets for the first financial year have been established, Member States shall make the Community interest-free advances which shall be deducted from their financial contributions to the implementation of these budgets.

3. Until the Staff Regulations of officials and the Conditions of Employment of other servants of the Community provided for in Article 186 have been laid down, each institution shall recruit the staff it needs and to this end conclude contracts of limited duration.

Each institution shall examine together with the Council any question concerning the number, remuneration and distribution of posts.

Section II

Provisions for the initial application of this Treaty

Article 215

1. An initial research and training programme, which is set out in Annex V to this Treaty and the cost of which shall not, unless the Council unanimously decides otherwise, exceed 215 million EPU units of account, shall be carried out within five years of the entry into force of this Treaty.

2. A breakdown of the expenditure necessary for the implementation of this programme is set out by way of illustration under main subdivisions in Annex V.

The Council may, acting by a qualified majority on a proposal from the Commission, modify this programme.

Article 216

The Commission proposals on the way in which the institution of university status referred to in Article 9 is to function shall be submitted to the Council within one year of the entry into force of this Treaty.

Article 217

The security regulations provided for in Article 24 concerning the security gradings applicable to the dissemination of information shall be adopted by the Council within six months of the entry into force of this Treaty.

Article 218

The basic standards shall be determined in accordance with the provisions of Article 31 within one year of the entry into force of this Treaty.

Article 219

Provisions laid down by law, regulation or administrative action to ensure the protection of the health of the general public and of workers in the territories of Member States against the dangers arising from ionizing radiations shall, in accordance with Article 33, be communicated to the Commission by these States within three months of the entry into force of this Treaty.

Article 220

The Commission proposals relating to the statutes of the Agency which are provided for in Article 54 shall be submitted to the Council within three months of the entry into force of this Treaty.

Transitional provisions

Article 221

The provisions of Articles 14 to 23 and of Articles 25 to 28 shall apply to patents, provisionally protected patent rights and utility models, and also to patent and utility model applications in existence before the entry into force of this Treaty, under the following conditions:

1. When assessing the period of time referred to in Article 17 (2), allowance shall be made, in favour of the owner, for the new situation created by the entry into force of this Treaty.

2. With regard to the communication of an invention which is not secret, where either or both of the periods of three and eighteen months referred to in Article 16 have expired at the date on which this Treaty enters into force, a further period of six months shall run from that date.

If either or both of those periods remain unexpired at that date, they shall be extended by six months from the date of their normal expiry.

3. The same provisions shall apply to the communication of a secret invention in accordance with Article 16 and Article 25 (1); in such case, however, the date of entry into force of the security regulations referred to in Article 24 shall be the date taken as the starting point for the new period or for the extension of a current period.

Article 222

During the period between the date of entry into force of this Treaty and the date fixed by the Commission on which the Agency takes up its duties, agreements and contracts for the supply of ores, source materials or special fissile materials shall be concluded or renewed only with the prior approval of the Commission.

The Commission shall refuse to approve the conclusion or renewal of any agreements and contracts which it considers would prejudice the implementation of this Treaty. It may in particular make its approval dependent upon the insertion in agreements and contracts of clauses permitting the Agency to take part in carrying them out.

Article 223

By way of derogation from the provisions of Article 60, reactors installed in the territories of a Member State which may go critical before the expiry of a period of seven years from the date of entry into force of this Treaty shall, during a period of not more than 10 years from that date, in order to take account of work and studies already initiated, be granted priority which may be exercised in respect both of supplies of ores or source materials coming from the territories of that State and also of supplies of source materials or special fissile materials which are the subject of a bilateral agreement concluded before the entry into force of this Treaty and communicated to the Commission in accordance with Article 105.

The same priority shall be granted during the same period of 10 years in respect of supplies for any isotope separation plant, whether or not it constitutes a Joint Undertaking, which comes into operation in the territory of a Member State before the expiry of a period of seven years from the date of entry into force of this Treaty.

The Agency shall conclude the appropriate contracts, after the Commission has ascertained that the conditions for the exercise of the right of priority have been fulfilled.

Final provisions

Article 224

This Treaty shall be ratified by the High Contracting Parties in accordance with their respective constitutional requirements. The instruments of ratification shall be deposited with the Government of the Italian Republic.

This Treaty shall enter into force on the first day of the month following the deposit of the instrument of ratification by the last signatory State to take this step. If, however, such deposit is made less than 15 days before the beginning of the following month, this Treaty shall not enter into force until the first day of the second month after the date of such deposit.

Article 225

This Treaty, drawn up in a single original in the Dutch, French, German and Italian languages, all four texts being equally authentic, shall be deposited in the archives of the Government of the Italian Republic, which shall transmit a certified copy to each of the Governments of the other signatory States.

IN WITNESS WHEREOF, the undersigned Plenipotentiaries have signed this Treaty.

Done at Rome this twenty-fifth day of March in the year one thousand nine hundred and fifty-seven.

P. H. SPAAK	J. Ch. SNOY ET D'OPPUERS
ADENAUER	HALLSTEIN
PINEAU	M. FAURE
Antonio SEGNI	Gaetano MARTINO
BECH	Lambert SCHAUS
J. LUNS	J. LINTHORST HOMAN

Annexes

ANNEX I

FIELDS OF RESEARCH CONCERNING
NUCLEAR ENERGY

referred to in Article 4 of this Treaty

I — Raw materials

1. Methods for the prospecting and mining of base materials (uranium, thorium and other products of particular importance in the field of nuclear energy).

2. Methods of concentrating these materials and converting them into technically pure compounds.

3. Methods of converting these technically pure compounds into nuclear-grade compounds and metals.

4. Methods for the conversion and processing of these compounds and metals — as well as plutonium, uranium-235 or uranium-233, either pure or combined with such compounds or metals — into fuel elements by the chemical, ceramic or metallurgical industries.

5. Methods of protecting such fuel elements against corrosion or erosion by external agents.

6. Methods of producing, refining, processing and preserving other special materials used in the field of nuclear energy, in particular:

   (a) moderators, such as heavy water, nuclear-grade graphite, beryllium and beryllium oxide;

   (b) structural materials such as zirconium (hafnium-free), niobium, lanthanum, titanium, beryllium and their oxides, carbides and other compounds capable of being used in the field of nuclear energy;

   (c) coolants, such as helium, organic liquids, sodium, sodium-potassium alloys, bismuth, lead-bismuth alloys.

7. Methods of isotope separation:

   (a) of uranium;

   (b) of materials in ponderable quantities which can be used in the production of nuclear energy, such as lithium-6, lithium-7, nitrogen-15 and boron-10;

   (c) of isotopes used in small quantities for research.

II — Physics applied to nuclear energy

1. Applied theoretical physics:

   (a) low-energy nuclear reactions, in particular neutron-induced reactions;

   (b) fission;

   (c) interaction of ionising radiation and photons with matter;

   (d) solid state theory;

(e) study of fusion, with particular reference to the behaviour of an ionised plasma under the action of electromagnetic forces and to the thermodynamics of extremely high temperatures.

2. Applied experimental physics:

   (a) the same subjects as those specified in 1 above;

   (b) study of the properties of transuranic elements of importance in the field of nuclear energy.

3. Reactor calculations:

   (a) theoretical macroscopic neutron physics;

   (b) experimental neutron measurements; exponential and critical experiments;

   (c) thermodynamic calculations and calculations of strength of materials;

   (d) corresponding experimental measurements;

   (e) reactor kinetics, reactor control problems and relevant experiments;

   (f) radiation protection calculations and relevant experiments.

III — Physical chemistry of reactors

1. Study of changes in the physical and chemical structure and of alterations in the technical properties of various materials in reactors brought about by:

   (a) heat;

   (b) the nature of the agents with which they are in contact;

   (c) mechanical factors.

2. Study of degradation and other phenomena produced by irradiation in:

   (a) fuel elements;

757

(b) structural materials and coolants;

(c) moderators.

3. Application of analytical chemistry and analytical physical chemistry to reactor components.

4. Physical chemistry of homogeneous reactors: radiochemistry, corrosion.

IV — Processing of radioactive material

1. Methods of extracting plutonium and uranium-233 from irradiated fuels, and possible recovery of uranium or thorium.

2. Chemistry and metallurgy of plutonium.

3. Methods of extracting and chemistry of other transuranic elements.

4. Methods of extracting and chemistry of useful radioisotopes:

   (a) fission products

   (b) radioisotopes obtained by irradiation.

5. Concentration and storage of useless radioactive waste.

V — Applications of radioisotopes

Application of radioisotopes as active elements or tracers in:

(a) industry and science;

(b) medicine and biology;

(c) agriculture.

VI — Study of the harmful affects of radiation on living organisms

1. Study of the detection and measurement of harmful radiations.

2. Study of adequate preventive and protective measures and the appropriate safety standards.

3. Study of the treatment of radiation effects.

VII — Equipment

Studies relating to the construction and improvement of equipment specially intended not only for reactors but also for any of the industrial and research installations required for the research activities listed above. As examples may be mentioned:

1. The following types of mechanical equipment:

    (a) pumps for special fluids;

    (b) heat exchangers;

    (c) apparatus for nuclear physics research, such as neutron velocity selectors;

    (d) remote handling equipment.

2. The following types of electrical equipment:

    (a) instruments for radiation detection and measurement, used particularly in:

    — prospecting for minerals;

    — scientific and technical research;

    — reactor control;

    — health and safety:

(b) reactor control equipment;

(c) low-energy particle accelerators (up to 10 MeV).

VIII — Economic aspects of energy production

1. Comparative studies, both theoretical and experimental, of the various reactor types.

2. Technical and economic study of fuel cycles.

ANNEX II

INDUSTRIAL ACTIVITIES

referred to in Article 41 of this Treaty

1. Mining of uranium and thorium ore.

2. Concentration of such ores.

3. Chemical processing and refining of uranium and thorium concentrates.

4. Preparation of nuclear fuels, in any form.

5. Fabrication of nuclear fuel elements.

6. Production of uranium hexafluoride.

7. Production of enriched uranium.

8. Processing of irradiated fuels for the purpose of separating some or all of the elements contained therein.

9. Production of reactor moderators.

10. Production of hafnium-free zirconium or compounds thereof.

11. Nuclear reactors of all types and for all purposes.

12. Facilities for the industrial processing of radioactive waste, set up in conjunction with one or more of the facilities specified in this list.

13. Semi-industrial installations intended to prepare the way for the construction of plants involved in any of activities 3 to 10.

ANNEX III

ADVANTAGES WHICH MAY BE CONFERRED ON JOINT UNDERTAKINGS

under Article 48 of this Treaty

1. *(a)* Recognition that public interest status in conformity with the national laws applies to the acquisition of immovable property required for the establishment of Joint Undertakings.

   (b) Application of national procedure for compulsory acquisition on the grounds of public interest, so that such acquisition may be effected where amicable agreement has not been reached.

2. The right to be granted licences, either through arbitration or under compulsory powers as provided in Articles 17 to 23.

3. Exemption from all duties and charges when Joint Undertakings are established and from all duties on assets contributed.

4. Exemption from all duties and charges levied upon acquisition of immovable property and from all registration and recording charges.

5. Exemption from all direct taxes to which Joint Undertakings, their property, assets and revenue might otherwise be liable.

6. Exemption from all customs duties and charges having equivalent effect and from all prohibitions and restrictions on imports or exports, whether of an economic or of a fiscal nature, with regard to:

   (a) scientific and technical equipment, excluding building materials and equipment for administrative purposes;

   (b) substances which have been or are to be processed in the Joint Undertaking.

7. Exchange arrangements provided for in Article 182 (6).

8. Exemption from restrictions on entry and residence for nationals of Member States employed by Joint Undertakings and for their spouses and dependent members of their families.

LIST OF GOODS AND PRODUCTS SUBJECT TO THE PROVISIONS OF CHAPTER IX

on the nuclear common market

List A[1]

Uranium ores containing more than 5 per cent by weight of natural uranium.

Pitchblende containing more than 5 per cent by weight of natural uranium.

Uranium oxide.

Inorganic compounds of natural uranium other than uranium oxide and uranium hexafluoride.

Organic compounds of natural uranium.

Crude or processed natural uranium.

Alloys containing plutonium.

Organic or inorganic compounds of uranium enriched in organic or inorganic compounds or uranium-235.

Organic or inorganic compounds or uranium-233.

Thorium enriched in uranium-233.

Organic or inorganic compounds of plutonium.

Uranium enriched in plutonium.

Uranium enriched in uranium-235.

Alloys containing uranium enriched in uranium-235 or uranium-233.

Plutonium.

Uranium-233.

Uranium hexafluoride.

Monazite.

Thorium ores containing more than 20 per cent by weight of thorium.

Urano-thorianite containing more than 20 per cent of thorium.

Crude or processed thorium.

Thorium oxide.

Inorganic compounds of thorium other than thorium oxide.

Organic compounds of thorium.

List A[2]

Deuterium and its compounds (including heavy water) in which the ratio
of the number of deuterium atoms to normal hydrogen atoms exceeds
1 : 5 000.

Heavy paraffin in which the ratio of the number of deuterium atoms to normal hydrogen atoms exceeds 1 : 5 000.

Mixtures and solutions in which the ratio of the number of deuterium atoms to normal hydrogen atoms exceeds 1 : 5 000.

Nuclear reactors.

Equipment for the separation of uranium isotopes by gaseous diffusion or other methods.

Equipment for the production of deuterium, its compounds (including heavy water) and derivates, and mixtures or solutions containing deuterium in which the ratio of the number of deuterium atoms to normal hydrogen atoms exceeds 1 : 5 000:

— equipment operating by the electrolysis of water;

— equipment operating by the distillation of water, liquid hydrogen, etc.;

— equipment operating by isotope exchange between hydrogen sulphide and water by means of a change of temperature;

— equipment operating by other techniques.

Equipment specially designed for the chemical processing of radioactive material:

— equipment for the separation of irradiated fuel:

— by chemical process (solvents, precipitation, ion exchange, etc.);

— by physical processes (fractional distillation, etc.);

— waste-processing equipment;

— fuel-recycling equipment.

Vehicles specially designed for the transport of highly radioactive substances:

— railway and tramway goods vans, goods wagons and trucks of any gauge;

— motor lorries;

— motorized works trucks for the handling of goods;

— trailers and semi-trailers and other non-motorized vehicles.

Containers with lead radiation shielding for the transport or storage of radioactive material.

Artifical radioactive isotopes and their inorganic or organic compounds.

Remote-controlled mechanical manipulators specially designed for handling highly radioactive substances:

— mechanical handling gear, fixed or mobile, but not being capable of being operated manually.

List B

. . . .*

Lithium ores and concentrates.

Nuclear-grade metals:

— crude beryllium;

— crude bismuth;

— crude niobium (columbium);

---

* Heading deleted by Article 1 of Regulation No 5 of the Council of the European Atomic Energy Community of 22 December 1958.
(*Official Journal of the European Communities*, No 7, 9 February 1959).

- crude zirconium (hafnium-free);

- crude lithium;

- crude aluminium;

- crude calcium;

- crude magnesium.

Boron trifluoride.

Anhydrous hydrofluoric acid.

Chlorine trifluoride.

Bromine trifluoride.

Lithium hydroxide.

Lithium fluoride.

Lithium chloride.

Lithium hydride.

Lithium carbonate.

Nuclear-grade beryllium oxide.

Refractory bricks of nuclear-grade beryllium oxide.

Other refractory products of nuclear-grade beryllium oxide.

Artificial graphite in the form of blocks or bars in which the boron content is less than or equal to one part per million and in which the total microscopic thermal neutron absorption cross-section is less than or equal to 5 millibarns.

Artificially separated stable isotopes.

Electromagnetic ion separators, including mass spectrographs and mass spectrometers.

Reactor simulators (special analog computers).

Remote-controlled mechanical manipulators:

— hand-controlled (i.e., operated manually like a tool).

Liquid-metal pumps.

High-vacuum pumps.

Heat exchangers specially designed for nuclear power stations.

Radiation detection instruments (and spare parts) of one of the following types, specially designed, or adaptable, for the detection of measurement of nuclear radiation, such as alpha and beta particles, gamma rays, neutrons and protons:

— Geiger counter tubes and proportional counters;

— detection or measuring instruments incorporating Geiger-Muller tubes or proportional counters;

— ionization chambers;

— instruments incorporating ionization chambers;

— radiation detection or measuring equipment for mineral prospecting and for reactor, air, water and soil monitoring;

— neutron detector tubes using boron, boron trifluoride, hydrogen or a fissile element;

— detection or measuring instruments incorporating neutron detector tubes using boron, boron trifluoride, hydrogen or a fissile element;

— scintillation crystals, mounted or in a metal casing (solid scintillators);

— detection or measuring instruments incorporating liquid, solid or gaseous scintillators;

— amplifiers specially designed for nuclear measurements, including linear amplifiers, preamplifiers, distributed amplifiers and pulse height analysers;

— coincidence devices for use with radiation detectors;

— electroscopes and electrometers, including dosimeters (but excluding instruments intended for instruction purposes, simple metal leaf electroscopes, dosimeters specially designed for use with medical X-ray equipment and electrostatic measuring instruments);

— instruments capable of measuring a current of less than one picoampere;

— photomultiplier tubes with a photocathode which gives a current of at least 10 microamperes per lumen and in which the average amplification is greater than 10^5, and any other types of electric multiplier activated by positive ions;

— scalers and electronic integrating meters for the detection of radiation.

Cyclotrons, Van de Graaff or Cockcroft-Walton electrostatic generators, linear accelerators and other machines capable of imparting an energy greater than 1 MeV to nuclear particles.

Magnets specially designed and constructed for the above-mentioned machines and equipment (cyclotrons, etc.).

Accelerating and focusing tubes of the type used in mass spectrometers and mass spectrographs.

Intense electronic sources of positive ions intended for use with particle accelerators, mass spectrometers and similar devices.

Anti-radiation plate glass:

— cast or rolled plate glass (including wired or flashed glass) in squares or rectangles, surface-ground or polished but not further worked;

— cast or rolled plate glass (whether or not ground or polished) cut to shape other than square or rectangular, or curved or otherwise worked (for example, bevelled or engraved);

— safety glass, consisting of toughened or laminated glass, shaped or not.

Airtight clothing affording protection against radiation or radioactive contamination:

— made of plastic;

— made of rubber;

— made of impregnated or coated fabric:

— for men;

— for women.

Diphenyl (when it is in fact the aromatic hydrocarbon $C_6H_5C_6H_5$).

Terphenyl.

INITIAL RESEARCH AND TRAINING PROGRAMME

referred to in Article 215 of this Treaty

I. Programme of the Joint Centre

1. *Laboratories, equipment and infrastructure*

The Joint Centre shall include:

(a) general laboratories for chemistry, physics, electronics and metallurgy;

(b) special laboratories for the following subjects:

— nuclear fusion;

— separation of isotopes other than uranium-235 (this laboratory shall be equipped with a high-resolution electromagnetic separator);

— prototypes of prospecting instruments;

— mineralogy;

— radiobiology;

(c) a bureau of standards specializing in nuclear measurements for isotope analysis and absolute measurements of radiation and neutron absorption, equipped with its own experimental reactor.

2. *Documentation, information and training*

The Joint Centre shall arrange for a large-scale exchange of information, particularly in the following fields:

— raw materials: methods of prospecting, mining, concentration, conversion, processing, etc.;

— physics applied to nuclear energy;

— physical chemistry of reactors;

— processing of radioactive material;

— applications of radioisotopes.

The Joint Centre shall organize specialized courses relating particularly to the training of prospectors and to the applications of radioisotopes.

The health and safety documentation and study section referred to in Article 39 shall collect the necessary documentation and information.

3. *Reactor prototypes*

A group of experts shall be set up as soon as this Treaty enters into force. After comparing the programmes of the Member States, it shall submit to the Commission, as soon as possible, appropriate recommendations on the choices before it in this field and the ways and means of implementing them.

It is planned to construct three or four low-power prototypes and to participate — e.g. by supplying fuel and moderators — in several power reactors.*

---

* Second subparagraph as amended by Article 1 of the Decision of the Council of the European Atomic Energy Community of 3 July 1961 (*Official Journal of the European Communities*, No 55, 16 August 1961).

4. *High-flux reactor*

The Centre shall within the shortest possible time have at its disposal a reactor with a high fast-neutron flux for the testing of materials under irradiation.

Preparatory studies shall be undertaken for this purpose as soon as this Treaty enters into force.

The high-flux reactor shall be provided with extensive experimental areas and suitable laboratories for users.

II. Research carried out under contract outside the Joint Centre

A considerable part of the research work shall be carried out under contract outside the Joint Centre in accordance with Article 10. Such research contracts may take the following forms:

1. Research complementary to that of the Joint Centre shall be carried out in the fields of nuclear fusion, separation of isotopes other than uranium-235, chemistry, physics, electronics, metallurgy and radiobiology.

2. The Centre may arrange to have use of space for experiments in high-flux reactors of Member States.*

3. The Centre may make use of the specialized installations of Joint Undertakings to be established in accordance with Chapter V, by assigning to them by contract certain research of a general scientific nature.

---

* Paragraph (2) as amended by Article 1 of the Decision of the Council of the European Atomic Energy Community of 19 July 1960 (*Official Journal of the European Communities*, No 75, 25 November 1960).

BREAKDOWN BY MAIN HEADINGS
of the expenditure required
to carry out the research and training programme

(in millions of EPU units of account)

	Equipment	Operation[1]	Equipment and/or Operation	Total
I — JOINT CENTRE				
1. *Laboratories, equipment and infrastructure:*				
(a) General laboratories for chemistry, physics, electronics and metallurgy	12			
(b) Special laboratories:				
nuclear fusion	3.5			
isotope separation (except U 235)	2			
prospecting and mineralogy	1	1st year 1.3		
(c) Central Bureau for nuclear measurements	3	2nd year 4.3 / 3rd year 6.5		
(d) Other equipment for the Centre and its establishments	8	4th year 7.4 / 5th year 8.5		
(e) Infrastructure	8.5	28		
	38			66
2. *Documentation, information and training*	1	1st year 0.6 / 2nd year 1.6 / 3rd year 1.6 / 4th year 1.6 / 5th year 1.6 / 7		8
3. *Reactor prototypes:*				
Group of experts to choose prototypes		1st year 0.7		
Programme			59.3[2]	60
4. *High-flux reactor:*				
Reactor	15			
Laboratory	6	4th year 5.2		
Replacement of equipment	3	5th year 5.2		
	24	10.4		34.4
II — RESEARCH CARRIED OUT UNDER CONTRACT OUTSIDE THE CENTRE				
1. *Work complementary to that of the Centre:*				
(a) Chemistry, physics, electronics, metallurgy			25	
(b) Nuclear fusion			7.5	
(c) Isotope separation (except U 235)			1	
(d) Radiobiology			3.1	
2. *Renting of space in high-flux reactors of Member States*			6	
3. *Research carried out in Joint Undertakings*			4	
			46.6	46.6
Total	....	....	....	215

[1] Estimate based on a staff of about 1 000.
[2] Part of this sum may be allocated to work carried out under contract outside the Centre.

II — PROTOCOLS

Protocol
on the application of the Treaty
establishing the
European Atomic Energy Community
to the non-European parts
of the Kingdom of the Netherlands

THE HIGH CONTRACTING PARTIES,

ANXIOUS, at the time of signature of the Treaty establishing the European Atomic Energy Community, to define the scope of the provisions of Article 198 of this Treaty in respect of the Kingdom of the Netherlands,

HAVE AGREED upon the following provisions, which shall be annexed to this Treaty:

The Government of the Kingdom of the Netherlands, by reason of the constitutional structure of the Kingdom resulting from the Statute of 29 December 1954, shall, by way of derogation from Article 198, be entitled to ratify this Treaty either on behalf of the Kingdom of the Netherlands in its entirety or on behalf of the Kingdom in Europe and Netherlands New Guinea. In the event of ratification being limited to the Kingdom in Europe and Netherlands New Guinea, the Government of the Kingdom of the Netherlands may at any time, by notification to the Government of the Italian Republic as depositary of the instruments of ratification, declare this Treaty also applicable either to Surinam, or to the Netherlands Antilles, or to both Surinam and the Netherlands Antilles.

Done at Rome this twenty-fifth day of March in the year one thousand nine hundred and fifty-seven.

P. H. SPAAK	J. Ch. SNOY ET D'OPPUERS
ADENAUER	HALLSTEIN
PINEAU	M. FAURE
Antonio SEGNI	Gaetano MARTINO
BECH	Lambert SCHAUS
J. LUNS	J. LINTHORST HOMAN

Protocol on the Statute
of the Court of Justice of the
European Atomic Energy Community

THE HIGH CONTRACTING PARTIES TO THE TREATY ESTABLISHING THE EUROPEAN ATOMIC ENERGY COMMUNITY,

DESIRING to lay down the Statute of the Court provided for in Article 160 of this Treaty,

HAVE DESIGNATED as their Plenipotentiaries for this purpose:

HIS MAJESTY THE KING OF THE BELGIANS:

Baron J. Ch. SNOY ET D'OPPUERS, Secretary-General of the Ministry of Economic Affairs, Head of the Belgian delegation to the Intergovernmental Conference;

THE PRESIDENT OF THE FEDERAL REPUBLIC OF GERMANY:

Professor Dr Carl Friedrich OPHÜLS, Ambassador of the Federal Republic of Germany, Head of the German delegation to the Intergovernmental Conference;

THE PRESIDENT OF THE FRENCH REPUBLIC:

Mr Robert MARJOLIN, Professor of Law, Deputy Head of the French delegation to the Intergovernmental Conference;

THE PRESIDENT OF THE ITALIAN REPUBLIC:

Mr V. BADINI CONFALONIERI, Under-Secretary of State in the Ministry of Foreign Affairs, Head of the Italian delegation to the Intergovernmental Conference;

HER ROYAL HIGHNESS THE GRAND DUCHESS OF LUXEMBOURG:

Mr Lambert SCHAUS, Ambassador of the Grand Duchy of Luxembourg, Head of the Luxembourg delegation to the Intergovernmental Conference;

HER MAJESTY THE QUEEN OF THE NETHERLANDS:

Mr J. LINTHORST HOMAN, Head of the Netherlands delegation to the Intergovernmental Conference;

WHO, having exchanged their Full Powers, found in good and due form,

HAVE AGREED upon the following provisions, which shall be annexed to the Treaty establishing the European Atomic Energy Community.

Article 1

The Court established by Article 3 of this Treaty shall be constituted and shall function in accordance with the provisions of this Treaty and of this statute.

TITLE I

JUDGES AND ADVOCATES-GENERAL

Article 2

Before taking up his duties each Judge shall, in open court, take an oath to perform his duties impartially and conscientiously and to preserve the secrecy of the deliberations of the Court.

Article 3

The Judges shall be immune from legal proceedings. After they have ceased to hold office, they shall continue to enjoy immunity in respect of acts performed by them in their official capacity, including words spoken or written.

The Court, sitting in plenary session, may waive the immunity.

Where immunity has been waived and criminal proceedings are instituted against a Judge, he shall be tried, in any of the Member States, only by the Court competent to judge the members of the highest national judiciary.

Article 4

The Judges may not hold any political or administrative office.

They may not engage in any occupation, whether gainful or not, unless exemption is exceptionally granted by the Council.

When taking up their duties, they shall give a solemn undertaking that, both during and after their term of office, they will respect the obligations arising therefrom, in particular the duty to behave with integrity and discretion as regards the acceptance, after they have ceased to hold office, of certain appointments or benefits.

Any doubt on this point shall be settled by decision of the Court.

Article 5

Apart from normal replacement, or death, the duties of a Judge shall end when he resigns.

Where a Judge resigns, his letter of resignation shall be addressed to the President of the Court for transmission to the President of the Council. Upon this notification a vacancy shall arise on the bench.

Save where Article 6 applies, a Judge shall continue to hold office until his successor takes up his duties.

Article 6

A Judge may be deprived of his office or of his right to a pension or other benefits in its stead only if, in the unanimous opinion of the Judges and Advocates-General of the Court, he no longer fulfils the requisite conditions or meets the obligations arising from his office. The Judge concerned shall not take part in any such deliberations.

The Registrar of the Court shall communicate the decision of the Court to the President of the European Parliament and to the President of the Commission and shall notify it to the President of the Council.

In the case of a decision depriving a Judge of his office, a vacancy shall arise on the bench upon this latter notification.

Article 7

A Judge who is to replace a member of the Court whose term of office has not expired shall be appointed for the remainder of his predecessor's term.

Article 8

The provisions of Articles 2 to 7 shall apply to the Advocates-General.

TITLE II

ORGANIZATION

Article 9

The Registrar shall take an oath before the Court to perform his duties impartially and conscientiously and to preserve the secrecy of the deliberations of the Court.

Article 10

The Court shall arrange for replacement of the Registrar on occasions when he is prevented from attending the Court.

Article 11

Officials and other servants shall be attached to the Court to enable it to function. They shall be responsible to the Registrar under the authority of the President.

Article 12

On a proposal from the Court, the Council may, acting unanimously, provide for the appointment of Assistant Rapporteurs and lay down the rules governing their service. The Assistant Rapporteurs may be required, under conditions laid down in the rules of procedure, to participate in preparatory inquiries in cases pending before the Court and to cooperate with the Judge who acts as Rapporteur.

The Assistant Rapporteurs shall be chosen from persons whose independence is beyond doubt and who possess the necessary legal qualifications; they shall be appointed by the Council. They shall take an oath before the Court to perform their duties impartially and conscientiously and to preserve the secrecy of the deliberations of the Court.

Article 13

The Judges, the Advocates-General and the Registrar shall be required to reside at the place where the Court has its seat.

Article 14

The Court shall remain permanently in session. The duration of the judicial vacations shall be determined by the Court with due regard to the needs of its business.

Article 15*

Decisions of the Court shall be valid only when an uneven number of its members is sitting in the deliberations. Decisions of the full Court shall be valid if seven members are sitting. Decisions of the Chambers shall be valid only it three Judges are sitting; in the event of one of the Judges of a Chamber being prevented from attending, a Judge of another Chamber may be called upon to sit in accordance with conditions laid down in the rules of procedure.

Article 16

No Judge or Advocate-General may take part in the disposal of any case in which he has previously taken part as agent or adviser or has acted for one of the parties, or on which he has been called up on to pronounce as a member of a court or tribunal, of a commission of inquiry or in any other capacity.

---

* Text as amended by Article 20 of the AA DK/IRL/UK.

If, for some special reason, any Judge or Advocate-General considers that he should not take part in the judgment or examination of a particular case, he shall so inform the President. If, for some special reason, the President considers that any Judge or Advocate-General should not sit or make submissions in a particular case, he shall notify him accordingly.

Any difficulty arising as to the application of this Article shall be settled by decision of the Court.

A party may not apply for a change in the composition of the Court or of one of its Chambers on the grounds of either the nationality of a Judge or the absence from the Court or from the Chamber of a Judge of the nationality of that party.

TITLE III

PROCEDURE

Article 17

The States and the institutions of the Community shall be represented before the Court by an agent appointed for each case; the agent may be assisted by an adviser or a lawyer entitled to practise before a court of a Member State.

Other parties must be represented by a lawyer entitled to practise before a court of a Member State.

Such agents, advisers and lawyers shall, when they appear before the Court, enjoy the rights and immunities necessary to the independent exercise of their duties, under conditions laid down in the rules of procedure.

As regards such advisers and lawyers who appear before it, the Court shall have the powers normally accorded to courts of law, under conditions laid down in the rules of procedure.

University teachers being nationals of a Member State whose law accords them a right of audience shall have the same rights before the Court as are accorded by this Article to lawyers entitled to practise before a court of a Member State.

Article 18

The procedure before the Court shall consist of two parts: written and oral.

The written procedure shall consist of the communication to the parties and to the institutions of the Community whose decisions are in dispute of applications, statements of case, defences and observations, and of replies, if any, as well as of all papers and documents in support or of certified copies of them.

Communications shall be made by the Registrar in the order and within the time laid down in the rules of procedure.

The oral procedure shall consist of the reading of the report presented by a Judge acting as Rapporteur, the hearing by the Court of agents, advisers and lawyers entitled to practice before a court of a Member State and of the submissions of the Advocate-General, as well as the hearing, if any, of witnesses and experts.

Article 19

A case shall be brought before the Court by a written application addressed to the Registrar. The application shall contain the applicant's name and permanent address and the description of the signatory, the name of the party against whom the application is made, the subject matter of the dispute, the submissions and a brief statement of the grounds on which the application is based.

The application shall be accompanied, where appropriate, by the measure the annulment of which is sought or, in the circumstances referred to in Article 148 of this Treaty, by documentary evidence of the date on which an institution was, in accordance with that Article, requested to act. If the documents are not submitted with the application, the Registrar shall ask the party concerned to produce them within a reasonable period, but in that event the rights of the party shall not lapse even if such documents are produced after the time limit for bringing proceedings.

Article 20

A case governed by Article 18 of this Treaty shall be brought before the Court by an appeal addressed to the Registrar. The appeal shall contain the name and permanent address of the applicant and the description of the signatory, a reference to the decision against which the appeal is brought, the names of the respondents, the subject matter of the dispute, the submissions and a brief statement of the grounds on which the appeal is based.

The appeal shall be accompanied by a certified copy of the decision of the Arbitration Committee which is contested.

If the Court rejects the appeal, the decision of the Arbitration Committee shall become final.

If the Court annuls the decision of the Arbitration Committee, the matter may be re-opened, where appropriate, on the initiative of one of the parties in the case, before the Arbitration Committee. The latter shall conform to any decisions on points of law given by the Court.

Article 21

In the cases governed by Article 150 of this Treaty, the decision of the court or tribunal of a Member State which suspends its proceedings and refers a case to the Court shall be notified to the Court by the court or tribunal concerned. The decision shall then be notified by the Registrar of the Court to the parties, to the Member States and to the Commission, and also to the Council if the act the validity or interpretation of which is in dispute originates from the Council.

Within two months of this notification, the parties, the Member States, the Commission and, where appropriate, the Council, shall be entitled to submit statements of case or written observations to the Court.

Article 22

The Court may require the parties to produce all documents and to supply all information which the Court considers desirable. Formal note shall be taken of any refusal.

The Court may also require the Member States and institutions not being parties to the case to supply all information which the Court considers necessary for the proceedings.

Article 23

The Court may at any time entrust any individual, body, authority, committee or other organization it chooses with the task of giving an expert opinion.

Article 24

Witnesses may be heard under conditions laid down in the rules of procedure.

Article 25

With respect to defaulting witnesses the Court shall have the powers generally granted to courts and tribunals and may impose pecuniary penalites under conditions laid down in the rules of procedure.

Article 26

Witnesses and experts may be heard on oath taken in the form laid down in the rules of procedure or in the manner laid down by the law of the country of the witness or expert.

Article 27

The Court may order that a witness or expert be heard by the judicial authority of his place of permanent residence.

The order shall be sent for implementation to the competent judicial authority under conditions laid down in the rules of procedure. The documents drawn up in compliance with the letters rogatory shall be returned to the Court under the same conditions.

The Court shall defray the expenses, without prejudice to the right to charge them, where appropriate, to the parties.

Article 28

A Member State shall treat any violation of an oath by a witness or expert in the same manner as if the offence had been committed before one of its courts with jurisdiction in civil proceedings. At the instance of the Court, the Member State concerned shall prosecute the offender before its competent court.

Article 29

The hearing in court shall be public, unless the Court, of its own motion or on application by the parties, decides otherwise for serious reasons.

Article 30

During the hearings the Court may examine the experts, the witnesses and the parties themselves. The latter, however, may address the Court only through their representatives.

Article 31

Minutes shall be made of each hearing and signed by the President and the Registrar.

Article 32

The cause list shall be established by the President.

Article 33

The deliberations of the Court shall be and shall remain secret.

Article 34

Judgments shall state the reasons on which they are based. They shall contain the names of the Judges who took part in the deliberations.

Article 35

Judgments shall be signed by the President and the Registrar. They shall be read in open court.

Article 36

The Court shall adjudicate upon costs.

Article 37

The President of the Court may, by way of summary procedure, which may, in so far as necessary, differ from some of the rules contained in this Statute and which shall be laid down in the rules of procedure, adjudicate upon applications to suspend execution, as provided for in Article 157 of this Treaty, or to prescribe interim measures in pursuance of Article 158, or to suspend enforcement in accordance with the last paragraph of Article 164.

Should the President be prevented from attending, his place shall be taken by another Judge under conditions laid down in the rules of procedure.

The ruling of the President or of the Judge replacing him shall be provisional and shall in no way prejudice the decision of the Court on the substance of the case.

Article 38

Member States and institutions of the Community may intervene in cases before the Court.

The same right shall be open to any other person establishing an interest in the result of any case submitted to the Court, save in cases between Member States, between institutions of the Community or between Member States and institutions of the Community.

Submissions made in an application to intervene shall be limited to supporting the submissions of one of the parties.

Article 39

Where the defending party, after having been duly summoned, fails to file written submissions in defence, judgment shall be given against that party by default. An objection may be lodged against the judgment within one month of it being notified. The objection shall not have the effect of staying enforcement of the judgment by default unless the Court decides otherwise.

Article 40

Member States, institutions of the Community and any other natural or legal persons may, in cases and under conditions to be determined by the rules of procedure, institute third-party proceedings to contest a judgment rendered without their being heard, where the judgment is prejudicial to their rights.

Article 41

If the meaning or scope of a judgment is in doubt, the Court shall construe it on application by any party or any institution of the Community establishing an interest therein.

Article 42

An application for revision of a judgment may be made to the Court only on discovery of a fact which is of such a nature as to be a decisive factor, and which, when the judgment was given, was unknown to the Court and to the party claiming the revision.

The revision shall be opened by a judgment of the Court expressly recording the existence of a new fact, recognizing, that it is of such a character as to lay the case open to revision and declaring the application admissible on this ground.

No application for revision may be made after the lapse of 10 years from the date of the judgment.

Article 43

Periods of grace based on considerations of distance shall be determined by the rules of procedure.

No right shall be prejudiced in consequence of the expiry of a time limit if the party concerned proves the existence of unforeseeable circumstances or of force majeure.

Article 44

Proceedings against the Community in matters arising from non-contractual liability shall be barred after a period of five years from the occurrence of the event giving rise thereto. The period of limitation shall be interrupted if proceedings are instituted before the Court or if prior to such proceedings an application is made by the aggrieved party to the relevant institution of the Community. In the latter event the proceedings must be instituted within the period of two months provided for in Article 146; the provisions of the second paragraph of Article 148 shall apply where appropriate.

Article 45

The rules of procedure of the Court provided for in Article 160 of this Treaty shall contain, apart from the provisions contemplated by this statute, any other provisions necessary for applying and, where required, supplementing it.

Article 46

The Council may, acting unanimously, make such further adjustments to the provisions of this statute as may be required by reason of measures taken by the Council in accordance with the last paragraph of Article 137 of this Treaty.

Article 47

Immediately after the oath has been taken, the President of the Council shall proceed to choose by lot the Judges and the Advocates-General whose terms of office are to expire at the end of the first three years in accordance with the second and third paragraphs of Article 139 of this Treaty.

IN WITNESS WHEREOF, the undersigned Plenipotentiaries have signed this Protocol.

Done at Brussels this seventeenth day of April in the year one thousand nine hundred and fifty-seven.

J. Ch. SNOY ET D'OPPUERS

C. F. OPHÜLS

Robert MARJOLIN

Vittorio BADINI CONFALONIERI

Lambert SCHAUS

J. LINTHORST HOMAN

Treaties revising the Treaties
establishing the European Communities
and
Acts relating to the Communities

Single European Act

Contents

---

* EDITORIAL NOTE:
Notwithstanding the provisions of Article 3 of the SEA, and for historical reasons, the term 'Assembly' has not been replaced by the terms 'European Parliament'.

I — CONVENTION
ON CERTAIN INSTITUTIONS COMMON
TO THE EUROPEAN COMMUNITIES

His Majesty the King of the Belgians, the President of the Federal Republic of Germany, the President of the French Republic, the President of the Italian Republic, Her Royal Highness the Grand Duchess of Luxembourg, Her Majesty the Queen of the Netherlands,

Anxious to limit the number of institutions responsible for carrying out similar tasks in the European Communities which they have constituted,

Have decided to create for these Communities certain single institutions and to this end have designated as their Plenipotentiaries:

His Majesty the King of the Belgians:

Mr Paul-Henri Spaak, Minister for Foreign Affairs;
Baron J. Ch. Snoy et d'Oppuers, Secretary-General of the Ministry of Economic Affairs, Head of the Belgian Delegation to the Intergovernmental Conference;

The President of the Federal Republic of Germany:

Dr Konrad Adenauer, Federal Chancellor;
Professor Dr Walter Hallstein, State Secretary of the Federal Foreign Office;

The President of the French Republic:

Mr Christian Pineau, Minister for Foreign Affairs;
Mr Maurice Faure, Under-Secretary of State for Foreign Affairs;

811

THE PRESIDENT OF THE ITALIAN REPUBLIC:

Mr Antonio SEGNI, President of the Council of Ministers;
Professor Gaetano MARTINO, Minister for Foreign Affairs;

HER ROYAL HIGHNESS THE GRAND DUCHESS OF LUXEMBOURG:

Mr Joseph BECH, President of the Government, Minister for Foreign Affairs;
Mr Lambert SCHAUS, Ambassador, Head of the Luxembourg Delegation to the Intergovernmental Conference;

HER MAJESTY THE QUEEN OF THE NETHERLANDS:

Mr Josef LUNS, Minister for Foreign Affairs;
Mr J. LINTHORST HOMAN, Head of the Netherlands Delegation to the Intergovernmental Conference.

WHO, having exchanged their Full Powers, found in good and due form, have agreed as follows:

SECTION I

THE ASSEMBLY*

Article 1

The powers and jurisdiction which the Treaty establishing the European Economic Community and the Treaty establishing the European Atomic Energy Community confer upon the Assembly shall be exercised, in accordance with those Treaties, by a single Assembly composed and

---

* EDITORIAL NOTE:
  Notwithstanding the provisions of Article 3 of the SEA, and for historical reasons, the term 'Assembly' has not been replaced by the terms 'European Parliament'.

designated as provided in Article 138 of the Treaty establishing the European Economic Community and in Article 108 of the Treaty establishing the European Atomic Energy Community.*

Article 2

1. Upon taking up its duties, the single Assembly referred to in Article 1 shall take the place of the Common Assembly provided for in Article 21 of the Treaty establishing the European Coal and Steel Community. It shall exercise the powers and jurisdiction conferred upon the Common Assembly by that Treaty in accordance with the provisions thereof.*

2. To this end, Article 21 of the Treaty establishing the European Coal and Steel Community shall be repealed on the date when the single Assembly referred to in Article 1 takes up its duties, and the following provisions substituted therefor:*

'Article 21

1. *The European Parliament shall consist of delegates who shall be designated by the respective Parliaments from among their members in accordance with the procedure laid down by each Member State.*

2. *The number of these delegates shall be as follows:*

Germany	*36*
Belgium	*14*
France	*36*
Italy	*36*
Luxembourg	*6*
Netherlands	*14*

---

* EDITORIAL NOTE:
  Notwithstanding the provisions of Article 3 of the SEA, and for historical reasons, the term 'Assembly' has not been replaced by the terms 'European Parliament'.

3.   *The European Parliament shall draw up proposals for elections by direct universal suffrage in accordance with a uniform procedure in all Member States.*

The Council shall, acting unanimously, lay down the appropriate provisions, which it shall recommend to Member States for adoption in accordance with their respective constitutional requirements.'

SECTION II

THE COURT OF JUSTICE

Article 3

The jurisdiction which the Treaty establishing the European Economic Community and the Treaty establishing the European Atomic Energy Community confer upon the Court of Justice shall be exercised, in accordance with those Treaties, by a single Court of Justice composed and appointed as provided in Articles 165 to 167 of the Treaty establishing the European Economic Community and in Articles 137 to 139 of the Treaty establishing the European Atomic Energy Community.

Article 4

1.   Upon taking up its duties, the single Court of Justice referred to in Article 3 shall take the place of the Court provided for in Article 32 of the Treaty establishing the European Coal and Steel Community. It shall exercise the jurisdiction conferred upon that Court by that Treaty in accordance with the provisions thereof.

The President of the single Court of Justice referred to in Article 3 shall exercise the powers conferred by the Treaty establishing the European

Coal and Steel Community upon the President of the Court provided for in that Treaty.

2. To this end, on the date when the single Court of Justice referred to in Article 3 takes up its duties:

(a) Article 32 of the Treaty establishing the European Coal and Steel Community shall be repealed and the following provisions substituted therefor:

'Article 32

The Court shall consist of seven Judges.

The Court shall sit in plenary session. It may, however, form chambers, each consisting of three or five Judges, either to undertake certain preparatory inquiries or to adjudicate on particular categories of cases in accordance with rules laid down for these purposes.

Whenever the Court hears cases brought before it by a Member State or by one of the institutions of the Community or has to give preliminary rulings on questions submitted to it pursuant to Article 41, it shall sit in plenary session.

Should the Court so request, the Council may, acting unanimously, increase the number of Judges and make the necessary adjustments to the second and third paragraphs of this Article and to the second paragraph of Article 32 b.'

'Article 32 *a*

The Court shall be assisted by two Advocates-General.

It shall be the duty of the Advocate-General acting with complete impartiality and independence, to make, in open court, reasoned submissions on cases brought before the Court, in order to assist the Court in the performance of the task assigned to it in Article 31.

Should the Court so request, the Council may, acting unanimously, in-crease the number of Advocates-General and make the necessary adjustments to the third paragraph of Article 32 b.'

'Article 32 *b*

The Judges and Advocates-General shall be chosen from persons whose independence is beyond doubt and who possess the qualifications required for appointment to the highest judicial offices in their respective countries or who are jurisconsults of recognized competence; they shall be appointed by com-mon accord of the Governments of the Member States for a term of six years.

Every three years there shall be a partial replacement of the Judges. Three and four Judges shall be replaced alternately. The three Judges whose terms of office are to expire at the end of the first three years shall be chosen by lot.

Every three years there shall be a partial replacement of the Advocates-General. The Advocate-General whose term of office is to expire at the end of the first three years shall be chosen by lot.

Retiring Judges and Advocates-General shall be eligible for reappoint-ment.

The Judges shall elect the President of the Court from among their num-ber for a term of three years. He may be re-elected.'

'Article 32 *c*

The Court shall appoint its Registrar and lay down the rules governing his service.'

(b) The provisions of the Protocol on the statute of the Court of Justice annexed to the Treaty establishing the European Coal and Steel Com-

munity, in so far as they are in conflict with Articles 32 to 32c of that Treaty, shall be repealed.

SECTION III

THE ECONOMIC AND SOCIAL COMMITTEE

Article 5

1. The functions which the Treaty establishing the European Economic Community and the Treaty establishing the European Atomic Energy Community confer upon the Economic and Social Committee shall be exercised, in accordance with those Treaties, by a single Economic and Social Committee composed and appointed as provided in Article 194 of the Treaty establishing the European Economic Community and in Article 166 of the Treaty establishing the European Atomic Energy Community.

2. The single Economic and Social Committee referred to in paragraph 1 shall include a section specializing in, and may include subcommittees competent for, the fields or questions dealt with in the Treaty establishing the European Atomic Energy Community.

3. The provisions of Articles 193 and 197 of the Treaty establishing the European Economic Community shall apply to the single Economic and Social Committee referred to in paragraph 1.

SECTION IV

THE FINANCING OF THESE INSTITUTIONS

Article 6

(repealed by Article 23 of the Merger Treaty)

[*See Article 20 of the Merger Treaty, which reads as follows:*

1. The administrative expenditure of the European Coal and Steel Community and the revenue relating thereto, the revenue and expenditure of the European Economic Community, and the revenue and expenditure of the European Atomic Energy Community, with the exception of that of the Supply Agency and the Joint Undertakings, shall be shown in the budget of the European Communities in accordance with the appropriate provisions of the Treaties establishing the three Communities. This budget, which shall be in balance as to revenue and expenditure, shall take the place of the administrative budget of the European Coal and Steel Community, the budget of the European Economic Community and the operating budget and research and investment budget of the European Atomic Energy Community.*

2. The portion of the expenditure covered by the levies provided for in Article 49 of the Treaty establishing the European Coal and Steel Community shall be fixed at 18 million units of account.

---

* Paragraph (1) as amended by Article 10 of the Treaty amending Certain Budgetary Provisions.

As from the financial year beginning 1 January 1967, the Commission shall submit annually to the Council a report on the basis of which the Council shall examine whether there is reason to adjust this figure to changes in the budget of the Communities. The Council shall act by the majority laid down in the first sentence of the fourth paragraph of Article 28 of the Treaty establishing the European Coal and Steel Community. The adjustment shall be made on the basis of an assessment of developments in expenditure arising from the application of the Treaty establishing the European Coal and Steel Community.

3. The portion of the levies assigned to cover expenditure under the budget of the Communities shall be allocated by the Commission for the implementation of that budget in accordance with the timetable provided for in the financial regulations adopted pursuant to Article 209(b) of the Treaty establishing the European Economic Community and Article 183(b) of the Treaty establishing the European Atomic Energy Community relating to the methods and procedure whereby the contributions of the Member States shall be made available.]

Final provisions

Article 7

This Convention shall be ratified by the High Contracting Parties in accordance with their respective constitutional requirements. The instruments of ratification shall be deposited with the Government of the Italian Republic.

This Convention shall enter into force at the same time as the Treaty establishing the European Economic Community and the Treaty establishing the European Atomic Energy Community.

Article 8

This Convention, drawn up in a single original in the Dutch, French, German and Italian languages, all four texts being equally authentic, shall be deposited in the archives of the Government of the Italian Republic, which shall transmit a certified copy to each of the Governments of the other signatory States.

IN WITNESS WHEREOF, the undersigned Plenipotentiaries have signed this Convention.

Done at Rome this twenty-fifth day of March in the year one thousand nine hundred and fifty-seven.

P. H. SPAAK	J. Ch. SNOY ET D'OPPUERS
ADENAUER	HALLSTEIN
PINEAU	M. FAURE
Antonio SEGNI	Gaetano MARTINO
BECH	Lambert SCHAUS
J. LUNS	J. LINTHORST HOMAN

II — TREATY
ESTABLISHING A SINGLE COUNCIL AND
A SINGLE COMMISSION OF
THE EUROPEAN COMMUNITIES

Official Journal of the European Communities, No 152, 13 July 1967.

1. Text of the Treaty

His Majesty the King of the Belgians, the President of the Federal Republic of Germany, the President of the French Republic, the President of the Italian Republic, His Royal Highness the Grand Duke of Luxembourg, Her Majesty the Queen of the Netherlands,

Having regard to Article 96 of the Treaty establishing the European Coal and Steel Community,

Having regard to Article 236 of the Treaty establishing the European Economic Community,

Having regard to Article 204 of the Treaty establishing the European Atomic Energy Community,

Resolved to continue along the road to European unity,

Resolved to effect the unification of the three Communities,

Mindful of the contribution which the creation of single Community institutions represents for such unification,

Have decided to create a single Council and a single Commission of the European Communities and to this end have designated as their Plenipotentiaries:

His Majesty the King of the Belgians:

Mr Paul-Henri Spaak, Deputy Prime Minister and Minister for Foreign Affairs;

THE PRESIDENT OF THE FEDERAL REPUBLIC OF GERMANY:

Mr Kurt SCHMÜCKER, Minister for Economic Affairs;

THE PRESIDENT OF THE FRENCH REPUBLIC:

Mr Maurice COUVE DE MURVILLE, Minister for Foreign Affairs;

THE PRESIDENT OF THE ITALIAN REPUBLIC:

Mr Amintore FANFANI, Minister for Foreign Affairs;

HIS ROYAL HIGHNESS THE GRAND DUKE OF LUXEMBOURG:

Mr Pierre WERNER, President of the Government, Minister for Foreign Affairs;

HER MAJESTY THE QUEEN OF THE NETHERLANDS:

Mr J. M. A. H. LUNS, Minister for Foreign Affairs;

WHO, having exchanged their Full Powers, found in good and due form, have agreed as follows:

CHAPTER 1

THE COUNCIL OF THE EUROPEAN COMMUNITIES

Article 1

A Council of the European Communities (hereinafter called the 'Council') is hereby established. This Council shall take the place of the Special Council of Ministers of the European Coal and Steel Community, the Council of the European Economic Community and the Council of the European Atomic Energy Community.

It shall exercise the powers and jurisdiction conferred on those institutions in accordance with the provisions of the Treaties establishing the European Coal and Steel Community, the European Economic Community and the European Atomic Energy Community, and of this Treaty.

Article 2

The Council shall consist of representatives of the Member States. Each Government shall delegate to it one of its members.

The office of President shall be held in turn by each Member State in the Council for a term of six months, in the following order of Member States:

— for a first cycle of six years: Belgium, Denmark, Germany, Greece, Spain, France, Ireland, Italy, Luxembourg, Netherlands, Portugal, United Kingdom,

— for the following cycle of six years: Denmark, Belgium, Greece, Germany, France, Spain, Italy, Ireland, Netherlands, Luxembourg, United Kingdom, Portugal.*

Article 3

The Council shall meet when convened by its President on his own initiative or at the request of one of its members or of the Commission.

Article 4

A committee consisting of the Permanent Representatives of the Member States shall be responsible for preparing the work of the Council and for carrying out the tasks assigned to it by the Council.

Article 5

The Council shall adopt its rules of procedure.

---

* Second paragraph as amended by Article 11 of the Act of Accession ESP/PORT.

Article 6

The Council shall, acting by a qualified majority, determine the salaries, allowances and pensions of the President and members of the Commission, and of the President, Judges, Advocates-General and Registrar of the Court of Justice. It shall also, again by a qualified majority, determine any payment to be made instead of remuneration.

Article 7

Article 27, the first paragraph of Article 28, and Articles 29 and 30 of the Treaty establishing the European Coal and Steel Community, Articles 146, 147, 151 and 154 of the Treaty establishing the European Economic Community, and Articles 116, 117, 121 and 123 of the Treaty establishing the European Atomic Energy Community are repealed.

Article 8

1. The conditions governing the exercise of the jurisdiction conferred on the Special Council of Ministers by the Treaty establishing the European Coal and Steel Community and by the Protocol on the Statute of the Court of Justice annexed thereto shall be amended as set out in paragraphs 2 and 3.

2. Article 28 of the Treaty establishing the European Coal and Steel Community shall be amended as follows:

(a) To the provisions of the third paragraph, worded thus:

'Wherever this Treaty requires a unanimous decision or unanimous assent, such decision or assent shall be duly given if all the members of the Council vote in favour.'

there shall be added the following provisions:

'However, for the purposes of applying Articles 21, 32, 32 a, 78 d and 78 f of this Treaty, and Article 16, the third paragraph of Article 20,

the fifth paragraph of Article 28 and Article 44 of the Protocol on the Statute of the Court of Justice, abstention by members present in person or represented shall not prevent the adoption by the Council of acts which require unanimity.'

(b) To the provisions of the fourth paragraph, worded thus:

'Decisions of the Council, other than those which require a qualified majority or unanimity, shall be taken by a vote of the majority of its members; this majority shall be considered to be attained if it represents an absolute majority of the representatives of the Member States, including the vote of the representative of one of the States which each produce at least one-sixth of the total value of the coal and steel output of the Community.'

there shall be added the following provisions:

'However, for the purposes of applying those provisions of Articles 78, 78 b and 78 d of this Treaty which require a qualified majority, the votes of the members of the Council shall be weighted as follows: Belgium 2, Germany 4, France 4, Italy 4, Luxembourg 1, Netherlands 2. For their adoption, acts shall require at least 12 votes in favour, cast by not less than four members.'

3. The Protocol on the Statute of the Court of Justice annexed to the Treaty establishing the European Coal and Steel Community shall be amended as follows:

(a) Articles 5 and 15 are repealed.

(b) Article 16 is repealed and the following substituted therefor:

'1. *Officials and other servants shall be attached to the Court to enable it to function. They shall be responsible to the Registrar under the authority of the President.*

2. *On a proposal from the Court, the Council may, acting unanimously, provide for the appointment of Assistant Rapporteurs and lay down the rules governing their service. The Assistant Rapporteurs may be required,*

under conditions laid down in the rules of procedure, to participate in prepara-
tory inquiries in cases pending before the Court and to cooperate with the
Judge who acts as Rapporteur.

The Assistant Rapporteurs shall be chosen from persons whose indepen-
dence is beyond doubt and who posses the necessary legal qualifications; they
shall be appointed by the Council. They shall take an oath before the Court to
perform their duties impartially and conscientiously and to preserve the
secrecy of the deliberations of the Court.'

(c) The third paragraph of Article 20 and the fifth paragraph of Article
28 shall be amended by the addition at the end of each paragraph of the
words:

'acting unanimously'.

(d) The first sentence of Article 44 is repealed and the following substituted therefor:

'The Court of Justice shall adopt its rules of procedure. These shall require
the unanimous approval of the Council.'

CHAPTER II

THE COMMISSION OF THE EUROPEAN COMMUNITIES

Article 9

A Commission of the European Communities (hereinafter called the
'Commission') is hereby established. This Commission shall take the place
of the High Authority of the European Coal and Steel Community, the
Commission of the European Economic Community and the Commission
of the European Atomic Energy Community.

It shall exercise the powers and jurisdiction conferred on those institutions in accordance with the provisions of the Treaties establishing the European Coal and Steel Community, the European Economic Community and the European Atomic Energy Community, and of this Treaty.

Article 10

1. The Commission shall consist of 17 members, who shall be chosen on the grounds of their general competence and whose independence is beyond doubt.*

The number of members of the Commission may be altered by the Council, acting unanimously.

Only nationals of Member States may be members of the Commission.

The Commission must include at least one national of each of the Member States, but may not include more than two members having the nationality of the same State.

2. The members of the Commission shall, in the general interest of the Communities, be completely independent in the performance of their duties.

In the performance of these duties, they shall neither seek nor take instructions from any Government or from any other body. They shall refrain from any action incompatible with their duties. Each Member State undertakes to respect this principle and not to seek to influence the members of the Commission in the performance of their tasks.

The members of the Commission may not, during their term of office, engage in any other occupation, whether gainful or not. When entering upon their duties they shall give a solemn undertaking that, both du-

---

* First subparagraph of paragraph 1 as amended by Article 15 of the Act of Accession ESP/PORT.

ring and after their term of office, they will respect the obligations arising therefrom and in particular their duty to behave with integrity and discretion as regards the acceptance, after they have ceased to hold office, of certain appointments or benefits. In the event of any breach of these obligations, the Court of Justice may, on application by the Council or the Commission, rule that the member concerned be, according to the circumstances, either compulsorily retired in accordance with the provisions of Article 13 or deprived of his right to a pension or other benefits in its stead.

Article 11

The members of the Commission shall be appointed by common accord of the Governments of the Member States.

Their term of office shall be four years. It shall be renewable.

Article 12

Apart from normal replacement, or death, the duties of a member of the Commission shall end when he resigns or is compulsorily retired.

The vacancy thus caused shall be filled for the remainder of the member's term of office. The Council may, acting unanimously, decide that such a vacancy need not be filled.

Save in the case of compulsory retirement under the provisions of Article 13, members of the Commission shall remain in office until they have been replaced.

Article 13

If any member of the Commission no longer fulfils the conditions required for the performance of his duties or if he has been guilty of serious misconduct, the Court of Justice may, on application by the Council or the Commission, compulsorily retire him.

Article 14

The President and the six Vice-Presidents of the Commission shall be appointed from among its members for a term of two years in accordance with the same procedure as that laid down for the appointment of members of the Commission. Their appointments may be renewed.*

The Council, acting unanimously, may amend the provisions concerning Vice-Presidents.**

Save where the entire Commission is replaced, such appointments shall be made after the Commission has been consulted.

In the event of retirement or death, the President and the Vice-Presidents shall be replaced for the remainder of their term of office in accordance with the preceding provisions.

Article 15

The Council and the Commission shall consult each other and shall settle by common accord their methods of cooperation.

Article 16

The Commission shall adopt its rules of procedure so as to ensure that both it and its departments operate in accordance with the provisions of the Treaties establishing the European Coal and Steel Community, the European Economic Community and the European Atomic Energy Community, and of this Treaty. It shall ensure that these rules are published.

Article 17

The Commission shall act by a majority of the number of members provided for in Article 10.

---

* First paragraph as amended by Article 16 of the Act of Accession ESP/PORT.
** Second paragraph as added by Article 16 of the said Act.

A meeting of the Commission shall be valid only if the number of members laid down in its rules of procedure is present.

Article 18

The Commission shall publish annually, not later than one month before the opening of the session of the European Parliament, a general report on the activities of the Communities.

Article 19

Articles 156 to 163 of the Treaty establishing the European Economic Community, Articles 125 to 133 of the Treaty establishing the European Atomic Energy Community and Articles 9 to 13, the third paragraph of Article 16, Article 17 and the sixth paragraph of Article 18 of the Treaty establishing the European Coal and Steel Community are repealed.

CHAPTER III

FINANCIAL PROVISIONS

Article 20

1. The administrative expenditure of the European Coal and Steel Community and the revenue relating thereto, the revenue and expenditure of the European Economic Community, and the revenue and expenditure of the European Atomic Energy Community, with the exception of that of the Supply Agency and the Joint Undertakings, shall be shown in the budget of the European Communities in accordance with the appropriate

provisions of the Treaties establishing the three Communities. This budget, which shall be in balance as to revenue and expenditure, shall take the place of the administrative budget of the European Coal and Steel Community, the budget of the European Economic Community and the operating budget and research and investment budget of the European Atomic Energy Community.*

2.   The portion of the expenditure covered by the levies provided for in Article 49 of the Treaty establishing the European Coal and Steel Community shall be fixed at 18 million units of account.

As from the financial year beginning 1 January 1967. the Commission shall submit annually to the Council a report on the basis of which the Council shall examine whether there is reason to adjust this figure to changes in the budget of the Communities. The Council shall act by the majority laid down in the first sentence of the fourth paragraph of Article 28 of the Treaty establishing the European Coal and Steel Community. The adjustment shall be made on the basis of an assessment of developments in expenditure arising from the application of the Treaty establishing the European Coal and Steel Community.

3.   The portion of the levies assigned to cover expenditure under the budget of the Communities shall be allocated by the Commission for the implementation of that budget in accordance with the timetable provided for in the financial regulations adopted pursuant to Article 209 *(b)* of the Treaty establishing the European Economic Community and Article 183 *(b)* of the Treaty establishing the European Atomic Energy Community relating to the methods and procedure whereby the contributions of the Member States shall be made available.

---

* Paragraph (1) as amended by Article 10 cf the Treaty amending Certain Budgetary Provisions.

Article 21

Article 78 of the Treaty establishing the European Coal and Steel Community is repealed and the following substituted therefor:

'Article 78

1.   *The financial year of the Community shall run from 1 January to 31 December.*

2.   *The administrative expenditure of the Community shall comprise the expenditure of the High Authority, including that relating to the functioning of the Consultative Committee, and that of the Court, the European Parliament and the Council.*

3.   *Each institution of the Community shall draw up estimates of its administrative expenditure. The High Authority shall consolidate these estimates in a preliminary draft administrative budget. It shall attach thereto an opinion which may contain different estimates.*

The High Authority shall place the preliminary draft budget before the Council not later than 30 September of the year preceding that in which the budget is to be implemented.

The Council shall consult the High Authority and, where appropriate, the other institutions concerned whenever it intends to depart from the preliminary draft budget.

4.   *The Council shall, acting by a qualified majority, establish the draft administrative budget and then forward it to the European Parliament.*

The draft administrative budget shall be placed before the European Parliament not later than 31 October of the year preceding that in which the budget is to be implemented.

The European Parliament shall have the right to propose to the Council modifications to the draft administrative budget.

5.   *If within one month of the draft administrative budget being placed before it, the European Parliament has given its approval or has not forwarded its opinion to the Council, the draft administrative budget shall be deemed to be finally adopted.*

If within this period the European Parliament has proposed modifications, the draft administrative budget so modified shall be forwarded to the Council. The Council shall discuss it with the High Authority and, where appropriate, with the other institutions concerned, and shall finally adopt the administrative budget, acting by a qualified majority.

6.   *The final adoption of the administrative budget shall have the effect of authorizing and requiring the High Authority to collect the corresponding revenue in accordance with the provisions of Article 49.*

Article 78a

The administrative budget shall be drawn up in the unit of account determined in accordance with the provisions of the regulations made pursuant to Article 78f.

The expenditure shown in the budget shall be authorized for one financial year, unless the regulations made pursuant to Article 78f provide otherwise.

In accordance with conditions to be laid down pursuant to Article 78f, any appropriations, other than those relating to staff expenditure, that are unexpended at the end of the financial year may be carried forward to the next financial year only.

Appropriations shall be classified under different chapters grouping items of expenditure according to their nature or purpose and subdivided, as far as may be necessary, in accordance with the regulations made pursuant to Article 78f.

The expenditure of the European Parliament, the Council, the High Authority and the Court shall be set out in separate parts of the administrative budget, without prejudice to special arrangements for certain common items of expenditure.

Article 78b

1.   If, at the beginning of a financial year, the administrative budget has not yet been voted, a sum equivalent to not more than one twelfth of the budget appropriations for the preceding financial year may be spent each month in respect of any chapter or other subdivision of the administrative budget in accordance with the provisions of the regulations made pursuant to Article 78f; this arrangement shall not, however, have the effect of placing at the disposal of the High Authority appropriations in excess of one-twelfth of those provided for in the draft administrative budget in course of preparation.

The High Authority is authorized and required to impose the levies up to the amount of the appropriations for the preceding financial year, but shall not thereby exceed the amount which would have resulted from the adoption of the draft administrative budget.

2.   The Council may, acting by a qualified majority, provided that the other conditions laid down in paragraph 1 are observed, authorize expenditure in excess of one twelfth. The authorization and requirement to impose the levies may be adjusted accordingly.

Article 78c

The High Authority shall implement the administrative budget, in accordance with the provisions of the regulations made pursuant to Article 78f, on its own responsibility and within the limits of the appropriations.

The regulations shall lay down detailed rules for each institution concerning its part in effecting its own expenditure.

Within the administrative budget, the High Authority may, subject to the limits and conditions laid down in the regulations made pursuant to Article 78f, transfer appropriations from one chapter to another or from one subdivision to another.

Article 78d

The accounts of all the administrative expenditure referred to in Article 78 (2), and of administrative revenue and of revenue derived from the tax for the benefit of the Community levied on the salaries, wages and emoluments of its officials and other servants, shall be examined by an Audit Board consisting of auditors whose independence is beyond doubt, one of whom shall be chairman. The Council shall, acting unanimously, determine the number of the auditors. The auditors and the chairman of the Audit Board shall be appointed by the Council, acting unanimously, for a period of five years. Their remuneration shall be determined by the Council, acting by a qualified majority.

The purpose of the audit, which shall be based on records and, if necessary, performed on the spot, shall be to establish that all revenue has been received and all expenditure incurred in a lawful and regular manner and that the financial management has been sound. After the close of each financial year, the Audit Board shall draw up a report, which shall be adopted by a majority of its members.

The High Authority shall submit annually to the Council and to the European Parliament the accounts of the preceding financial year relating to the implementation of the administrative budget, together with the report of the Audit Board. The High Authority shall also forward to them a financial statement of the assets and liabilities of the Community in the field covered by that budget.

The Council shall, acting by a qualified majority, give the High Authority a discharge in respect of the implementation of the budget. It shall communicate its decision to the European Parliament.

Article 78e

The Council shall appoint an auditor to serve for three years; he shall draw up an annual report stating whether the accounting and the financial management of the High Authority have been effected in a regular manner; this report shall not cover entries relating to the administrative expenditure referred to in Article 78 (2), to administrative revenue or to revenue derived from the tax for the benefit of the Community levied on the salaries, wages and emoluments of its officials and other servants. He shall draw up this report within six months of the close of the financial year to which the accounts refer and shall submit it to the High Authority and the Council. The High Authority shall forward it to the European Parliament.

The auditor shall be completely independent in the performance of his duties. The office of auditor shall be incompatible with any other office in an institution or department of the Communities other than that of member of the Audit Board provided for in Article 78d. His term of office shall be renewable.

Article 78f

The Council shall, acting unanimously on a proposal from the High Authority:

(a) make financial regulations specifying in particular the procedure to be adopted for establishing and implementing the administrative budget and for presenting and auditing accounts.

(b) *lay down rules concerning the responsibility of authorizing officers and accounting officers and concerning appropriate arrangements for inspection.'*

Article 22*

1. The powers and jurisdiction conferred upon the Court of Auditors established by Article 78e of the Treaty establishing the European Coal and Steel Community, by Article 206 of the Treaty establishing the European Economic Community, and by Article 180 of the Treaty establishing the European Atomic Energy Community shall be exercised in accordance with those Treaties by a single Court of Auditors of the European Communities constituted as provided in these Articles.

2. Without prejudice to the powers and jurisdiction referred to in paragraph 1, the Court of Auditors of the European Communities shall exercise the powers and jurisdiction conferred, before the entry into force of this Treaty, upon the Audit Board of the European Communities and upon the Auditor of the European Coal and Steel Community under the conditions laid down in the various instruments referring to the Audit Board and to the Auditor. In all these instruments the words 'Audit Board' and 'Auditors' shall be replaced by the words 'Court of Auditors'.

Article 23

Article 6 of the Convention on Certain Institutions Common to the European Communities is repealed.

---

* As amended by Article 27 of the Treaty amending Certain Financial Provisions.

CHAPTER IV

OFFICIALS AND OTHER SERVANTS
OF THE EUROPEAN COMMUNITIES

Article 24

1. The officials and other servants of the European Coal and Steel Community, the European Economic Community and the European Atomic Energy Community shall, at the date of entry into force of this Treaty, become officials and other servants of the European Communities and form part of the single administration of those Communities.

The Council shall, acting by a qualified majority on a proposal from the Commission and after consulting the other institutions concerned, lay down the Staff Regulations of officials of the European Communities and the Conditions of Employment of other servants of those Communities.

2. The third paragraph of Article 7 of the Convention on the Transitional Provisions annexed to the Treaty establishing the European Coal and Steel Community, Article 212 of the Treaty establishing the European Economic Community and Article 186 of the Treaty establishing the European Atomic Energy Community are repealed.

Article 25

Until the uniform Staff Regulations and Conditions of Employment provided for in Article 24 and the Protocol annexed to this Treaty enter into force, officials and other servants recruited before the date of entry into force of this Treaty shall continue to be governed by the provisions which were until then applicable to them.

Officials and other servants recruited on or after the date of entry into force of this Treaty shall, pending the adoption of the uniform Staff Regulations and Conditions of Employment provided for in Article 24 and of regulations to be made pursuant to Article 13 of the Protocol annexed to this Treaty, be governed by the provisions applicable to officials and other servants of the European Economic Community and of the European Atomic Energy Community.

Article 26

The second paragraph of Article 40 of the Treaty establishing the European Coal and Steel Community is repealed and the following substituted therefor:

'*The Court shall also have jurisdiction to order the Community to make good any injury caused by a personal wrong by a servant of the Community in the performance of his duties. The personal liability of its servants towards the Community shall be governed by the provisions laid down in their Staff Regulations or the Conditions of Employment applicable to them.*'

CHAPTER V

GENERAL AND FINAL PROVISIONS

Article 27

1. The first paragraph of Article 22 of the Treaty establishing the European Coal and Steel Community, the first paragraph of Article 139 of the Treaty establishing the European Economic Community, and the first paragraph of Article 109 of the Treaty establishing the European Atomic Energy Community are repealed and the following substituted therefor:

'The European Parliament shall hold an annual session. It shall meet, without requiring to be convened, on the second Tuesday in March.'

2.   The second paragraph of Article 24 of the Treaty establishing the European Coal and Steel Community is repealed and the following substituted therefor:

'If a motion of censure on the activities of the High Authority is tabled before it, the European Parliament shall not vote thereon until at least three days after the motion has been tabled and only by open vote.'

Article 28

The European Communities shall enjoy in the territories of the Member States such privileges and immunities as are necessary for the performance of their tasks, under the conditions laid down in the Protocol annexed to this Treaty. The same shall apply to the European Investment Bank.

Article 76 of the Treaty establishing the European Coal and Steel Community, Article 218 of the Treaty establishing the European Economic Community and Article 191 of the Treaty establishing the European Atomic Energy Community; the Protocols on Privileges and Immunities annexed to these three Treaties; the fourth paragraph of Article 3 and the second paragraph of Article 14 of the Protocol on the Statute of the Court of Justice annexed to the Treaty establishing the European Coal and Steel Community; and the second subparagraph of Article 28 (1) of the Protocol on the Statute of the European Investment Bank annexed to the Treaty establishing the European Economic Community are repealed.

Article 29

The jurisdiction conferred upon the Council by Articles 5, 6, 10, 12, 13, 24, 34 and 35 of this Treaty and by the Protocol annexed thereto shall be exercised according to the rules laid down in Articles 148, 149 and 150 of the Treaty establishing the European Economic Community and Articles 118, 119 and 120 of the Treaty establishing the European Atomic Energy Community.

Article 30

The provisions of the Treaties establishing the European Economic Community and the European Atomic Energy Community relating to the jurisdiction of the Court of Justice and to the exercise of that jurisdiction shall be applicable to the provisions of this Treaty and of the Protocol annexed thereto, with the exception of those which represent amendments to Articles of the Treaty establishing the European Coal and Steel Community, in respect of which the provisions of the Treaty establishing the European Coal and Steel Community shall remain applicable.

Article 31

The Council shall take up its duties on the date of entry into force of this Treaty.

On that date the office of President of the Council shall be held by the member of the Council who, in accordance with the rules laid down in the Treaties establishing the European Economic Community and the European Atomic Energy Community, was to take up the office of President of the Council of the European Economic Community and of the European Atomic Energy Community; this will apply for the remainder of his term of office. On expiry of this term, the office of President shall then be held in the order of Member States laid down in Article 2 of this Treaty.

Article 32

1. Until the date of entry into force of the Treaty establishing a Single European Community, or until three years after the appointment of its

members, whichever is the earlier, the Commission shall consist of 14 members.

During this period, not more than three members may have the nationality of the same State.

2. The President, the Vice-President and the members of the Commission shall be appointed upon the entry into force of this Treaty. The Commission shall take up its duties on the fifth day after the appointment of its members. The term of office of the members of the High Authority and of the Commission of the European Economic Community and of the European Atomic Energy Community shall end at the same time.

Article 33

The term of office of the members of the Commission provided for in Article 32 shall expire on the date determined by Article 32 (1). The members of the Commission provided for in Article 10 shall be appointed one month before that date at the latest.

If any or all of these appointments are not made within the required time, the provisions of the third paragraph of Article 12 shall not be applicable to that member who, among the nationals of each State, has least seniority as a member of a Commission or of the High Authority or, where two or more members have the same seniority, to the youngest of them. The provisions of the third paragraph of Article 12 shall remain applicable, however, to all members of the same nationality, where, before the date determined by Article 32 (1), a member of that nationality has ceased to hold office and has been replaced.

Article 34

The Council shall, acting unanimously, make financial arrangements for past members of the High Authority and of the Commissions of the European Economic Community and of the European Atomic Energy Community who, having ceased to hold office in pursuance of Article 32, have not been appointed members of the Commission.

Article 35

1. The first budget of the Communities shall be established and adopted for the financial year beginning 1 January following the entry into force of this Treaty.

2. If this Treaty enters into force before 1 July 1965, the general estimates of the administrative expenditure of the European Coal and Steel Community which expire on 1 July shall be extended until 31 December of the same year; the appropriations made in these estimates shall be proportionately increased, unless the Council, acting by a qualified majority, decides otherwise.

If this Treaty enters into force after 20 June 1965, the Council shall, acting unanimously on a proposal from the Commission, take the appropriate decisions, taking account of the need to ensure that the Communities function smoothly and that the first budget of the Communities is adopted at as early a date as possible.

Article 36

The chairman and members of the Audit Board of the European Economic Community and of the European Atomic Energy Community shall take up the duties of chairman and members of the Audit Board of the European Communities upon the entry into force of this Treaty and for the remainder of their former term of office.

The auditor who, until the entry into force of this Treaty, is performing his duties pursuant to Article 78 of the Treaty establishing the European Coal and Steel Community shall take up the duties of the auditor provided for in Article 78e of that Treaty for the remainder of his former term of office.*

---

* See Article 22 above.

Article 37

Without prejudice to the application of Article 77 of the Treaty establishing the European Coal and Steel Community, Article 216 of the Treaty establishing the European Economic Community, Article 189 of the Treaty establishing the European Atomic Energy Community and the second paragraph of Article 1 of the Protocol on the Statute of the European Investment Bank, the representatives of the Governments of the Member States shall by common accord lay down the provisions required in order to settle certain problems peculiar to the Grand Duchy of Luxembourg which arise out of the creation of a single Council and a single Commission of the European Communities.

The decision of the representatives of the Governments of the Member States shall enter into force on the same date as this Treaty.

Article 38

This Treaty shall be ratified by the High Contracting Parties in accordance with their respective constitutional requirements. The instruments of ratification shall be deposited with the Government of the Italian Republic.

This Treaty shall enter into force on the first day of the month following the deposit of the instrument of ratification by the last signatory State to take this step.

Article 39

This Treaty, drawn up in a single original in the Dutch, French, German and Italian languages, all four texts being equally authentic, shall be deposited in the archives of the Government of the Italian Republic, which shall transmit a certified copy to each of the Governments of the other signatory States.

IN WITNESS WHEREOF, the undersigned Plenipotentiaries have signed this Treaty.

Done at Brussels this eighth day of April in the year one thousand nine hundred and sixty-five.

Pour Sa Majesté le roi des Belges
Voor Zijne Majesteit de Koning der Belgen
    Paul-Henri SPAAK

Für den Präsidenten der Bundesrepublik Deutschland
    Kurt SCHMÜCKER

Pour le Président de la République française
    Maurice COUVE DE MURVILLE

Per il Presidente della Repubblica italiana
    Amintore FANFANI

Pour Son Altesse Royale le grand-duc de Luxembourg
    Pierre WERNER

Voor Hare Majesteit de Koningin der Nederlanden
    J. M. A. H. LUNS

2. Protocol on the privileges and immunities of the European Communities

THE HIGH CONTRACTING PARTIES,

CONSIDERING that, in accordance with Article 28 of the Treaty establishing a Single Council and a Single Commission of the European Communities, these Communities and the European Investment Bank shall enjoy in the territories of the Member States such privileges and immunities as are necessary for the performance of their tasks,

HAVE AGREED upon the following provisions, which shall be annexed to this Treaty:

CHAPTER I

PROPERTY, FUNDS, ASSETS AND OPERATIONS OF THE EUROPEAN COMMUNITIES

Article 1

The premises and buildings of the Communities shall be inviolable. They shall be exempt from search, requisition, confiscation or expropriation. The property and assets of the Communities shall not be the subject of any administrative or legal measure of constraint without the authorization of the Court of Justice.

Article 2

The archives of the Communities shall be inviolable.

Article 3

The Communities, their assets, revenues and other property shall be exempt from all direct taxes.

The Governments of the Member States shall, wherever possible, take the appropriate measures to remit or refund the amount of indirect taxes or sales taxes included in the price of movable or immovable property, where the Communities make, for their official use, substantial purchases the price of which includes taxes of this kind. These provisions shall not be applied, however, so as to have the effect of distorting competition within the Communities.

No exemption shall be granted in respect of taxes and dues which amount merely to charges for public utility services.

Article 4

The Communities shall be exempt from all customs duties, prohibitions and restrictions on imports and exports in respect of articles intended for their official use: articles so imported shall not be disposed of, whether or not in return for payment, in the territory of the country into which they have been imported, except under conditions approved by the Government of that country.

The Communities shall also be exempt from any customs duties and any prohibitions and restrictions on imports and exports in respect of their publications.

Article 5

The European Coal and Steel Community may hold currency of any kind and operate accounts in any currency.

CHAPTER II

COMMUNICATIONS AND *LAISSEZ-PASSER*

Article 6

For their official communications and the transmission of all their documents, the institutions of the Communities shall enjoy in the territory of each Member State the treatment accorded by that State to diplomatic missions.

Official correspondence and other official communications of the institutions of the Communities shall not be subject to censorship.

Article 7

1. Laissez-passer in a form to be prescribed by the Council, which shall be recognized as valid travel documents by the authorities of the Member States, may be issued to members and servants of the institutions of the Communities by the Presidents of these institutions. These laissez-passer shall be issued to officials and other servants under conditions laid down in the Staff Regulations of officials and the Conditions of Employment of other servants of the Communities.

The Commission may conclude agreements for these laissez-passer to be recognized as valid travel documents within the territory of third countries.

2. The provisions of Article 6 of the Protocol on the Privileges and Immunities of the European Coal and Steel Community shall, however, remain applicable to members and servants of the institutions who are at the date of entry into force of this Treaty in possession of the laissez-passer provided for in that Article, until the provisions of paragraph 1 of this Article are applied.

CHAPTER III

MEMBERS OF THE EUROPEAN PARLIAMENT

Article 8

No administrative or other restriction shall be imposed on the free movement of members of the European Parliament travelling to or from the place of meeting of the European Parliament.

Members of the European Parliament shall, in respect of customs and exchange control, be accorded:

(a) by their own Government, the same facilities as those accorded to senior officials travelling abroad on temporary official missions;

(b) by the Governments of other Member States, the same facilities as those accorded to representatives of foreign Governments on temporary official missions.

Article 9

Members of the European Parliament shall not be subject to any form of inquiry, detention or legal proceedings in respect of opinions expressed or votes cast by them in the performance of their duties.

Article 10

During the sessions of the European Parliament, its members shall enjoy:

(a) in the territory of their own State, the immunities accorded to members of their parliament;

(b) in the territory of any other Member State, immunity from any measure of detention and from legal proceedings.

Immunity shall likewise apply to members while they are travelling to and from the place of meeting of the European Parliament.

Immunity cannot be claimed when a member is found in the act of committing an offence and shall not prevent the European Parliament from exercising its right to waive the immunity of one of its members.

CHAPTER IV

REPRESENTATIVES OF MEMBER STATES TAKING PART IN THE WORK OF THE INSTITUTIONS OF THE EUROPEAN COMMUNITIES

Article 11

Representatives of Member States taking part in the work of the institutions of the Communities, their advisers and technical experts shall, in the performance of their duties and during their travel to and from the place of meeting, enjoy the customary privileges, immunities and facilities.

This Article shall also apply to members of the advisory bodies of the Communities.

CHAPTER V

OFFICIALS AND OTHER SERVANTS OF THE EUROPEAN COMMUNITIES

Article 12

In the territory of each Member State and whatever their nationality, officials and other servants of the Communities shall:

(a) subject to the provisions of the Treaties relating, on the one hand, to the rules on the liability of officials and other servants towards the Communities and, on the other hand, to the jurisdiction of the Court in disputes between the Communities and their officials and other servants, be immune from legal proceedings in respect of acts performed by them in their official capacity, including their words spoken or written. They shall continue to enjoy this immunity after they have ceased to hold office.

(b) together with their spouses and dependent members of their families, not be subject to immigration restrictions or to formalities for the registration of aliens;

(c) in respect of currency or exchange regulations, be accorded the same facilities as are customarily accorded to officials of international organizations;

(d) enjoy the right to import free of duty their furniture and effects at the time of first taking up their post in the country concerned, and the right to re-export free of duty their furniture and effects, on termination of their duties in that country, subject in either case to the conditions considered to be necessary by the Government of the country in which this right is exercised;

(e) have the right to import free of duty a motor car for their personal use, acquired either in the country of their last residence or in the country of which they are nationals on the terms ruling in the home market in that country, and to re-export it free of duty, subject in either case to the conditions considered to be necessary by the Government of the country concerned.

Article 13

Officials and other servants of the Communities shall be liable to a tax for the benefit of the Communities on salaries, wages and emoluments paid to them by the Communities, in accordance with the conditions and procedure laid down by the Council, acting on a proposal from the Commission.

They shall be exempt from national taxes on salaries, wages and emoluments paid by the Communities.

Article 14

In the application of income tax, wealth tax and death duties and in the application of conventions on the avoidance of double taxation concluded between Member States of the Communities, officials and other servants of the Communities who, solely by reason of the performance of their duties in the service of the Communities, establish their residence in the territory of a Member State other than their country of domicile for tax purposes at the time of entering the service of the Communities, shall be considered, both in the country of their actual residence and in the country of domicile for tax purposes, as having maintained their domicile in the latter country provided that it is a member of the Communities. This provision shall also apply to a spouse, to the extent that the latter is not separately engaged in a gainful occupation, and to children dependent on and in the care of the persons referred to in this Article.

Movable property belonging to persons referred to in the preceding paragraph and situated in the territory of the country where they are staying shall be exempt from death duties in that country; such property shall, for the assessment of such duty, be considered as being in the country of domicile for tax purposes, subject to the rights of third countries and to the possible application of provisions of international conventions on double taxation.

Any domicile acquired solely by reason of the performance of duties in the service of other international organizations shall not be taken into consideration in applying the provisions of this Article.

Article 15

The Council shall, acting unanimously on a proposal from the Commission, lay down the scheme of social security benefits for officials and other servants of the Communities.

Article 16

The Council shall, acting on a proposal from the Commission and after consulting the other institutions concerned, determine the categories of officials and other servants of the Communities to whom the provisions of Article 12, the second paragraph of Article 13, and Article 14 shall apply, in whole or in part.

The names, grades and addresses of officials and other servants included in such categories shall be communicated periodically to the Governments of the Member States.

CHAPTER VI

PRIVILEGES AND IMMUNITIES OF MISSIONS OF THIRD COUNTRIES ACCREDITED TO THE EUROPEAN COMMUNITIES

Article 17

The Member State in whose territory the Communities have their seat shall accord the customary diplomatic immunities and privileges to missions of third countries accredited to the Communities.

CHAPTER VII

GENERAL PROVISIONS

Article 18

Privileges, immunities and facilities shall be accorded to officials and other servants of the Communities solely in the interests of the Communities.

Each institution of the Communities shall be required to waive the immunity accorded to an official or other servant wherever that institution considers that the waiver of such immunity is not contrary to the interests of the Communities.

Article 19

The institutions of the Communities shall, for the purpose of applying this Protocol, cooperate with the responsible authorities of the Member States concerned.

Article 20

Articles 12 to 15 and Article 18 shall apply to members of the Commission.

Article 21

Articles 12 to 15 and Article 18 shall apply to the Judges, the Advocates-General, the Registrar and the Assistant Rapporteurs of the Court of Justice, without prejudice to the provisions of Article 3 of the Protocols on the Statute of the Court of Justice concerning immunity from legal proceedings of Judges and Advocates-General.

Article 22

This Protocol shall also apply to the European Investment Bank, to the members of its organs, to its staff and to the representatives of the Member States taking part in its activities, without prejudice to the provisions of the Protocol on the Statute of the Bank.

The European Investment Bank shall in addition be exempt from any form of taxation or imposition of a like nature on the occasion of any increase in its capital and from the various formalities which may be connected therewith in the State where the Bank has its seat. Similarly, its dissolution or liquidation shall not give rise to any imposition. Finally, the activities of the Bank and of its organs carried on in accordance with its Statute shall not be subject to any turnover tax.

IN WITNESS WHEREOF, the undersigned Plenipotentiaries have signed this Protocol.

Done at Brussels this eighth day of April in the year one thousand nine hundred and sixty-five.

Paul-Henri SPAAK

Kurt SCHMÜCKER

Maurice COUVE DE MURVILLE

Amintore FANFANI

Pierre WERNER

J. M. A. H. LUNS

3. Final Act

The plenipotentiaries

of His Majesty the King of the Belgians, the President of the Federal Republic of Germany, the President of the French Republic, the President of the Italian Republic, His Royal Highness the Grand Duke of Luxembourg, Her Majesty the Queen of the Netherlands.

Assembled at Brussels on 8 April 1965 for the signature of the Treaty establishing a Single Council and a Single Commission of the European Communities,

Have adopted the following texts:

The Treaty establishing a Single Council and a Single Commission of the European Communities,

The Protocol on the Privileges and Immunities of the European Communities.

At the time of signature of these texts, the Plenipotentiaries have:

— assigned to the Commission of the European Communities the task set out in Annex I; and

— taken note of the Declaration by the Government of the Federal Republic of Germany set out in Annex II.

In witness whereof, the undersigned Plenipotentiaries have signed this Final Act.

Done at Brussels this eighth day of April in the year one thousand nine hundred and sixty-five.

Paul-Henri SPAAK

Kurt SCHMÜCKER

Maurice COUVE DE MURVILLE

Amintore FANFANI

Pierre WERNER

J. M. A. H. LUNS

Annexes

ANNEX I

TASK ASSIGNED TO THE COMMISSION
OF THE EUROPEAN COMMUNITIES

The commission of the European Communities shall, within the framework of its responsibilities, have the task of taking the necessary steps to rationalize its departments within a reasonable and relatively short period of time not exceeding one year. To this end, the Commission may seek all appropriate opinions. To enable the Council to follow the progress of this operation, the Commission is requested to report periodically to the Council.

ANNEX II

DECLARATION
BY THE GOVERNMENT
OF THE FEDERAL REPUBLIC
OF GERMANY

on the Application to Berlin of the Treaty establishing
a Single Council and a Single Commission of the
European Communities and of the Treaty establishing
the European Coal and Steel Community

The Government of the Federal Republic of Germany reserves the right to declare, when depositing its instrument of ratification, that the Treaty establishing a Single Council and a Single Commission of the European Communities and the Treaty establishing the Coal and Steel Community shall equally apply to Land Berlin.

III — DECISION

OF THE REPRESENTATIVES OF THE GOVERNMENTS OF THE MEMBER STATES OF THE PROVISIONAL LOCATION OF CERTAIN INSTITUTIONS AND DEPARTMENTS OF THE COMMUNITIES

Official Journal of the European Communities, No 152, 13 July 1967.

THE REPRESENTATIVES OF THE GOVERNMENTS OF THE MEMBER STATES,

HAVING REGARD to Article 37 of the Treaty establishing a single Council and a single Commission of the European Communities,

CONSIDERING that it is appropriate, at the time of setting up a single Council and a single Commission of the European Communities, in order to settle certain problems peculiar to the Grand Duchy of Luxembourg, to designate Luxembourg as the provisional place of work of certain institutions and departments, without prejudice to the application of Article 77 of the Treaty establishing the European Coal and Steel Community, Article 216 of the Treaty establishing the European Economic Community, Article 189 of the Treaty establishing the European Atomic Energy Community and of the second paragraph of Article 1 of the Protocol on the Statute of the European Investment Bank,

HAVE DECIDED:

Article 1

Luxembourg, Brussels and Strasbourg shall remain the provisional places of work of the institutions of the Communities.

Article 2

During the months of April, June and October, the Council shall hold its sessions in Luxembourg.

Article 3

The Court of Justice shall remain in Luxembourg.

There shall also be located in Luxembourg the judicial and quasi-judicial bodies, including those competent to apply the rules on competition, already existing or yet to be set up pursuant to the Treaties establishing the European Coal and Steel Community, the European Economic Community and the European Atomic Energy Community, or to conventions concluded within the framework of the Communities, whether between Member States or with third countries.

Article 4

The General Secretariat of the European Parliament and its departments shall remain in Luxembourg.

Article 5

The European Investment Bank shall be located in Luxembourg, where its governing bodies shall meet and all its activities shall be carried on.

This provision relates in particular to the development of its present activities, especially those mentioned in Article 130 of the Treaty establishing the European Economic Community, to the possible extension of those activities to other fields and to such new tasks as may be assigned to the Bank.

An office for liaison between the Commission and the European Investment Bank shall be located in Luxembourg, with the particular task of facilitating the operations of the European Development Fund.

Article 6

The Monetary Committee shall meet in Luxembourg and in Brussels.

Article 7

The financial departments of the European Coal and Steel Community shall be located in Luxembourg. These comprise the Directorate-General for Credit and Investments, the department responsible for collecting the levy and the accounts departments attached thereto.

Article 8

An Official Publications Office of the European Communities with a joint sales office and a medium- and long-term translation service attached shall be located in Luxembourg.

Article 9

Further, the following departments of the Commission shall be located in Luxembourg:

(a) the Statistical Office and the Data Processing Department;

(b) the hygiene and industrial safety departments of the European Economic Community and of the European Coal and Steel Community;

(c) the Directorate-General for the Dissemination of Information, the Directorate for Health Protection and the Directorate for Safeguards of the European Atomic Energy Community;

and the appropriate administrative and technical infrastructure.

Article 10

The Governments of the Member States are willing to locate in Luxembourg, or to transfer thereto, other Community bodies and departments, particularly those concerned with finance, provided that their proper functioning can be ensured.

To this end, they request the Commission to present to them annually a report on the current situation concerning the location of Community bodies and departments and on the possibility of taking new steps to give effect to this provision, account being taken of the need to ensure the proper functioning of the Communities.

Article 11

In order to ensure the proper functioning of the European Coal and Steel Community, the Commission is requested to transfer the various departments in a gradual and coordinated manner, transferring last the departments which manage the coal and steel markets.

Article 12

Subject to the preceding provisions, this decision shall not affect the provisional places of work of the institutions and departments of the European Communities, as determined by previous decisions of the Governments, nor the regrouping of departments occasioned by the establishing of a single Council and a single Commission.

Article 13

This decision shall enter into force on the same date as the Treaty establishing a Single Council and a Single Commission of the European Communities.

Done at Brussels this eighth day of April in the year one thousand nine hundred and sixty-five.

Paul-Henri SPAAK

Kurt SCHMÜCKER

Maurice COUVE DE MURVILLE

Amintore FANFANI

Pierre WERNER

J. M. A. H. LUNS

IV — TREATY
AMENDING CERTAIN BUDGETARY PROVISIONS OF THE TREATIES ESTABLISHING THE EUROPEAN COMMUNITIES AND OF THE TREATY ESTABLISHING A SINGLE COUNCIL AND A SINGLE COMMISSION OF THE EUROPEAN COMMUNITIES*

Official Journal of the European Communities, No L 2, 2 January 1971.

* EDITORIAL NOTE:
  The Resolutions and Declarations recorded in the minutes of the Council Meeting of 22 April 1970 are reproduced on pp. 1089 to 1094 of this volume.

His Majesty the King of the Belgians, the President of the Federal Republic of Germany, the President of the French Republic, the President of the Italian Republic, His Royal Highness the Grand Duke of Luxembourg, Her Majesty the Queen of the Netherlands,

Having regard to Article 96 of the Treaty establishing the European Coal and Steel Community;

Having regard to Article 236 of the Treaty establishing the European Economic Community;

Having regard to Article 204 of the Treaty establishing the European Atomic Energy Community;

Considering that the Communities will have at their disposal their own resources in order to cover their total expenditure,

Considering that the replacement of financial contributions of Member States by the Communities' own resources requires a strengthening of the budgetary powers of the European Parliament,

Resolved to associate the European Parliament closely in the supervision of the implementation of the budget of the Communities,

Have decided to amend certain budgetary provisions of the Treaties establishing the European Communities and of the Treaty establishing a Single Council and a Single Commission of the European Communities and to this end have designated as their Plenipotentiaries:

His Majesty the King of the Belgians:
Mr Pierre Harmel, Minister for Foreign Affairs;

THE PRESIDENT OF THE FEDERAL REPUBLIC OF GERMANY:
   Mr Walter SCHEEL, Minister for Foreign Affairs;

THE PRESIDENT OF THE FRENCH REPUBLIC:
   Mr Maurice SCHUMANN, Minister for Foreign Affairs;

THE PRESIDENT OF THE ITALIAN REPUBLIC:
   Mr Aldo MORO, Minister for Foreign Affairs;

HIS ROYAL HIGHNESS THE GRAND DUKE OF LUXEMBOURG:
   Mr Gaston THORN, Minister for Foreign Affairs and for External Trade;

HER MAJESTY THE QUEEN OF THE NETHERLANDS:
   Mr H. J. DE KOSTER, Under-Secretary of State for Foreign Affairs;

WHO, having exchanged their Full Powers, found in good and due form,

HAVE AGREED as follows:

CHAPTER I

PROVISIONS AMENDING THE TREATY ESTABLISHING THE EUROPEAN COAL AND STEEL COMMUNITY

Article 1

The following provisions shall be substituted for Article 78 of the Treaty establishing the European Coal and Steel Community:

'Article 78

1. The financial year shall run from 1 January to 31 December.

The administrative expenditure of the Community shall comprise the expenditure of the High Authority, including that relating to the functioning of the Consultative Committee, and that of the Court, the European Parliament and the Council.

2. Each institution of the Community shall, before 1 July, draw up estimates of its administrative expenditure. The High Authority shall consolidate these estimates in a preliminary draft administrative budget. It shall attach thereto an opinion which may obtain different estimates.

The preliminary draft budget shall contain an estimate of revenue and an estimate of expenditure.

3. The High Authority shall place the preliminary draft administrative budget before the Council not later than 1 September of the year preceding that in which the budget is to be implemented.

The Council shall consult the High Authority and, where appropriate, the other institutions concerned whenever it intends to depart from the preliminary draft budget.

The Council shall, acting by a qualified majority, establish the draft administrative budget and forward it to the European Parliament.

4. The draft administrative budget shall be placed before the European Parliament not later than 5 October of the year preceding that in which the budget is to be implemented.

The European Parliament shall have the right to amend the draft administrative budget, acting by a majority of its members, and to propose to the Council, acting by an absolute majority of the votes cast, modifications to the draft budget relating to expenditure necessarily resulting from this Treaty or from acts adopted in accordance therewith.

If, within 45 days of the draft administrative budget being placed before it, the European Parliament has given its approval, the administrative budget shall stand as finally adopted. If within this period the European Parliament has not amended the draft administrative budget nor proposed any modifications thereto, the administrative budget shall be deemed to be finally adopted.

If within this period the European Parliament has adopted amendments or proposed modifications, the draft administrative budget together with the amendments or proposed modifications shall be forwarded to the Council.

5.   After discussing the draft administrative budget with the High Authority and, where appropriate, with the other institutions concerned, the Council may, acting by a qualified majority, modify any of the amendments adopted by the European Parliament and shall pronounce, also by a qualified majority, on the modifications proposed by the latter. The draft administrative budget shall be modified on the basis of the proposed modifications accepted by the Council.

If, within 15 days of the draft administrative budget being placed before it, the Council has not modified any of the amendments adopted by the European Parliament and has accepted the modifications proposed by the latter, the administrative budget shall be deemed to be finally adopted. The Council shall inform the European Parliament that it has not modified any of the amendments and has accepted the proposed modifications.

If within this period the Council has modified one or more of the amendments adopted by the European Parliament or has not accepted the modifications proposed by the latter, the draft administrative budget shall again be forwarded to the European Parliament. The Council shall inform the European Parliament of the results of its deliberations.

6.   Within 15 days of the draft administrative budget being placed before it, the European Parliament, which shall have been notified of the action taken

on its proposed modifications, shall act, by a majority of its members and three-fifths of the votes cast, on the modifications to its amendments made by the Council, and shall adopt the administrative budget accordingly. If within this period the European Parliament has not acted, the administrative budget shall be deemed to be finally adopted.

7.   When the procedure provided for in this Article has been completed, the President of the European Parliament shall declare that the administrative budget has been finally adopted.

8.   A maximum rate of increase in relation to the expenditure of the same type to be incurred during the current year shall be fixed annually for the total expenditure other than that necessarily resulting from this Treaty or from acts adopted in accordance therewith.

The High Authority shall, after consulting the Conjunctural Policy Committee and the Budgetary Policy Committee, declare what this maximum rate is as it results from:

— the trend, in terms of volume, of the gross national product within the Community;

— the average variation in the budgets of the Member States;

and

— the trend of the cost of living during the preceding financial year.

The maximum rate shall be communicated, before 1 May, to all the institutions of the Community. The latter shall be required to conform to this during the budgetary procedure, subject to the provisions of the fourth and fifth subparagraphs of this paragraph.

If, in respect of expenditure other than that necessarily resulting from this Treaty or from acts adopted in accordance therewith, the actual rate of increase in the draft administrative budget established by the Council is over half the maximum rate, the European Parliament may, exercising its right of amendment, further increase the total amount of that expenditure to a limit not exceeding half the maximum rate.

Where, in exceptional cases, the European Parliament, the Council or the High Authority considers that the activities of the Communities require that the rate determined according to the procedure laid down in this paragraph should be exceeded, another rate may be fixed by agreement between the Council, acting by a qualified majority, and the European Parliament, acting by a majority of its members and three-fifths of the votes cast.

9. *Each institution shall exercise the powers conferred upon it by this Article, with due regard for the provisions of this Treaty and for acts adopted in accordance therewith, in particular those relating to the Communities' own resources and to the balance between revenue and expenditure.*

10. *Final adoption of the administrative budget shall have the effect of authorizing and requiring the High Authority to collect the corresponding revenue in accordance with the provisions of Article 49.'*

Article 2

The following provisions shall be added to the Treaty establishing the European Coal and Steel Community:

'Article 78a

By way of derogation from the provisions of Article 78, the following provisions shall apply to budgets for financial years preceding the financial year 1975:

1.   *The financial year shall run from 1 January to 31 December.*

   The administrative expenditure of the Community shall comprise the expenditure of the High Authority, including that relating to the functioning of the Consultative Committee, and that of the Court, the European Parliament and the Council.

2.   *Each institution of the Community shall, before 1 July, draw up estimates of its administrative expenditure. The High Authority shall consolidate these estimates in a preliminary draft administrative budget. It shall attach thereto an opinion which may contain different estimates.*

   The preliminary draft budget shall contain an estimate of revenue and an estimate of expenditure.

3.   *The High Authority shall place the preliminary draft administrative budget before the Council not later than 1 September of the year preceding that in which the budget is to be implemented.*

   The Council shall consult the High Authority and, where appropriate, the other institutions concerned whenever it intends to depart from the preliminary draft budget.

   The Council shall, acting by a qualified majority, establish the draft administrative budget and forward it to the European Parliament.

4.   *The draft administrative budget shall be placed before the European Parliament not later then 5 October of the year preceding that in which the budget is to be implemented.*

   The European Parliament shall have the right to propose to the Council modifications to the draft administrative budget.

   If, within 45 days of the draft administrative budget being placed before it, the European Parliament has given its approval or has not proposed any modifications to the draft budget, the administrative budget shall be deemed to be finally adopted.

If within this period the European Parliament has proposed modifications, the draft administrative budget together with the proposed modifications shall be forwarded to the Council.

5.   *The Council shall, after discussing the draft administrative budget with the High Authority and, where appropriate, with the other institutions concerned, adopt the administrative budget, within 30 days of the draft budget being placed before it, under the following conditions.*

Where a modification proposed by the European Parliament does not have the effect of increasing the total amount of the expenditure of an institution, owing in particular to the fact that the increase in expenditure which it would involve would be expressly compensated by one or more proposed modifications correspondingly reducing expenditure, the Council may, acting by a qualified majority, reject the proposed modification. In the absence of a decision to reject it, the proposed modification shall stand as accepted.

Where a modification proposed by the European Parliament has the effect of increasing the total amount of the expenditure of an institution, the Council must act by a qualified majority in accepting the proposed modification.

Where, in pursuance of the second or third subparagraphs of this paragraph, the Council has rejected or has not accepted a proposed modification, it may, acting by a qualified majority, either retain the amount shown in the draft administrative budget or fix another amount.

6.   *When the procedure provided for in this Article has been completed, the President of the Council shall declare that the administrative budget has been finally adopted.*

7.   *Each institution shall exercise the powers conferred upon it by this Article, with due regard for the provisions of this Treaty and for acts adopted in*

accordance therewith, in particular those relating to the Communities' own resources and to the balance between revenue and expenditure.

8. *Final adoption of the administrative budget shall have the effect of authorizing and requiring the High Authority to collect the corresponding revenue in accordance with the provisions of Article 49.'*

Article 3

The following provisions shall be substituted for the last paragraph of Article 78d of the Treaty establishing the European Coal and Steel Community:

'*The Council and the European Parliament shall give a discharge to the High Authority in respect of the implementation of the administrative budget. To this end, the report of the Audit Board shall be examined in turn by the Council, which shall act by a qualified majority, and by the European Parliament. The High Authority shall stand discharged only after the Council and the European Parliament have acted.'*

CHAPTER II

PROVISIONS AMENDING THE TREATY
ESTABLISHING THE EUROPEAN
ECONOMIC COMMUNITY

Article 4

The following provisions shall be substituted for Article 203 of the Treaty establishing the European Economic Community:

'Article 203

1. *The financial year shall run from 1 January to 31 December.*

2. *Each institution of the Community shall, before 1 July, draw up estimates of its expenditure. The Commission shall consolidate these estimates in a preliminary draft budget. It shall attach thereto an opinion which may contain different estimates.*

The preliminary draft budget shall contain an estimate of revenue and an estimate of expenditure.

3. *The Commission shall place the preliminary draft budget before the Council not later than 1 September of the year preceding that in which the budget is to be implemented.*

The Council shall consult the Commission and, where appropriate, the other institutions concerned whenever it intends to depart from the preliminary draft budget.

The Council shall, acting by a qualified majority, establish the draft budget and forward it to the European Parliament.

4. *The draft budget shall be placed before the European Parliament not later than 5 October of the year preceding that in which the budget is to be implemented.*

The European Parliament shall have the right to amend the draft budget, acting by a majority of its members, and to propose to the Council, acting by an absolute majority of the votes cast, modifications to the draft budget relating to expenditure necessarily resulting from this Treaty or from acts adopted in accordance therewith.

If, within 45 days of the draft budget being placed before it, the European Parliament has given its approval, the budget shall stand as finally adopted. If within this period the European Parliament has not amended the draft budget nor proposed any modifications thereto, the budget shall be deemed to be finally adopted.

If within this period the European Parliament has adopted amendments or proposed modifications, the draft budget together with the amendments or proposed modifications shall be forwarded to the Council.

5.   *After discussing the draft budget with the Commission and, where appropriate, with the other institutions concerned, the Council may, acting by a qualified majority, modify any of the amendments adopted by the European Parliament and shall pronounce, also by a qualified majority, on the modifications proposed by the latter. The draft budget shall be modified on the basis of the proposed modifications accepted by the Council.*

If, within 15 days of the draft being placed before it, the Council has not modified any of the amendments adopted by the European Parliament and has accepted the modifications proposed by the latter, the budget shall be deemed to be finally adopted. The Council shall inform the European Parliament that it has not modified any of the amendments and has accepted the proposed modifications.

If within this period the Council has modified one or more of the amendments adopted by the European Parliament or has not accepted the modifications proposed by the latter, the draft budget shall again be forwarded to the European Parliament. The Council shall inform the European Parliament of the results of its deliberations.

6.   *Within 15 days of the draft budget being placed before it, the European Parliament, which shall have been notified of the action taken on its proposed modifications, shall act, by a majority of its members and three fifths of the votes cast, on the modifications to its amendments made by the Council, and shall adopt the budget accordingly. If within this period the European Parliament has not acted, the budget shall be deemed to be finally adopted.*

7.   When the procedure provided for in this Article has been completed, the President of the European Parliament shall declare that the budget has been finally adopted.

8.   A maximum rate of increase in relation to the expenditure of the same type to be incurred during the current year shall be fixed annually for the total expenditure other than that necessarily resulting from this Treaty or from acts adopted in accordance therewith.

The Commission shall, after consulting the Conjuntural Policy Committee and the Budgetary Policy Committee, declare what this maximum rate is as it results from:

— the trend, in terms of volume, of the gross national product within the Community;

— the average variation in the budgets of the Member States;

and

— the trend of the cost of living during the preceding financial year.

The maximum rate shall be communicated, before 1 May, to all the institutions of the Community. The latter shall be required to conform to this during the budgetary procedure, subject to the provisions of the fourth and fifth subparagraphs of this paragraph.

If, in respect of expenditure other than that necessarily resulting from this Treaty or from acts adopted in accordance therewith, the actual rate of increase in the draft budget established by the Council is over half the maximum rate, the European Parliament may, exercising its right of amendment, further increase the total amount of that expenditure to a limit not exceeding half the maximum rate.

Where, in exceptional cases, the European Parliament, the Council or the Commission considers that the activities of the Communities require that the rate determined according to the procedure laid down in this paragraph *should be exceeded, another rate may be fixed by agreement between the Council, acting by a qualified majority, and the European Parliament, acting by a majority of its members and three fifths of the votes cast.*

9.   *Each institution shall exercise the powers conferred upon it by this Article, with due regard for the provisions of this Treaty and for acts adopted in accordance therewith, in particular those relating to the Communities' own resources and to the balance between revenue and expenditure.'*

Article 5

The following provisions shall be added to the Treaty establishing the European Economic Community.

'Article 203a

By way of derogation from the provisions of Article 203, the following provisions shall apply to budgets for financial years preceding the financial year 1975:

1.   *The financial year shall run from 1 January to 31 December.*

2.   *Each institution of the Community shall, before 1 July, draw up estimates of its expenditure. The Commission shall consolidate these estimates in a preliminary draft budget. It shall attach thereto an opinion which may contain different estimates.*

The preliminary draft budget shall contain an estimate of revenue and an estimate of expenditure.

3.   *The Commission shall place the preliminary draft budget before the Council not later than 1 September of the year preceding that in which the budget is to be implemented.*

The Council shall consult the Commission and, where appropriate the other institutions concerned whenever it intends to depart from the preliminary draft budget.

The Council shall, acting by a qualified majority, establish the draft budget and forward it to the European Parliament.

4. The draft budget shall be placed before the European Parliament not later than 5 October of the year preceding that in which the budget is to be implemented.

The European Parliament shall have the right to propose to the Council modifications to the draft budget.

If, within 45 days of the draft budget being placed before it, the European Parliament has given its approval or has not proposed any modifications to the draft budget, the budget shall be deemed to be finally adopted.

If within this period the European Parliament has proposed modifications, the draft budget together with the proposed modifications shall be forwarded to the Council.

5. The Council shall, after discussing the draft budget with the Commission and, where appropriate, with the other institutions concerned, adopt the budget, within 30 days of the draft budget being placed before it, under the following conditions.

Where a modification proposed by the European Parliament does not have the effect of increasing the total amount of the expenditure of an institution, owing in particular to the fact that the increase in expenditure which it would involve would be expressly compensated by one or more proposed modifications correspondingly reducing expenditure, the Council may, acting by a qualified majority, reject the proposed modification. In the absence of a decision to reject it, the proposed modification shall stand as accepted.

Where a modification proposed by the European Parliament has the effect of increasing the total amount of the expenditure of an institution, the Council must act by a qualified majority in accepting the proposed modification.

Where, in pursuance of the second or third subparagraph of this paragraph, the Council has rejected or has not accepted a proposed modification, it may, acting by a qualified majority, either retain the amount shown in the draft budget or fix another amount.

6.   When the procedure provided for in this Article has been completed, the President of the Council shall declare that the budget has been finally adopted.

7.   Each institution shall exercise the powers conferred upon it by this Article, with the due regard for the provisions of this Treaty and for acts adopted in accordance therewith, in particular those relating to the Communities' own resources and to the balance between revenue and expenditure.'

Article 6

The following provisions shall be substituted for the last paragraph of Article 206 of the Treaty establishing the European Economic Community:

'The Council and the European Parliament shall give a discharge to the Commission in respect of the implementation of the budget. To this end, the report of the Audit Board shall be examined in turn by the Council, which shall act by a qualified majority, and by the European Parliament. The Commission shall stand discharged only after the Council and the European Parliament have acted.'

CHAPTER III

PROVISIONS AMENDING THE TREATY
ESTABLISHING THE EUROPEAN
ATOMIC ENERGY COMMUNITY

Article 7

The following provisions shall be substituted for Article 177 of the Treaty establishing the European Atomic Energy Community:

'Article 177

1.   *The financial year shall run from 1 January to 31 December.*

Within the meaning of this Article, 'budget' shall include the operating budget and the research and investment budget.

2.   *Each institution of the Community shall, before 1 July, draw up estimates of its expenditure. The Commission shall consolidate these estimates in a preliminary draft budget. It shall attach thereto an opinion which may contain different estimates.*

The preliminary draft budget shall contain an estimate of revenue and an estimate of expenditure.

3.   *The Commission shall place the preliminary draft budget before the Council not later than 1 September of the year preceding that in which the budget is to be implemented.*

The Council shall consult the Commission and, where appropriate, the other institutions concerned whenever it intends to depart from the preliminary draft budget.

The Council shall, acting by a qualified majority, establish the draft budget and forward it to the European Parliament.

4.   *The draft budget shall be placed before the European Parliament not later than 5 October of the year preceding that in which the budget is to be implemented.*

The European Parliament shall have the right to amend the draft budget, acting by a majority of its members, and to propose to the Council, acting by an absolute majority of the votes cast, modifications to the draft budget relating to expenditure necessarily resulting from this Treaty or from acts adopted in accordance therewith.

If, within 45 days of the draft budget being placed before it, the European Parliament has given its approval, the budget shall stand as finally adopted. If within this period the European Parliament has not amended the draft budget nor proposed any modifications thereto, the budget shall be deemed to be finally adopted.

If within this period the European Parliament has adopted amendments or proposed modifications, the draft budget together with the amendments or proposed modifications shall be forwarded to the Council.

5.   *After discussing the draft budget with the Commission and, where appropriate, with the other institutions concerned, the Council may, acting by a qualified majority, modify any of the amendments adopted by the European Parliament and shall pronounce, also by a qualified majority, on the modifications proposed by the latter. The draft budget shall be modified on the basis of the proposed modifications accepted by the Council.*

If, within 15 days of the draft budget being placed before it, the Council has not modified any of the amendments adopted by the European Parliament and has accepted the modifications proposed by the latter, the budget shall be deemed to be finally adopted. The Council shall inform the European Parliament that it has not modified any of the amendments and has accepted the proposed modifications.

If within this period the Council has modified one or more of the amendments adopted by the European Parliament or has not accepted the modifications proposed by the latter, the draft budget shall again be forwarded to the European Parliament. The Council shall inform the European Parliament of the results of its deliberations.

6. *Within 15 days of the draft budget being placed before it, the European Parliament, which shall have been notified of the action taken on its proposed modifications, shall act, by a majority of its members and three fifths of the votes cast, on the modifications to its amendments made by the Council, and shall adopt the budget accordingly. If within this period the European Parliament has not acted, the budget shall be deemed to be finally adopted.*

7. *When the procedure provided for in this Article has been completed, the President of the European Parliament shall declare that the budget has been finally adopted.*

8. *A maximum rate of increase in relation to the expenditure of the same type to be incurred during the current year shall be fixed annually for the total expenditure other than that necessarily resulting from the Treaty or from acts adopted in accordance therewith.*

The Commission shall, after consulting the Conjunctural Policy Committee and the Budgetary Policy Committee, declare what this maximum rate is as it results from:

— *the trend, in terms of volume, of the gross national product within the Community;*

— *the average variation in the budgets of the Member States;*

and

— *the trend of the cost of living during the preceding financial year.*

The maximum rate shall be communicated, before 1 May, to all the institutions of the Community. The latter shall be required to conform to this during the budgetary procedure, subject to the provisions of the fourth and fifth subparagraphs of this paragraph.

If, in respect of expenditure other than that necessarily resulting from this Treaty or from acts adopted in accordance therewith, the actual rate of increase in the draft budget established by the Council is over half the maximum rate, the European Parliament may, exercising its right of amendment, further increase the total amount of that expenditure to a limit not exceeding half the maximum rate.

Where, in exceptional cases, the European Parliament, the Council or the Commission considers that the activities of the Communities require that the rate determined according to the procedure laid down in this paragraph should be exceeded, another rate may be fixed by agreement between the Council, acting by a qualified majority, and the European Parliament, acting by a majority of its members and three-fifths of the votes cast.

9.   *Each institution shall exercise the powers conferred upon it by this Article, with due regard for the provisions of this Treaty and for acts adopted in accordance therewith, in particular those relating to the Communities' own resources and to the balance between revenue and expenditure.'*

Article 8

The following provisions shall be added to the Treaty establishing the European Atomic Energy Community:

'Article 177a

By way of derogation from the provisions of Article 177, the following provisions shall apply to budgets for financial years preceding the financial year 1975:

1.   *The financial year shall run from 1 January to 31 December.*

Within the meaning of this Article, 'budget' shall include the operating budget and the research and investment budget.

2.   *Each institution of the Community shall, before 1 July, draw up estimates of its expenditure. The Commission shall consolidate these estimates in a preliminary draft budget. It shall attach thereto an opinion which may contain different estimates.*

The preliminary draft budget shall contain an estimate of revenue and an estimate of expenditure.

3.   *The Commission shall place the preliminary draft budget before the Council not later than 1 September of the year preceding that in which the budget is to be implemented.*

The Council shall consult the Commission and, where appropriate, the other institutions concerned whenever it intends to depart from the preliminary draft budget.

The Council shall, acting by a qualified majority, establish the draft budget and forward it to the European Parliament.

4.   *The draft budget shall be placed before the European Parliament not later than 5 October of the year preceding that in which the budget is to be implemented.*

The European Parliament shall have the right to propose to the Council modifications to the draft budget.

If, within 45 days of the draft budget being placed before it, the European

Parliament has given its approval or has not proposed any modifications to the draft budget, the budget shall be deemed to be finally adopted.

If within this period the European Parliament has proposed modifications, the draft budget together with the proposed modifications shall be forwarded to the Council.

5. *The Council shall, after discussing the draft budget with the Commission and, where appropriate, with the other institutions concerned, adopt the budget, within 30 days of the draft budget being placed before it, under the following conditions.*

Where a modification proposed by the European Parliament does not have the effect of increasing the total amount of the expenditure of an institution, owing in particular to the fact that the increase in expenditure which it would involve would be expressly compensated by one or more proposed modifications correspondingly reducing expenditure, the Council may, acting by a qualified majority, reject the proposed modification. In the absence of a decision to reject it, the proposed modification shall stand as accepted.

Where a modification proposed by the European Parliament has the effect of increasing the total amount of the expenditure of an institution, the Council must act by a qualified majority in accepting the proposed modification.

Where, in pursuance of the second or third subparagraph of this paragraph, the Council has rejected or has not accepted a proposed modification, it may, acting by a qualified majority, either retain the amount shown in the draft budget or fix another amount.

6. *When the procedure provided for in this Article has been completed, the President of the Council shall declare that the budget has been finally adopted.*

7. *Each institution shall exercise the powers conferred upon it by this Article, with due regard for the provisions of this Treaty and for acts adopted in*

accordance therewith, in particular those relating to the Communities' own resources and to the balance between revenue and expenditure.'

Article 9

The following provisions shall be substituted for the last paragraph of Article 180 of the Treaty establishing the European Atomic Energy Community:

'The Council and the European Parliament shall give a discharge to the Commission in respect of the implementation of each budget. To this end, the report of the Audit Board shall be examined in turn by the Council, which shall act by a qualified majority, and by the European Parliament. The Commission shall stand discharged only after the Council and the European Parliament have acted.'

CHAPTER IV

PROVISIONS AMENDING THE TREATY ESTABLISHING A SINGLE COUNCIL AND A SINGLE COMMISSION OF THE EUROPEAN COMMUNITIES

Article 10

The following provisions shall be substituted for Article 20 (1) of the Treaty establishing a Single Council and a Single Commission of the European Communities:

'1. The administrative expenditure of the European Coal and Steel Community and the revenue relating thereto, the revenue and expenditure

of the European Economic Community, and the revenue and expenditure of the European Atomic Energy Community, with the exception of that of the Supply Agency and the Joint Undertakings, shall be shown in the budget of the European Communities in accordance with the appropriate provisions of the Treaties establishing the three Communities. This budget, which shall be in balance as to revenue and expenditure, shall take the place of the administrative budget of the European Coal and Steel Community, the budget of the European Economic Community and the operating budget and research and investment budget of the European Atomic Energy Community.'

CHAPTER V

FINAL PROVISIONS

Article 11

This Treaty shall be ratified by the High Contracting Parties in accordance with their respective constitutional requirements. The instruments of ratification shall be deposited with the Government of the Italian Republic.

Article 12

This Treaty shall enter into force on the first day of the month following the deposit of the instrument of ratification by the last signatory State to take this step.

If, however, the notification provided for in Article 7 of the Decision of 21 April 1970 on the replacement of financial contributions from Member States by the Communities' own resources has not been given before that date by all the signatory States, this Treaty shall enter into force on the first day of the month after the last notification has been given.

If this Treaty enters into force during the budgetary procedure, the Council shall, after consulting the Commission, lay down the measures required in order to facilitate the application of this Treaty to the remainder of the budgetary procedure.

Article 13

This Treaty, drawn up in a single original in the Dutch, French, German and Italian languages, all four texts being equally authentic, shall be deposited in the archives of the Government of the Italian Republic, which shall transmit a certified copy to each of the Governments of the other signatory States.

IN WITNESS WHEREOF, the undersigned Plenipotentiaries have signed this Treaty.

Done at Luxembourg this twenty-second day of April in the year one thousand nine hundred and seventy.

Pour Sa Majesté le roi des Belges
Voor Zijne Majesteit de Koning der Belgen
    Pierre HARMEL

Für den Präsidenten der Bundesrepublik Deutschland
    Walter SCHEEL

Pour le Président de la République française
    Maurice SCHUMANN

Per il Presidente della Repubblica italiana
    Aldo MORO

Pour Son Altesse Royale le grand-duc de Luxembourg
    Gaston THORN

Voor Hare Majesteit de Koningin der Nederlanden
    H. J. DE KOSTER

V — TREATY
AMENDING CERTAIN PROVISIONS
OF THE PROTOCOL ON THE STATUTE
OF THE EUROPEAN INVESTMENT BANK

Official Journal of the European Communities, No L 91, 6 April 1978.

HIS MAJESTY THE KING OF THE BELGIANS, HER MAJESTY THE QUEEN OF DENMARK, THE PRESIDENT OF THE FEDERAL REPUBLIC OF GERMANY, THE PRESIDENT OF THE FRENCH REPUBLIC, THE PRESIDENT OF IRELAND, THE PRESIDENT OF THE ITALIAN REPUBLIC, HIS ROYAL HIGHNESS THE GRAND DUKE OF LUXEMBOURG, HER MAJESTY THE QUEEN OF THE NETHERLANDS, HER MAJESTY THE QUEEN OF THE UNITED KINGDOM OF GREAT BRITAIN AND NORTHERN IRELAND,

HAVING REGARD to Article 236 of the Treaty establishing the European Economic Community,

WHEREAS the Protocol on the Statute of the European Investment Bank which is annexed to the Treaty establishing the European Economic Community is an integral part thereof;

WHEREAS the definition of the unit of account and the methods of conversion as between this unit and the currencies of the Member States contained in the present text of the second subparagraph of Article 4 (1), and Article 7 (3) and (4) of the Statute of the Bank are no longer entirely in keeping with the circumstances of international monetary relations;

WHEREAS the future evolution of the international monetary system cannot be foreseen: whereas, consequently, rather than adopting immediately a new definition of the unit of account in the Statute of the Bank, it is desirable, particularly taking into account the position of the Bank in relation to capital markets, to give the Bank the means to adapt the definition of the unit of account and the methods of conversion to changes, where necessary and on appropriate conditions;

WHEREAS, in order to permit this rapid and flexible adaptation it is appropriate to give the Board of Governors of the Bank powers to alter, if

911

necessary, the definition of the unit of account and the methods of conversion as between the unit of account and the various currencies;

HAVE DECIDED to amend certain provisions of the Protocol on the Statute of the European Investment Bank, hereinafter called 'the Protocol', and to this end have designated as their Plenipotentiaries:

HIS MAJESTY THE KING OF THE BELGIANS:
   Willy DE CLERCQ,
   Minister of Finance;

HER MAJESTY THE QUEEN OF DENMARK:
   Per HÆKKERUP,
   Minister for Economic Affairs;

THE PRESIDENT OF THE FEDERAL REPUBLIC OF GERMANY:
   Dr Hans APEL,
   Federal Minister of Finance;

THE PRESIDENT OF THE FRENCH REPUBLIC:
   Jean-Pierre FOURCADE,
   Minister for Economic Affairs and Finance;

THE PRESIDENT OF IRELAND:
   Charles MURRAY,
   Secretary, Department of Finance of Ireland;

THE PRESIDENT OF THE ITALIAN REPUBLIC:
   Emilio COLOMBO,
   Minister of the Treasury;

HIS ROYAL HIGHNESS THE GRAND DUKE OF LUXEMBOURG:
   Jean DONDELINGER,
   Ambassador Extraordinary and Plenipotentiary,
   Permanent Representative to the European Communities;

HER MAJESTY THE QUEEN OF THE NETHERLANDS:

L. J. BRINKHORST,
State Secretary for Foreign Affairs;

HER MAJESTY THE QUEEN OF THE UNITED KINGDOM OF GREAT BRITAIN
AND NORTHERN IRELAND:

Sir Michael PALLISER, KCMG,
Ambassador Extraordinary and Plenipotentiary,
Permanent Representative to the European Communities;

WHO, having exchanged their Full Powers, found in good and due
form, have agreed as follows:

Article 1

The following sentence shall be added to the second subparagraph of
Article 4 (1) of the Protocol:

*'The Board of Governors, acting unanimously on a proposal from the
Board of Directors, may alter the definition of the unit of account.'*

Article 2

The following sentence shall be added to Article 7 (4) of the Protocol:

*'Furthermore it may, acting unanimously on a proposal from the Board of
Directors, alter the method of converting sums expressed in units of account
into national currencies and vice versa.'*

Article 3

Article 9 (3) (g) of the Protocol shall be replaced by the following:

913

'(g) exercise the powers and functions provided for in Articles 4, 7, 14, 17, 26 and 27;'

Article 4

This Treaty will be ratified by the High Contracting Parties in accordance with their respective constitutional requirements. The instruments of ratification will be deposited with the Government of the Italian Republic.

Article 5

This Treaty shall enter into force on the first day of the month following the deposit of the instrument of ratification by the last signatory State to take this step.

Article 6

This Treaty, drawn up in a single original in the Danish, Dutch, English, French, German, Irish and Italian languages, all seven texts being authentic, shall be deposited in the archives of the Government of the Italian Republic, which will transmit a certified copy to each of the Governments of the other signatory States.

TIL BEKRÆFTELSE HERAF har undertegnede befuldmægtigede underskrevet denne Traktat.

ZU URKUND DESSEN haben die unterzeichneten Bevollmächtigten ihre Unterschriften unter diesen Vertrag gesetzt.

IN WITNESS WHEREOF, the undersigned Plenipotentiaries have affixed their signatures below this Treaty.

EN FOI DE QUOI, les plénipotentiaires soussignés ont apposé leurs signatures au bas du présent traité.

DÁ FHIANÚ SIN, chuir na Lánchumhachtaigh thíos-sínithe a lámh leis an gConradh seo.

IN FEDE DI CHE, i plenipotenziari sottoscritti hanno apposto le loro firme in calce al presente trattato.

TEN BLIJKE WAARVAN de ondergetekende gevolmachtigden hun hand-tekening onder dit Verdrag hebben gesteld.

Udfærdiget i Bruxelles, den tiende juli nitten hundrede og femog-halvfjerds.

Geschehen zu Brüssel am zehnten Juli neunzehnhundertfünfundsieb-zig.

Done at Brussels on the tenth day of July in the year one thousand nine hundred and seventy-five.

Fait à Bruxelles, le dix juillet mil neuf cent soixante-quinze.

Arna dhéanamh sa Bhruiséil, an deichiú lá de mhí Iúil, míle naoi gcéad seachtó a cúig.

Fatto a Bruxelles, addì dieci luglio millenovecentosettantacinque.

Gedaan te Brussel, de tiende juli negentienhonderdvijfenzeventig.

W. DE CLERCQ
Per HÆKKERUP
Hans APEL
J.-P. FOURCADE
Ch. MURRAY
E. COLOMBO
J. DONDELINGER
L. J. BRINKHORST
Michael PALLISER

VI — TREATY
AMENDING CERTAIN FINANCIAL PROVISIONS OF THE TREATIES ESTABLISHING THE EUROPEAN COMMUNITIES AND OF THE TREATY ESTABLISHING A SINGLE COUNCIL AND A SINGLE COMMISSION OF THE EUROPEAN COMMUNITIES

DECLARATIONS

Official Journal of the European Communities, No L 359, 31 December 1977.

His Majesty the King of the Belgians, Her Majesty the Queen of Denmark, the President of the Federal Republic of Germany, the President of the French Republic, the President of Ireland, the President of the Italian Republic, His Royal Highness the Grand Duke of Luxembourg, Her Majesty the Queen of the Netherlands, Her Majesty the Queen of the United Kingdom of Great Britain and Northern Ireland,

Having regard to Article 96 of the Treaty establishing the European Coal and Steel Community,

Having regard to Article 236 of the Treaty establishing the European Economic Community,

Having regard to Article 204 of the Treaty establishing the European Atomic Energy Community,

Whereas, as of 1 January 1975, the budget of the Communities is financed entirely from the Communities' own resources;

Whereas the complete replacement of financial contributions of Member States by the Communities' own resources requires a strengthening of the budgetary powers of the European Parliament;

Whereas, for the same reasons, the implementation of the budget should be more closely supervised,

Have decided to amend certain financial provisions of the Treaties establishing the European Communities and of the Treaty establishing a

Single Council and a Single Commission of the European Communities, and to this end have designated as their Plenipotentiaries:

HIS MAJESTY THE KING OF THE BELGIANS:

R. VAN ELSLANDE,

Minister for Foreign Affairs and for Cooperation with the Developing Countries;

HER MAJESTY THE QUEEN OF DENMARK:

Niels ERSBØLL,

Ambassador Extraordinary and Plenipotentiary,
Permanent Representative to the European Communities;

THE PRESIDENT OF THE FEDERAL REPUBLIC OF GERMANY:

Hans-Dietrich GENSCHER,
Federal Minister for Foreign Affairs;

THE PRESIDENT OF THE FRENCH REPUBLIC:

Jean-Marie SOUTOU,

Ambassador of France,
Permanent Representative to the European Communities;

THE PRESIDENT OF IRELAND:

Garret FITZGERALD,
Minister for Foreign Affairs;

THE PRESIDENT OF THE ITALIAN REPUBLIC:

Mariano RUMOR,

Minister for Foreign Affairs,
President-in-Office of the Council of the European Communities;

HIS ROYAL HIGHNESS THE GRAND DUKE OF LUXEMBOURG:

Jean DONDELINGER,

Ambassador Extraordinary and Plenipotentiary,
Permanent Representative to the European Communities;

HER MAJESTY THE QUEEN OF THE NETHERLANDS:

L. J. BRINKHORST,
State Secretary for Foreign Affairs;

HER MAJESTY THE QUEEN OF THE UNITED KINGDOM OF GREAT BRITAIN
AND NORTHERN IRELAND:

Sir Michael PALLISER, KCMG,

Ambassador Extraordinary and Plenipotentiary,
Permanent Representative to the European Communities;

WHO, having exchanged their Full Powers, found in good and due
form, have agreed as follows:

CHAPTER I

PROVISIONS AMENDING THE TREATY
ESTABLISHING THE
EUROPEAN COAL AND STEEL COMMUNITY

Article 1

After Article 7 of the Treaty establishing the European Coal and Steel
Community the following subparagraph is added:

'*The audit shall be carried out by a Court of Auditors acting within the
limits of the powers conferred upon it by this Treaty.*'

Article 2

Article 78 of the Treaty establishing the European Coal and Steel Community is replaced by the following:

'Article 78

1.   *The financial year shall run from 1 January to 31 December.*

The administrative expenditure of the Community shall comprise the expenditure of the High Authority, including that relating to the functioning of the Consultative Committee, and that of the European Parliament, the Council, and of the Court of Justice.

2.   *Each institution of the Community shall, before 1 July, draw up estimates of its administrative expenditure. The High Authority shall consolidate these estimates in a preliminary draft administrative budget. It shall attach thereto an opinion which may contain different estimates.*

The preliminary draft budget shall contain an estimate of revenue and an estimate of expenditure.

3.   *The High Authority shall place the preliminary draft administrative budget before the Council not later than 1 September of the year preceding that in which the budget is to be implemented.*

The Council shall consult the High Authority and, where appropriate, the other institutions concerned whenever it intends to depart from the preliminary draft budget.

The Council shall, acting by a qualified majority establish the draft administrative budget and forward it to the European Parliament.

4.   *The draft administrative budget shall be placed before the European Parliament not later than 5 October of the year preceding that in which the budget is to be implemented.*

The European Parliament shall have the right to amend the draft administrative budget, acting by a majority of its members and to propose to the Council, acting by an absolute majority of the votes cast, modifications to the draft budget relating to expenditure necessarily resulting from this Treaty or from acts adopted in accordance therewith.

If, within 45 days of the draft administrative budget being placed before it, the European Parliament has given its approval, the administrative budget shall stand as finally adopted. If within, this period the European Parliament has not amended the draft administrative budget nor proposed any modifications thereto, the administrative budget shall be deemed to be finally adopted.

If within this period the European Parliament has adopted amendments or proposed modifications, the draft administrative budget together with the amendments or proposed modifications shall be forwarded to the Council.

5. After discussing the draft administrative budget with the High Authority and, where appropriate, with the other institutions concerned, the Council shall act under the following conditions:

(a) the Council may, acting by a qualified majority, modify any of the amendments adopted by the European Parliament;

(b) with regard to the proposed modifications:

— where a modification proposed by the European Parliament does not have the effect of increasing the total amount of the expenditure of an institution, owing in particular to the fact that the increase in expenditure which it would involve would be expressly compensated by one or more proposed modifications correspondingly reducing expenditure, the Council may, acting by a qualified majority, reject the proposed modification. In the absence of a decision to reject it, the proposed modification shall stand as accepted,

— where a modification proposed by the European Parliament has the effect of increasing the total amount of the expenditure of an institution, the Council may, acting by a qualified majority, accept this proposed modifica-

tion. In the absence of a decision to accept it, the proposed modification shall stand as rejected,

— where, in pursuance of one of the two preceding subparagraphs, the Council has rejected a proposed modification, it may, acting by a qualified majority, either retain the amount shown in the draft administrative budget or fix another amount.

The draft administrative budget shall be modified on the basis of the proposed modifications accepted by the Council.

If, within 15 days of the draft administrative budget being placed before it, the Council has not modified any of the amendments adopted by the European Parliament and if the modifications proposed by the latter have been accepted, the administrative budget shall be deemed to be finally adopted. The Council shall inform the European Parliament that it has not modified any of the amendments and that the proposed modifications have been accepted.

If within this period the Council has modified one or more of the amendments adopted by the European Parliament or if the modifications proposed by the latter have been rejected or modified, the modified draft administrative budget shall again be forwarded to the European Parliament. The Council shall inform the European Parliament of the results of its deliberations.

6.   Within 15 days of the draft administrative budget being placed before it, the European Parliament, which shall have been notified of the action taken on its proposed modification, may, acting by a majority of its members and three-fifths of the votes cast, amend or reject the modifications to its amendments made by the Council and shall adopt the administrative budget accordingly. If within this period the European Parliament has not acted, the administrative budget shall be deemed to be finally adopted.

7.   When the procedure provided for in this Article has been completed, the President of the European Parliament shall declare that the administrative budget has been finally adopted.

924

8. However, the European Parliament, acting by a majority of its members and two-thirds of the votes cast, may, if there are important reasons, reject the draft administrative budget and ask for a new draft to be submitted to it.

9. A maximum rate of increase in relation to the expenditure of the same type to be incurred during the current year shall be fixed annually for the total expenditure other than that necessarily resulting from this Treaty or from acts adopted in accordance therewith.

The High Authority shall, after consulting the Economic Policy Committee, declare what this maximum is as it results from:

— the average variation in the budgets of the Member States,

and

— the trend of the cost of living during the preceding financial year.

The maximum rate shall be communicated, before 1 May, to all the institutions of the Community. The latter shall be required to conform to this during the budgetary procedure, subject to the provisions of the fourth and fifth subparagraphs of this paragraph.

If, in respect of expenditure other than that necessarily resulting from this Treaty or from acts adopted in accordance therewith, the actual rate of increase in the draft administrative budget established by the Council is over half the maximum rate, the European Parliament may, exercising its right of amendment, further increase the total amount of that expenditure to a limit not exceeding half the maximum rate.

Where the European Parliament, the Council or the High Authority considers that the activities of the Communities require that the rate determined according to the procedure laid down in this paragraph should be exceeded, another rate may be fixed by agreement between the Council, acting by a *qualified majority, and the European Parliament, acting by a majority of its members and three-fifths of the votes cast.*

10.   *Each institution shall exercise the powers conferred upon it by this Article, with due regard for the provisions of this Treaty and for acts adopted in accordance therewith, in particular those relating to the Communities' own resources and to the balance between revenue and expenditure.*

11.   *Final adoption of the administrative budget shall have the effect of authorizing and requiring the High Authority to collect the corresponding revenue in accordance with the provisions of Article 49.'*

Article 3

In Article 78a of the Treaty establishing the European Coal and Steel Community, '78f' is replaced by '78h'.

Article 4

Article 78b of the Treaty establishing the European Coal and Steel Community is replaced by the following:

'Article 78b

1.   *If, at the beginning of a financial year, the administrative budget has not yet been voted, a sum equivalent to not more than one-twelfth of the budget appropriations for the preceding financial year may be spent each month in respect of any chapter or other subdivision of the administrative budget in accordance with the provisions of the Regulations made pursuant to Article 78h; this arrangement shall not, however, have the effect of placing at the disposal of the High Authority appropriations in excess of one-twelfth of those provided for in the draft administrative budget in course of preparation.*

The High Authority is authorized and required to impose the levies up to the amount of the appropriations for the preceding financial year, but shall not thereby exceed the amount which would have resulted from the adoption of the draft administrative budget.

2. The Council may, acting by a qualified majority, provided that the other conditions laid down in paragraph 1 are observed, authorize expenditure in excess of one-twelfth. The authorization and requirement to impose the levies may be adjusted accordingly.

If the decision relates to expenditure which does not necessarily result from this Treaty or from acts adopted in accordance therewith, the Council shall forward it immediately to the European Parliament; within 30 days the European Parliament, acting by a majority of its members and three-fifths of the votes cast, may adopt a different decision on the expenditure in excess of the one-twelfth referred to in paragraph 1. This part of the decision of the Council shall be suspended until the European Parliament has taken its decision. If within the said period the European Parliament has not taken a decision which differs from the decision of the Council, the latter shall be deemed to be finally adopted.'

Article 5

In Article 78c of the Treaty establishing the European Coal and Steel Community, '78f' is replaced by '78h'.

Article 6

Article 78d of the Treaty establishing the European Coal and Steel Community is replaced by the following:

'Article 78d

The High Authority shall submit annually to the Council and to the European Parliament the accounts of the preceding financial year relating to the implementation of the administrative budget. The High Authority shall also forward to them a financial statement of the assets and liabilities of the Community in the field covered by that budget.'

Article 7

Article 78e of the Treaty establishing the European Coal and Steel Community is replaced by the following:

'Article 78e

1.   *A Court of Auditors is hereby established.*

2.   *The Court of Auditors shall consist of nine members.*

3.   *The members of the Court of Auditors shall be chosen from among persons who belong or have belonged in their respective countries to external audit bodies or who are especially qualified for this office. Their independence must be beyond doubt.*

4.   *The members of the Court of Auditors shall be appointed for a term of six years by the Council, acting unanimously after consulting the European Parliament.*

However, when the first appointments are made, four members of the Court of Auditors, chosen by lot, shall be appointed for a term of office of four years only.

The members of the Court of Auditors shall be eligible for reappointment.

They shall elect the President of the Court of Auditors from among their number for a term of three years. The President may be re-elected.

5.   *The members of the Court of Auditors shall, in the general interest of the Community, be completely independent in the performance of their duties.*

In the performance of these duties, they shall neither seek nor take instructions from any government or from any other body. They shall refrain from any action incompatible with their duties.

6.   *The members of the Court of Auditors may not, during their term of office, engage in any other occupation, whether gainful or not. When entering upon their duties they shall give a solemn undertaking that, both during and after their term of office, they will respect the obligations arising therefrom and in particular their duty to behave with integrity and discretion as regards the acceptance, after they have ceased to hold office, of certain appointments or benefits.*

7.   *Apart from normal replacement, or death, the duties of a member of the Court of Auditors shall end when he resigns, or is compulsorily retired by a ruling of the Court of Justice pursuant to paragraph 8.*

The vacancy thus caused shall be filled for the remainder of the member's term of office.

Save in the case of compulsory retirement, members of the Court of Auditors shall remain in office until they have been replaced.

8.   *A member of the Court of Auditors may be deprived of his office or of his right to a pension or other benefits in its stead only if the Court of Justice, at the request of the Court of Auditors, finds that he no longer fulfils the requisite conditions or meets the obligations arising from his office.*

9.   The Council, acting by a qualified majority, shall determine the conditions of employment of the President and the members of the Court of Auditors and in particular their salaries, allowances and pensions. It shall also, by the same majority, determine any payment to be made instead of remuneration.

10.   The provisions of the Protocol on the Privileges and Immunities of the European Communities applicable to the Judges of the Court of Justice shall also apply to the members of the Court of Auditors.'

Article 8

Article 78f of the Treaty establishing the European Coal and Steel Community is replaced by the following:

'Article 78f

1.   The Court of Auditors shall examine the accounts of all administrative expenditure and administrative revenue of the Community, including the revenue from the tax for the benefit of the Community levied on the salaries, wages and emoluments of officials and other servants of the latter. It shall also examine the accounts of all revenue and expenditure of all bodies set up by the Community in so far as the relevant constituent instrument does not preclude such examination.

2.   The Court of Auditors shall examine whether all revenue referred to in paragraph 1 has been received and all expenditure referred to in that paragraph has been incurred in a lawful and regular manner and whether the financial management had been sound.

The audit of revenue shall be carried out on the basis both of the amounts established as due and the amounts actually paid to the Community.

The audit of expenditure shall be carried out on the basis both of commitments undertaken and payments made.

These audits may be carried out before the closure of accounts for the financial year in question.

3.   *The audit shall be based on records and, if necessary, performed on the spot in the institutions of the Community and in the Member States. In the Member States the audit shall be carried out in liaison with the national audit bodies or, if these do not have the necessary powers, with the competent national departments. These bodies or departments shall inform the Court of Auditors whether they intend to take part in the audit.*

The institutions of the Community and the national audit bodies or, if these do not have the necessary powers, the competent national departments, shall forward to the Court of Auditors, at its request, any document or information necessary to carry out its task.

4.   *The Court of Auditors shall draw up an annual report after the close of each financial year. It shall be forwarded to the institutions of the Community and shall be published, together with the replies of these institutions to the observations of the Court of Auditors, in the* Official Journal of the European Communities.

The Court of Auditors may also, at any time, submit observations on specific questions and deliver opinions at the request of one of the institutions of the Community.

It shall adopt its annual reports or opinions by a majority of its members.

It shall assist the European Parliament and the Council in exercising their powers of control over the implementation of the budget.

5.   *The Court of Auditors shall also draw up a separate annual report stating whether the accounting other than that for the expenditure and revenue re-*

931

ferred to in paragraph 1 and the financial management by the High Authority relating thereto have been effected in a regular manner. It shall draw up this report within six months of the end of the financial year to which the accounts refer and shall submit it to the High Authority and the Council. The High Authority shall forward it to the European Parliament.'

Article 9

The following provisions shall be added to the Treaty establishing the European Coal and Steel Community:

'Article 78g

The European Parliament, acting on a recommendation from the Council which shall act by a qualified majority, shall give a discharge to the High Authority in respect of the implementation of the administrative budget. To this end, the Council and the European Parliament in turn shall examine the accounts and the financial statement referred to in Article 78d, and the annual report by the Court of Auditors together with the replies of the institutions under audit to the observations of the Court of Auditors.'

Article 10

The following provisions shall be added to the Treaty establishing the European Coal and Steel Community:

'Article 78h

The Council, acting unanimously on a proposal from the High Authority and after consulting the European Parliament and obtaining the opinion of the Court of Auditors, shall:

(a) make Financial Regulations specifying in particular the procedure to be adopted for establishing and implementing the administrative budget and for presenting and auditing accounts;

(b) lay down rules concerning the responsibility of authorizing officers and accounting officers and concerning appropriate arrangements for inspection.'

CHAPTER II

PROVISIONS AMENDING THE TREATY ESTABLISHING THE EUROPEAN ECONOMIC COMMUNITY

Article 11

After Article 4 of the Treaty establishing the European Economic Community the following paragraph is added:

'3.   *The audit shall be carried out by a Court of Auditors acting within the limits of the powers conferred upon it by this Treaty.*'

Article 12

Article 203 of the Treaty establishing the European Economic Community is replaced by the following:

'Article 203

1.   *The financial year shall run from 1 January to 31 December.*

2.   *Each institution of the Community shall, before 1 July, draw up estimates of its expenditure. The Commission shall consolidate these estimates in a preliminary draft budget. It shall attach thereto an opinion which may contain different estimates.*

The preliminary draft budget shall contain an estimate of revenue and an estimate of expenditure.

3. The Commission shall place the preliminary draft budget before the Council not later than 1 September of the year preceding that in which the budget is to be implemented.

The Council shall consult the Commission and, where appropriate, the other institutions concerned whenever it intends to depart from the preliminary draft budget.

The Council, acting by a qualified majority, shall establish the draft budget and forward it to the European Parliament.

4. The draft budget shall be placed before the European Parliament not later than 5 October of the year preceding that in which the budget is to be implemented.

The European Parliament shall have the right to amend the draft budget, acting by a majority of its members, and to propose to the Council, acting by an absolute majority of the votes cast, modifications to the draft budget relating to expenditure necessarily resulting from this Treaty or from acts adopted in accordance therewith.

If, within 45 days of the draft budget being placed before it, the European Parliament has given its approval, the budget shall stand as finally adopted. If within this period the European Parliament has not amended the draft budget nor proposed any modifications thereto, the budget shall be deemed to be finally adopted.

If within this period the European Parliament has adopted amendments or proposed modifications, the draft budget together with the amendments or proposed modifications shall be forwarded to the Council.

5. After discussing the draft budget with the Commission and, where appropriate, with the other institutions concerned, the Council shall act under the following conditions:

(a) the Council may, acting by a qualified majority, modify any of the amendments adopted by the European Parliament.

(b) *With regard to the proposed modifications:*

— *where a modification proposed by the European Parliament does not have the effect of increasing the total amount of the expenditure of an institution, owing in particular to the fact that the increase in expenditure which it would involve would be expressly compensated by one or more proposed modifications correspondingly reducing expenditure, the Council may, acting by a qualified majority, reject the proposed modification. In the absence of a decision to reject it, the proposed modification shall stand as accepted,*

— *where a modification proposed by the European Parliament has the effect of increasing the total amount of the expenditure of an institution, the Council may, acting by a qualified majority, accept this proposed modification. In the absence of a decision to accept it, the proposed modification shall stand as rejected,*

— *where, in pursuance of one of the two preceding subparagraphs, the Council has rejected a proposed modification, it may, acting by a qualified majority, either retain the amount shown in the draft budget or fix another amount.*

The draft budget shall be modified on the basis of the proposed modifications accepted by the Council.

If, within 15 days of the draft budget being placed before it, the Council has not modified any of the amendments adopted by the European Parliament and if the modifications proposed by the latter have been accepted, the budget shall be deemed to be finally adopted. The Council shall inform the European Parliament that it has not modified any of the amendments and that the proposed modifications have been accepted.

If within this period the Council has modified one or more of the amendments adopted by the European Parliament or if the modifications proposed by the latter have been rejected or modified, the modified draft budget shall again be forwarded to the European Parliament. The Council shall inform the European Parliament of the results of its deliberations.

6.   Within 15 days of the draft budget being placed before it, the European Parliament, which shall have been notified of the action taken on its proposed modifications, may, acting by a majority of its members and three-fifths of the votes cast, amend or reject the modifications to its amendments made by the Council and shall adopt the budget accordingly. If within this period the European Parliament has not acted, the budget shall be deemed to be finally adopted.

7.   When the procedure provided for in this Article has been completed, the President of the European Parliament shall declare that the budget has been finally adopted.

8.   However, the European Parliament, acting by a majority of its members and two-thirds of the votes cast, may, if there are important reasons, reject the draft budget and ask for a new draft to be submitted to it.

9.   A maximum rate of increase in relation to the expenditure of the same type to be incurred during the current year shall be fixed annually for the total expenditure other than that necessarily resulting from this Treaty or from acts adopted in accordance therewith.

The Commission shall, after consulting the Economic Policy Committee, declare what this maximum rate is as it results from:

— the trend, in terms of volume, of the gross national product within the Community,

— the average variation in the budgets of the Member States,

and

— the trend of the cost of living during the preceding financial year.

The maximum rate shall be communicated, before 1 May, to all the institutions of the Community. The latter shall be required to conform to this *during the budgetary procedure, subject to the provisions of the fourth and fifth subparagraphs of this paragraph.*

If, in respect of expenditure other than that necessarily resulting from this Treaty or from acts adopted in accordance therewith, the actual rate of increase in the draft budget established by the Council is over half the maximum rate, the European Parliament may, exercising its right of amendment, further increase the total amount of that expenditure to a limit not exceeding half the maximum rate.

Where the European Parliament, the Council or the Commission consider that the activities of the Communities require that the rate determined according to the procedure laid down in this paragraph should be exceeded, another rate may be fixed by agreement between the Council, acting by a qualified majority, and the European Parliament, acting by a majority of its members and three-fifths of the votes cast.

10. *Each institution shall exercise the powers conferred upon it by this Article, with due regard for the provisions of the Treaty and for acts adopted in accordance therewith, in particular those relating to the Communities' own resources and to the balance between revenue and expenditure.'*

Article 13

Article 204 of the Treaty establishing the European Economic Community is replaced by the following:

'Article 204

If, at the beginning of a financial year, the budget has not yet been voted, a sum equivalent to not more than one-twelfth of the budget appropriations for the preceding financial year may be spent each month in respect of any chapter or other subdivision of the budget in accordance with the provisions of the Regulations made pursuant to Article 209, this arrangement shall not, however, have the effect of placing at the disposal of the Commission appropriations in excess of one-twelfth of those provided for in the draft budget in course of preparation.

The Council may, acting by a qualified majority, provided that the other conditions laid down in the first subparagraph are observed, authorize expenditure in excess of one-twelfth.

If the decision relates to expenditure which does not necessarily result from this Treaty or from acts adopted in accordance therewith, the Council shall forward it immediately to the European Parliament, within 30 days the European Parliament, acting by a majority of its members and three-fifths of the votes cast, may adopt a different decision on the expenditure in excess of the one-twelfth referred to in the first subparagraph. This part of the decision of the Council shall be suspended until the European Parliament has taken its decision. If within the said period the European Parliament has not taken a decision which differs from the decision of the Council, the latter shall be deemed to be finally adopted.

The decisions referred to in the second and third subparagraphs shall lay down the necessary measures relating to resources to ensure application of this Article.'

Article 14

The following provisions shall be added to the Treaty establishing the European Economic Community:

'Article 205a

The Commission shall submit annually to the Council and to the European Parliament the accounts of the preceding financial year relating to the implementation of the budget. The Commission shall also forward to them a financial statement of the assets and liabilities of the Community.'

Article 15

Article 206 of the Treaty establishing the European Economic Community shall be replaced by the following:

'Article 206

1.   *A Court of Auditors is hereby established.*

2.   *The Court of Auditors shall consist of nine members.*

3.   *The members of the Court of Auditors shall be chosen from among persons who belong or have belonged in their respective countries to external audit bodies or who are especially qualified for this office. Their independence must be beyond doubt.*

4.   *The members of the Court of Auditors shall be appointed for a term of six years by the Council, acting unanimously after consulting the European Parliament.*

However, when the first appointments are made, four members of the Court of Auditors, chosen by lot, shall be appointed for a term of office of four years only.

The members of the Court of Auditors shall be eligible for reappointment.

They shall elect the President of the Court of Auditors from among their number for a term of three years. The President may be re-elected.

5.   The members of the Court of Auditors shall, in the general interest of the Community, be completely independent in the performance of their duties.

In the performance of these duties, they shall neither seek nor take instructions from any government or from any other body. They shall refrain from any action incompatible with their duties.

6.   The members of the Court of Auditors may not, during their term of office, engage in any other occupation, whether gainful or not. When entering upon their duties they shall give a solemn undertaking that, both during and after their term of office, they will respect the obligations arising therefrom and in particular their duty to behave with integrity and discretion as regards the acceptance, after they have ceased to hold office, of certain appointments or benefits.

7.   Apart from normal replacement, or death, the duties of a member of the Court of Auditors shall end when he resigns, or is compulsorily retired by a ruling of the Court of Justice pursuant to paragraph 8.

The vacancy thus caused shall be filled for the remainder of the member's term of office.

Save in the case of compulsory retirement, members of the Court of Auditors shall remain in office until they have been replaced.

8.   A member of the Court of Auditors may be deprived of his office or of his right to a pension or other benefits in its stead only if the Court of Justice, at the request of the Court of Auditors, finds that he no longer fulfils the requisite conditions or meets the obligations arising from his office.

9.   The Council, acting by a qualified majority, shall determine the conditions of employment of the President and the members of the Court of Auditors and in particular their salaries, allowances and pensions. It shall also, by the same majority, determine any payment to be made instead of remuneration.

10.   The provisions of the Protocol on the Privileges and Immunities of the European Communities applicable to the Judges of the Court of Justice shall also apply to the members of the Court of Auditors.'

Article 16

The following provisions shall be added to the Treaty establishing the European Economic Community:

'Article 206a

1.   *The Court of Auditors shall examine the accounts of all revenue and expenditure of the Commmunity. It shall also examine the accounts of all revenue and expenditure of all bodies set up by the Community in so far as the relevant constituent instrument does not preclude such examination.*

2.   *The Court of Auditors shall examine whether all revenue has been received and all expenditure incurred in a lawful and regular manner and whether the financial management has been sound.*

The audit of revenue shall be carried out on the basis both of the amounts established as due and the amounts actually paid to the Community.

The audit of expenditure shall be carried out on the basis both of commitments undertaken and payments made.

These audits may be carried out before the closure of accounts for the financial year in question.

3. *The audit shall be based on records and, if necessary, performed on the spot in the institutions of the Community and in the Member States. In the Member States the audit shall be carried out in liaison with the national audit bodies or, if these do not have the necessary powers, with the competent national departments. These bodies or departments shall inform the Court of Auditors whether they intend to take part in the audit.*

The institutions of the Community and the national audit bodies or, if these do not have the necessary powers, the competent national departments, shall forward to the Court of Auditors, at its request, any document or information necessary to carry out its task.

4. *The Court of Auditors shall draw up an annual report after the close of each financial year. It shall be forwarded to the institutions of the Community and shall be published, together with the replies of these institutions to the observations of the Court of Auditors, in the* Official Journal of the European Communities.

The Court of Auditors may also, at any time, submit observations on specific questions and deliver opinions at the request of one of the institutions of the Community.

It shall adopt its annual reports or opinions by a majority of its members.

It shall assist the European Parliament and the Council in exercising their powers of control over the implementation of the budget.'

Article 17

The following provisions shall be added to the Treaty establishing the European Economic Community:

'Article 206b

The European Parliament, acting on a recommendation from the Council which shall act by a qualified majority, shall give a discharge to the Commission in respect of the implementation of the budget. To this end, the Council and the European Parliament in turn shall examine the accounts and the financial statement referred to in Article 205a and the annual report by the Court of Auditors together with the replies of the institutions under audit to the observations of the Court of Auditors.'

Article 18

Article 209 of the Treaty establishing the European Economic Community shall be replaced by the following:

'Article 209

The Council, acting unanimously on a proposal from the Commission and after consulting the European Parliament and obtaining the opinion of the Court of Auditors, shall:

(a) make Financial Regulations specifying in particular the procedure to be adopted for establishing and implementing the budget and for presenting and auditing accounts;

(b) determine the methods and procedure whereby the budget revenue provided under the arrangements relating to the Communities' own resources shall be made available to the Commission, and determine the measures to be applied, if need be, to meet cash requirements;

(c) lay down rules concerning the responsibility of authorizing officers and accounting officers and concerning appropriate arrangements for inspection.'

CHAPTER III

PROVISIONS AMENDING THE TREATY ESTABLISHING THE EUROPEAN ATOMIC ENERGY COMMUNITY

Article 19

After Article 3 of the Treaty establishing the European Atomic Energy Community the following paragraph is added:

'3.   *The audit shall be carried out by a Court of Auditors acting within the limits of the powers conferred upon it by this Treaty.*'

Article 20

Article 177 of the Treaty establishing the European Atomic Energy Community is replaced by the following:

'Article 177

1.   *The financial year shall run from 1 January to 31 December.*

Within the meaning of this Article, 'budget' shall include the operating budget and the research and investment budget.

2.   *Each institution of the Community shall, before 1 July, draw up estimates of its expenditure. The Commission shall consolidate these estimates in a preliminary draft budget. It shall attach thereto an opinion which may contain different estimates.*

The preliminary draft budget shall include an estimate of revenue and an estimate of expenditure.

3. The Commission shall place the preliminary draft budget before the Council not later than 1 September of the year preceding that in which the budget is to be implemented.

The Council shall consult the Commission and, where appropriate, the other institutions concerned whenever in intends to depart from the preliminary draft budget.

The Council shall, acting by a qualified majority, establish the draft budget and forward it to the European Parliament.

4. The draft budget shall be placed before the European Parliament not later than 5 October of the year preceding that in which the budget is to be implemented.

The European Parliament shall have the right to amend the draft budget acting by a majority of its members, and to propose to the Council, acting by an absolute majority of the votes cast, modifications to the draft budget relating to expenditure necessarily resulting from this Treaty or from acts adopted in accordance therewith.

If, within 45 days of the draft budget being placed before it, the European Parliament has given its approval, the budget shall stand as finally adopted. If within this period the European Parliament has not amended the draft budget or proposed any modifications thereto, the budget shall be deemed to be finally adopted.

If within this period the European Parliament has adopted amendments or proposed modifications, the draft budget together with the amendments or proposed modifications shall be forwarded to the Council.

5. After discussing the draft budget with the Commission and, where appropriate, with the other institutions concerned, the Council shall act under the following conditions:

(a) the Council may, acting by a qualified majority, modify any of the amendments adopted by the European Parliament;

(b) *with regard to the proposed modifications:*

— *where a modification proposed by the European Parliament does not have the effect of increasing the total amount of the expenditure of an institution, owing in particular to the fact that the increase in expenditure which it would involve would be expressly compensated by one or more proposed modifications correspondingly reducing expenditure, the Council may, acting by a qualified majority, reject the proposed modification. In the absence of a decision to reject it, the proposed modification shall stand as accepted,*

— *where a modification proposed by the European Parliament has the effect of increasing the total amount of the expenditure on an institution, the Council may, acting by a qualified majority, accept this proposed modification. In the absence of a decision to accept it, the proposed modification shall stand as rejected,*

— *where, in pursuance of one of the two preceding subparagraphs, the Council has rejected a proposed modification, it may, acting by a qualified majority, either retain the amount shown in the draft budget or fix another amount.*

The draft budget shall be modified on the basis of the proposed modifications accepted by the Council.

If, within 15 days of the draft budget being placed before it, the Council has not modified any of the amendments adopted by the European Parliament and if the modifications proposed by the latter have been accepted, the budget shall be deemed to be finally adopted. The Council shall inform the European Parliament that it has not modified any of the amendments and that the proposed modifications have been accepted.

If within this period the Council has modified one or more of the amendments adopted by the European Parliament or if the modifications proposed by the latter have been rejected or modified, the modified draft budget shall again be forwarded to the European Parliament. The Council shall inform the European Parliament of the results of its deliberations.

6.   Within 15 days of the draft budget being placed before it, the European Parliament, which shall have been notified of the action taken on its proposed modifications may, acting by a majority of its members and three-fifths of the votes cast, amend or reject the modifications to its amendments made by the Council and shall adopt the budget accordingly. If within this period the European Parliament has not acted, the budget shall be deemed to be finally adopted.

7.   When the procedure provided for in this Article has been completed, the President of the European Parliament shall declare that the budget has been finally adopted.

8.   However, the European Parliament, acting by a majority of its members and two-thirds of the votes cast may, if there are important reasons, reject the draft budget and ask for a new draft to be submitted to it.

9.   A maximum rate of increase in relation to the expenditure of the same type to be incurred during the current year shall be fixed annually for the total expenditure other than that necessarily resulting from this Treaty or from acts adopted in accordance therewith.

    The Commission shall after consulting the Economic Policy Committee, declare what this maximum rate is, as it results from:

    — the trend, in terms of volume, of the gross national product within the Community,

    — the average variation in the budgets of the Member States

and

    — the trend of the cost of living during the preceding financial year.

    The maximum rate shall be communicated, before 1 May, to all the institutions of the Community. The latter shall be required to conform to this *during the budgetary procedure, subject to the provisions of the fourth and fifth subparagraphs of this paragraph.*

If, in respect of expenditure other than that necessarily resulting from this Treaty or from acts adopted in accordance therewith, the actual rate of increase in the draft budget established by the Council is over half the maximum rate, the European Parliament may, exercising its right of amendment, further increase the total amount of that expenditure to a limit not exceeding half the maximum rate.

Where the European Parliament, the Council or the Commission considers that the activities of the Communities require that the rate determined according to the procedure laid down in this paragraph should be exceeded, another rate may be fixed by agreement between the Council, acting by a qualified majority, and the European Parliament, acting by a majority of its members and three-fifths of the votes cast.

10. *Each institution shall exercise the powers conferred upon it by this Article, with due regard for the provisions of this Treaty and for acts adopted in accordance therewith, in particular those relating to the Communities' own resources and to the balance between revenue and expenditure.'*

Article 21

Article 178 of the Treaty establishing the European Atomic Energy Community is replaced by the following:

'Article 178

If, at the beginning of a financial year, the budget has not yet been voted, a sum equivalent to not more than one-twelfth of the budget appropriations for the preceding financial year may be spent each month in respect of any chapter or other subdivision of the budget in accordance with the provisions of

948

the Regulations made pursuant to Article 183; this arrangement shall not, however, have the effect of placing at the disposal of the Commission appropriations in excess of one-twelfth of those provided for in the draft budget in the course of preparation.

The Council may, acting by a qualified majority, provided that the other conditions laid down in the first subparagraph are observed, authorize expenditure in excess of one-twelfth.

If the decision relates to expenditure which does not necessarily result from this Treaty or from acts adopted in accordance therewith, the Council shall forward it immediately to the European Parliament; within 30 days the European Parliament, acting by a majority of its members and three-fifths of the votes cast, may adopt a different decision on the expenditure in excess of the one-twelfth referred to in the first subparagraph. This part of the decision of the Council shall be suspended until the European Parliament has taken its decision. If, within this period, the European Parliament has not taken a decision which differs from the decision of the Council, the latter shall be deemed to be finally adopted.

The decisions referred to in the second and third subparagraphs shall lay down the necessary measures relating to resources to ensure application of this Article.'

Article 22

The following provisions shall be added to the Treaty establishing the European Atomic Energy Community:

'Article 179a

The Commission shall submit annually to the Council and to the European Parliament the accounts of the preceding financial year relating to the implementation of the budget. The Commission shall also forward to them a financial statement of the assets and liabilities of the Community.'

Article 23

Article 180 of the Treaty establishing the European Atomic Energy Community is replaced by the following:

'Article 180

1. *A Court of Auditors is hereby established.*

2. *The Court of Auditors shall consist of nine members.*

3. *The members of the Court of Auditors shall be chosen from among persons who belong or have belonged in their respective countries to external audit bodies or who are especially qualified for this office. Their independence must be beyond doubt.*

4. *The members of the Court of Auditors shall be appointed for a term of six years by the Council, acting unanimously after consulting the European Parliament.*

   However, when the first appointments are made, four members of the Court of Auditors, chosen by lot, shall be appointed for a term of office of four years only.

   The members of the Court of Auditors shall be eligible for reappointment.

   They shall elect the President of the Court of Auditors from among their number for a term of three years. The President may be re-elected.

5. *The members of the Court of Auditors shall, in the general interest of the Community, be completely independent in the performance of their duties.*

   In the performance of these duties, they shall neither seek nor take instructions from any government, or from any other body. They shall refrain from any action incompatible with their duties.

6. *The members of the Court of Auditors may not, during their term of office, engage in any other occupation, whether gainful or not. When entering upon their duties they shall give a solemn undertaking that, both during and*

after their term of office, they will respect the obligations arising therefrom and in particular their duty to behave with integrity and discretion as regards the acceptance, after they have ceased to hold office, of certain appointments or benefits.

7.   *Apart from normal replacement, or death, the duties of a member of the Court of Auditors shall end when he resigns, or is compulsorily retired by a ruling of the Court of Justice pursuant to paragraph 8.*

The vacancy thus caused shall be filled for the remainder of the member's term of office.

Save in the case of compulsory retirement under the provisions of paragraph 8, members of the Court of Auditors shall remain in office until they have been replaced.

8.   *A member of the Court of Auditors may be deprived of his office or of his right to a pension or other benefits in its stead only if the Court of Justice, at the request of the Court of Auditors, finds that he no longer fulfils the requisite conditions or meets the obligations arising from his office.*

9.   *The Council, acting by a qualified majority, shall determine the conditions of employment of the President and the members of the Court of Auditors and in particular their salaries, allowances and pensions. It shall also, by the same majority, determine any payment to be made instead of remuneration.*

10.   *The provisions of the Protocol on the Privileges and Immunities of the European Communities applicable to the Judges of the Court of Justice shall also apply to the members of the Court of Auditors.'*

Article 24

The following provisions shall be added to the Treaty establishing the European Atomic Energy Community:

'Article 180a

1. *The Court of Auditors shall examine the accounts of all revenue and expenditure of the Community. It shall also examine the accounts of all revenue and expenditure of all bodies set up by the Community in so far as the relevant constituent instrument does not preclude such examination.*

2. *The Court of Auditors shall examine whether all revenue has been received and all expenditure incurred in a lawful and regular manner and whether the financial management has been sound.*

The audit of revenue shall be carried out on the basis both of the amounts established as due and the amounts actually paid to the Communities.

The audit of expenditure shall be carried out on the basis both of commitments undertaken and payments made.

These audits may be carried out before the closure of accounts for the financial year in question.

3. *The audit shall be based on records and, if necessary, performed on the spot in the institutions of the Community and in the Member States. In the Member States the audit shall be carried out in liaison with the national audit bodies or, if these do not have the necessary powers, with the competent national departments. These bodies or departments shall inform the Court of Auditors whether they intend to take part in the audit.*

The institutions of the Community and the national audit bodies or, if the latter do not have the necessary powers, the competent national departments, shall forward to the Court of Auditors, at its request, any document or information necessary to carry out its task.

4. *The Court of Auditors shall draw up an annual report after the close of each financial year. It shall be forwarded to the institutions of the Community and shall be published, together with the replies of these institutions to the*

observations of the Court of Auditors, in the Official Journal of the European Communities.

The Court of Auditors may also, at any time, submit observations on specific questions and deliver opinions at the request of one of the institutions of the Community.

It shall adopt its annual reports or opinions by a majority of its members.

It shall assist the European Parliament and the Council in exercising their powers of control over the implementation of the budget.'

Article 25

The following provisions shall be added to the Treaty establishing the European Atomic Energy Community:

'Article 180b

The European Parliament, acting on a recommendation from the Council which shall act by a qualified majority, shall give a discharge to the Commission in respect of the implementation of the budget. To this end, the Council and the European Parliament in turn shall examine the accounts and the financial statement referred to in Article 179a, and the annual report by the Court of Auditors together with the replies of the institutions under audit to the observations of the Court of Auditors.'

Article 26

The following provisions shall be substituted for Article 183 of the Treaty establishing the European Atomic Energy Community:

'Article 183

The Council, acting unanimously on a proposal from the Commission and after consulting the European Parliament and obtaining the opinion of the Court of Auditors, shall:

(a) *make Financial Regulations specifying in particular the procedure to be adopted for establishing and implementing the budget and for presenting and auditing accounts;*

(b) *determine the methods and procedure whereby the budget revenue provided for under the arrangements relating to the Communities' own resources, shall be made available to the Commission, and determine the measures to be applied, if need be, to meet cash requirements;*

(c) *lay down rules concerning the responsibility of authorizing officers and accounting officers and concerning appropriate arrangements for inspection.'*

CHAPTER IV

PROVISIONS AMENDING THE TREATY ESTABLISHING A SINGLE COUNCIL AND A SINGLE COMMISSION OF THE EUROPEAN COMMUNITIES

Article 27

Article 22 of the Treaty establishing a Single Council and a Single Commission of the European Communities shall be replaced by the following:

'Article 22

1. *The powers and jurisdiction conferred upon the Court of Auditors established by Article 78e of the Treaty establishing the European Coal and Steel Community, by Article 206 of the Treaty establishing the European Economic Community, and by Article 180 of the Treaty establishing the Euro-*

pean Atomic Energy Community shall be exercised in accordance with those Treaties by a single Court of Auditors of the European Communities constituted as provided in these Articles.

2.   *Without prejudice to the powers and jurisdiction referred to in paragraph 1, the Court of Auditors of the European Communities shall exercise the powers and jurisdiction conferred, before the entry into force of this Treaty, upon the Audit Board of the European Communities and upon the Auditor of the European Coal and Steel Community under the conditions laid down in the various instruments referring to the Audit Board and to the Auditor. In all these instruments the words "Audit Board" and "Auditor" shall be replaced by the words "Court of Auditors".'*

CHAPTER V

FINAL PROVISIONS

Article 28

1. The members of the Court of Auditors shall be appointed upon the entry into force of this Treaty.

2. The terms of office of the members of the Audit Board and that of the auditor shall expire on the day they submit their report on the financial year preceding that in which the members of the Court of Auditors are appointed; their powers of audit shall be confined to operations relating to that financial year.

Article 29

This Treaty shall be ratified by the High Contracting Parties in accordance with their respective constitutional requirements. The instruments of ratification shall be deposited with the Government of the Italian Republic.

Article 30

This Treaty shall enter into force on the first day of the month following the deposit of the instrument of ratification by the last signatory State to take this step.

If this Treaty enters into force during the budgetary procedure, the Council shall, after consulting the European Parliament and the Commission, adopt the measures required in order to facilitate the application of this Treaty to the remainder of the budgetary procedure.

Article 31

This Treaty, drawn up in a single original in the Danish, Dutch, English, French, German, Irish and Italian languages, all seven texts being authentic, shall be deposited in the archives of the Government of the Italian Republic, which shall transmit a certified copy to each of the Governments of the other signatory States.

TIL BEKRÆFTELSE HERAF har undertegnede befuldmægtigede underskrevet denne Traktat.

ZU URKUND DESSEN haben die unterzeichneten Bevollmächtigten ihre Unterschriften unter diesen Vertrag gesetzt.

IN WITNESS WHEREOF, the undersigned Plenipotentiaries have affixed their signatures below this Treaty.

EN FOI DE QUOI, les plénipotentiaires soussignés ont apposé leurs signatures au bas du présent traité.

Dá FHIANÚ SIN, chuir na Lánchumhachtaigh thíos-sínithe a lámh leis an gConradh seo.

IN FEDE DI CHE, i plenipotenziari sottoscritti hanno apposto le loro firme in calce al presente trattato.

TEN BLIJKE WAARVAN de ondergetekende gevolmachtigden hun handtekening onder dit Verdrag hebben gesteld.

Udfærdiget i Bruxelles, den toogtyvende juli nitten hundrede og femoghalvfjerds.

Geschehen zu Brüssel am zweiundzwanzigsten Juli neunzehnhundertfünfundsiebzig.

Done at Brussels on the twenty-second day of July in the year one thousand nine hundred and seventy-five.

Fait à Bruxelles, le vingt-deux juillet mil neuf cent soixante-quinze.

Arna dhéanamh sa Bhruiséil, an dóú lá is fiche de mhí Iúil, míle naoi gcéad seachtó a cúig.

Fatto a Bruxelles, addì ventidue luglio millenovecentosettantacinque.

Gedaan te Brussel, de tweeëntwintigste juli negentienhonderdvijfenzeventig.

R. VAN ELSLANDE
Niels ERSBØLL
Hans-Dietrich GENSCHER
Jean-Marie SOUTOU
Gearóid MAC GEARAILT
Mariano RUMOR
J. DONDELINGER
L. J. BRINKHORST
Michael PALLISER

STATEMENTS

1. *Re first subparagraph of Article 206a (1) of the EEC Treaty:*

'It is agreed that the Court of Auditors shall have jurisdiction to audit the operations of the European Development Fund.'

2. *Re second subparagraph of Articles 78f (2) of the ECSC Treaty, 206a (2) of the EEC Treaty and 180a (2) of the Euratom Treaty:*

'With regard to entitlements established by the Member States in accordance with Article 2 of Regulation (EEC, Euratom, ECSC) No 2/71 of the Council of 2 January 1971 implementing the Decision of 21 April 1970 on the replacement of financial contributions from Member States by the Communities' own resources, the provisions of the second subparagraph of paragraph 2 of the abovementioned Articles must be interpreted to mean that the audit shall not cover substantive transactions properly so called shown in the supporting documents which relate to such establishment; accordingly, the audit on the spot shall not be carried out by recourse to the debtor.'

3. *Re first subparagraph of Article 78f (3) of the ECSC Treaty, re Article 206a (3) of the EEC Treaty and re Article 180a (3) of the Euratom Treaty:*

'Member States shall notify the Court of Auditors of the institutions and departments concerned and of their respective powers.'

VII — ACT CONCERNING THE ELECTION OF THE REPRESENTATIVES OF THE EUROPEAN PARLIAMENT BY DIRECT UNIVERSAL SUFFRAGE

ANNEXED TO THE COUNCIL DECISION OF 20 SEPTEMBER 1976

Official Journal of the European Communities, No L 278, 8 October 1976.

Council

DECISION
(76/787/ECSC, EEC, Euratom)

THE COUNCIL,

COMPOSED of the representatives of the Member States and acting unanimously,

HAVING regard to Article 21 (3) of the Treaty establishing the European Coal and Steel Community,

HAVING regard to Article 138 (3) of the Treaty establishing the European Economic Community,

HAVING regard to Article 108 (3) of the Treaty establishing the European Atomic Energy Community,

HAVING regard to the proposal from the European Parliament,

INTENDING to give effect to the conclusions of the European Council in Rome on 1 and 2 December 1975, that the election of the European Parliament should be held on a single date within the period May/June 1978,

HAS LAID DOWN the provisions annexed to this Decision which it recommends to the Member States for adoption in accordance with their respective constitutional requirements.

This Decision and the provisions annexed hereto shall be published in the *Official Journal of the European Communities*.

The Member States shall notify the Secretary-General of the Council of the European Communities without delay of the completion of the procedures necessary in accordance with their respective constitutional requirements for the adoption of the provisions annexed to this Decision.

This Decision shall enter into force on the day of its publication in the *Official Journal of the European Communities*.

Udfærdiget i Bruxelles, den tyvende september nitten hundrede og seksoghalvfjerds.

Geschehen zu Brüssel am zwanzigsten September neunzehnhundert-sechsundsiebzig.

Done at Brussels on the twentieth day of September in the year one thousand nine hundred and seventy-six.

Fait à Bruxelles, le vingt septembre mil neuf cent soixante-seize.

Arna dhéanamh sa Bhruiséil, an fichiú lá de mhí Mhéan Fómhair, míle naoi gcéad seachtó a sé.

Fatto a Bruxelles, addì venti settembre millenovecentosettantasei.

Gedaan te Brussel, de twintigste september negentienhonderdzesenze-ventig.

For Rådet for De europæiske Fællesskaber
Für den Rat der Europäischen Gemeinschaften
For the Council of the European Communities
Pour le Conseil des Communautés européennes
Thar céann Chomhairle na gComhphobal Eorpach
Per il Consiglio delle Comunità europee
Voor de Raad van de Europese Gemeenschappen

Formand
Der Präsident
The President
Le Président
An t-Uachtarán
Il Presidente
De Voorzitter
M. van der Stoel

Le ministre des affaires étrangères du royaume de Belgique
De Minister van Buitenlandse Zaken van het Koninkrijk België
R. van Elslande

Kongeriget Danmarks udenrigsøkonomiminister
Ivar Nørgaard

Der Bundesminister des Auswärtigen der Bundesrepublik Deutschland
Hans-Dietrich Genscher

Le ministre des affaires étrangères de la République française
Louis de Guiringaud

The Minister for Foreign Affairs of Ireland
Aire Gnóthaí Eachtracha na hÉireann
Gearóid Mac Gearailt

Il ministro degli Affari esteri della Repubblica italiana
Arnaldo Forlani

Membre du gouvernement du grand-duché de Luxembourg
Jean Hamilius

De Staatssecretaris van Buitenlandse Zaken van het Koninkrijk der
Nederlanden
L. J. Brinkhorst

The Secretary of State for Foreign and Commonwealth Affairs of the United Kingdom of Great Britain and Northern Ireland

A. CROSLAND

ACT

concerning the election of the representatives of the European Parliament
by direct universal suffrage

Article 1

The representatives in the European Parliament of the peoples of the States brought together in the Community shall be elected by direct universal suffrage.

Article 2*

The number of representatives elected in each Member State shall be as follows:

Belgium	24
Denmark	16
Germany	81
Greece	24
Spain	60
France	81
Ireland	15
Italy	81
Luxembourg	6
Netherlands	25
Portugal	24
United Kingdom	81

---

* Article as replaced by Article 10 of the Act of Accession ESP/PORT.

Article 3

1. Representatives shall be elected for a term of five years.

2. This five-year period shall begin at the opening of the first session following each election.

It may be extended or curtailed pursuant to the second subparagraph of Article 10 (2).

3. The term of office of each representative shall begin and end at the same time as the period referred to in paragraph 2.

Article 4

1. Representatives shall vote on an individual and personal basis. They shall not be bound by any instructions and shall not receive a binding mandate.

2. Representatives shall enjoy the privileges and immunities applicable to members of the European Parliament by virtue of the Protocol on the Privileges and Immunities of the European Communities annexed to the Treaty establishing a Single Council and a Single Commission of the European Communities.

Article 5

The office of representative in the European Parliament shall be compatible with membership of the Parliament of a Member State.

Article 6

1. The office of representative in the European Parliament shall be incompatible with that of:

— member of the Government of a Member State,

— member of the Commission of the European Communities,

— Judge, Advocate-General or Registrar of the Court of Justice of the European Communities,

— member of the Court of Auditors of the European Communities,

— member of the Consultative Committee of the European Coal and Steel Community or member of the Economic and Social Committee of the European Economic Community and of the European Atomic Energy Community,

— member of committees or other bodies set up pursuant to the Treaties establishing the European Coal and Steel Community, the European Economic Community and the European Atomic Energy Community for the purpose of managing the Communities' funds or carrying out a permanent direct administrative task,

— member of the Board of Directors, Management Committee or staff of the European Investment Bank,

— active official or servant of the institutions of the European Communities or of the specialized bodies attached to them.

2.   In addition, each Member State may, in the circumstances provided for in Article 7 (2), lay down rules at national level relating to incompatibility.

3.   Representatives in the European Parliament to whom paragraphs 1 and 2 become applicable in the course of the five-year period referred to in Article 3 shall be replaced in accordance with Article 12.

Article 7

1.   Pursuant to Article 21 (3) of the Treaty establishing the European Coal and Steel Community, Article 138 (3) of the Treaty establishing the European Economic Community and 108 (3) of the Treaty establishing

the European Atomic Energy Community, the European Parliament shall draw up a proposal for a uniform electoral procedure.

2.   Pending the entry into force of a uniform electoral procedure and subject to the other provisions of this Act, the electoral procedure shall be governed in each Member State by its national provisions.

Article 8

No one may vote more than once in any election of representatives to the European Parliament.

Article 9

1.   Elections to the European Parliament shall be held on the date fixed by each Member State; for all Member States this date shall fall within the same period starting on a Thursday morning and ending on the following Sunday.

2.   The counting of votes may not begin until after the close of polling in the Member State whose electors are the last to vote within the period referred to in paragraph 1.

3.   If a Member State adopts a double ballot system for elections to the European Parliament, the first ballot must take place during the period referred to in paragraph 1.

Article 10

1.   The Council, acting unanimously after consulting the European Parliament, shall determine the period referred to in Article 9 (1) for the first elections.

2. Subsequent elections shall take place in the corresponding period in the last year of the five-year period referred to in Article 3.

Should it prove impossible to hold the elections in the Community during that period, the Council acting unanimously shall, after consulting the European Parliament, determine another period which shall be not more than one month before or one month after the period fixed pursuant to the preceding subparagraph.

3. Without prejudice to Article 22 of the Treaty establishing the European Coal and Steel Community, Article 139 of the Treaty establishing the European Economic Community and Article 109 of the Treaty establishing the European Atomic Energy Community, the European Parliament shall meet, without requiring to be convened, on the first Tuesday after expiry of an interval of one month from the end of the period referred to in Article 9 (1).

4. The powers of the outgoing European Parliament shall cease upon the opening of the first sitting of the new European Parliament.

Article 11

Pending the entry into force of the uniform electoral procedure referred to in Article 7 (1), the European Parliament shall verify the credentials of representatives. For this purpose it shall take note of the results declared officially by the Member States and shall rule on any disputes which may arise out of the provisions of this Act other than those arising out of the national provisions to which the Act refers.

Article 12

1. Pending the entry into force of the uniform electoral procedure referred to in Article 7 (1) and subject to the other provisions of this Act, each Member State shall lay down appropriate procedures for filling any seat which falls vacant during the five-year term of office referred to in Article 3 for the remainder of that period.

2. Where a seat falls vacant pursuant to national provisions in force in a Member State, the latter shall inform the European Parliament, which shall take note of that fact.

In all other cases, the European Parliament shall establish that there is a vacancy and inform the Member State thereof.

Article 13

Should it appear necessary to adopt measures to implement this Act, the Council acting unanimously on a proposal from the European Parliament after consulting the Commission, shall adopt such measures after endeavouring to reach agreement with the European Parliament in a conciliation committee consisting of the Council and representatives of the European Parliament.

Article 14

Article 21 (1) and (2) of the Treaty establishing the European Coal and Steel Community, Article 138 (1) and (2) of the Treaty establishing the European Economic Community and Article 108 (1) and (2) of the Treaty establishing the European Atomic Energy Community shall lapse on the date of the sitting held in accordance with Article 10 (3) by the first European Parliament elected pursuant to this Act.

Article 15

This Act is drawn up in the Danish, Dutch, English, French, German, Irish and Italian languages, all the texts being equally authentic.

Annexes I to III shall form an integral part of this Act.

A declaration by the Government of the Federal Republic of Germany is attached hereto.

Article 16

The provisions of this Act shall enter into force on the first day of the month following that during which the last of the notifications referred to in the Decision is received.

Udfærdiget i Bruxelles den tyvende september nitten hundrede og seks-oghalvfjerds.

Geschehen zu Brüssel am zwanzigsten September neunzehnhundert-sechsundsiebzig.

Done at Brussels on the twentieth day of September in the year one thousand nine hundred and seventy-six.

Fait à Bruxelles, le vingt septembre mil neuf cent soixante-seize.

Arna dhéanamh sa Bhruiséil, an fichiú lá de mhí Mhéan Fómhair, míle naoi gcéad seachtó a sé.

Fatto a Bruxelles, addì venti settembre millenovecentosettantasei.

Gedaan te Brussel, de twintigste september negentienhonderdzesenze-
ventig.

R. VAN ELSLANDE

Ivar NØRGAARD

Hans-Dietrich GENSCHER

Louis DE GUIRINGAUD

Gearóid MAC GEARAILT

Arnaldo FORLANI

Jean HAMILIUS

L. J. BRINKHORST

A. CROSLAND

ANNEX I

The Danish authorities may decide on the dates on which the election of members to the European Parliament shall take place in Greenland.

ANNEX II

The United Kingdom will apply the provisions of this Act only in respect of the United Kingdom.

ANNEX III

DECLARATION ON ARTICLE 13

As regards the procedure to be followed by the Conciliation Committee, it is agreed to have recourse to the provisions of paragraphs 5, 6 and 7 of the procedure laid down in the Joint Declaration of the European Parliament, the Council and the Commission of 4 March 1975.* **

DECLARATION BY THE GOVERNMENT OF THE FEDERAL REPUBLIC OF GERMANY

The Government of the Federal Republic of Germany declares that the Act concerning the election of the members of the European Parliament by direct universal suffrage shall equally apply to *Land* Berlin.

---

* *Official Journal of the European Communities*, No C 89, 22 April 1975.
** This Joint Declaration is given on pp. 1095 to 1098 of this volume.

In consideration of the rights and responsibilities of France, the United Kingdom of Great Britain and Northern Ireland, and the United States of America, the Berlin House of Deputies will elect representatives to those seats within the quota of the Federal Republic of Germany that fall to *Land* Berlin.

VIII — DECISION OF THE REPRESENTATIVES OF THE GOVERNMENTS OF THE MEMBER STATES OF 5 APRIL 1977 ON THE PROVISIONAL LOCATION OF THE COURT OF AUDITORS

Official Journal of the European Communities, No L 104, 28 April 1977.

THE REPRESENTATIVES OF THE GOVERNMENTS OF THE MEMBER STATES,

HAVING regard to the Treaty establishing a Single Council and a Single Commission of the European Communities, and in particular Article 37 thereof,

HAVING regard to the Decision of the Representatives of the Governments of the Member States of 8 April 1965 on the provisional location of certain institutions and departments of the Communities,* and in particular Article 10 thereof,

HAVING regard to the opinion of the Commission,

WHEREAS, without prejudice to the application of Article 77 of the Treaty establishing the European Coal and Steel Community, of Article 216 of the Treaty establishing the European Economic Community, and of Article 189 of the Treaty establishing the European Atomic Energy Community, it is necessary to make arrangements for the provisional place of work of the Court of Auditors, set up by the Treaty of 22 July 1975, amending certain financial provisions of the Treaties establishing the European Communities and of the Treaty establishing a Single Council and a Single Commission of the European Communities,

HAVE DECIDED:

Article 1

The Court of Auditors shall be located at Luxembourg which shall be the provisional place of work within the meaning of the Decision of the

---

* See ante at point III, p. 875.

Representatives of the Governments of the Member States of 8 April 1965 on the provisional location of certain institutions and departments of the Communities.

Article 2

This Decision shall enter into force on the same date as the Treaty of 22 July 1975 amending certain financial provisions of the Treaties establishing the European Communities and the Treaty establishing a Single Council and a Single Commission of the European Communities.

Done at Luxembourg, 5 April 1977.

The President

D. Owen

IX — TREATY
AMENDING, WITH REGARD TO GREENLAND, THE TREATIES ESTABLISHING THE EUROPEAN COMMUNITIES

Official Journal of the European Communities, No L 29, 1 February 1985.

1. Text of the Treaty

HIS MAJESTY THE KING OF THE BELGIANS, HER MAJESTY THE QUEEN OF DENMARK, THE PRESIDENT OF THE FEDERAL REPUBLIC OF GERMANY, THE PRESIDENT OF THE HELLENIC REPUBLIC, THE PRESIDENT OF THE FRENCH REPUBLIC, THE PRESIDENT OF IRELAND, THE PRESIDENT OF THE ITALIAN REPUBLIC, HIS ROYAL HIGHNESS THE GRAND DUKE OF LUXEMBOURG, HER MAJESTY THE QUEEN OF THE NETHERLANDS, HER MAJESTY THE QUEEN OF THE UNITED KINGDOM OF GREAT BRITAIN AND NORTHERN IRELAND,

HAVING REGARD to Article 96 of the Treaty establishing the European Coal and Steel Community,

HAVING REGARD to Article 236 of the Treaty establishing the European Economic Community,

HAVING REGARD to Article 204 of the Treaty establishing the European Atomic Energy Community,

WHEREAS the Government of the Kingdom of Denmark has submitted a proposal to the Council for the purpose of revising the Treaties establishing the European Communities so that they cease to apply to Greenland and introducing new arrangements governing relations between the Communities and Greenland;

WHEREAS, in view of the special features of Greenland, this proposal should be accepted by arrangements being introduced which permit close and lasting links between the Community and Greenland to be maintained and mutual interests, notably the development needs of Greenland, to be taken into account;

WHEREAS the arrangements applicable to overseas countries and territories set out in Part Four of the Treaty establishing the European Economic Community provide an appropriate framework for these relations, although additional specific provisions are needed to cater for Greenland,

HAVE DECIDED to determine by common agreement new arrangements applicable to Greenland and have, to this end, designated as their Plenipotentiaries;

HIS MAJESTY THE KING OF THE BELGIANS:

Leo TINDEMANS, Minister for External Relations of the Kingdom of Belgium;

HER MAJESTY THE QUEEN OF DENMARK:

Uffe ELLEMAN-JENSEN, Minister for Foreign Affairs of Denmark;

Gunnar RIBERHOLDT, Ambassador Extraordinary and Plenipotentiary, Permanent Representative of Denmark;

THE PRESIDENT OF THE FEDERAL REPUBLIC OF GERMANY:

Hans-Dietrich GENSCHER, Minister for Foreign Affairs of the Federal Republic of Germany;

THE PRESIDENT OF THE HELLENIC REPUBLIC:

Theodoros PANGALOS, Secretary of State for Foreign Affairs of the Hellenic Republic;

THE PRESIDENT OF THE FRENCH REPUBLIC:

Roland DUMAS, Minister for European Affairs of the French Republic;

THE PRESIDENT OF IRELAND:

Peter BARRY, Minister for Foreign Affairs of Ireland;

THE PRESIDENT OF THE ITALIAN REPUBLIC:

Giulio ANDREOTTI, Minister for Foreign Affairs of the Italian Republic;

HIS ROYAL HIGHNESS THE GRAND DUKE OF LUXEMBOURG:

Colette FLESCH, Minister for Foreign Affairs of the Government of the Grand Duchy of Luxembourg;

HER MAJESTY THE QUEEN OF THE NETHERLANDS:

W. F. VAN EEKELEN, Secretary of State for Foreign Affairs of the Netherlands;
H. J. Ch. RUTTEN, Ambassador Extraordinary and Plenipotentiary, Permanent Representative of the Netherlands;

HER MAJESTY THE QUEEN OF THE UNITED KINGDOM OF GREAT BRITAIN AND NORTHERN IRELAND:

The Right Honourable Sir Geoffrey HOWE, QC, MP, Secretary of State for Foreign and Commonwealth Affairs;

WHO, having exchanged their full powers, found in good and due form,

HAVE AGREED as follows:

Article 1

The following subparagraph shall be added to point *(a)* of the second paragraph of Article 79 of the Treaty establishing the European Coal and Steel Community:

'This Treaty shall not apply to Greenland.'

Article 2

Denmark shall be added to the Member States specified in the first sentence of the first paragraph of Article 131 of the Treaty establishing the European Economic Community.

Article 3

1. The following Article 136a shall be added to Part Four of the Treaty establishing the European Economic Community:

'*Article 136a*

The provisions of Articles 131 to 136 shall apply to Greenland, subject to the specific provisions for Greenland set out in the Protocol on special arrangements for Greenland, annexed to this Treaty.'

2. The Protocol on special arrangements for Greenland attached to this Treaty shall be annexed to the Treaty establishing the European Economic Community. Protocol 4 on Greenland, annexed to the Act of Accession of 22 January 1972, is hereby repealed.

Article 4

Greenland shall be added to the list in Annex IV to the Treaty establishing the European Economic Community.

Article 5

The following subparagraph shall be added to point *(a)* of the third paragraph of Article 198 of the Treaty establishing the European Atomic Energy Community:

'This Treaty shall not apply to Greenland.'

Article 6

1. This Treaty shall be ratified by the High Contracting Parties in accordance with their respective constitutional requirements. The instruments of ratification shall be deposited with the Government of the Italian Republic.

2. This Treaty shall enter into force on 1 January 1985. If all the instruments of ratification have not been deposited by that date, this Treaty shall enter into force on the first day of the month following the deposit of the instrument of ratification by the last Signatory State to take this step.

Article 7

This Treaty, drawn up in a single original in the Danish, Dutch, English, French, German, Greek, Irish, and Italian languages, all eight texts being equally authentic, shall be deposited in the archives of the Government of the Italian Republic, which shall transmit a certified copy to each of the Governments of the other Signatory States.

TIL BEKRÆFTELSE HERAF har undertegnede befuldmægtigede underskrevet denne Traktat.

ZU URKUND DESSEN haben die unterzeichneten Bevollmächtigten ihre Unterschriften unter diesen Vertrag gesetzt.

ΣΕ πίστωση των ανωτέρω οι υπογεγραμμένοι πληρεξούσιοι υπέγραψαν την παρούσα συνθήκη.

IN WITNESS WHEREOF, the undersigned Plenipotentiaries have affixed their signatures below this Treaty.

EN FOI DE QUOI, les plénipotentiaires soussignés ont apposé leur signature au bas du présent traité.

DÁ FHIANÚ SIN, chuir na Lánchumhachtaigh thíos-sínithe a lámh leis an gConradh seo.

IN FEDE DI CHE, i plenipotenziari sottoscritti hanno apposto le loro firme in calce al presente trattato.

TEN BLIJKE WAARVAN de ondergetekende gevolmachtigden hun handtekening onder dit Verdrag hebben gesteld.

Udfærdiget i Bruxelles, den trettende marts nitten hundrede og fireogfirs.

Geschehen zu Brüssel am dreizehnten März neunzehnhundertvierundachtzig.

Έγινε στις Βρυξέλλες στις δεκατρείς Μαρτίου χίλια εννιακόσια ογδόντα τέσσερα.

Done at Brussels on the thirteenth day of March in the year one thousand nine hundred and eighty-four.

Fait à Bruxelles, le treize mars mil neuf cent quatre-vingt-quatre.

Arna dhéanamh sa Bruiséil an tríú lá déag de mhí Márta sa bhliain míle naoi gcéad ochtó a ceathair.

988

Fatto a Bruxelles, addì tredici marzo millenovecentottantaquattro.

Gedaan te Brussel, de dertiende maart negentienhonderdvierentachtig.

L. TINDEMANS

U. ELLEMANN-JENSEN

H.-D. GENSCHER

T. PANGALOS

R. DUMAS

P. BARRY

G. ANDREOTTI

C. FLESCH

W. F. van EEKELEN

Sir G. HOWE QC, MP.

2. Protocol
on special arrangements
for Greenland

Article 1

1. The treatment on import into the Community of products subject to the common organization of the market in fishery products, originating in Greenland, shall, while complying with the mechanisms of the common market organization, involve exemption from customs duties and charges having equivalent effect and the absence of quantitative restrictions or measures having equivalent effect if the possibilities for access to Greenland fishing zones granted to the Community pursuant to an agreement between the Community and the authority responsible for Greenland are satisfactory to the Community.

2. All measures relating to the import arrangements for such products, including those relating to the adoption of such measures, shall be adopted in accordance with the procedure laid down in Article 43 of the Treaty establishing the European Economic Community.

Article 2

The Commission shall make proposals to the Council, which shall act by a qualified majority, for the transitional measures which it considers necessary, by reason of the entry into force of the new arrangements, with regard to the maintenance of rights acquired by natural or legal persons during the period when Greenland was part of the Community and the regularization of the situation with regard to financial assistance granted by the Community to Greenland during that period.

Article 3

The following text shall be added to Annex I to the Council Decision of 16 December 1980 on the association of the overseas countries and territories with the European Economic Community:

'6. Distinct community of the Kingdom of Denmark:

— Greenland.'

X — COUNCIL DECISION
OF 7 MAY 1985
ON THE COMMUNITIES' SYSTEM OF OWN RESOURCES*

Official Journal of the European Communities, No L 128, 14 May 1985

* EDITORIAL NOTES:
  This Decision repealed the Decision of 21 April 1970 on the replacement of financial contributions from Member States by the Communities' own resources (*Official Journal of the European Communities*, No L 94, 28 April 1970).
  The declaration recorded in the Council minutes and adopted on 7 May 1985 is reproduced on page 1111 of this volume.

THE COUNCIL OF THE EUROPEAN COMMUNITIES,

HAVING REGARD to the Treaty establishing the European Economic Community, and in particular Article 201 thereof,

HAVING REGARD to the Treaty establishing the European Atomic Energy Community, and in particular Article 173 thereof,

HAVING REGARD to the proposal from the Commission,

HAVING REGARD to the opinion of the European Parliament,

HAVING REGARD to the opinion of the Economic and Social Committee,

WHEREAS the Decision of 21 April 1970 on the replacement of financial contributions from Member States by the Communities' own resources, hereinafter referred to as 'the Decision of 21 April 1970', introduced a Community system of own resources;

WHEREAS, in order to augment own resources, while retaining the existing sources of revenue introduced by the Decision of 21 April 1970, the 1 % limit to the rate applied to the uniform basis for assessing value-added tax should be increased;

WHEREAS the European Council which met in Fontainebleau on 25 and 26 June 1984 reached certain conclusions;

WHEREAS, by the terms of those conclusions, the maximum rate of mobilization of value-added tax own resources will be 1.4 % on 1 January 1986; whereas this maximum rate applies to every Member State and will enter into force as soon as the ratification procedures are completed and

997

by 1 January 1986 at the latest; whereas the maximum rate may be increased to 1.6 % on 1 January 1988 by unanimous decision of the Council and after agreement has been given in accordance with national procedures;

WHEREAS, in those same conclusions, the European Council considered that expenditure policy is ultimately the essential means of resolving the question of budgetary imbalances;

WHEREAS, however, the European Council decided that any Member State bearing an excessive budgetary burden in relation to its relative prosperity may benefit at the appropriate time from a correction;

WHEREAS such a correction must now be applied to the United Kingdom,

HAS LAID DOWN these provisions, which it recommends to the Member States for adoption:

Article 1

The Communities shall be allocated resources of their own in accordance with the following Articles in order to ensure that their budget is in balance.

The budget of the Communities shall, irrespective of other revenue, be financed entirely from the Communities' own resources.

Article 2

Revenue from:

(a) levies, premiums, additional or compensatory amounts, additional amounts or factors and other duties established or to be established by the

institutions of the Communities in respect of trade with non-member countries within the framework of the common agricultural policy, and also contributions and other duties provided for within the framework of the common organization of the markets in sugar;

(b) Common Customs Tariff duties and other duties established or to be established by the institutions of the Communities in respect of trade with non-member countries,

shall constitute own resources entered in the budget of the Communities.

In addition, revenue accruing from other charges introduced within the framework of a common policy in accordance with the Treaty establishing the European Economic Community or the Treaty establishing the European Atomic Energy Community shall constitute own resources entered in the budget of the Communities, subject to the procedure laid down in Article 201 of the Treaty establishing the European Economic Community or in Article 173 of the Treaty establishing the European Atomic Energy Community having been followed.

Article 3

1. Own resources shall also include revenue accruing, in accordance with this Article, from the application of rates to the assessment basis for value-added tax which is determined in a uniform manner for Member States according to Community rules.

2. None of the rates referred to in paragraph 1 shall exceed 1.4 %. The rates shall be fixed, taking into account all other revenue, within the framework of the budgetary procedure.

3. The rates shall be calculated as follows:

  (a) a uniform rate shall be determined in relation to the assessment basis referred to in paragraph *1*;

  (b) as regards the rate to be applied to the United Kingdom, a deduction shall be made from the amount payable under the uniform rate by:

  (i) calculating the difference, in the preceding budgetary year, between the percentage share of the United Kingdom in the value-added tax which would have been paid in that year, including adjustments in respect of previous years, had the uniform rate been applied, and the percentage share of the United Kingdom in total allocated expenditure;

  (ii) applying the difference thus obtained to total allocated expenditure;

  (iii) multiplying the result by 0.66.

  The reduced amount shall be divided by the assessment basis of the United Kingdom;

  (c) as regards the rates to be applied to the other Member States, a sum equivalent to the deduction referred to in *(b)* shall be borne by them. The allocation of this sum shall first be calculated according to their respective shares in value-added tax payments payable under the uniform rate, the United Kingdom being excluded; it shall subsequently be adjusted so as to limit the participation of the Federal Republic of Germany to two-thirds of the share produced by that calculation.

  The rates to be applied to these Member States shall be obtained by dividing the total obtained by adding together the amounts payable under the uniform rate and their shares in the additional sum by the assessment basis of each Member State;

(d) where paragraph *7* applies, financial contributions shall be substituted for payments of value-added tax in the calculations referred to in this paragraph for any Member State concerned.

4. On the entry into force of this paragraph, and by way of derogation from the Decision of 21 April 1970, a lump-sum deduction of 1 000 million ECU shall be made from the amount of value-added tax payable by the United Kingdom. A sum equivalent to the deduction shall be borne by the other Member States, being allocated in accordance with paragraph *3 (c)*.

The operations referred to in the preceding subparagraph shall constitute modifications to own resources accruing from value-added tax in respect of the financial year 1985. If necessary, the corresponding amounts shall be entered in the accounts for the financial year 1985 by the Commission.

5. The Commission shall carry out the calculations necessary for the application of paragraphs *3* and *4.*

6. If, at the beginning of the financial year, the budget has not been adopted, the rates of value-added tax previously fixed shall remain applicable until the entry into force of new rates.

7. By way of derogation from paragraph *1,* if, on 1 January of the financial year in question, the rules determining the uniform basis for assessing value-added tax have not yet been applied in all Member States, the financial contribution to the budget of the Communities to be made by a Member State not yet applying this uniform basis shall be determined according to the proportion of its gross national product to the sum total of the gross national products of the Member States. The balance of the budget shall be covered by revenue accruing from value-added tax in accordance with

paragraph *1* and collected by the other Member States. This derogation shall cease to have effect as soon as the rules for determining the uniform basis for assessing value-added tax are applied in all Member States.

8. For the purpose of paragraph *7,* 'gross national product' shall mean gross national product at market prices.

Article 4

1. The revenue referred to in Articles 2 and 3 shall be used without distinction to finance all expenditure entered in the budget of the Communities.

2. Financing from the Communities' own resources of the expenditure connected with research programmes of the European Communities shall exclude neither entry in the budget of the Communities of expenditure relating to supplementary programmes nor the financing of this expenditure by means of financial contributions from Member States, the level and scale of funding of which will be fixed pursuant to a decision of the Council, acting by a qualified majority after obtaining the agreement of the Member States concerned.*

Article 5

The Communities shall refund to each Member State 10 % of the amounts paid in accordance with the first paragraph of Article 2 in order to cover expense incurred in collection.

---

* Last part of the sentence amended by Article 29 of the SEA — see pages 1005 *et seq.* of this volume.

Article 6

Any surplus of the Communities' own resources over and above the actual expenditure during a financial year shall be carried over to the following financial year.

Article 7

1. The Community resources referred to in Articles 2 and 3 shall be collected by the Member States in accordance with national provisions imposed by law, regulation or administrative action, which shall, where necessary, be amended for that purpose. Member States shall make these resources available to the Commission.

2. Without prejudice to the auditing of accounts provided for in Article 206a of the Treaty establishing the European Economic Community, or to the inspection arrangements made pursuant to Article 209 *(c)* of that Treaty, the Council shall, acting unanimously on a proposal from the Commission and after consulting the European Parliament, adopt provisions relating to the supervision of collection, the making available to the Commission, and the payment of the revenue referred to in Articles 2 and 3.

Article 8

Member States shall be notified of this Decision by the Secretary-General of the Council of the European Communities; it shall be published in the *Official Journal of the European Communities.*

Member States shall notify the Secretary-General of the Council of the European Communities without delay of the completion of the procedures for the adoption of this Decision in accordance with their respective constitutional requirements.

This Decision shall enter into force:

— as regards the provisions of Article 3 (4), on the second day after receipt of the last of the notifications referred to in the second paragraph;

— as regards its other provisions, on the second day after receipt of the last such notification or after the deposit, by the present Member States of the Communities, of the last of the instruments of ratification of the Treaties of Accession of Spain and Portugal, whichever occurs later, unless the Council, acting unanimously, decides otherwise.

Without prejudice to Article 3 (4), this Decision shall enter into effect on 1 January 1986 and the Decision of 21 April 1970 shall be repealed on the same date. To the extent necessary, any reference to the Decision of 21 April 1970 shall be understood as referring to this Decision.

Done at Brussels, 7 May 1985.

For the Council
The President
G. ANDREOTTI

XI — SINGLE EUROPEAN ACT

Official Journal of the European Communities, No L 169, 29 June 1987.

1. Text of the Treaty

His Majesty the King of the Belgians, Her Majesty the Queen of Denmark, the President of the Federal Republic of Germany, the President of the Hellenic Republic, His Majesty the King of Spain, the President of the French Republic, the President of Ireland, the President of the Italian Republic, His Royal Highness the Grand Duke of Luxembourg, Her Majesty the Queen of the Netherlands, the President of the Portuguese Republic, Her Majesty the Queen of the United Kingdom of Great Britain and Northern Ireland,

Moved by the will to continue the work undertaken on the basis of the Treaties establishing the European Communities and to transform relations as a whole among their States into a European Union, in accordance with the Solemn Declaration of Stuttgart of 19 June 1983,

Resolved to implement this European Union on the basis, firstly, of the Communities operating in accordance with their own rules and, secondly, of European Cooperation among the Signatory States in the sphere of foreign policy and to invest this union with the necessary means of action,

Determined to work together to promote democracy on the basis of the fundamental rights recognized in the constitutions and laws of the Member States, in the Convention for the Protection of Human Rights and Fundamental Freedoms and the European Social Charter, notably freedom, equality and social justice,

Convinced that the European idea, the results achieved in the fields of economic integration and political cooperation, and the need for new developments correspond to the wishes of the democratic peoples of Europe, for whom the European Parliament, elected by universal suffrage, is an indispensable means of expression,

AWARE of the responsibility incumbent upon Europe to aim at speaking ever increasingly with one voice and to act with consistency and solidarity in order more effectively to protect its common interests and independence, in particular to display the principles of democracy and compliance with the law and with human rights to which they are attached, so that together they may make their own contribution to the preservation of international peace and security in accordance with the undertaking entered into by them within the framework of the United Nations Charter,

DETERMINED to improve the economic and social situation by extending common policies and pursuing new objectives, and to ensure a smoother functioning of the Communities by enabling the institutions to exercise their powers under conditions most in keeping with Community interests,

WHEREAS at their Conference in Paris from 19 to 21 October 1972 the Heads of State or of Government approved the objective of the progressive realization of Economic and Monetary Union,

HAVING REGARD to the Annex to the conclusions of the Presidency of the European Council in Bremen on 6 and 7 July 1978 and the Resolution of the European Council in Brussels on 5 December 1978 on the introduction of the European Monetary System (EMS) and related questions, and noting that in accordance with that Resolution, the Community and the Central Banks of the Member States have taken a number of measures intended to implement monetary cooperation,

HAVE DECIDED to adopt this Act and to this end have designated as their plenipotentiaries:

HIS MAJESTY THE KING OF THE BELGIANS:

Mr Leo TINDEMANS, Minister for External Relations;

HER MAJESTY THE QUEEN OF DENMARK:
Mr Uffe ELLEMANN-JENSEN, Minister for Foreign Affairs;

THE PRESIDENT OF THE FEDERAL REPUBLIC OF GERMANY:
Mr Hans-Dietrich GENSCHER, Federal Minister for Foreign Affairs;

THE PRESIDENT OF THE HELLENIC REPUBLIC:
Mr Karolos PAPOULIAS, Minister for Foreign Affairs;

HIS MAJESTY THE KING OF SPAIN:
Mr Francisco FERNÁNDEZ ORDÓÑEZ, Minister for Foreign Affairs;

THE PRESIDENT OF THE FRENCH REPUBLIC:
Mr Roland DUMAS, Minister for External Relations;

THE PRESIDENT OF IRELAND:
Mr Peter BARRY, T D, Minister for Foreign Affairs;

THE PRESIDENT OF THE ITALIAN REPUBLIC:
Mr Giulio ANDREOTTI, Minister for Foreign Affairs;

HIS ROYAL HIGHNESS THE GRAND DUKE OF LUXEMBOURG:
Mr Robert GOEBBELS, State Secretary, Minister for Foreign Affairs;

HER MAJESTY THE QUEEN OF THE NETHERLANDS:
Mr Hans VAN DEN BROEK, Minister for Foreign Affairs;

THE PRESIDENT OF THE PORTUGUESE REPUBLIC:
Mr Pedro PIRES DE MIRANDA, Minister for Foreign Affairs;

HER MAJESTY THE QUEEN OF THE UNITED KINGDOM OF GREAT BRITAIN AND NORTHERN IRELAND:

Mrs Lynda CHALKER, Minister of State for Foreign and Commonwealth Affairs;

WHO, having exchanged their full powers, found in good and due form, have agreed as follows.

TITLE I

Common provisions

Article 1

The European Communities and European Political Cooperation shall have as their objective to contribute together to making concrete progress towards European unity.

The European Communities shall be founded on the Treaties establishing the European Coal and Steel Community, the European Economic Community, the European Atomic Energy Community and on the subsequent Treaties and Acts modifying or supplementing them.

Political Cooperation shall be governed by Title III. The provisions of that Title shall confirm and supplement the procedures agreed in the reports of Luxembourg (1970), Copenhagen (1973), London (1981), the Solemn Declaration on European Union (1983) and the practices gradually established among the Member States.

Article 2

The European Council shall bring together the Heads of State or of Government of the Member States and the President of the Commission of the European Communities. They shall be assisted by the Ministers for Foreign Affairs and by a Member of the Commission.

The European Council shall meet at least twice a year.

Article 3

1. The institutions of the European Communities, henceforth designated as referred to hereafter, shall exercise their powers and jurisdiction under

the conditions and for the purposes provided for by the Treaties establishing the Communities and by the subsequent Treaties and Acts modifying or supplementing them and by the provisions of Title II.

2. The institutions and bodies responsible for European Political Cooperation shall exercise their powers and jurisdiction under the conditions and for the purposes laid down in Title III and in the documents referred to in the third paragraph of Article 1.

TITLE II

Provisions amending the Treaties establishing the European Communities

CHAPTER I

PROVISIONS AMENDING THE TREATY ESTABLISHING THE EUROPEAN COAL AND STEEL COMMUNITY

Article 4

The ECSC Treaty shall be supplemented by the following provisions:

'Article 32 d

1.   *At the request of the Court of Justice and after consulting the Commission and the European Parliament, the Council may, acting unanimously, attach to the Court of Justice a court with jurisdiction to hear and determine at first instance, subject to a right of appeal to the Court of Justice on points of law only and in accordance with the conditions laid down by the Statute, certain classes of action or proceeding brought by natural or legal persons. That court shall not be competent to hear and determine actions brought by Member States or by Community institutions or questions referred for a preliminary ruling under Article 41.*

2.   *The Council, following the procedure laid down in paragraph 1, shall determine the composition of that court and adopt the necessary adjustments and additional provisions to the Statute of the Court of Justice. Unless the Council decides otherwise, the provisions of this Treaty relating to the Court of Justice, in particular the provisions of the Protocol on the Statute of the Court of Justice, shall apply to that court.*

3.   The members of that court shall be chosen from persons whose independence is beyond doubt and who possess the ability required for appointment to judicial office; they shall be appointed by common accord of the Governments of the Member States for a term of six years. The membership shall be partially renewed every three years. Retiring members shall be eligible for re-appointment.

4.   That court shall establish its rules of procedure in agreement with the Court of Justice. Those rules shall require the unanimous approval of the Council.'

Article 5

Article 45 of the ECSC Treaty shall be supplemented by the following paragraph:

'The Council may, acting unanimously at the request of the Court of Justice and after consulting the Commission and the European Parliament, amend the provisions of Title III of the Statute.'

CHAPTER II

PROVISIONS AMENDING THE TREATY ESTABLISHING THE EUROPEAN ECONOMIC COMMUNITY

Section I

Institutional provisions

Article 6

1.   A cooperation procedure shall be introduced which shall apply to acts based on Articles 7, 49, 54 (2), 56 (2), second sentence, 57 with the exception of the second sentence of paragraph 2 thereof, 100a, 100b, 118a, 130e and 130q (2) of the EEC Treaty.

2.   In Article 7, second paragraph of the EEC Treaty the terms *'after consulting the Assembly'* shall be replaced by *'in cooperation with the European Parliament'*.

3.   In Article 49 of the EEC Treaty the terms *'the Council shall, acting on a proposal from the Commission and after consulting the Economic and Social Committee'* shall be replaced by *'the Council shall, acting by a qualified majority on a proposal from the Commission, in cooperation with the European Parliament and after consulting the Economic and Social Committee'*.

4.   In Article 54 (2) of the EEC Treaty the terms *'the Council shall, on a proposal from the Commission and after consulting the Economic and Social Committee and the Assembly'* shall be replaced by *'the Council shall, acting on a proposal from the Commission, in cooperation with the European Parliament and after consulting the Economic and Social Committee'*.

5.   In Article 56 (2) of the EEC Treaty the second sentence shall be replaced by the following:

'After the end of the second stage, however, the Council shall, acting by a qualified majority on a proposal from the Commission and in cooperation with the European Parliament, issue directives for the coordination of such provisions as, in each Member State, are a matter for regulation or administrative action.'

6.   In Article 57 (1) of the EEC Treaty the terms *'and after consulting the Assembly'* shall be replaced by *'and in cooperation with the European Parliament'*.

7.   In Article 57 (2) of the EEC Treaty, the third sentence shall be replaced by the following:

'In other cases the Council shall act by a qualified majority, in cooperation with the European Parliament.'

Article 7

Article 149 of the EEC Treaty shall be replaced by the following provisions:

'Article 149

1.   *Where, in pursuance of this Treaty, the Council acts on a proposal from the Commission, unanimity shall be required for an act constituting an amendment to that proposal.*

2.   *Where, in pursuance of this Treaty, the Council acts in cooperation with the European Parliament, the following procedure shall apply:*

(a) *The Council, acting by a qualified majority under the conditions of paragraph 1, on a proposal from the Commission and after obtaining the Opinion of the European Parliament, shall adopt a common position.*

(b) *The Council's common position shall be communicated to the European Parliament. The Council and the Commission shall inform the European Parliament fully of the reasons which led the Council to adopt its common position and also of the Commission's position.*

   If, within three months of such communication, the European Parliament approves this common position or has not taken a decision within that period, the Council shall definitively adopt the act in question in accordance with the common position.

(c) *The European Parliament may within the period of three months referred to in point (b), by an absolute majority of its component members, propose amendments to the Council's common position. The European Parliament may also, by the same majority, reject the Council's common position. The result of the proceedings shall be transmitted to the Council and the Commission.*

If the European Parliament has rejected the Council's common position, unanimity shall be required for the Council to act on a second reading.

(d) The Commission shall, within a period of one month, re-examine the proposal on the basis of which the Council adopted its common position, by taking into account the amendments proposed by the European Parliament.

The Commission shall forward to the Council, at the same time as its re-examined proposal, the amendments of the European Parliament which it has not accepted, and shall express its opinion on them. The Council may adopt these amendments unanimously.

(e) The Council, acting by a qualified majority, shall adopt the proposal as re-examined by the Commission.

Unanimity shall be required for the Council to amend the proposal as re-examined by the Commission.

(f) In the cases referred to in points (c), (d) and (e), the Council shall be required to act within a period of three months. If no decision is taken within this period, the Commission proposal shall be deemed not to have been adopted.

(g) The periods referred to in points (b) and (f) may be extended by a maximum of one month by common accord between the Council and the European Parliament.

3. As long as the Council has not acted, the Commission may alter its proposal at any time during the procedures mentioned in paragraphs 1 and 2.'

Article 8

The first paragraph of Article 237 of the EEC Treaty shall be replaced by the following provision:

'Any European State may apply to become a member of the Community. It shall address its application to the Council, which shall act unanimously

after consulting the Commission and after receiving the assent of the Euro-
pean Parliament which shall act by an absolute majority of its component
members.'

Article 9

The second paragraph of Article 238 of the EEC Treaty shall be replaced by the following provision:

'These agreements shall be concluded by the Council, acting unanimously
and after receiving the assent of the European Parliament which shall act by
an absolute majority of its component members.'

Article 10

Article 145 of the EEC Treaty shall be supplemented by the following
provision:

'— confer on the Commission, in the acts which the Council adopts, pow-
ers for the implementation of the rules which the Council lays down. The
Council may impose certain requirements in respect of the exercise of these
powers. The Council may also reserve the right, in specific cases, to exercise
directly implementing powers itself. The procedures referred to above must be
consonant with principles and rules to be laid down in advance by the Coun-
cil, acting unanimously on a proposal from the Commission and after obtain-
ing the Opinion of the European Parliament.'

Article 11

The EEC Treaty shall be supplemented by the following provisions:

' Article 168a

1.   *At the request of the Court of Justice and after consulting the Commis-*
sion and the European Parliament, the Council may, acting unanimously, at-

tach to the Court of Justice a court with jurisdiction to hear and determine at first instance, subject to a right of appeal to the Court of Justice on points of law only and in accordance with the conditions laid down by the Statute, certain classes of action or proceeding brought by natural or legal persons. That court shall not be competent to hear and determine actions brought by Member States or by Community institutions or questions referred for a preliminary ruling under Article 177.

2. The Council, following the procedure laid down in paragraph 1, shall determine the composition of that court and adopt the necessary adjustments and additional provisions to the Statute of the Court of Justice. Unless the Council decides otherwise, the provisions of this Treaty relating to the Court of Justice, in particular the provisions of the Protocol on the Statute of the Court of Justice, shall apply to that court.

3. The members of that court shall be chosen from persons whose independence is beyond doubt and who possess the ability required for appointment to judicial office; they shall be appointed by common accord of the Governments of the Member States for a term of six years. The membership shall be partially renewed every three years. Retiring members shall be eligible for reappointment.

4. That court shall establish its rules of procedure in agreement with the Court of Justice. Those rules shall require the unanimous approval of the Council.'

Article 12

A second paragraph worded as follows shall be inserted in Article 188 of the EEC Treaty:

'The Council may, acting unanimously at the request of the Court of Justice and after consulting the Commission and the European Parliament, amend the provisions of Title III of the Statute.'

Section II

Provisions relating to the foundations and the policy of the Community

Subsection I — Internal market

Article 13

The EEC Treaty shall be supplemented by the following provisions:

'Article 8a

The Community shall adopt measures with the aim of progressively establishing the internal market over a period expiring on 31 December 1992, in accordance with the provisions of this Article and of Articles 8b, 8c, 28, 57 (2), 59, 70 (1), 84, 99, 100a and 100b and without prejudice to the other provisions of this Treaty.

The internal market shall comprise an area without internal frontiers in which the free movement of goods, persons, services and capital is ensured in accordance with the provisions of this Treaty.'

Article 14

The EEC Treaty shall be supplemented by the following provisions:

'Article 8b

The Commission shall report to the Council before 31 December 1988 and again before 31 December 1990 on the progress made towards achieving the internal market within the time limit fixed in Article 8a.

The Council, acting by a qualified majority on a proposal from the Commission, shall determine the guidelines and conditions necessary to ensure balanced progress in all the sectors concerned.'

Article 15

The EEC Treaty shall be supplemented by the following provisions:

'Article 8c

When drawing up its proposals with a view to achieving the objectives set out in Article 8a, the Commission shall take into account the extent of the effort that certain economies showing differences in development will have to sustain during the period of establishment of the internal market and it may propose appropriate provisions.

If these provisions take the form of derogations, they must be of a temporary nature and must cause the least possible disturbance to the functioning of the common market.'

Article 16

1. Article 28 of the EEC Treaty shall be replaced by the following provisions:

'Article 28

Any autonomous alteration or suspension of duties in the common customs tariff shall be decided by the Council acting by a qualified majority on a proposal from the Commission.'

2. In Article 57 (2) of the EEC Treaty, the second sentence shall be replaced by the following:

'Unanimity shall be required for directives the implementation of which involves in at least one Member State amendment of the existing principles laid

down by law governing the professions with respect to training and conditions of access for natural persons.'

3.   In the second paragraph of Article 59 of the EEC Treaty, the term *'unanimously'* shall be replaced by *'by a qualified majority'*.

4.   In Article 70 (1) of the EEC Treaty, the last two sentences shall be replaced by the following:

   'For this purpose the Council shall issue directives, acting by a qualified majority. It shall endeavour to attain the highest possible degree of liberalization. Unanimity shall be required for measures which constitute a step back as regards the liberalization of capital movements.'

5.   In Article 84 (2) of the EEC Treaty, the term *'unanimously'* shall be replaced by *'by a qualified majority'*.

6.   Article 84 of the EEC Treaty shall be supplemented by the following paragraph:

   'The procedural provisions of Article 75 (1) and (3) shall apply.'

Article 17

   Article 99 of the EEC Treaty shall be replaced by the following provisions:

'Article 99

   The Council shall, acting unanimously on a proposal from the Commission and after consulting the European Parliament, adopt provisions for the harmonization of legislation concerning turnover taxes, excise duties and other forms of indirect taxation to the extent that such harmonization is necessary to ensure the establishment and the functioning of the internal market within the time-limit laid down in Article 8a.'

Article 18

The EEC Treaty shall be supplemented by the following provisions:

'Article 100a

1.   *By way of derogation from Article 100 and save where otherwise provided in this Treaty, the following provisions shall apply for the achievement of the objectives set out in Article 8a. The Council shall, acting by a qualified majority on a proposal from the Commission in cooperation with the European Parliament and after consulting the Economic and Social Committee, adopt the measures for the approximation of the provisions laid down by law, regulation or administrative action in Member States which have as their object the establishment and functioning of the internal market.*

2.   *Paragraph 1 shall not apply to fiscal provisions, to those relating to the free movement of persons nor to those relating to the rights and interests of employed persons.*

3.   *The Commission, in its proposals envisaged in paragraph 1 concerning health, safety, environmental protection and consumer protection, will take as a base a high level of protection.*

4.   *If, after the adoption of a harmonization measure by the Council acting by a qualified majority, a Member State deems it necessary to apply national provisions on grounds of major needs referred to in Article 36, or relating to*

protection of the environment or the working environment, it shall notify the Commission of these provisions.

The Commission shall confirm the provisions involved after having verified that they are not a means of arbitrary discrimination or a disguised restriction on trade between Member States.

By way of derogation from the procedure laid down in Articles 169 and 170, the Commission or any Member State may bring the matter directly before the Court of Justice if it considers that another Member State is making improper use of the powers provided for in this Article.

5. *The harmonization measures referred to above shall, in appropriate cases, include a safeguard clause authorizing the Member States to take, for one or more of the non-economic reasons referred to in Article 36, provisional measures subject to a Community control procedure.'*

Article 19

The EEC Treaty shall be supplemented by the following provisions:

'Article 100b

1. *During 1992, the Commission shall, together with each Member State, draw up an inventory of national laws, regulations and administrative provisions which fall under Article 100a and which have not been harmonized pursuant to that Article.*

The Council, acting in accordance with the provisions of Article 100a, may decide that the provisions in force in a Member State must be recognized as being equivalent to those applied by another Member State.

2. *The provisions of Article 100a (4) shall apply by analogy.*

3. The Commission shall draw up the inventory referred to in the first sub-paragraph of paragraph 1 and shall submit appropriate proposals in good time to allow the Council to act before the end of 1992.'

Subsection II — Monetary capacity

Article 20

1. A new Chapter 1 shall be inserted in Part Three, Title II of the EEC Treaty reading as follows:

'CHAPTER 1

COOPERATION IN ECONOMIC
AND MONETARY POLICY
(ECONOMIC AND MONETARY UNION)

Article 102a

1. *In order to ensure the convergence of economic and monetary policies which is necessary for the further development of the Community, Member States shall cooperate in accordance with the objectives of Article 104. In so doing, they shall take account of the experience acquired in cooperation within the framework of the European Monetary System (EMS) and in developing the ECU, and shall respect existing powers in this field.*

2. *Insofar as further development in the field of economic and monetary policy necessitates institutional changes, the provisions of Article 236 shall be applicable. The Monetary Committee and the Committee of Governors of the Central Banks shall also be consulted regarding institutional changes in the monetary area.'*

2.   Chapters 1, 2 and 3 shall become Chapters 2, 3 and 4 respectively.

Subsection III — Social policy

Article 21

The EEC Treaty shall be supplemented by the following provisions:

'Article 118a

1.   *Member States shall pay particular attention to encouraging improvements, especially in the working environment, as regards the health and safety of workers, and shall set as their objective the harmonization of conditions in this area, while maintaining the improvements made.*

2.   *In order to help achieve the objective laid down in the first paragraph, the Council, acting by a qualified majority on a proposal from the Commission, in cooperation with the European Parliament and after consulting the Economic and Social Committee, shall adopt, by means of directives, minimum requirements for gradual implementation, having regard to the conditions and technical rules obtaining in each of the Member States.*

   Such directives shall avoid imposing administrative, financial and legal constraints in a way which would hold back the creation and development of small and medium-sized undertakings.

3.   *The provisions adopted pursuant to this Article shall not prevent any Member State from maintaining or introducing more stringent measures for the protection of working conditions compatible with this Treaty.'*

Article 22

The EEC Treaty shall be supplemented by the following provision:

'Article 118b

The Commission shall endeavour to develop the dialogue between management and labour at European level which could, if the two sides consider it desirable, lead to relations based on agreement.'

Subsection IV — Economic and social cohesion

Article 23

A Title V shall be added to Part Three of the EEC Treaty reading as follows:

'TITLE V

Economic and social cohesion

Article 130a

In order to promote its overall harmonious development, the Community shall develop and pursue its actions leading to the strengthening of its economic and social cohesion.

In particular the Community shall aim at reducing disparities between the various regions and the backwardness of the least-favoured regions.

Article 130b

Member States shall conduct their economic policies, and shall coordinate them, in such a way as, in addition, to attain the objectives set out in Article 130a. The implementation of the common policies and of the internal market shall take into account the objectives set out in Article 130a and in Article 130c and shall contribute to their achievement. The Community shall support the achievement of these objectives by the action it takes through the structural Funds (European Agricultural Guidance and Guarantee Fund, Guidance Section, European Social Fund, European Regional Development Fund), the European Investment Bank and the other existing financial instruments.

Article 130c

The European Regional Development Fund is intended to help redress the principal regional imbalances in the Community through participating in the development and structural adjustment of regions whose development is lagging behind and in the conversion of declining industrial regions.

Article 130d

Once the Single European Act enters into force the Commission shall submit a comprehensive proposal to the Council, the purpose of which will be to make such amendments to the structure and operational rules of the existing structural Funds (European Agricultural Guidance and Guarantee Fund, Guidance Section, European Social Fund, European Regional Development Fund) as are necessary to clarify and rationalize their tasks in order to contribute to the achievement of the objectives set out in Article 130a and Article 130c, to increase their efficiency and to coordinate their activities between themselves and with the operations of the existing financial instruments. The Council shall act unanimously on this proposal within a period of one year, after consulting the European Parliament and the Economic and Social Committee.

Article 130e

After adoption of the decision referred to in Article 130d, implementing decisions relating to the European Regional Development Fund shall be taken by the Council, acting by a qualified majority on a proposal from the Commission and in cooperation with the European Parliament.

With regard to the European Agricultural Guidance and Guarantee Fund, Guidance Section and the European Social Fund, Articles 43, 126 and 127 remain applicable respectively.'

Subsection V — Research and technological development

Article 24

A Title VI shall be added to Part Three of the EEC Treaty reading as follows:

'TITLE VI

Research and technological development

Article 130f

1. The Community's aim shall be to strengthen the scientific and technological basis of European industry and to encourage it to become more competitive at international level.

2.   In order to achieve this, it shall encourage undertakings including small and medium-sized undertakings, research centres and universities in their research and technological development activities; it shall support their efforts to cooperate with one another, aiming notably at enabling undertakings to exploit the Community's internal market potential to the full, in particular through the opening up of national public contracts, the definition of common standards and the removal of legal and fiscal barriers to that cooperation.

3.   In the achievement of these aims, special account shall be taken of the connection between the common research and technological development effort, the establishment of the internal market and the implementation of common policies, particularly as regards competition and trade.

Article 130g

In pursuing these objectives the Community shall carry out the following activities, complementing the activities carried out in the Member States:

(a) implementation of research, technological development and demonstration programmes, by promoting cooperation with undertakings, research centres and universities;

(b) promotion of cooperation in the field of Community research, technological development and demonstration with third countries and international organizations;

(c) dissemination and optimization of the results of activities in Community research, technological development and demonstration;

(d) stimulation of the training and mobility of researchers in the Community.

Article 130h

Member States shall, in liaison with the Commission, coordinate among themselves the policies and programmes carried out at national level. In close contact with the Member States, the Commission may take any useful initiative to promote such coordination.

Article 130i

1. *The Community shall adopt a multiannual framework programme setting out all its activities. The framework programme shall lay down the scientific and technical objectives, define their respective priorities, set out the main lines of the activities envisaged and fix the amount deemed necessary, the detailed rules for financial participation by the Community in the programme as a whole and the breakdown of this amount between the various activities envisaged.*

2. *The framework programme may be adapted or supplemented, as the situation changes.*

Article 130k

The framework programme shall be implemented through specific programmes developed within each activity. Each specific programme shall define the detailed rules for implementing it, fix its duration and provide for the means deemed necessary.

The Council shall define the detailed arrangements for the dissemination of knowledge resulting from the specific programmes.

Article 130l

In implementing the multiannual framework programme, supplementary programmes may be decided on involving the participation of certain Member

States only, which shall finance them subject to possible Community participation.

The Council shall adopt the rules applicable to supplementary programmes, particularly as regards the dissemination of knowledge and the access of other Member States.

Article 130m

In implementing the multiannual framework programme, the Community
may make provisions, with the agreement of the Member States concerned,
for participation in research and development programmes undertaken by several Member States, including participation in the structures created for the
execution of those programmes.

Article 130n

In implementing the multiannual framework programme, the Community
may make provision for cooperation in Community research, technological
development and demonstration with third countries or international organizations.

The detailed arrangements for such cooperation may be the subject of international agreements between the Community and the third parties concerned which shall be negotiated and concluded in accordance with
Article 228.

Article 130o

The Community may set up joint undertakings or any other structure
necessary for the efficient execution of programmes of Community research,
technological development and demonstration.

Article 130p

1.   *The detailed arrangements for financing each programme, including any Community contribution, shall be established at the time of the adoption of the programme.*

2.   *The amount of the Community's annual contribution shall be laid down under the budgetary procedure, without prejudice to other possible methods of Community financing. The estimated cost of the specific programmes must not in aggregate exceed the financial provision in the framework programme.*

Article 130q

1.   *The Council shall, acting unanimously on a proposal from the Commission and after consulting the European Parliament and the Economic and Social Committee, adopt the provisions referred to in Articles 130i and 130o.*

2.   *The Council shall, acting by a qualified majority on a proposal from the Commission, after consulting the Economic and Social Committee, and in cooperation with the European Parliament, adopt the provisions referred to in Articles 130k, 130l, 130m, 130n and 130p (1). The adoption of these supplementary programmes shall also require the agreement of the Member States concerned.'*

Subsection VI — Environment

Article 25

A Title VII shall be added to Part Three of the EEC Treaty reading as follows:

Environment

Article 130r

1. *Action by the Community relating to the environment shall have the following objectives:*

— *to preserve, protect and improve the quality of the environment;*

— *to contribute towards protecting human health;*

— *to ensure a prudent and rational utilization of natural resources.*

2. *Action by the Community relating to the environment shall be based on the principles that preventive action should be taken, that environmental damage should as a priority be rectified at source, and that the polluter should pay. Environmental protection requirements shall be a component of the Community's other policies.*

3. *In preparing its action relating to the environment, the Community shall take account of:*

— *available scientific and technical data;*

— *environmental conditions in the various regions of the Community,*

— *the potential benefits and costs of action or of lack of action;*

— *the economic and social development of the Community as a whole and the balanced development of its regions.*

4. *The Community shall take action relating to the environment to the extent to which the objectives referred to in paragraph 1 can be attained better*

at Community level than at the level of the individual Member States. Without prejudice to certain measures of a Community nature, the Member States shall finance and implement the other measures.

5. Within their respective spheres of competence, the Community and the Member States shall cooperate with third countries and with the relevant international organizations. The arrangements for Community cooperation may be the subject of agreements between the Community and the third parties concerned, which shall be negotiated and concluded in accordance with Article 228.

The previous paragraph shall be without prejudice to Member States' competence to negotiate in international bodies and to conclude international agreements.

Article 130s

The Council, acting unanimously on a proposal from the Commission and after consulting the European Parliament and the Economic and Social Committee, shall decide what action is to be taken by the Community.

The Council shall, under the conditions laid down in the preceding subparagraph, define those matters on which decisions are to be taken by a qualified majority.

Article 130t

The protective measures adopted, in common pursuant to Article 130s shall not prevent any Member State from maintaining or introducing more stringent protective measures compatible with this Treaty.'

1041

CHAPTER III

PROVISIONS AMENDING THE TREATY
ESTABLISHING
THE EUROPEAN ATOMIC ENERGY COMMUNITY

Article 26

The EAEC Treaty shall be supplemented by the following provisions:

'Article 140a

1. *At the request of the Court of Justice and after consulting the Commission and the European Parliament, the Council may, acting unanimously, attach to the Court of Justice a court with jurisdiction to hear and determine at first instance, subject to a right of appeal to the Court of Justice on points of law only and in accordance with the conditions laid down by the Statute, certain classes of action or proceeding brought by natural or legal persons. That court shall not be competent to hear and determine actions brought by Member States or by Community institutions or questions referred for a preliminary ruling under Article 150.*

2. *The Council, following the procedure laid down in paragraph 1, shall determine the composition of that court and adopt the necessary adjustments and additional provisions to the Statute of the Court of Justice. Unless the Council decides otherwise, the provisions of this Treaty relating to the Court of Justice, in particular the provisions of the Protocol on the Statute of the Court of Justice, shall apply to that court.*

3. *The members of that court shall be chosen from persons whose independence is beyond doubt and who possess the ability required for appointment to judicial office; they shall be appointed by common accord of the Governments*

*of the Member States for a term of six years. The membership shall be par-
tially renewed every three years. Retiring members shall be eligible for reappointment.*

4. *That court shall establish its rules of procedure in agreement with the
Court of Justice. Those rules shall require the unanimous approval of the
Council.'*

Article 27

A second paragraph shall be inserted in Article 160 of the EAEC Treaty
worded as follows:

*'The Council may, acting unanimously at the request of the Court of Jus-
tice and after consulting the Commission and the European Parliament,
amend the provisions of Title III of the Statute.'*

CHAPTER IV

GENERAL PROVISIONS

Article 28

The provisions of this Act shall be without prejudice to the provisions
of the Instruments of Accession of the Kingdom of Spain and the Portuguese Republic to the European Communities.

Article 29

In Article 4 (2) of the Council Decision 85/257/EEC, Euratom of
7 May 1985 on the Communities' system of own resources, the words *'the
level and scale of funding of which will be fixed pursuant to a decision of the
Council acting unanimously'* shall be replaced by the words *'the level*

and scale of funding of which shall be fixed pursuant to a decision of the Council acting by a qualified majority after obtaining the agreement of the Member States concerned'.

This amendment shall not affect the legal nature of the aforementioned Decision.

TITLE III

Treaty provisions
on European Cooperation
in the sphere of foreign policy

Article 30

European Cooperation in the sphere of foreign policy shall be governed by the following provisions:

1. The High Contracting Parties, being members of the European Communities, shall endeavour jointly to formulate and implement a European foreign policy.

2. (a) The High Contracting Parties undertake to inform and consult each other on any foreign policy matters of general interest so as to ensure that their combined influence is exercised as effectively as possible through coordination, the convergence of their positions and the implementation of joint action.

(b) Consultations shall take place before the High Contracting Parties decide on their final position.

(c) In adopting its positions and in its national measures each High Contracting Party shall take full account of the positions of the other partners and shall give due consideration to the desirability of adopting and implementing common European positions.

In order to increase their capacity for joint action in the foreign policy field, the High Contracting Parties shall ensure that common principles and objectives are gradually developed and defined.

The determination of common positions shall constitute a point of reference for the policies of the High Contracting Parties.

(d) The High Contracting Parties shall endeavour to avoid any action or position which impairs their effectiveness as a cohesive force in international relations or within internationl organizations.

3. (a) The Ministers for Foreign Affairs and a member of the Commission shall meet at least four times a year within the framework of European Political Cooperation. They may also discuss foreign policy matters within the framework of Political Cooperation on the occasion of meetings of the Council of the European Communities.

(b) The Commission shall be fully associated with the proceedings of Political Cooperation.

(c) In order to ensure the swift adoption of common positions and the implementation of joint action, the High Contracting Parties shall, as far as possible, refrain from impeding the formation of a consensus and the joint action which this could produce.

4. The High Contracting Parties shall ensure that the European Parliament is closely associated with European Political Cooperation. To that end the Presidency shall regularly inform the European Parliament of the foreign policy issues which are being examined within the framework of Political Cooperation and shall ensure that the views of the European Parliament are duly taken into consideration.

5. The external policies of the European Community and the policies agreed in European Political Cooperation must be consistent.

The Presidency and the Commission, each within its own sphere of competence, shall have special responsibility for ensuring that such consistency is sought and maintained.

6. (a) The High Contracting Parties consider that closer cooperation on questions of European security would contribute in an essential way to the development of a European identity in external policy matters. They are ready to coordinate their positions more closely on the political and economic aspects of security.

(b) The High Contracting Parties are determined to maintain the technological and industrial conditions necessary for their security. They shall work to that end both at national level and, where appropriate, within the framework of the competent institutions and bodies.

(c) Nothing in this Title shall impede closer cooperation in the field of security between certain of the High Contracting Parties within the framework of the Western European Union or the Atlantic Alliance.

7. (a) In international institutions and at international conferences which they attend, the High Contracting Parties shall endeavour to adopt common positions on the subjects covered by this Title.

(b) In international institutions and at international conferences in which not all the High Contracting Parties participate, those who do participate shall take full account of positions agreed in European Political Cooperation.

8. The High Contracting Parties shall organize a political dialogue with third countries and regional groupings whenever they deem it necessary.

9. The High Contracting Parties and the Commission, through mutual assistance and information, shall intensify cooperation between their representations accredited to third countries and to international organizations.

10. (a) The Presidency of European Political Cooperation shall be held by the High Contracting Party which holds the Presidency of the Council of the European Communities.

(b) The Presidency shall be responsible for initiating action and coordinating and representing the positions of the Member States in relations with third countries in respect of European Political Cooperation activities. It shall also be responsible for the management of Political Cooperation and in particular for drawing up the timetable of meetings and for convening and organizing meetings.

(c) The Political Directors shall meet regularly in the Political Committee in order to give the necessary impetus, maintain the continuity of European Political Cooperation and prepare Ministers' discussions.

(d) The Political Committee or, if necessary, a ministerial meeting shall convene within forty-eight hours at the request of at least three Member States.

(e) The European Correspondents' Group shall be responsible, under the direction of the Political Committee, for monitoring the implementation of European Political Cooperation and for studying general organizational problems.

(f) Working Groups shall meet as directed by the Political Committee.

(g) A Secretariat based in Brussels shall assist the Presidency in preparing and implementing the activities of European Political Cooperation and in administrative matters. It shall carry out its duties under the authority of the Presidency.

11. As regards privileges and immunities, the members of the European Political Cooperation Secretariat shall be treated in the same way as mem-

bers of the diplomatic missions of the High Contracting Parties based in the same place as the Secretariat.

12.   Five years after the entry into force of this Act the High Contracting Parties shall examine whether any revision of Title III is required.

TITLE IV

General and final provisions

Article 31

The provisions of the Treaty establishing the European Coal and Steel Community, the Treaty establishing the European Economic Community and the Treaty establishing the European Atomic Energy Community concerning the powers of the Court of Justice of the European Communities and the exercise of those powers shall apply only to the provisions of Title II and to Article 32; they shall apply to those provisions under the same conditions as for the provisions of the said Treaties.

Article 32

Subject to Article 3 (1), to Title II and to Article 31, nothing in this Act shall affect the Treaties establishing the European Communities or any subsequent Treaties and Acts modifying or supplementing them.

Article 33

1. This Act will be ratified by the High Contracting Parties in accordance with their respective constitutional requirements. The instruments of ratification will be deposited with the Government of the Italian Republic.

2. This Act will enter into force on the first day of the month following that in which the instrument of ratification is deposited of the last Signatory State to fulfil that formality.

Article 34

This Act, drawn up in a single original in the Danish, Dutch, English, French, German, Greek, Irish, Italian, Portuguese and Spanish languages, the texts in each of these languages being equally authentic, will be deposited in the archives of the Government of the Italian Republic, which will remit a certified copy to each of the Governments of the other Signatory States.

TIL BEKRÆFTELSE HERAF har undertegnede befuldmægtigede underskrevet denne europæiske fælles akt.

ZU URKUND DESSEN haben die unterzeichneten Bevollmächtigten ihre Unterschriften unter diese Einheitliche Europäische Akte gesetzt.

ΣΕ ΠΙΣΤΩΣΗ ΤΩΝ ΑΝΩΤΕΡΩ, ΟΙ υπογεγραμμένοι πληρεξούσιοι υπέγραψαν την παρούσα Ενιαία Ευρωπαϊκή Πράξη.

IN WITNESS WHEREOF the undersigned Plenipotentiaries have signed this Single European Act.

EN FE DE LO CUAL, los plenipotenciarios abajo firmantes suscriben la presente Acta Única Europea.

EN FOI DE QUOI, les plénipotentiaires soussignés ont apposé leurs signatures au bas du présent Acte unique européen.

DÁ FHIANÚ SIN, chuir na Lánchumhachtaigh thíos-sínithe a lámh leis an Ionstraim Eorpach Aonair seo.

IN FEDE DI CHE, i plenipotenziari sottoscritti hanno apposto le loro firme in calce al presente Atto unico europeo.

TEN BLIJKE WAARVAN de ondergetekende gevolmachtigden hun handtekening onder deze Europese Akte hebben gesteld.

EM FÉ DO QUE os plenipotenciários abaixo assinados apuseram as suas assinaturas no final do presente Acto Único Europeu.

Udfærdiget i Luxembourg den syttende februar nitten hundrede og seksogfirs og i Haag den otteogtyvende februar nitten hundrede og seksogfirs.

Geschehen zu Luxemburg am siebzehnten Februar neunzehnhundertsechsundachtzig und in Den Haag am achtundzwanzigsten Februar neunzehnhundertsechsundachtzig.

Έγινε στο Λουξεμβούργο στις δεκαεπτά Φεβρουαρίου χίλια εννιακόσια ογδόντα έξι και στη Χάγη στις είκοσι οκτώ Φεβρουαρίου χίλια εννιακόσια ογδόντα έξι.

Done at Luxembourg on the seventeenth day of February in the year one thousand nine hundred and eighty-six and at the Hague on the twenty-eighth day of February in the year one thousand nine hundred and eighty-six.

Hecho en Luxemburgo, el diecisiete de febrero de mil novecientos ochenta y seis y en La Haya el veintiocho de febrero de mil novecientos ochenta y seis.

Fait à Luxembourg le dix-sept février mil neuf cent quatre-vingt-six et à La Haye le vingt-huit février mil neuf cent quatre-vingt-six.

Arna dhéanamh i Lucsamburg an seachtú lá déag de mhí Feabhra sa bhliain míle naoi gcéad ochtó a sé agus sa Háig an t-ochtú lá is fiche de mhí Feabhra míle naoi gcéad ochtó a sé.

Fatto a Lussemburgo, addì diciassette febbraio millenovecentottantasei e all'Aia, addì ventotto febbraio millenovecentottantasei.

Gedaan te Luxemburg, zeventien februari negentienhonderdzesentachtig en te 's-Gravenhage achtentwintig februari negentienhonderdzesentachtig.

Feito no Luxemburgo, aos dezassete de Fevereiro de mil novecentos e oitenta e seis e em Haia aos vinte e oito de Fevereiro de mil novecentos e oitenta e seis.

Leo TINDEMANS

Uffe ELLEMANN-JENSEN

Hans-Dietrich GENSCHER

Karolos PAPOULIAS

Francisco FERNÁNDEZ ORDÓÑEZ

Roland DUMAS

Peter BARRY

Giulio ANDREOTTI

Robert GOEBBELS

Hans VAN DEN BROEK

Pedro PIRES DE MIRANDA

Lynda CHALKER

2. Final Act

The Conference of the Representatives of the Governments of the Member States convened at Luxembourg on 9 September 1985, which carried on its discussions in Luxembourg and Brussels and adopted the following text:

I

Single European Act

II

At the time of signing this text, the Conference adopted the declarations listed hereinafter and annexed to this Final Act:

1. Declaration on the powers of implementation of the Commission,

2. Declaration on the Court of Justice,

3. Declaration on Article 8a of the EEC Treaty,

4. Declaration on Article 100a of the EEC Treaty,

5. Declaration on Article 100b of the EEC Treaty,

6. General Declaration on Articles 13 to 19 of the Single European Act,

7. Declaration on Article 118a (2) of the EEC Treaty,

8. Declaration on Article 130d of the EEC Treaty,

9. Declaration on Article 130r of the EEC Treaty,

10. Declaration by the High Contracting Parties on Title III of the Single European Act,

11. Declaration on Article 30 (10) (g) of the Single European Act.

The Conference also notes the declarations listed hereinafter and annexed to this Final Act:

1. Declaration by the Presidency on the time limit within which the Council will give its opinion following a first reading (Article 149 (2) of the EEC Treaty),

2. Political Declaration by the Governments of the Member States on the free movement of persons,

3. Declaration by the Government of the Hellenic Republic on Article 8a of the EEC Treaty,

4. Declaration by the Commission on Article 28 of the EEC Treaty,

5. Declaration by the Government of Ireland on Article 57 (2) of the EEC Treaty,

6. Declaration by the Government of the Portuguese Republic on Articles 59, second paragraph, and 84 of the EEC Treaty,

7. Declaration by the Government of the Kingdom of Denmark on Article 100a of the EEC Treaty,

8. Declaration by the Presidency and the Commission on the monetary capacity of the Community,

9. Declaration by the Government of the Kingdom of Denmark on European Political Cooperation.

Udfærdiget i Luxembourg den syttende februar nitten hundrede og seksogfirs og i Haag den otteogtyvende februar nitten hundrede og seksogfirs.

Geschehen zu Luxemburg am siebzehnten Februar neunzehnhundertsechsundachtzig und in Den Haag am achtundzwanzigsten Februar neunzehnhundertsechsundachtzig.

Έγινε στο Λουξεμβούργο στις δεκαεπτά Φεβρουαρίου χίλια εννιακόσια ογδόντα έξι και στη Χάγη στις είκοσι οκτώ Φεβρουαρίου χίλια εννιακόσια ογδόντα έξι.

Done at Luxembourg on the seventeenth day of February in the year one thousand nine hundred and eighty-six and at The Hague on the twenty-eighth day of February in the year one thousand nine hundred and eighty-six.

Hecho en Luxemburgo, el diecisiete de febrero de mil novecientos ochenta y seis y en La Haya el veintiocho de febrero de mil novecientos ochenta y seis.

Fait à Luxembourg le dix-sept février mil neuf cent quatre-vingt-six et à La Haye le vingt-huit février mil neuf cent quatre-vingt-six.

Arna dhéanamh i Lucsamburg an seachtú lá déag de mhí Feabhra sa bhliain míle naoi gcéad ochtó a sé agus sa Háig an t-ochtú lá is fiche de mhí Feabhra míle naoi gcéad ochtó a sé.

Fatto a Lussemburgo, addì diciassette febbraio millenovecentottantasei e all'Aia, addì ventotto febbraio millenovecentottantasei.

Gedaan te Luxemburg, zeventien februari negentienhonderdzesentachtig en te 's-Gravenhage achtentwintig februari negentienhonderdzesentachtig.

Feito no Luxemburgo, aos dezassete de Fevereiro de mil novecentos e oitenta e seis e em Haia aos vinte e oito de Fevereiro de mil novecentos e oitenta e seis.

Leo TINDEMANS	Peter BARRY
Uffe ELLEMANN-JENSEN	Giulio ANDREOTTI
Hans-Dietrich GENSCHER	Robert GOEBBELS
Karolos PAPOULIAS	Hans VAN DEN BROEK
Francisco FERNÁNDEZ ORDÓÑEZ	Pedro PIRES DE MIRANDA
Roland DUMAS	Lynda CHALKER

DECLARATION

on the powers of implementation of the Commission

The Conference asks the Community authorities to adopt, before the Act enters into force, the principles and rules on the basis of which the Commission's powers of implementation will be defined in each case.

In this connection the Conference requests the Council to give the Advisory Committee procedure in particular a predominant place in the interests of speed and efficiency in the decision-making process, for the exercise of the powers of implementation conferred on the Commission within the field of Article 100a of the EEC Treaty.

DECLARATION

on the Court of Justice

The Conference agrees that the provisions of Article 32 d (1) of the ECSC Treaty, Article 168a (1) of the EEC Treaty and Article 140a (1) of the EAEC Treaty do not prejudge any conferral of judicial competence likely to be provided for in the context of agreements concluded between the Member States.

DECLARATION

on Article 8a of the EEC Treaty

The Conference wishes by means of the provisions in Article 8a to express its firm political will to take before 1 January 1993 the decisions necessary to complete the internal market defined in those provisions, and more particularly the decisions necessary to implement the Commission's programme described in the White Paper on the Internal Market.

Setting the date of 31 December 1992 does not create an automatic legal effect.

DECLARATION

on Article 100a of the EEC Treaty

In its proposals pursuant to Article 100a (1) the Commission shall give precedence to the use of the instrument of a directive if harmonization involves the amendment of legislative provisions in one or more Member States.

DECLARATION

on Article 100b of the EEC Treaty

The Conference considers that, since Article 8c of the EEC Treaty is of general application, it also applies to the proposals which the Commission is required to make under Article 100b of that Treaty.

GENERAL DECLARATION

on Articles 13 to 19 of the Single European Act

Nothing in these provisions shall affect the right of Member States to take such measures as they consider necessary for the purpose of controlling immigration from third countries, and to combat terrorism, crime, the traffic in drugs and illicit trading in works of art and antiques.

DECLARATION

on Article 118a (2) of the EEC Treaty

The Conference notes that in the discussions on Article 118a (2) of the EEC Treaty it was agreed that the Community does not intend, in laying down minimum requirements for the protection of the safety and health of employees, to discriminate in a manner unjustified by the circumstances against employees in small and medium-sized undertakings.

DECLARATION

on Article 130d of the EEC Treaty

In this context the Conference refers to the conclusions of the European Council in Brussels in March 1984, which read as follows:

'The financial resources allocated to aid from the Funds, having regard to the IMPs, will be significantly increased in real terms within the limits of financing possibilities.'

DECLARATION

on Article 130r of the EEC Treaty

Re paragraph 1, third indent

The Conference confirms that the Community's activities in the sphere of the environment may not interfere with national policies regarding the exploitation of energy resources.

Re paragraph 5, second subparagraph

The Conference considers that the provisions of Article 130r (5), second subparagraph do not affect the principles resulting from the judgment handed down by the Court of Justice in the AETR case.

DECLARATION
BY THE HIGH CONTRACTING PARTIES

on Title III of the Single European Act

The High Contracting Parties to Title III on European Political Cooperation reaffirm their openness to other European nations which share the same ideals and objectives. They agree in particular to strengthen their links with the member countries of the Council of Europe and with other democratic European countries with which they have friendly relations and close cooperation.

DECLARATION

on Article 30 (10) (g)
of the Single European Act

The Conference considers that the provisions of Article 30 (10) (g) do not affect the provisions of the Decision of the Representatives of the Governments of the Member States of 8 April 1965 on the provisional location of certain institutions and departments of the Communities.

DECLARATION BY THE PRESIDENCY

on the time limit within which the Council will give
its Opinion following a first reading
(Article 149 (2) of the EEC Treaty)

As regards the declaration by the European Council in Milan, to the effect that the Council must seek ways of improving its decision-making procedures, the Presidency states its intention of completing the work in question as soon as possible.

POLITICAL DECLARATION
BY THE GOVERNMENTS OF THE MEMBER STATES

on the free movement of persons

In order to promote the free movement of persons, the Member States shall cooperate, without prejudice to the powers of the Community, in particular as regards the entry, movement and residence of nationals of third countries. They shall also cooperate in the combating of terrorism, crime, the traffic in drugs and illicit trading in works of art and antiques.

DECLARATION BY THE GOVERNMENT
OF THE HELLENIC REPUBLIC

on Article 8a of the EEC Treaty

Greece considers that the development of Community policies and actions, and the adoption of measures on the basis of Articles 70 (1) and 84, must both take place in such a way as not to harm sensitive sectors of Member States' economies.

DECLARATION BY THE COMMISSION

on Article 28 of the EEC Treaty

With regard to its own internal procedures, the Commission will ensure that the changes resulting from the amendment of Article 28 EEC will not lead to delays in responding to urgent requests for the alteration or suspension of Common Customs Tariff duties.

DECLARATION
BY THE GOVERNMENT OF IRELAND

on Article 57 (2) of the EEC Treaty

Ireland, in confirming its agreement to qualified majority voting under Article 57 (2), wishes to recall that the insurance industry in Ireland is a particularly sensitive one and that special arrangements have had to be made by the Government of Ireland for the protection of insurance policy holders and third parties. In relation to harmonization of legislation on insurance, the Government of Ireland would expect to be able to rely on a sympathetic attitude from the Commission and from the other Member States of the Community should Ireland later find itself in a situation where the Government of Ireland considers it necessary to have special provision made for the position of the industry in Ireland.

DECLARATION BY THE GOVERNMENT OF THE PORTUGUESE REPUBLIC

on Articles 59, second paragraph, and 84 of the EEC Treaty

Portugal considers that as the change from unanimous to qualified majority voting in Articles 59, second paragraph, and 84 was not contemplated in the negotiations for the accession of Portugal to the Community and substantially alters the Community *acquis,* it must not damage sensitive and vital sectors of the Portuguese economy, and, wherever necessary, appropriate and specific transitional measures should be introduced to forestall the adverse consequences that could ensue for these sectors.

DECLARATION BY THE GOVERNMENT
OF THE KINGDOM OF DENMARK

on Article 100a of the EEC Treaty

The Danish Government notes that in cases where a Member State is of the opinion that measures adopted under Article 100a do not safeguard higher requirements concerning the working environment, the protection of the environment or the needs referred to in Article 36, the provisions of Article 100a (4) guarantee that the Member State in question can apply national provisions. Such national provisions are to be taken to fulfil the above-mentioned aim and may not entail hidden protectionism.

DECLARATION BY THE PRESIDENCY
AND THE COMMISSION

on the monetary capacity of the Community

The Presidency and the Commission consider that the provisions inserted in the EEC Treaty with reference to the Community's monetary capacity are without prejudice to the possibility of further development within the framework of the existing powers.

DECLARATION BY THE GOVERNMENT
OF THE KINGDOM OF DENMARK

on European Political Cooperation

The Danish Government states that the conclusion of Title III on European Political Cooperation in the sphere of foreign policy does not affect Denmark's participation in Nordic cooperation in the sphere of foreign policy.

Resolutions and Declarations*

* EDITORIAL NOTE:
   For the reader's convenience, a certain number of Resolutions and Declarations are reproduced
   in this section.

Summary

I — RESOLUTIONS AND DECLARATIONS RECORDED IN THE MINUTES OF THE MEETING OF THE COUNCIL ON 22 APRIL 1970

Resolutions

1. Resolution relating to the section of the budget concerning the European Parliament for the period referred to in Article 78a of the ECSC Treaty, Article 203a of the EEC Treaty and Article 177a of the EAEC Treaty

The Council undertakes to make no amendments to the estimate of expenditure of the European Parliament. This undertaking shall only be binding in so far as this estimate of expenditure does not conflict with Community provisions, in particular with regard to the Staff Regulations of officials and Conditions of Employment of other servants, and to the seat of the institutions.

2. Resolution relating to Community acts having financial implications and to cooperation between the Council and the European Parliament

In order to provide the European Parliament with such information as will enable it to give its opinion on Community acts having financial implications, the Council shall invite the Commission to append to the proposals which it forwards to the European Parliament estimates of the financial implications of those acts.

The Council undertakes to maintain the closest cooperation with the European Parliament in the examination of such acts and to explain to it such reasons as may have led it to depart from the European Parliament's opinion.

3. Resolution on cooperation between the Council and the European Parliament in matters of budgetary procedure

In matters of budgetary procedure everything possible should be done by common agreement between the Council and the European Parliament to ensure close cooperation at all levels between the two institutions; in particular the President in office or another member of the Council should be present at the deliberations of the European Parliament on the draft budget.

Declarations

1. Re the first subparagraph of Article 78 (8) of the ECSC Treaty, of Article 203 (8) of the EEC Treaty and of Article 177 (8) of the EAEC Treaty:

In adopting these provisions, the Council has taken as its basis the classification of budget expenditure as set out in the list prepared by the President on 3 February 1970, while at the same time recognizing that this classification may change in the light of the operational requirements of the Communities.

2. Re the second subparagraph of paragraph 8 of the same Articles:

The Council assumes that the method of calculation to be established by the Commission of the European Communities in order to determine the reference values will remain unchanged.

3. Re Article 78a (7) of the ECSC Treaty, Article 203 a (7) of the EEC Treaty and Article 177 a (7) of the EAEC Treaty:

These provisions must be interpreted in the sense that the European Parliament may not, by proposed modifications entailing a reduction in expenditure, call into question acts adopted pursuant to the Treaties.

4. Declaration of the Council

(a) On the occasion of the signature of the Treaty amending Certain Budgetary Provisions of the Treaties establishing the European Communities and of the Treaty establishing a Single Council and a Single Commission of the European Communities, the Council took careful note of the points of view expressed by the European Parliament and communicated to it in the Resolutions of 10 December 1969, 3 February and 11 March 1970, and in an *aide mémoire* dated 19 April 1970.

(b) Accordingly, the Commission notified to the Council its intention to submit proposals on this subject subsequent to the ratification by all Member States of the Treaty signed on 22 April and at the latest within two years.

(c) The Council, in accordance with the procedure laid down in Article 236 of the Treaty, will examine these proposals in the light of the discussions which will take place in the Parliaments of the Member States, of the development of the European situation and of the institutional problems which will be posed by the enlargement of the Community.

II — JOINT DECLARATION BY THE EUROPEAN PARLIAMENT, THE COUNCIL AND THE COMMISSION ON THE INSTITUTION OF A CONCILIATION PROCEDURE,

OF 4 MARCH 1975

Official Journal of the European Communities. No C 89, 22 April 1975.

Joint Declaration
of the European Parliament, the Council and the Commission

THE EUROPEAN PARLIAMENT, THE COUNCIL AND THE COMMISSION,

Whereas from 1 January 1975, the Budget of the Communities will be financed entirely from the Communities' own resources;

Whereas in order to implement this system the European Parliament will be given increased budgetary powers;

Whereas the increase in the budgetary powers of the European Parliament must be accompanied by effective participation by the latter in the procedure for preparing and adopting decisions which give rise to important expenditure or revenue to be charged or credited to the budget of the European Communities,

HAVE AGREED AS FOLLOWS:

1. A conciliation procedure between the European Parliament and the Council with the active assistance of the Commission is hereby instituted.

2. This procedure may be followed for Community acts of general application which have appreciable financial implications, and of which the adoption is not required by virtue of acts already in existence.

3. When submitting its proposal the Commission shall indicate whether the act in question is, in its opinion, capable of being the subject of the conciliation procedure. The European Parliament, when giving its Opinion, and the Council may request that this procedure be initiated.

4. The procedure shall be initiated if the criteria laid down in paragraph 2 are met and if the Council intends to depart from the Opinion adopted by the European Parliament.

5. The conciliation shall take place in a 'Conciliation Committee' consisting of the Council and representatives of the European Parliament. The Commission shall participate in the work of the Conciliation Committee.

6. The aim of the procedure shall be to seek an agreement between the European Parliament and the Council.

   The procedure should normally take place during a period not exceeding three months, unless the act in question has to be adopted before a specific date or if the matter is urgent, in which case the Council may fix an appropriate time limit.

7. When the positions of the two institutions are sufficiently close, the European Parliament may give a new Opinion, after which the Council shall take definitive action.

Done at Brussels, 4 March 1975.

For the *Parliament*	*For the* *Council*	*For the* *Commission*
C. BERKHOUWER	G. FITZGERALD	François-Xavier ORTOLI

III — JOINT DECLARATION BY THE EUROPEAN PARLIAMENT, THE COUNCIL AND THE COMMISSION ON FUNDAMENTAL RIGHTS,

OF 5 APRIL 1977

Official Journal of the European Communities No C 103, 27 April 1977.

Joint Declaration

by the European Parliament, the Council and the Commission

THE EUROPEAN PARLIAMENT, THE COUNCIL AND THE COMMISSION,

Whereas the Treaties establishing the European Communities are based on the principle of respect for the law;

Whereas, as the Court of Justice has recognized, that law comprises, over and above the rules embodied in the treaties and secondary Community legislation, the general principles of law and in particular the fundamental rights, principles and rights on which the constitutional law of the Member States is based;

Whereas, in particular, all the Member States are Contracting Parties to the European Convention for the Protection of Human Rights and Fundamental Freedoms signed in Rome on 4 November 1950,

HAVE ADOPTED THE FOLLOWING DECLARATION:

1. The European Parliament, the Council and the Commission stress the prime importance they attach to the protection of fundamental rights, as derived in particular from the constitutions of the Member States and the European Convention for the Protection of Human Rights and Fundamental Freedoms.

2. In the exercise of their powers and in pursuance of the aims of the European Communities they respect and will continue to respect these rights.

Done at Luxembourg on the fifth day of April in the year one thousand nine hundred and seventy-seven.

For the *Parliament*	*For the* *Council*	*For the* *Commission*
E. COLOMBO	D. OWEN	R. JENKINS

IV — JOINT DECLARATION BY THE EUROPEAN PARLIAMENT, THE COUNCIL AND THE COMMISSION ON VARIOUS MEASURES TO IMPROVE THE BUDGETARY PROCEDURE,

OF 30 JUNE 1982

Official Journal of the European Communities. No C 194, 28 July 1982.

Joint Declaration by the European Parliament, the Council and the Commission on various measures to improve the budgetary procedure

The European Parliament, the Council and the Commission,

Whereas harmonious cooperation between the institutions is essential to the smooth operation of the Communities;

Whereas various measures to improve the operation of the budgetary procedure under Article 78 of the Treaty establishing the European Coal and Steel Community, Article 203 of the Treaty establishing the European Economic Community and Article 177 of the Treaty establishing the European Atomic Energy Community should be taken by agreement between the institutions of the Communities, due regard being had to their respective powers under the Treaties,

Agree as follows:

I. CLASSIFICATION OF EXPENDITURE

1. Criteria

In the light of this agreement and of the classification of expenditure proposed by the Commission for the budget for 1982, the three institutions consider compulsory expenditure such expenditure as the budgetary authority is obliged to enter in the budget to enable the Community to meet its obligations, both internally and externally, under the Treaties and acts adopted in accordance therewith.

2. *Application on the basis of this agreement*

Items in the budget are hereby classified as set out in the Annex hereto.*

II. CLASSIFICATION OF NEW BUDGET ITEMS OR EXISTING ITEMS FOR WHICH THE LEGAL BASIS HAS CHANGED

1. New budget items and the expenditure relating to them shall be classified having regard to the data set out in Section I hereof by agreement between the two institutions which make up the budgetary authority, acting on a proposal from the Commission.

2. The preliminary draft budget shall contain a reasoned proposal for the classification of each new budget item.

3. If one of the two institutions which make up the budgetary authority is unable to accept the Commission's proposal for classification, the disagreement shall be referred to a meeting of the Presidents of Parliament, of the Council and of the Commission, which shall undertake the chairmanship.

4. The three Presidents shall endeavour to resolve any disagreements before the draft budget is established.

5. The Chairman of the Tripartite Dialogue shall report to the inter-institutional conciliation meeting which precedes the first reading by the Coun-

---

* This Annex is not reproduced in this volume (See *Official Journal of the European Communities,* No C 194, 28 July 1982)

cil and shall, if necessary, speak in Council and Parliament debates on the first reading.

6.   The agreed classification, which shall be considered provisional if the basic act has not yet been adopted, may be reviewed by mutual agreement in the light of the basic act when it is adopted.

III. INTER-INSTITUTIONAL COLLABORATION IN THE CONTEXT OF THE BUDGETARY PROCEDURE

1.   The discussion of Parliament's views on the Commission's preliminary draft budget, which is scheduled to precede the Council's establishment of the draft budget, shall be held early enough for the Council to be able to give due weight to Parliament's proposals.

2.   (a) If it appears in the course of the budgetary procedure that completion of the procedure might require agreement on fixing a new rate of increase in relation to non-compulsory expenditure for payment appropriations and/or a new rate for commitment appropriations (the latter rate may be at a different level from the former), the Presidents of Parliament, the Council and the Commission shall meet immediately.

(b) In the light of the positions put forward every effort shall be made to identify those elements on which the two institutions which make up the budgetary authority can agree so that the budget procedure can be completed before the end of the year.

(c) To this end, all parties will use their best endeavours to respect this deadline, which is essential to the smooth running of the Community.

3. If, however, agreement has not been reached by 31 December, the budgetary authority shall continue its efforts to reach agreement so that the budget can be adopted by the end of January.

4. The agreement between the two institutions which make up the budgetary authority on the new rate shall determine the level of non-compulsory expenditure at which the budget shall be adopted.

5. The Presidents of Parliament, the Council and the Commission shall meet whenever necessary, at the request of one of them:

— to assess the results of the application of this declaration,

— to consider unresolved problems in order to prepare joint proposals for solutions to be submitted to the institutions.

IV. OTHER MATTERS

1. Parliament's margin for manoeuvre — which is to be at least half the maximum rate — shall apply as from the draft budget, including any letters of amendment, as adopted by the Council at the first reading.

2. The maximum rate is to be observed in respect of the annual budget, including amending and/or supplementary budgets, if any. Without prejudice to the determination of a new rate, any portion of the maximum rate which has not been utilized shall remain available for use and may be used when draft amending and/or supplementary budgets are to be considered.

3. (a) Ceilings fixed in existing regulations will be respected.

(b) In order that the full importance of the budget procedure may be preserved, the fixing of maximum amounts by regulation must be avoided, as must the entry in the budget of amounts in excess of what can actually be expended.

(c) The implementation of appropriations entered for significant new Community action shall require a basic regulation. If such appropriations are entered the Commission is invited, where no draft regulation exists, to present one by the end of January at the latest.

The Council and the Parliament undertake to use their best endeavours to adopt the regulation by the end of May at the latest.

If by this time the regulation has not been adopted, the Commission shall present alternative proposals (transfers) for the use during the financial year of the appropriations in question.

4. The institutions note that the procedure for revision of the Financial Regulation is in progress and that some problems should be resolved in that context. They undertake to do all in their power to bring that procedure to a swift conclusion.

Done at Brussels, 30 June 1982.

For the *Parliament*	*For the* *Council*	*For the* *Commission*
P. DANKERT	L. TINDEMANS	G. THORN

V — DECLARATION RECORDED IN THE COUNCIL
MINUTES AND ADOPTED
ON 7 MAY 1985

Declaration concerning Article 1 of the Council Decision on the Communities' system of own resources

The Council agrees that revenue from Community loans contracted on capital markets is not part of 'other revenue' within the meaning of Article 1 of this Decision.

VI — JOINT DECLARATION BY THE EUROPEAN PARLIAMENT, THE COUNCIL, THE REPRESENTATIVES OF THE MEMBER STATES, MEETING WITHIN THE COUNCIL, AND THE COMMISSION AGAINST RACISM AND XENOPHOBIA,

OF 11 JUNE 1986

Official Journal of the European Communities, No C 158, 25 June 1986.

Declaration against racism and xenophobia

THE EUROPEAN PARLIAMENT, THE COUNCIL, THE REPRESENTATIVES OF THE MEMBER STATES, MEETING WITHIN THE COUNCIL, AND THE COMMISSION,

Recognizing the existence and growth of xenophobic attitudes, movements and acts of violence in the Community which are often directed against immigrants;

Whereas the Community institutions attach prime importance to respect for fundamental rights, as solemnly proclaimed in the Joint Declaration of 5 April 1977, and to the principle of freedom of movement as laid down in the Treaty of Rome;

Whereas respect for human dignity and the elimination of forms of racial discrimination are part of the common cultural and legal heritage of all the Member States;

Mindful of the positive contribution which workers who have their origins in other Member States or in third countries have made, and can continue to make, to the development of the Member State in which they legally reside and of the resulting benefits for the Community as a whole,

1. vigorously condemn all forms of intolerance, hostility and use of force against persons or groups of persons on the grounds of racial, religious, cultural, social or national differences;

2. affirm their resolve to protect the individuality and dignity of every member of society and to reject any form of segregation of foreigners;

3. look upon it as indispensable that all necessary steps be taken to guarantee that this joint resolve is carried through;

4. are determined to pursue the endeavours already made to protect the individuality and dignity of every member of society and to reject any form of segregation of foreigners;

5. stress the importance of adequate and objective information and of making all citizens aware of the dangers of racism and xenophobia, and the need to ensure that all acts or forms of discrimination are prevented or curbed.

Done at Strasbourg, 11 June 1986.

For the European Parliament	*For the Council and the Representatives of the Member States, meeting within the Council*	*For the Commission of the European Communities*
P. PFLIMLIN	H. VAN DEN BROEK	J. DELORS

European Communities

Treaties establishing the European Communities
Treaties amending these Treaties
Single European Act

1987 edition — Vol. I

Luxembourg: Office for Official Publications of the European
Communities

1987 — 1118 pp. — 11.5 × 17 cm

ES, DA, DE, GR, EN, FR, GA, IT, NL, PT

Vol. I + II: ISBN 92-77-19294-1 — Vol. I: ISBN 92-77-19225-9

Catalogue number (Vol. I): FX-80-86-001-EN-C

Price (excluding VAT) in Luxembourg:

Vol. I + II:		ECU 104	BFR 4 500	IRL 80	UKL 75	USD 110
Vol. I	:	ECU 46.20	BFR 2 000	IRL 35.20	UKL 33	USD 48

**OFFICE FOR OFFICIAL PUBLICATIONS
OF THE EUROPEAN COMMUNITIES**

L - 2985 Luxembourg   Catalogue number: FX-80-86-001-EN-C